STABILITY WITH GROWTH

D1456481

THE INITATIVE FOR POLICY DIALOGUE SERIES

The Initiative for Policy Dialogue (IPD) brings together the top voices in development to address some of the most pressing and controversial debates in economic policy today. The IPD book series approaches topics such as capital market liberalization, macroeconomics, environmental economics, and trade policy from a balanced perspective, presenting alternatives and analyzing their consequences on the basis of the best available research. Written in a language accessible to policymakers and civil society, this series will rekindle the debate on economic policy and facilitate a more democratic discussion of development around the world.

Stability with Growth

Macroeconomics, Liberalization, and Development

Joseph E. Stiglitz, José Antonio Ocampo,
Shari Spiegel, Ricardo Ffrench-Davis, and
Deepak Nayyar

OXFORD
UNIVERSITY PRESS

OXFORD

UNIVERSITY PRESS

Great Clarendon Street, Oxford OX2 6DP

Oxford University Press is a department of the University of Oxford.
It furthers the University's objective of excellence in research, scholarship,
and education by publishing worldwide in

Oxford New York

Auckland Cape Town Dar es Salaam Hong Kong Karachi
Kuala Lumpur Madrid Melbourne Mexico City Nairobi
New Delhi Shanghai Taipei Toronto

With offices in

Argentina Austria Brazil Chile Czech Republic France Greece
Guatemala Hungary Italy Japan Poland Portugal Singapore
South Korea Switzerland Thailand Turkey Ukraine Vietnam

Oxford is a registered trade mark of Oxford University Press
in the UK and in certain other countries

Published in the United States
by Oxford University Press Inc., New York

British Library Cataloguing in Publication Data

Data available

Library of Congress Cataloging in Publication Data

Data available

Typeset by Newgen Imaging Systems (P) Ltd., Chennai, India
Printed in Great Britain
on acid-free paper by
Biddles Ltd., King's Lynn, Norfolk

ISBN 0-19-928813-5   978-0-19-928813-7
ISBN 0-19-928814-3   978-0-19-928814-4 (Pbk.)

10 9 8 7 6 5 4 3 2

Acknowledgements

This book is based on the work of the Initiative for Policy Dialogue (IPD) Macroeconomics and Capital Market Liberalization task forces. IPD is a network of some two hundred economists, development researchers, and practitioners throughout the developed and developing world, who are committed to furthering the understanding of the development process. The Macroeonomics and Capital Market Liberalization task forces each include 12 additional members from top universities, international institutions, governments, and NGOs, covering 11 countries across 4 continents. In many ways this book is an overview of the task force findings, though not everyone on the task forces will agree with everything we've written. We'd like to thank all the task force members for their contributions to this book. (for a full list of the IPD Macroeconomics and CML task force members, see the IPD website: www.policydialogue.org).

We'd like to thank everyone at the Initiative for Policy Dialogue who helped manage the project, edit, and comment on this book. Special thanks go to Shana Hofstetter and Lauren Anderson. Additional thanks go to Kira Brunner, Siddhartha Gupta, Laura Limonic, Akbar Noman, Maria Papadakis, Ariel Schwartz, and Sylvia Wu. We'd also like to thank Anya Schiffrin for her support.

Joanne Barkan edited an early version of the book, and Siddhartha Gupta helped edit the final version. We would also like to thank several of Joseph Stiglitz's research assistants for input, including Francesco Brindisi, Anton Korinek, Stephan Litschig, and Hamid Rashid for their work on this project. IPD interns and Columbia University students Raymond Koytcheff, Shruti Kumar, Niglmoro Okuk, Chhandasi Pandya, Santitarn Sathirathai, Man Tat Sun, and Ann Warner helped format and correct the text.

We are indebted to Sarah Caro and Jennifer Wilkinson at Oxford University Press, and to the anonymous reviewers who provided useful comments on the manuscript.

We'd also like to acknowledge the financial support of the Ford Foundation, the John D. and Catherine T. MacArthur Foundation, the

Acknowledgements

Charles Stewart Mott Foundation, Rockefeller Brothers Fund, the Canadian International Development Agency (CIDA), and the Swedish International Development Cooperation Agency (SIDA) for their financial support of IPD.

Finally, Shari Spiegel would like to thank Eli Berliner (who arrived in the middle of this project) for his inspiration.

Preface

Alternative Perspectives on Macroeconomics and Capital Market Liberalization for Developing Countries

By mid-2000, the debate on globalization had already begun. Protests in Seattle had brought the most recent round of World Trade Organization (WTO) trade negotiations to a temporary halt. The negotiators wouldn't resume their work until November 2001, until after the advanced industrial countries had made a commitment that the next round, called the 'Development Round', would rectify some of the inequities of the past.

Just a few months earlier, protestors had also demonstrated against the spring meetings of the International Monetary Fund (IMF) and World Bank to call attention to what they viewed as serious problems at both institutions, including the limited participation in economic decision-making for developing countries and the narrow range of perspectives and policies that were often recommended. For over two decades, these Washington-based institutions had imposed a set of policies that had come to be called 'the Washington consensus'. Although many of the policies had more subtlety and texture than are sometimes acknowledged, the Washington consensus reflected conventional wisdom that emphasized low inflation, fiscal stringency, privatization, and liberalization. This so-called consensus, however, mainly included policy-makers located between 15th Street and 19th Street in Washington, site of the US Treasury and IMF headquarters, respectively. The consensus did not include *many other people* in Washington, academia, or the developing world.

In response to the debate, a group of economists and other social scientists met in Washington, DC in mid-2000 to launch a new initiative. Participants at the meeting agreed there was a pressing need to broaden the policy dialogue in developing countries, and the *Initiative for Policy Dialogue (IPD)* was born. Initially headquartered at the Carnegie Endowment for International Peace and at Stanford University, after one year IPD moved to Columbia University where it is now housed. The Initiative receives core financial support from the Ford and MacArthur Foundations, and also receives funding from the Mott Foundation, the Open Society Institute, the Swedish and Canadian Development Agencies, and the United Nations Development Program. Since its inception, IPD has grown into a network of nearly 250 top economists, political scientists, policy-makers, and civil society representatives who voice a wide range of views. The Initiative has committed itself to giving all perspectives due attention.

As its first order of business, IPD organized a group of task forces to look at specific policy debates. The goal of these task forces is *not* to arrive at a consensus about the best set of policies, but rather to make sure that major alternative perspectives are given full voice. Each task force has at least two co-chairs—one from a developed and one from a developing country. While most task force members come from academia, practitioners and representatives from international economic institutions, think-tanks, non-governmental organizations (NGOs), and governments also participate.

At that first meeting many participants from developing countries argued that excessive fiscal restraint had stifled growth; others worried that capital market liberalization had contributed to economic instability. Macroeconomic policy and capital market liberalization (CML) became the focus of two of the first task forces. Several participants pointed out that capital market liberalization had made macroeconomic management all the more difficult. It soon became clear that the two issues were intricately interconnected in some regions of the world, and that the two task forces should work in conjunction with each other. The capital markets liberalization task force began work with an online dialogue, and the two task forces met in New York in 2002, and then in Barcelona in 2003.[1] The meetings established that the task forces would consider macroeconomics and capital market liberalization in the context of the significant differences between developed and less developed countries, and the diversity among developing countries. These included differences in economic structures, institutions, and goals, all of which had important implications for policy.

Since the task forces first met, much has changed in the world of policy. Only a few years before our first meeting, the IMF tried to change its charter to include a mandate to promote capital market liberalization. Now, even the IMF is far more circumspect about the virtues of this policy and far more aware of its costs. Similarly, the discussion of inflation has shifted. In the 1970s, the world faced a threat of inflation; in the 1980s, the threat

[1] The Barcelona meeting was hosted by the Centro de relaciones internacionales y cooperacion internacional.

abated; by the 1990s, huge devaluations, which in earlier decades might have set off another bout of inflation, had no such effect; and early in the new millennium, the world worried about deflation.

Over the past several years, many developing countries, especially those in Latin America, have noted that the two decades during which the Washington consensus held sway were among their worst performing decades of the twentieth century in terms of economic growth. Not only has disillusionment with globalization increased; disillusionment with the Washington consensus has grown as well. Yet no alternative theory or single alternative policy with widespread support has emerged. The need for a pragmatic and broad-ranging overview has never been greater.

This book is co-authored by the chairs of the CML task force (José Antonio Ocampo and Joseph Stiglitz), the chairs of the Macroeconomic task force (Ricardo Ffrench Davis, Deepak Nayyar, and Joseph Stiglitz), and the Managing Director of IPD (Shari Spiegel). It presents an overview of the task forces' findings in what we hope is an accessible style. The discussions in this book have also benefited enormously from a series of policy meetings organized by IPD in Vietnam, the Philippines, Nigeria, Serbia, Colombia, Brazil, Ethiopia, Moldova, and Argentina. These IPD 'country dialogues' bring together legislators, government officials, academics, business people, international economic institutions, and NGOs in open, sometimes heated, debate. We believe that such conversations are essential for deliberative democracy, and we hope that they will help incorporate a fuller range of views into the standard debate, ultimately resulting in better decision-making. Although we haven't been able to dispense completely with economic jargon, we've tried to make this volume comprehensible for policy-makers and citizens who wish to become more informed and to participate more actively in policy debates.

This book attempts to develop a new framework within which one can assess alternative policies. The task force reached a broad consensus that the Washington consensus has too narrow goals (focused on price stability), too few instruments (emphasizing monetary and fiscal policy), and an excessive focus on markets. The new framework focuses on *real* stability and long-term sustainable, equitable growth, and stresses the importance of separating intermediate goals (such as inflation) and final objectives (long-term, equitable growth). It emphasizes a balance between markets and government: market imperfections necessitate government interventions.

Economists have traditionally divided their field into macroeconomics and microeconomics, with macroeconomics further divided into stabilization policy and growth. Most policy discussions and much of the assignment of institutional responsibilities have followed these divisions. This has meant that policy-makers have pursued stabilization goals with little concern for growth consequences, while also trying to increase growth through structural reforms focused on improving economic efficiency. This book challenges these divisions. We argue that stabilization policy has important consequences for long-term growth and has often been implemented with adverse consequences. Moreover, structural policies, such as capital market liberalization, have had major consequences for economic stability. This connection explains why we have brought macroeconomic stabilization and capital market liberalization together in one book. Ideally, we would have included other macroeconomic and structural policies aimed at growth and examined how they affect stability. But that is too daunting a task for now. We hope this book as it is will demonstrate the risks of excessive compartmentalization.

This book has three parts. The first part introduces the key questions and looks at the objectives of economic policy from different perspectives. In the second part, 'Macroeconomics', we examine the central issues of macroeconomics, presenting an analysis of economic models and policy perspectives on stabilization from conservative, Keynesian, and heterodox perspectives. In Part III, we present a similar analysis for capital market liberalization.

Some readers might complain that, while we present a wide variety of views, we are not balanced. We must plead guilty, but we offer two exculpating factors. First, substantial evidence already exists on one side of the debate about capital market liberalization. Second, the Washington consensus (also known as 'conventional wisdom') has received so much attention elsewhere that most readers will be familiar with the arguments. Instead, we would like to bring more balance to the overall debate, of which this book is just one part.

Contents

Part I

Overview

1

Introducing the Key Questions

Few things matter more to society than economic growth and stability; yet few issues are more controversial. More than a decade after economic integration, Europeans are still debating the European Union's (EU's) stability pact and the European Central Bank's almost exclusive focus on avoiding inflation at the expense of employment. Is the EU approach the cornerstone of a successful stabilization policy, or are its institutional structures sentencing Europe to ongoing stagnation, if not recession? In the United States, some Republicans have become Keynesians, arguing that deficits will provide the stimulation that the economy needs. Meanwhile, some Democrats argue not only that the Bush administration's tax cuts have provided little stimulation in the short run but also that the resulting deficits will inhibit growth in the long run.

Economic growth and stability are of even greater concern in the developing world. In general, conservative economists have pursued a counterintuitive course in many developing countries. They've advised pro-cyclical, contractionary fiscal policy during downturns—just the opposite of the strategy regularly adopted by governments in the developed world, and just the opposite of what students of macroeconomics learn.[1] For example, in response to crises in Argentina, Korea, Thailand, and Indonesia, during which there were clear signs of severe economic downturns, the International Monetary Fund (IMF) advocated contractionary fiscal and monetary policies. This is an ironic twist of history, as the IMF was created under the intellectual aegis of John Maynard Keynes who ardently advocated the use of counter-cyclical fiscal policies—increasing expenditures and cutting taxes to stimulate the economy during downturns.[2]

According to its critics, the contractionary policies advocated by the Fund made the downturns worse. Even the IMF now agrees that it erred in

3

the case of the East Asian countries.[3] A study produced by its Independent Evaluation Office[4] reported that the IMF consistently overestimated growth and investment prospects, even in countries not in crisis. This inevitably led it to advocate for excessively austere fiscal and monetary policies.

More generally, conservative policies pushed in the 1990s emphasized price stability, liberalization, and privatization. Critics have argued that these policies were misguided and have pointed out that, in the long run, these policies have impeded growth. Instead of focusing exclusively on fighting inflation, they argue that policy-makers should focus on real economic stability, and long-term sustainable, equitable growth; with a balanced emphasis on growth, employment, and inflation.

In addition, the critics argue that conservative economists have largely ignored the relationship between structural reforms and macro-stability. Some of the structural reforms pushed during the 1990s, such as reforms that encouraged countries to live within their means, have had positive impacts. But other central reforms, such as capital and financial market liberalization,[5] have exposed developing countries to external shocks, and also reduced their capacity to respond to them. In addition, some reforms like privatization were implemented without the proper institutional framework in place, resulting in inefficient allocations of resources (due for example, to unbridled monopoly power) and widespread corruption (so much so that privatizations in many countries were nicknamed 'briberizations').

Although most economists now agree that institutions matter, international advisers have not had much to say on how such institutions should be created, and economists differ on what is meant by 'good institutions'. For example, debates exist on the role of the central bank, the structure of financial regulations, and bankruptcy laws. All of the debates have major implications on stability and growth,[6] as we'll discuss in this book. In addition, the link between policies and institutions is still not adequately recognized. Not only are good institutions necessary for stability, but instability can affect the development of good institutions. For instance, high interest rate policies in Russia (and the failure to create viable financial institutions to supply credit to new and expanding enterprises) made asset stripping more attractive than wealth creation, and weakened support for the creation of the kind of rule of law that would have supported capital accumulation.

As evidenced above, economists differ greatly in their views and policy prescriptions. All economic policies, though, have trade-offs. Policy choices come with risks, and the risks involve different beneficiaries and victims. Who makes the decisions also matters. Political processes play a key role in macroeconomic policy just as they do in most arenas of economic decision-making. If there were no alternative policies, or if one approach were best for everyone, then we could leave the design of economic policy to domestic and international technocrats and bureaucrats. But there are always alternatives and trade-offs. Choices are political in nature and cannot be left to technocrats.

The role of the economic adviser (in foreign or domestic policy) should be to identify the trade-offs and explain and (where possible) quantify the risks. The international financial institutions have sometimes failed to do this in their role as adviser to developing countries. Even if their policies achieved what they promised, they could still be criticized for putting certain concerns above others. In addition, the process by which these institutions have pushed their policies has sometimes undermined democracy by not allowing the political process to determine what weight to attach to the different objectives and risks.

In situations of uncertainty, good decisions *ex ante* (based on the best information available at the time) often turn out to be wrong *ex post*. Sometimes the opposite of what's expected happens. But policy-makers should not be blamed for the former or given credit for the latter. What policy-makers and their advisers should be held responsible for is whether *ex ante* they correctly assessed the trade-offs and the impact of the alternative policies (including the risks to employment and growth). They should be criticized if they pretended that there was only a single 'correct policy', a policy that Pareto dominated' all others.

Advisers, in particular, bear a special responsibility not to advocate policies that reflect their own objectives under the guise that they advocate the single best policy. Their job is to convey the range of alternatives, their assessment of the consequences of alternative policies, and a fair and accurate portrayal of the uncertainties—especially in the areas where there is active debate among economists (e.g. about how best to stimulate the economy). The widespread concern is that the advice of conservative economists is too often based on models that lead to excessively contractionary fiscal and monetary policies. As noted above, they put too much emphasis on inflation, and too little on growth, unemployment, and the impact on the poor.

Much of the advice given to developing countries has failed to identify these alternatives and provide countries with advice about the trade-offs. Moreover policy designers have failed to consider the marked differences not only between developing and developed countries, but also among developing countries and within regions (such as differences between East Asia and Latin America). The one-size-fits-all advice has been insensitive to these differences.[8]

For example, constraints are more binding on some countries than on others. Countries with smaller domestic capital markets and a limited ability to borrow abroad are less able to use counter-cyclical fiscal policies. Wage and price volatility might be higher in general in the developing world, but some regions have much greater volatility than others.

Similarly, financial markets, which play an important role in many economic crises, are far more developed in some regions than in others. Securities markets, which are essential for risk sharing, provide only a limited source of finance for new investment in the most advanced industrial countries,[9] but are particularly weak in most developing countries. In more developed countries, the role of banks in finance has diminished. This has increased concern about the efficacy of monetary policy, which focuses on banks as a source of credit.[10] In most developing countries, however, banks remain the most important source of finance, but in some of the poorest countries, money and credit play a far less significant role; in these countries (as in the most advanced countries), monetary policy often has limited scope.

Open capital markets often impose further constraints on monetary and fiscal policies. The conduct of monetary policy is largely dependent on the extent to which capital markets are liberalized. With open capital markets, attempts to stimulate the economy by lowering interest rates or increasing government deficits provoke capital outflows, weakening rather than strengthening the economy.

As a result of these differences, developing countries experience more economic volatility than developed countries (in part, because developing countries often have less diversified economies), so attention to stabilization is particularly relevant. In this book, we take a broad perspective on stabilization policy. We include day-to-day management of the economy, responses to crises, and policies (including structural reforms) that affect economic stability.

Day-to-day economic management includes how much emphasis to put on using monetary policy to control inflation, how aggressively monetary authorities should respond to the first signs of inflation, what kinds of tax cuts or expenditure increases best stimulate an economy when it's in a recession, and whether policy-makers should use a wide range of *microeconomic instruments* to manage the macro-economy. Responses to crises include whether or not to focus on reducing the deficits that typically arise when an economy goes into crisis, whether raising interest rates significantly is an appropriate response, and whether governments should use alternative instruments, such as capital controls or other capital account regulations.

The objective of this book is to show that there are alternatives, both for day-to-day macro-management of the economy, and for responding to crises. For instance, in September 1998, Malaysia reacted to the East Asia crisis by instituting capital controls while Thailand did not. Malaysia's downturn was shorter and shallower—and it emerged from the crisis with less of a legacy of debt. While there are a multitude of differences between the two countries, we would argue that at least part of Malaysia's superior performance is related to the fact that it imposed capital controls and did not follow orthodox prescriptions.[11] During the crisis, China implemented standard Keynesian policies and not only avoided a downturn, but also sustained its rapid economic growth. China's experience demonstrates the possibility of complementarities. When exports and growth were threatened, investments were increased. China's policy not only promoted higher incomes in the present, but also promoted higher income for the future. Similarly, India's prudence with capital market liberalization not only sheltered it from contagion in the financial crisis but also enabled it to follow macroeconomic policies that sustained rapid economic growth.[12]

The above discussion highlights the importance of integrating macroeconomic management and capital market liberalization. We have therefore divided this book into three parts. The first part is a general overview, the second part focuses on issues in macroeconomics, and the third part lays out the debates on capital market liberalization.

In the next chapter we'll discuss one of the most fundamental (but often poorly articulated) questions: what are the objectives of macroeconomic policy? Many of the differences in policy stances arise because analysts have differing views about objectives. For example, for most people, controlling inflation is a means to achieve faster, more stable, and more equitable growth. But sometimes economists and policy-makers turn price stability into an end in itself, and this jeopardizes more fundamental objectives, such as increasing growth and reducing poverty.

In addition to having different objectives, economists often disagree about how an economy functions and often operate using different assumptions. One of the great advances of modern economics is that analysts strive to develop formal and quantitative models that can be used to forecast the evolution of an economy. The precision that models give does help economists identify the critical differences in their assumptions and why they differ in their assessment of the consequences of a policy. Once this is accomplished, it becomes possible to consider which of the assumptions are reasonable and which are not. If the assumptions of the models don't make sense, then the conclusions derived from the models won't make sense either. In the second part of Chapter 2, we take a look at the assumptions that have given rise to some of the most important policy differences.

In Part II, we look at the current debates in macroeconomics in more detail. In Chapter 3, we take a closer look at alternative policy positions, to understand why economists have such different prescriptions for the same events. We approach this complex subject using three prototypical policy perspectives: the conventional Keynesian perspective, the conservative perspective, and a third perspective that attempts to integrate several alternative approaches. We call this third approach 'the heterodox perspective', although we use this with caution since economists use this term in a variety of ways.

Chapter 4 examines the differences in macroeconomic policy between developing and developed countries. The basic macroeconomic identities and aggregates, such as growth, inflation, and unemployment, of course, remain the same. But the institutional setting, including the level of development, gives rise to large variation in economic outcomes and policy choices.

In the following chapters we use the framework set up in Chapters 3 and 4 to examine the main policy instruments from the three alternative perspectives. Chapter 5 looks at monetary and fiscal policy in a closed economy. Chapter 6 extends the analysis to an open economy. In this chapter, we introduce exchange rate policy and analyze the complex relationships between exchange rate, fiscal, and monetary policies as well as the ways in which capital flows complicate traditional analyses. Chapter 7 then looks at exchange rate management and other policy options for an open economy.

Chapter 8 deals with three key issues that affect all policy perspectives. The first is the accounting framework of economic policy; this is the lens used to ascertain whether an economy is likely to overheat or to slip into recession. We find that widely used accounting frameworks often provide misleading information and bear some responsibility for poor economic advice and performance. Chapter 8 next considers the issue of risk, and how understanding and managing risk is crucial for policy-making. Reforms can modify both the vulnerability of an economy to shocks and its ability to respond to these shocks. Ideally, stabilization policy should do more than steady an economy sinking into recession or facing a crisis; it should create an economy less prone to these problems to begin with. Economists have paid remarkably little attention to this basic issue. The final section of this chapter looks at an aspect of policy to which economists have increasingly become sensitive: the institutional frameworks within which policy decisions are made. Chapter 9 then revisits some of the key issues of economic stabilization. In this chapter, we examine how different positions among economists arise from the different assumptions they make and the different models they use.

We then move onto the issue of capital market liberalization in Part III. Capital market liberalization (CML) has been one of the most important sources of macroeconomic instability facing countries in the developing world. The IMF and other international institutions pushed for capital market liberalization throughout most of the 1990s, based on the expectation that it would reduce volatility. Although there is now general agreement that capital market liberalization has not led to growth and stability (but has led to instability), several important debates still remain. In Chapter 10, we look at the basic arguments for and against CML, and examine why capital market liberalization failed to live up to the expectations of its supporters. We continue this discussion in Chapter 11, with a more in-depth examination of the capital market failures that lead to greater risk. Capital market regulations are an important tool for policy-makers in developing countries, but economists don't agree on the most appropriate ways to regulate flows. We devote Chapter 12 to an analysis of the alternative modes of intervention. In Chapter 13, we examine some of the other outstanding debates on CML.

One of the major differences between stabilization policy for developing and developed countries is that developing countries are more concerned with growth. Some economists worry that badly managed stabilization and liberalization policies will impede economic growth. In Chapter 14, we conclude by reviewing some of the key links between stabilization, liberalization, and growth.

2

Objectives

We begin our discussion by focusing on the objectives of economic policy-making. At the most general level, the goal of economic policy is to maximize long-run societal *well-being* in an *equitable* and *sustainable* manner.

To focus on well-being, we need to take into account how today's economic policies affect long-term growth and development.[1] But we also need to go further. Individuals are concerned about their health, the environment, the quality of civic life, and their leisure. Growth, as measured by gross domestic product (GDP), could be increasing, and yet individuals could be worse off because the measurement of GDP doesn't take these factors into account, as we'll discuss in Chapter 8.

To focus on equity we need to assess the impact of policies on income distribution, employment creation, and poverty. To focus on sustainable development we need to ensure that today's growth is not based on, say, the deterioration of the environment or the depletion of natural resources.[2] We can also view sustainable development more broadly as an aspect of equity, since it encompasses fairness between current and future generations.

Another objective of economic policy should be to promote *democratic development*. We believe that politics and economics are inextricably linked. Economic institutions, and the manner in which economic policy-making is conducted, can contribute towards (or undermine) democratic development.[3]

Within this broad perspective, the debates on economic policies concentrate on questions such as: What is the best way to increase incomes? Is there a relationship between that choice and equity, future growth, and stability? Are there changes in the structure of the economy that can enhance equity, growth, and stability?[4]

Much of the recent discussion of economic policy has focused on intermediate variables. But intermediate variables are not important in their own right. Their importance derives largely from their role as possible indicators

11

of economic performance in terms of the truly significant variables, such as growth, development, and equity. As a result, the debate has often confused ends with means and ignored or given short shrift to the important long-run goals. For example, economists and policy-makers often focus on price stability as an objective in its own right. But it's more accurate to see this as a tool for achieving other objectives, such as greater efficiency and long-term growth.

We believe that the center of attention should be on 'real macroeconomics'. We place the use of productive capacity—the employment of capital and labor at their highest potential level—and the growth of that productive capacity at the center of the debate. Significant underutilization of a country's capacity obviously represents a great waste of resources, but there are additional consequences. Unemployment contributes to poverty, insecurity, and inequity. Lower incomes are typically associated with lower levels of investment and higher government deficits, and these impair future growth and potential incomes.

Economists who advocate policies that result in the economy possibly falling short of its potential bear a heavy burden of proof. For example, if they oppose steps that might lead to higher output today because they believe the policies could have adverse effects on future growth, they must show that the likely long-run negative effects *on the real economy* are so great that they more than offset the short-run benefit, so that the overall impact is negative.

In this chapter, we discuss in greater detail the meaning and relevance of the goals of economic policy that are often put forward—from enhancing economic security and reducing unemployment, to reducing inflation, enhancing growth, maintaining external balance, reducing poverty, and increasing equality. *goals of economic policy.*

Economic Security and Unemployment

The standard analysis of economic security focuses on the individual and his or her family:[5] individuals are risk averse and value security. Moreover, they like to have a smooth income stream over time. Losing a job has the obvious direct consequence of a loss in income, but there is an additional consequence of uncertainty—how long will the individual remain unemployed? What will his or her wage be when and if he or she gets re-employed? In the United States, he or she faces an additional anxiety: how will he or she pay for his family's health insurance? There is a great deal of uncertainty in answering these questions. If the economy is in a recession, the worker knows that, on average, his or her next job will pay substantially less than his or her last, and he or she faces the risk of an extended period of unemployment.

Unemployment is the most significant risk that individuals face. Most people don't have enough savings to sustain their ordinary levels of consumption through a period of unemployment, especially when it's prolonged, and even fewer can borrow against the prospect of future income. Most respond by cutting back on consumption, slowing the economy further. That is why economists place a high value on policies, such as unemployment insurance, that mitigate these risks.

In developed countries, however the period of unemployment for most individuals is relatively short compared to total lifetime employment.[6] In addition, there are reasonably good social insurance benefits (unemployment benefits and welfare systems).[7] Better-off individuals have savings to turn to, and some individuals can borrow money to tide themselves over.[8] All of these factors reduce the social costs of economic fluctuations.[9]

For most developing countries, the consequences of unemployment are often far more severe. Individuals have less wealth to serve as a buffer, financial markets are less developed so fewer individuals can borrow,[10] and government-provided safety nets, if they exist, are even more inadequate than in developed countries. Because many developing countries have also implemented 'partial cost recovery' (people have to pay for at least part of the costs of health services and their children's education) even for those who are quite poor, there can be serious long-term consequences associated with periods of unemployment. When, for instance, a child's education is interrupted, there is a high probability that the child will not return to school; an episode of malnutrition or an untreated illness can have lifelong effects.

When a less developed economy goes into a downturn, many families make ends meet by taking jobs in the informal sector where they have no health or safety protections, let alone the fringe benefits that exist in the formal sector.[11] Intense competition for jobs drives down real wages so that even those who do not lose their jobs suffer. The prevalence of low-paid jobs in the informal sector in most developing countries implies that *under*employment, or when people engage in part time work because full time work is not available, is usually more important than *un*employment. In such situations, having a job is necessary but clearly not sufficient. What matters most is the income it yields. The most important consequence of widespread unemployment or underemployment in developing countries is persistent poverty and absolute deprivation. The reason is simple. For the poor, without assets and with only limited capabilities, work is the only source of income.[12] In the analysis below, even if we do not say it explicitly, we consider under- and unemployment in developing countries as dual manifestations of the underutilization of the available labor force.

There is one factor, however, that favors developing countries. The 'social insurance' available outside of government is higher because of closer kinship relationships and mores that require those who are better off to help their less fortunate relatives. The family, as a social institution, provides a safety net. Moreover, agricultural labor markets tend to be more flexible, so that the unemployed who migrate back to rural areas can often obtain agricultural jobs. In this way, there is more effective 'work-sharing' in developing countries; that is, work is more evenly distributed among workers when demand for their labor decreases. Of course, the consequences for societal welfare can still be great. Backward migration often leads to large wage reductions and increased underemployment.[13] This is what seems to have happened during the 1997 crisis in Thailand: rural wages fell dramatically as urban employment decreased.

However, as countries develop, kinship relationships weaken, re-migration becomes more difficult, and there is less of this form of socialization of risk. An additional problem is that changes typically occur before governments can provide adequate safety nets and before individuals have accumulated sufficient capital to create a buffer against unemployment.

There are other long-run economic costs of un- and underemployment. The most important is the deterioration of job-market skills that comes from spending long periods out of the labor force or in sub par jobs. Unemployed individuals lose skills—including the ordinary 'social' skills associated with the workplace—and they become less productive. Workers who are pessimistic about job prospects will not invest in the acquisition of skills. This is one reason why it often seems difficult to bring the unemployment rate down after an extended period of high unemployment. Europe saw the consequences of this in the 1980s (the so-called hysteresis effect that led to higher long-term unemployment);[14] the United States saw the converse benefits of low unemployment in the 1990s, when marginalized individuals returned to the labor market.[15]

In addition to these economic costs of unemployment, there are huge social costs. Extended bouts of unemployment are associated with a myriad of problems, from increased rates of family dissolution to higher suicide rates, increased crime, and violence. Extended periods of unemployment often lead to a variety of forms of social exclusion.

Most countries monitor their unemployment rate carefully. However, even in developed countries, the unemployment rate may underestimate the true weaknesses in the labor market, especially when there has been an extended downturn in the economy. Workers who search and fail to find a job often become discouraged, and stop actively looking. These workers are not treated as unemployed—though they really are. In many developed countries, disability pays more than unemployment insurance, so that those who cannot get a job and can qualify for disability often do so. Again, they are not really disabled; if an appropriate job came along, they would gladly take it. In the United States between 2001 and 2004 almost a million people were added to the disability roles. These are not included in the unemployed pool. (In 1989 in the Netherlands, the disability roles soared to 139 per 1,000 working population.[16]) At the other extreme, many young people, seeing that jobs are not available, stay in school, though again, if jobs were available, they would gladly take them. Older individuals, those say over 55, who have been laid off, may know that the prospects of a job are so bleak that they simply take early retirement.

A vast number of individuals may have jobs, but only part-time ones, when they would gladly work full time. In the United States, the numbers of such individuals increased around 25 percent between 2001 and 2004,[17] another indicator that all was not well with the labor market. In developing countries, these numbers can be much larger. An overall summary statistic that provides a good indicator for the short run is the fraction of those of working age that are working. While this number is subject to long-run changes (as women decide, for instance, to work outside the home), in the short run, decreases reflect a shortage of jobs.

Monitoring underemployment is even more difficult than monitoring unemployment, as it tends to have more varied forms and can only be indirectly inferred from the information provided in household surveys about self-employment or dissatisfaction with the number of hours worked or wage earned. In more elaborate household surveys (which may not exist in some countries and are less frequent in others), better measurements of informality can be done. But in all cases, it's difficult to gauge the magnitude of the underutilization of the labor force in a precise manner.

One of the problems policy-makers face is at what level they should start to be concerned with unemployment. Any unemployment is a waste of resources, but some unemployment is considered necessary since it takes time for workers to move from one job to another. As we discuss later, there is generally a trade-off between unemployment and inflation. How low can the unemployment rate be pushed without setting off inflationary pressures? (A similar question could probably be asked in relation to underemployment in developing countries, but this has not been subject to systematic research.) Many economists define full employment as the level of unemployment below which inflation would increase. The problem is that this number (sometimes referred to as the NAIRU, the non-accelerating inflation rate of unemployment) is elusive and variable. In 1993, the conventional wisdom in the United States was that the NAIRU was around 6.0 to 6.2 percent. When unemployment fell well below that and inflation did not rise, it became clear that the economy was capable of operating at a much lower level of unemployment than the 'inflation hawks' had said. But those who worry about inflation still raised the concern that inflation would eventually kick in. The debate continued, even as unemployment fell from 6 to 5 to 4 percent. Had the economy shown that it could function without inflation at a much lower rate? Or was the inflation just about to hit?

Clearly, one central policy objective should be to maintain the economy as close to full employment[18] or full utilization of the labor force as possible, and to ensure that there are as few bouts of unemployment or increased underemployment as possible. But there will be downturns even with the best economic management, and when the economy slips into a downturn, policy should be designed to ensure that the recession is as short and shallow as possible and that individuals are protected as best they can be.[19]

Unemployment, Inequality, and Poverty

Most societies are concerned not only with income levels and growth rates, but also with inequality and poverty. In some cases, the various objectives come into conflict; in other cases, they are complementary. As we argued earlier, un- or underemployment are two of the most important sources of poverty and inequality; without a job, individuals in most developing countries are condemned to a life of poverty and exclusion. But there are further reasons why unemployment may have a particularly strong impact on poverty and inequality.

First, high unemployment typically hurts the least skilled people the most. There is a 'job ladder', with the most skilled taking jobs from the less skilled in times of a job shortage. That is why the unskilled are most likely to experience bouts of unemployment.[20] Second, high unemployment pushes down wages, and this increases inequality even more.

Third, in many countries, especially developing countries, unemployment insurance is non-existent or woefully inadequate, and most workers have only a small buffer of savings. Hence, after an extended period of unemployment, savings are consumed, and individuals generally lose any assets that have been collateralized. The poor can sustain minimum levels of consumption for a time by selling their scarce assets at bargain prices or by borrowing from money lenders, driving them into a debt trap. A downward spiral has begun. Expenditures on items like medicine and health are postponed, health deteriorates, and the individual is marginalized further.

It's clear that two key objectives—maintaining low un- and underemployment and reducing poverty—typically complement one another. By the same token, some policies that promote growth also help to reduce poverty. Still, there can be important trade-offs, especially when policymakers focus on an intermediate variable like inflation. Fighting inflation can lead to higher unemployment and greater poverty, as we'll discuss in the next section. While we noted that some policies promote both growth and equality, there are other policies that purportedly help growth but increase inequality. In Chapter 10, we'll examine one such policy that we've already referred to: capital market liberalization (CML). Even if CML has a positive effect on growth (the evidence shows otherwise), it still might increase poverty and inequality.

Inflation

Although mainstream economics has focused on price stability as one of its primary policy objectives, there is considerable confusion as to its role. High inflation has come to signal that the government (fiscal and monetary authorities) isn't doing its job well. Inflation is thus a variable that is of concern not in its own right, but as an easy-to-see *indicator* of economic malperformance. There are, however, two problems with this analysis. First, many people have started to view the indicator as the policy objective itself. Second, the links between inflation and real variables may be weaker than usually assumed. Because these links may not be clear, it's often better to focus on the variables that are of direct concern, when they are observable.

Much of the importance placed on fighting inflation in developing countries today stems from the history of *hyperinflation* in Latin America in the 1980s. (There were also episodes of very high inflation in some transition economies of Central and Eastern Europe in the early 1990s. But, as we'll discuss below, countries in Asia have rarely experienced hyperinflation, and the African experience has been quite different from the Latin American experience.) There is general agreement that hyperinflation has large economic costs, and that defeating it should be a top priority. Hyperinflation, and even high and uncertain inflation, creates huge uncertainty about changes in relative prices, which can be devastating for the information quality of prices and for the efficiency with which resources (including individuals' energies) are used. Behavior gets distorted as firms and individuals work to spend money quickly, before it diminishes in value. In some countries, huge amounts have been spent on institutional arrangements to protect individuals from the effects of inflation.[21]

Under more moderate inflation levels (let's say 15 to 30 percent), these costs will be much lower, as economic agents learn to protect themselves against inflation through indexation of nominal contracts (i.e. cost of living clauses in wage and independent labor service contracts, and indexation of financial contracts). Indexation reduces the costs of inflation but at the same time creates more 'inertia'. Inflation inertia makes it more difficult- more costly- to disinflate. Moreover, while indexation reduces the short-run costs of inflation, it has proven difficult to develop fully indexed long-term contracts, perhaps because of concerns about agents' abilities to fulfill such contracts.[22]

All economic policies involve trade-offs; the question here is whether the benefits of further reducing inflation outweigh its costs. Since 1991, most developed and developing countries have experienced low or moderate inflation, with many countries experiencing relatively low inflation in the late 1990s and early 2000s. When inflation is low or moderate, efforts to reduce it further may have smaller benefits and increasing costs, especially when traditional contractionary monetary policy is the only instrument used to fight it. As we'll discuss below, this may dampen employment in the short term and growth in the longer term.

The Impact of Inflation on Growth

There is little evidence that moderate inflation has a significantly adverse impact on growth. Some inflation 'hawks', while admitting this, argue that once inflation starts, it takes off on its own, is hard to control, and is very expensive to dis-inflate. Therefore, prudence requires paying attention even to moderate levels of inflation. As we note below, there is very little evidence or theory behind these contentions.[23]

In fact, contrary to the folklore, real growth rates in periods of fairly high inflation have sometimes been impressive—and far better than growth rates in seemingly similar countries that have brought inflation down.

Table 2.1 examines growth in several countries that have experienced episodes of both high inflation or hyperinflation, and of low and moderate inflation. Very high inflation and hyperinflation have been generally associated with low growth or open economic recession, although there are exceptions to the rule, as in Israel in 1979–85. On the contrary, *moderate* rates of inflation (of the order of 20 or 30 percent per year) have been accompanied by rapid economic growth quite often, as in Argentina in 1965–74, Brazil in 1965–80, Chile in 1986–96, Poland in 1992–8, and Turkey in several periods during the last three decades of the twentieth century. The view that low inflation facilitates economic growth is *not*

Table 2.1. Countries where inflation has not impeded growth

Country	Years	Low inflation		Moderate inflation		High/hyperinflation	
		Inflation	Growth	Inflation	Growth	Inflation	Growth
Argentina	1965–74			30.5	5.1		
	1975–87					259.4	0.9
	1988–90					1912.2	−4.2
	1991–3			69.1	10.1		
	1994–2001	0.7	1.4				
	2002–4			12.2	1.6		
Brazil	1965–80			36.2	7.9		
	1981–6					150.4	2.2
	1987–95					1187.8	2.0
	1996–2003	8.5	1.7				
Chile	1965–71			25.7	4.6		
	1972–7					269.9	−0.6
	1978–85			26.9	3.5		
	1986–94			18.9	7.4		
	1995–2003	4.8	4.5				
Israel	1965–70	4.7	8.0				
	1971–8			30.3	5.5		
	1979–85					181.5	4.0
	1986–96			17.9	5.4		
	1997–2003	3.8	2.2				
Poland	1981–7			31.2	1.0		
	1988–91					233.8	−3.7
	1992–8			27.2	5.4		
	1999–2003	5.1	3.5				
Turkey	1968–70	5.4	4.7				
	1971–7			17.5	6.1		
	1978–80					71.4	−0.5
	1981–7			37.9	5.8		
	1988–2001					72.8	2.8
	2002–3			35.1	6.9		

Sources: World Bank WDI/EBRD. Data set from Bruno and Easterly (1998).

valid as a general proposition. For several of these countries, the periods of low inflation have been among those with slowest rates of economic growth, such as Argentina in 1994–2001, Brazil in 1996–2003, and Israel in recent years.[24]

The hard question, of course, is why the experiences of these countries differ so markedly. Standard statistical techniques are, in theory, able to show whether inflation across countries has been associated with lower growth or more inequality, while controlling for all other variables. These cross-country regressions,[25] although imperfect,[26] suggest that inflation is not closely related to growth, so long as inflation is not too high—below a threshold of some 20 to 30 percent.[27]

The problem is that the simple regression models seldom account fully for some of the most important differences in economic structures across countries.

For example, the history of inflation in a country matters: it affects both the institutional arrangements and the behavior of households, governments, and the business sector. As pointed out, Table 2.1 shows that some countries have managed to adapt even to high levels of inflation, although in most cases, the inflation rate has been relatively predictable. Turkey's economy managed to grow despite high inflation because it seems to have 'adjusted' well to inflation. One reason might be that firms in Turkey typically did not borrow heavily from banks; investment was self-financed so that high inflation imposed only limited costs on firms.[28]

Unexpected or volatile inflation has been more problematic. For example, the high variability in interest rates associated with volatile inflation can pose a serious problem in economies where firms have borrowed extensively, say to finance their plant and equipment.[29] This was apparent during the Asian crisis. The rise in interest rates to usurious levels led to widespread bankruptcies because firms were carrying high levels of short-term debt that had to be refinanced at extremely high rates. Of course, had there been a history of high volatility of interest rates prior to the crisis, firms probably wouldn't have held so much short-term leverage in the first place, and the volatility in inflation would have had far less impact. However, if firms come to believe that there will be periodic episodes of high interest rates, they will limit their borrowing, and as we explain below, this can have a significant adverse effect on growth.

The implication is that the inflation threshold differs from country to country. However, in general, we can say that the thershold is significantly higher than the extremely low levels advocated in most of the inflation-targeting regimes of the early late 1990s and early 2000s. A second problem in interpreting the data is that shocks to the economic system often lead to inflation, but inflation isn't necessarily the cause of the problem—it's merely a symptom of the external shock. Inflation itself is an endogenous variable that should be explained *within* the model. For example, the oil price rise in the 1970s led to inflation in much of the world; growth slowed and poverty increased. The underlying cause of the problem, however, was not the inflation rate but the higher price of oil. Because greater resources were being spent on oil, fewer resources were available for growth. Countries became poorer and had to adjust to new circumstances.

Policy-makers should, of course, undertake policies that mitigate the effects and facilitate a broad adjustment to the "shock"; but when governments respond to inflation by tightening macroeconomic policy, while doing little to facilitate the broader adjustment, the country is likely to be worse off,[30] especially when the shock has already led to an economic slowdown.

The effect that the oil price shock had on countries in Latin America is particularly telling. Latin American countries had borrowed heavily to maintain growth during the 1970s,[31] but the long-run costs of this strategy turned out to be enormous. When the United States raised interest rates to extreme levels after the oil crisis, most Latin American countries were forced into bankruptcy, ushering in the lost decade of the 1980s.[32]

The Issue of Deflation

Some economists now worry that too low a rate of inflation can be problematic. Greenwald and Stiglitz[33] (following on Fisher[34]) have argued that deflation[35] can be as problematic for an economy as inflation. The real value of what debtors have to repay increases with deflation, so that many debtors may be forced into bankruptcy and default, resulting in enormous human costs and loss of organization and informational capital. Periods of extended deflation—such as the late nineteenth century United States and more recently in Japan—have also been associated with low growth and, in some cases, high levels of social strife.[36]

Japan's experience has made economists pay more attention to deflation, as well as rethink the desirable rate of inflation. It's now widely recognized that even if central banks target inflation, they cannot completely control it: there are a number of random disturbances that cannot be anticipated. For example, the rise in oil prices in the fall of 2004 was far larger than most forecasters had thought, so that the inflation rate turned out higher than 'planned'. Random disturbances, such as a more bountiful harvest than anticipated, can also lead to lower levels of inflation. If policy-makers try to target zero inflation, there is a significant chance that the economy will experience deflation if random disturbances occur. So if, as we have suggested, there is a large cost associated with deflation (and it cannot easily be reversed), the central bank should target an inflation rate above zero.

There is another argument for targeting an inflation rate somewhat higher than zero.[37] There is considerable evidence of downward rigidity in prices and wages—deflation is possible, but there is resistance to falling prices, especially from workers who don't want to see their wages cut. But a dynamic economy requires large changes in *relative* prices. When it's difficult for prices to drop, some level of inflation can facilitate the necessary change in relative prices. Large adjustments in relative prices are important for economies going through massive transformation (as was the case in the former Eastern European economies after the end of communism). From this perspective, Poland did a better job of managing its transition with a 15 to 20 percent inflation rate than did the Czech Republic, which pushed inflation down to 9.9 percent in 1994.

There is one further argument against targeting inflation at too low a number and risking the economy moving into deflation. When the economy is in deflation, monetary policy may be less effective. When prices fall, real interest rates may rise. Even if banks charge a zero interest rate, the real interest rate is positive because prices are falling. For example, during the Great Depression, real interest rates rose as high as 10 percent depressing the economy further.[38,39] Central bankers once assumed the goal was to get inflation down to zero (price stability), and many still do. The above analysis suggests, however, that the optimal inflation rate (if such a thing can be defined) is greater than zero.

For countries facing deflation, a moderate amount of money-financed deficit spending can yield double benefits. It can reverse the deflation (avoiding deflation's adverse redistributive consequences) and stimulate the economy at the same time. Critics of such a policy worry that governments won't be able to use it with restraint: if a government prints any money at all, it will print an excess. Some governments have done this in the past, but that doesn't make it inevitable that others won't act with moderation.

22

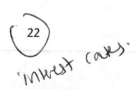
interest rates.

Indeed, a democratic government that hopes for re-election has a strong incentive to act with moderation since popular aversion to high inflation can be strong. Lags between policy implementation and consequences, however, mean that sometimes the costs of immoderation will emerge only after the election.

The Impact of Inflation on Inequality

The litany against inflation begins with how inflation is bad for growth, and goes on to assert that 'inflation is the cruelest tax of all'—that it especially hurts the poor. The previous paragraphs have questioned the conventional wisdom: moderate inflation does not seem particularly bad for growth, and too low inflation (aiming at price stability) may actually be bad for growth.

Here, we examine the second allegation that inflation contributes to poverty and inequality. There are some cases where the distributive effects of inflation are clearly adverse. For example, hyperinflation in Argentina in the late 1980s severely hurt the poor, and price stabilization had a positive effect. However, in broader terms, the evidence is actually ambiguous as to whom—poor or rich—inflation hurts more. The impact of inflation on inequality depends on social and market institutions, as well as on the level of indexation in the economy.

Creditors and holders of nominal financial instruments such as bonds and loans are clearly hurt by unexpected increases in the rate of inflation. The wealthy tend to hold financial assets (these assets are less equally distributed than income) so inflation has a negative impact on the rich. Middle-income individuals are likely to hold most of their assets in housing (financed in many countries by non-indexed mortgages), and thus benefit from unexpected inflation.[40] In most advanced industrial countries, social security is indexed, so that poor retirees, who depend on social security, are fully protected.[41] In contrast to industrial societies, social security is limited or non-existent in many developing countries. In these countries, inflation can have a greater effect on the elderly poor; though stronger family ties and informal networks in developing countries can somewhat mitigate the impact.

The effect of inflation on workers depends on whether their wages adjust. In places where inflation has been a problem, longer-term contracts often have cost of living adjustment clauses. However, in developing countries, many workers are not in organized labor. For these countries, as

23

well as for those without an inflationary history, indexation is not the norm for a significant proportion of the workforce. Here the extent to which inflation impacts workers depends on whether firms are forced to raise wages due to competition in the labor market, or to maintain worker productivity as 'efficiency wage' theory indicates they should.[42]

How inflation affects different groups of society is also determined by which sectors of the economy it hits. If inflation is strongest in basic food or necessities, it may have a larger impact on the urban poor, assuming their incomes don't adjust. On the other hand, higher food prices can help agricultural workers and the rural poor. In addition, if inflation mostly affects imported luxury items, the impact on the poor will be low.

Overall, though, depending on market institutions, it seems that inflation—so long as it doesn't have serious adverse effects on the economy—is worse for bondholders than for most other parts of society. As a result, it reduces inequality.[43] This conclusion conforms to the observed 'political economy': financial markets or Wall Street seem most concerned about fighting inflation, far more concerned than most workers or corporations on Main Street.

As we discussed earlier, it's important to differentiate the effects of inflation from its causes in assessing the effects on the poor. Inflation can be the result of an adjustment to a crisis, and not the cause of the crisis. When inflation is due to outside shocks, such as the oil price rise in the 1970s or the currency shocks of the 1990s, typical measures of fighting inflation (tightening macroeconomic policy) can lead to bankruptcies and higher unemployment. As we'll discuss in the next section, the cost of fighting inflation can outweigh the costs of inflation, especially for the poor, who suffer the most from unemployment.

The Costs of Fighting Inflation

The benefits of maintaining low inflation have to be offset against the costs. The costs depend, of course, on how inflation is fought. But whatever the specific tools employed, one casualty is almost always jobs: the fight against inflation leads to higher unemployment, at least in the short run,[44] and the risk of lower growth in the medium term. The well-off may be more likely to bear the costs of inflation, but the less well-off, especially unskilled workers, bear more of the costs of fighting inflation.

One of the arguments against excessive inflation is that it impairs the efficiency of the economy, but using tight monetary policy to fight inflation can be equally damaging. In Russia, excessively tight money in the years 1993 to 1998—defended on the grounds that it was needed to combat inflation—had extremely adverse effects on efficiency to the point that between 60 and 80 percent of all transactions were conducted in barter.

More generally, the high interest rates used to fight inflation makes funds more expensive, discourages investment, and limits growth. A heavy reliance on monetary policy to stabilize the economy may also lead to interest rates being highly variable. This was especially the case during the years in which monetarism was in vogue, in the 1980s in the United States[45], and was also evident during the East Asian crisis. Both high or excessively variable interest rates make debt financing less attractive. In developing countries, equity markets work poorly, and most outside financing is in the form of debt. If firms are reluctant to take on debt because of high and variable interest rates, they will have to rely on self-finance. Firms also find it difficult to meet their working capital needs. Thus, high and variable interest rates impair the efficiency of capital markets, further lowering growth rates. In addition, as mentioned above, high interest rates[46] used to fight inflation can also cause widespread bankruptcies, with all the associated economic and social losses, especially when an economy is characterized by a significant amount of leverage.

To fight inflation, governments sometimes deliberately try to strengthen the exchange rate. The price of imported goods is a key determinant of the price level, especially in small open economies, and a strong exchange rate lowers the price of imports, as we'll discuss in more detail in Chapter 6. But even when governments do not deliberately focus on the currency, the exchange rate typically strengthens when the government fights inflation by raising interest rates. So long as interest rates are raised moderately (so probabilities of default are not increased significantly), capital may flow into the country, leading to currency appreciation. But even this policy, while it may reduce inflation, can have enormous costs. The strong currency can hurt exports, hurt the sectors that compete with imports, and hurt employment generation. To make matters worse, the funds that are attracted to the higher interest rates are often short term, making the country more vulnerable to shocks. In several Latin American countries in the 1990s, strong exchange rate policies led to long-term vulnerability due to increased indebtedness and diminished competitiveness. The Argentinian case provides an example of this, as we'll see in the next section.

Combating Inflation as a Policy Goal

It's important to note the fundamental difference between combating inflation and combating un- and underemployment as policy goals. Involuntary unemployment and underemployment are direct evidence of an important inefficiency in the economy, a waste of a productive resource.[47] Both have social consequences and almost always lead to inequality in income. Even moderate levels of unemployment can have large social costs.

By contrast, the costs of moderate levels of inflation, when prices and wages rise commensurately, may be lower than usually assumed by conservative economists, while excessively low levels of inflation may actually impair economic efficiency. As we've noted, inflation, especially high inflation, is often a symptom of other economic maladies.

To the extent possible, economic policy should focus on the variables of ultimate concern, such as efficiency, growth, and equity. This means that one must assess the benefits and costs of lowering inflation in terms of these other goals. Tight monetary policies are sometimes associated with inefficiencies (we've mentioned the growth of barter in Russia); growth can suffer when investment is stifled; and equity can be undermined when unemployment soars. The one justification for these seeming counterproductive policies is a counterfactual: but for the fight against inflation, growth would have been even lower, markets would have been even less efficient, and equity would have been even worse. The burden of establishing this is not easy, and unfortunately, those who advocated these and similar policies in Russia and elsewhere have seldom succeeded in doing so.

In countries that have experienced high levels of inflation in the past, people inevitably still worry about inflation. But even in these countries, economic advisers need to emphasize the links between fighting inflation and more fundamental goals, and put the benefits and costs into perspective.

External Balance

The governments of most developing countries worry about trade deficits, or more broadly, their 'external balance'. In the world of fixed exchange rates that prevailed before the early 1970s, the reason for focusing on external balance was clear. A country that was buying more from abroad than it was selling had to pay for the gap either by borrowing abroad or selling international reserves. But eventually, a country's reserves would run out, and creditors would no longer be willing to lend to it.[48] Countries would then suddenly have to cut back imports, leading to a crisis. Often, countries imposed exchange controls to stop funds from leaving the country. But controls sometimes turned into a nightmare to enforce and gave rise to black markets. In some countries, the shortage of foreign exchange meant that cars couldn't get spare parts, gasoline was rationed, and the economy appeared on the threshold of chaos.

With flexible exchange rates, the sequence is slightly different, but the outcome is not dissimilar. If the country seems to be borrowing excessively, lenders and other investors may suddenly lose confidence in the country and want their money back. The exchange rate depreciates as investors take money out of the country, making it even more difficult for those in the country to repay dollar-denominated short-term debt. As the stock market also plunges, the country goes into crisis.

Like inflation, external balance is an intermediate variable, less important in its own right and more important for its impact on variables that are of greater concern, such as stability and growth. It's not always easy to evaluate the links between external balance and the more fundamental objectives (just as it's difficult to evaluate the links between inflation and the fundamental objectives). Unfortunately, external balance constraints tend to be 'binding' for developing countries during crises: when lending drops or becomes excessively costly, countries may be forced to adjust due to the inability to finance the deficit. We'll discuss the issue of external balance in more detail in Chapter 7.

Sometimes governments have addressed one problem, while exacerbating another. There have been instances when countries have avoided inflation by creating an external imbalance. One way to check inflation is to allow the currency to appreciate, reducing aggregate demand and domestic price pressures at the same time that imported prices in local currencies fall. But the resulting trade deficit portends a problem for the future even worse than the problems that might otherwise have resulted from the inflation. Turkey provides one example of this and Latin America provides many more.

As we discussed above, Turkey has a history of high inflation. In December 1999, with inflation at 65 percent, Turkey entered an agreement with the IMF that attempted to break the inflation rate through a fixed exchange rate mechanism. At first, the program appeared to be working, with inflation falling to 40 percent. But the fixed currency led to massive short-term capital inflows. By the fall of 2000, imbalances began to appear, with the trade deficit widening due to the overvalued exchange rate. In February 2001, investors pulled their funds out of the country, the lira devalued approximately 40 percent, and the country went into crisis. Stabilization with a floating exchange rate after this episode seems to have been more successful.

Another example is Argentina. Argentina experienced zero inflation and a strong recovery in 1996–7, with GDP growth averaging over 6.7 percent per year. But the current account deficit as a percentage of GDP nearly doubled, and even during the growth period, unemployment remained high. The recovery was then followed by a four-year recession (1999–2002) during which GDP fell 18 percent.

Stabilization and Growth

Most recent discussions of stabilization policies have focused on price stability. Indeed, stabilization has come to mean price stability in some professional circles. But what people truly care about[49] is the stability and growth of their real incomes. It should be obvious why growth is important: even small changes in the rate of growth, say, from 2.5 percent to 3 percent, add up significantly over time because of the effect of compounding. With a growth rate of 2.5 percent, incomes double every 28 years; with a growth rate of 3 percent, they double every 23 years.

In this section, we'll show that the issues of stabilization and growth cannot be separated. Stabilization policy should focus exclusively on current output and employment only if current policies have no effect on future growth. But, in general, the conduct of short-run stabilization policy does have long-term effects.

The traditional debates about macroeconomic stabilization have not only given short shrift to the link between current policies and future growth, but even when the topic has been discussed, there has been little agreement. For instance, conservative economists often advise countries, in effect, not to try to maintain the economy at full employment. They urge them to face the pain of adjustment, implying that future output will be higher if there is a deeper economic downturn today.

This policy recommendation conforms to the strong spring analogy: the harder you push the spring down, the more forcefully it bounces back. Critics respond that a better analogy for the economy is the weak spring:

push it down too hard and it will remain permanently distorted—its restorative forces will be destroyed. These are just analogies, but statistical analysis[50] suggests that the critics are closer to the mark. If the economy's output is lowered 10 percent today, the best estimate is that the output path will be 10 percent lower 10 years from now than it otherwise would have been.[51] That means that downturns have long-lasting effects. Even Korea and Malaysia, countries that economists regard as having recovered well from the Asian crisis, are moving on a path some 10 points below the trend they set in the pre-crisis decades.

The implications of thinking about policy in this framework are profound. If a decline in the economy today leads to lower output far into the future,[52] then even the cost of a 1 percent decline in GDP today is enormous. For example, if an economy grows at 4 percent annually for the next 20 years and there is a 6 percent discount rate, the present discounted value of GDP will be approximately 50 times today's GDP. *The loss is not 1 percent of today's GDP, but 50 times higher.*

There are several links between stabilization (how it's pursued and to what extent) and growth. Instability leads to higher risk premiums. Risk-averse firms require a higher rate of return in order to invest, and this impedes growth. It's the overall stability of the real economy, and not just price stability, that concerns firms when they make investment decisions.

As we've seen, an exclusive or even excessive focus on price stability can have a negative impact on growth. Tight monetary policy used to stabilize prices can limit growth by making funds for investment less available and more expensive. High interest rates lead to more firm and bank failures, and impose higher costs on the government during restructurings.

We've also seen that the issue of stabilization and how it's pursued can't be separated from standard microeconomic issues of efficiency.[53] If policy-makers rely too much on higher interest rates to stabilize prices, firms become reluctant to use debt financing and will rely more heavily on self-financing. Capital, which is so scarce in developing countries, will be allocated less efficiently in the short run, and growth will be hampered in the long run.

Relying on alternative measures to stabilize the economy (such as the government expenditures used by Korea and Malaysia during the Asian crisis or the regulations on capital inflows used by Chile and Malaysia in the 1990s) may have less adverse effects on long-term growth than relying exclusively on modifying interest rates.

The links between growth and stability go two ways. Some of the structural reforms that international financial institutions promoted as enhancing growth, such as capital market liberalization, led to greater instability. (In the end, as we show in Chapter 10, capital market liberalization did not lead to higher growth or even improved resource allocation.)

A key variable that links the goals of current stability, social equity, and growth is the use of the potential capacity of the economy. High instability generates an 'unfriendly' domestic macro-environment that appears to be a crucial factor in explaining low rates of capital formation: firms have less incentive to invest. As a result, growth will be lower. Because adjustments are slow, economies with greater instability are likely to have higher average levels of unemployment and the attendant increases in poverty and inequality. If this view is correct, then there may be less of a trade-off between growth and stabilization policy (pursued in the right way) than conservatives often suggest. Economic policies that lead to fuller utilization of resources today may also lead to higher incomes in the future.[54] This perspective informs much of the policy analysis in the following chapters.

Short-Term Growth versus Sustainable Growth

Policy-makers should, of course, be concerned not just with income today and short-run growth, but also with long-run economic performance. There may be trade-offs between growth in the near term and sustainable growth in the long run. For example, governments often incur short-term debt, which boosts GDP today and makes growth appear more robust. Short-term and private liquid capital inflows (for example, inflows to domestic stock markets) can contribute to exchange rate appreciation, reduce inflation, improve consumer confidence, and help finance imported consumer goods. But such debt makes a country increasingly vulnerable to interest rate and exchange rate fluctuations and to abrupt halts to the inflow of capital. These are often beyond the control of the government and put the country's future growth at risk.

Similarly, a country can exploit its resources today, leaving future generations poorer. In this case, it might look as if growth is increasing and the country is better off, but in reality, it's just an accounting charade. Because the resources are being depleted without offsetting investments in human and physical capital, the country is actually poorer. If markets worked well, they would recognize this and 'send a signal' (e.g. by offering to lend only at increasingly high interest rates). But markets are typically myopic and often don't recognize the 'charade' until there's a crisis.

In order to ascertain whether growth is sustainable, we need an analysis of balance sheets that show a country's physical, human, social, and institutional capital matched with its financial liabilities, as we'll discuss in greater detail in Chapter 8.

Beyond Economics

The 'individualistic' approach (which forms the basis of most standard economic analyses) leaves out many issues of vital concern to all countries, and to developing countries in particular. For example, economic policy, including the unemployment rate, can have a major effect on the level of crime.[55] Violence and crime can deter potential investors, but their impact is more profound: violence and crime affect the very nature of society. Low unemployment in the United States in the 1990s contributed to a reduction in poverty, violence, and crime: the Clinton administration's full-employment policy was perhaps its most important social policy. By contrast, high unemployment in Latin America during the 1980s is often cited as one cause of the region's high levels of crime.

In addition, unemployment probably has important hysteresis effects beyond those associated with the deterioration of human capital discussed above: even after the unemployment rate falls, many young people who've taken up a life of crime will not change their ways quickly.

The riots that resulted from the IMF's shortsighted policy of cutting of food and fuel subsidies to the very poor in Indonesia in 1998 destroyed an enormous amount of social capital. Similarly, the bankruptcies caused by high interest rate policies in East Asia almost surely destroyed capital (including organization and informational capital) whose value exceeded the value of the loans extended.

Some social capital inevitably erodes in the process of development. For example, traditional communities become weaker when young people leave to find work elsewhere. But if development processes are managed well, they can enable the creation of new social capital. Just as badly managed trade liberalization led to the destruction of old jobs before enough new ones were created, badly managed structural adjustment policies can lead to the destruction of old social capital without providing space for the creation of new capital.

There is still another approach to many of these issues: individuals have certain economic and social rights, and economic policy should help ensure that they achieve those rights. From this perspective, employment is not just another economic benefit to be traded off against others; having a job is a right.[56] A government that fails to provide employment for essentially everyone who is willing to work has failed in one of its primary obligations.

Some economists have concerns about the impact of economic policies on democracy. They see democracy not only as an instrument but also as a social good to protect. We can evaluate policies in terms of whether they strengthen or weaken democracy. Some economists, for example, have criticized capital market liberalization not just because it leads to greater economic instability and poverty, but also because it undermines democracy: it circumscribes the economic choices of countries in an unacceptable way and gives greater weight to the views of outsiders (such as Wall Street money managers) than to domestic citizens. We'll take a closer look at these issues in Chapter 10.

Integrating Objectives

We began this chapter with a simple assertion: the goal of economic policy is to maximize the long-term well-being of society in an equitable and sustainable manner. We've tried to articulate what this entails, arguing that economists should focus on real variables (growth, the stability of real output, unemployment, poverty, and inequality) rather than on intermediate variables (inflation and external balance), which are of concern mainly because of their impact on the real variables. We've also described the links between these intermediate variables and the ultimate objectives.

Economics is the science of choice. Economic policy would be easy if there were no trade-offs. Everyone would agree: let's have low inflation, high employment, rapid growth, and no instability or poverty. But there are trade-offs, and much of this chapter—indeed, much of this book—is about the trade-offs and how we ought to think about them.

Because there are trade-offs, we need a general approach to how to balance different concerns. Much of the political discourse in society implicitly revolves around getting the right balance: one party might stress the importance of investment and long-term growth; another might stress unemployment. But this kind of political discourse often misses some key points.[57] There are some policies that promote multiple objectives and some instances in which key trade-offs can be avoided. Some policies can promote both growth and equality (so-called pro-poor growth policies, such as universal education). Other policies might lead to more instability and increased poverty with little increased growth (an example is capital market liberalization). We have shown that some ways of pursuing stabilization policies adversely affect long-term growth, but other ways might not undermine growth and might even lead to higher incomes in the future. And, inevitably, redistributive politics lies beneath the different emphases: different macroeconomic policies, motivated or justified in part by particular objectives, will have different impacts on the various groups in society.

One cannot approach the problems of unemployment, inflation, and growth piecemeal. Doing so risks confronting the essential trade-offs. All of the problems have to be addressed in a single comprehensive framework. Economists have traditionally approached the problem of balancing different objectives through a social welfare function. Such a function attempts to reflect on all the variables that go into determining the well-being of society. It reflects, for instance, the loss of societal welfare (at a particular moment and over time) generated by the loss of individual well-being from insecurity and an unequal distribution of income.[58,59] Over the last quarter-century, research in this area has found that, under plausible assumptions, the loss of welfare either from inequality or from insecurity can be substantial and that societies and individuals are willing to give up large fractions of their income in order to reduce insecurity and risk.[60]

This chapter—and this book—focuses on economic well-being, but economics is set within a social context, and there are broader values to consider. For example, economic policies that are likely to provoke riots are objectionable, not just because they destroy current income and create uncertainty about future income. Riots create unemployment, and the social costs go well beyond loss of income.[61] Although we'll focus on the economic consequences of alternative policies in this book, the broader social consequences shouldn't be ignored.

Summary

We hope this discussion has driven home three major points. First, there is no Pareto-dominant policy, no one single policy that ensures that all individuals in society will be better off than they would be under any other policy. Different policies have different repercussions on different groups within society (workers versus financial markets, domestic creditors versus foreign creditors; borrowers versus creditors). Second, different groups are forced to bear different risks, including risks associated with the success or failure of a policy. And third, because of different repercussions on different groups, democracies cannot leave macroeconomic policy to technocrats, no matter how well informed or well intentioned they may be. Of course, the political process can then delegate specific tasks to technocrats, but macroeconomic policy is intrinsically political; it involves trade-offs that should be decided only within a political process.

Part II

Macroeconomics

3

Three Perspectives on Policy

After all the advances in economic science, the unfortunate truth is that economists cannot agree on the best set of policies. It's not just a matter of fine tuning, with some economists saying that taxes should be lowered 5 percent, and others that they should be lowered 7 percent; or some saying that a tax cut should be across the board, and others saying that it should be targeted to the poor. Some economists view one set of policies as a cure, while others believe the same set of policies will aggravate the disease.

For example, East Asian countries, as recommended by the IMF, raised interest rates and cut deficits during the Asian financial crisis. The IMF believed these policies would help the countries recover quickly. Other economists worried that the same policies would make matters even worse. The most remarkable aspect of this debate was that the economic controversies continued to rage long *after* the crisis ended. To some, it seemed as if the level of scientific advancement in economic policy was on the level of medieval medicine, when doctors debated whether bloodletting made patients better or worse.

Though the IMF prescriptions in East Asia generated strong contractionary effects, all of the countries eventually recovered, some more quickly than anticipated, some more slowly. The key question was the *counterfactual*: what would have happened had an alternative policy been followed? Would Thailand have recovered more quickly if it had an IMF program? Would Malaysia have recovered more quickly if it had an IMF program and followed the IMF's advice?

Given that economists continue to debate these issues, we cannot provide a definitive resolution of these and other policy controversies. What we can do is better understand why economists differ. Previous chapters laid the groundwork, describing the different objectives, some of the different models, and some of the ways developing countries differ from developed countries and from each other. Here, we identify three broad policy positions and look at the theory and evidence concerning each, in the hope that the reader can come to a more informed judgment.

We'll label the first approach 'conservative' (or 'neoclassical'), the second, 'standard Keynesian', and the third, 'heterodox'. The approaches differ not only in what they focus on, but also in their assumptions concerning the structure and behavior of the economy and the behavior of the government. The conservative approach focuses on inflation and deficits, which it attempts to address through tight monetary and restrictive fiscal policy. The standard Keynesian approach is more concerned with unemployment and stagnation, which it attempts to address through expansionary monetary and fiscal policy. The heterodox approach looks for non-standard ways (including the use of microeconomic interventions) to stabilize the economy, stimulate growth and employment, and contain inflation.

The conservative approach is based largely on the neoclassical model that assumes competitive markets, rational consumers, and profit-maximizing firms. As we noted earlier, the economy is seen as normally well functioning and efficient, and episodes of unemployment are temporary aberrations. From this perspective, there are strong restorative forces, which means that most government intervention is unnecessary. Even when markets behave imperfectly, government actions are likely to be ineffective or make matters worse. Government interventions, such as job protection for workers, are the cause of much of the unemployment around the world. Government is seen as part of the problem more often than it's seen as part of the solution.

The Keynesian and heterodox approaches take the existence of extensive periods of unemployment into account. As Keynes put it, 'in the long run, we are all dead', meaning that we can't simply wait for the economy to return to full employment on its own. From this perspective, the restorative forces in an economy work sufficiently slowly, and government has a role to play. The standard Keynesian approach assumes that households will increase consumption when their disposable income[1] rises, and that government interventions, such as lowering taxes, can be used to raise disposable incomes. Likewise, firms can be induced to increase investment if the government lowers the interest rate (although the Keynesian approach does recognize that government is sometimes unable to lower interest rates, and that firms sometimes fail to respond to lower rates).

Neoclassical economists typically attacked the Keynesian model for not being based on 'rational' individuals and profit-maximizing firms, as we'll discuss in Chapter 9. The Keynesians responded that the neoclassical model does not provide a good description of the behavior of firms, households, or the economy. They argued that even if behavior in the Keynesian model is not derived through solving the maximization problem of perfectly informed and rational firms and households operating in perfectly competitive markets, it still provides a better description of actual behavior than the neoclassical model with a single representative firm and household.

The heterodox approach attempts to bridge the gap by building a coherent model of the economy, based on realistic micro-foundations, which recognize that information and markets are imperfect.[2] In this approach, expectations, wealth variables, and relative prices (including relative prices between the present and the future) play a more important role than they do in standard Keynesian models. In contrast to the conservative model, the heterodox model gives a much more important role to constraints (such as credit constraints), market imperfections (in capital markets in particular, but also imperfections in competition and information, and incomplete markets), and wage and price rigidities. In the heterodox model, wages and prices are not fully flexible for reasons that can be explained in terms of the costs or risks of adjustment.

The best way to see the difference between the alternative approaches is to examine how each responds to an impending economic slowdown[3] when government revenues decline,[4] and when a balanced budget turns into a deficit.[5] This chapter presents the three basic alternative policy frameworks. The next chapter examines how macroeconomic policies differ for developing, versus developed, countries. Chapter 5 then looks at monetary and fiscal policy prescriptions for a *closed* economy facing an economic downturn, and Chapters 6 and 7 extend the analysis to an open economy.

Alternative Policy Frameworks

We'll start by briefly introducing each of the three frameworks. We could, perhaps, simplify the discussion by dividing the world into two schools of thought: those who believe in very limited government interventions that are focused on price stability and those who believe in more expansive government interventions focused more on employment and growth. But the contrast in arguments and analysis between the traditional Keynesians and the heterodox school is sufficiently large that it is important to have an extensive discussion of each.

The Standard Keynesian Approach

For more than half a century, the conventional policy prescription for an economic downturn was based on the response formulated by Keynes: increase government spending, cut taxes, and lower interest rates to stimulate the economy. The conventional Keynesian approach for developing countries that wish to increase long-term growth puts priority on investment. If it's possible to stimulate private investment, either through lower interest rates or through investment tax credits, it should be done. The Keynesians express some preference for monetary over fiscal policy, especially in developing countries because lower interest rates and greater credit availability encourage investment, stimulating growth.

However, this approach recognizes that when an economy is in a severe downturn or when there is large excess capacity (as in the US recession of 2001), lowering interest rates may fail to stimulate investment, perhaps because firms already face large excess capacity. Or it might be difficult for the government or central bank to lower *real* interest rates (taking into account inflation). In Japan in the 1990s, for example, *nominal* interest rates were close to zero, yet falling prices meant that real interest rates were positive. As Keynes pointed out, in these situations, monetary policy is like pushing on a string. The government should then place greater emphasis on fiscal policy.[6]

The Keynesian approach argues that, even when government investment is totally unproductive, the expenditure itself will lead to an expansion of output because of a multiplier effect[7] throughout the economy (pump priming). And if the expenditure is on productive investments, the social benefits of government spending can be enormous. Not only will output increase today, but it will also increase tomorrow: if today's income increases, future growth will rise as well. Estimates put the marginal return on government investments in certain areas (such as research and development) at a far higher rate than investments in the private sector.[8]

Tax cuts can also play a role in the conventional Keynesian approach, but considerable attention is paid to *who* gets the tax reduction. Tax cuts for the poor and middle class are likely to stimulate the economy far more than tax cuts for the wealthy, because the poor and middle class spend more of their tax savings on consumption. Moreover, in developing countries where growth is a top priority, Keynesians generally put a greater emphasis on stimulating investment than on tax cuts.

If monetry policy and tax cuts fail to stimulate private investment, reliance needs to be placed on increases in government investment expenditures. But even when it's possible to stimulate private investment, one wants a balanced strategy, reflecting the overall marginal *social* returns to public and private investments. Public investments, such as on infrastructure, can yield high returns, and actually increase the returns to private investment. There are often significant complementarities between public investment and private investment.

Of course, excessive stimulation to the economy may lead to inflation. Most Keynesians see a trade-off. For them, the Phillips curve (which shows the extent to which inflation increases as unemployment is reduced) slopes downward, meaning that looser monetary or expansionary fiscal policy will lead to both higher employment and higher inflation. But, as long as inflation remains moderate, its costs are low or even negative (as we saw in the last chapter). Moreover, if inflation does increase beyond an 'acceptable' level, it's possible to bring it down again.

Any expansionary macroeconomic policy during a crisis also means that, at any given exchange rate, external resources will be required to finance the larger trade deficits that such a policy implies, as we'll discuss in Chapter 7. This may prove problematic, particularly in developing countries, which can run into an external financing 'gap'. Providing such financing when it's not available in the market, so as to guarantee that full employment policies can be pursued, was precisely one of the roles envisaged for the IMF when it was created in 1944. Exchange rate devaluation is another alternative, but at times "excessive devaluation" may run contrary to the objective of supporting the recovery of economic activity, as we'll see in Chapter 6.

The Conservative Approach

Conservatives base their criticisms of the conventional Keynesian approach on the belief that Keynesian policy prescriptions are ineffective,[9] unfeasible, or have undesirable side-effects. The conservative approach is pessimistic about the efficacy of both fiscal and monetary policy. This pessimism about government goes hand in hand with optimism about markets, and conservatives consider government intervention by and large unnecessary.

Although the conservatives differ in their arguments, they share a common conclusion that government is more often part of the problem than part of the solution. In their view, the best thing the government can do is figure out how it's distorting the economy and eliminate the distortions, for instance by reducing regulations and taxation. When the government does take action, such as loosening monetary policy, it should rely on broad-based market mechanisms, like lowering interest rates.

One conservative view that is popular in academic circles (although less popular outside academics) states that there's no need for stabilization policy at all. In this view, the economy is (almost) always at full employment. Any deviation from full employment will be short-lived because the economy has strong restorative forces (unless they're inhibited by government intervention). Variations in observed levels of employment—even from 1929 to 1933 during the Great Depression—reflect for the most part *voluntary* decisions on the part of workers. Workers choose leisure over work, sometimes markedly decreasing the labor supply because of the particular configuration of relative prices (such as wages and interest rates). We can think of those workers who have decided to take a protracted vacation as happy to be relieved of the burdens of ordinary toil. For conservatives who believe that the unemployed have chosen not to work the mystery of the unemployed's profound unhappiness is a matter for psychologists more than economists. Today, however, most governments recognize that there are cyclical fluctuations in the economy and that restorative forces are sufficiently weak, so that if governments and central banks can help maintain full employment, they should.[10]

The conservative 'mainstream', always worried about an expansion of the public sector, begins with the assumption that government expenditures (investments and consumption) are not only unproductive, but also ineffective at stimulating the economy. For example, conservatives believe that the private sector will generally respond to government actions in ways that offset any positive effects. For example, when government expenditures increase, households see the associated increased deficits, anticipate future increases in taxes, and increase savings and decrease consumption. If savings do not increase, government spending pushes up interest rates and 'crowds out' private investment.

Furthermore, conservatives often see the economy through the eyes of the financial community. They argue that fiscal deficits (whatever their source) are counterproductive because they destroy investor confidence.[11] In making this argument, conservatives ignore the differences between the perspectives of the financial community and 'real' investors, the firms that actually build factories. Financial markets tend to be myopic, focusing on the short run; real investors look at the long run. Financial markets' anxiety is increased by rising deficits; real investors are equally or more worried about a decaying infrastructure or a weak economy.

There is some disagreement among conservatives about the extent to which tax cuts stimulate the economy. One strand argues that they do, as a result of increased household disposable income.[12] But this strand also worries that when the government tries to intervene to strengthen the economy, it will get the timing wrong; it will fail to recognize the lags, and the effect of a tax cut will be felt just as the economy is facing inflation. Another strand is more skeptical. They believe that individuals will see the increased deficits associated with tax cuts and save more—just as they would were the deficits the result of increased government expenditure (and possibly even more so, if the increased government expenditures go to investment).

Given that conservatives believe the economy operates at close to full employment, they worry more about inflation than unemployment. They focus more on how economic policies affect supply—the productive capacity of the economy—than on how they affect demand. To many conservatives, tax cuts are desirable because they induce individuals to work more, by increasing the after-tax return to labor (though the evidence that they do so is limited at best).[13] This is in contrast to Keynesians, who believe increasing the supply of labor when there already is high unemployment will simply add to unemployment; output will not increase.

Conservatives tend to like tax cuts on investment returns because the tax cuts encourage savings. Here the conservatives are assuming that a savings increase automatically translates into an increase in investment. Again, this would be true if the economy were always operating at full employment (and there was no borrowing from abroad). But if the economy is not fully using its resources, an increase in savings will lead to a reduction in national output.

To conservatives, looser monetary policy will typically result in higher prices, not more output, and accordingly monetary policy is largely irrelevant in determining output and employment. In what is called 'the classical dichotomy',[14] money affects only price levels and has no impact on output whatsoever. Only the real fundamentals of the economy determine real variables.[15] Most of these theories again *assume* the economy is at full employment—in which case it's obvious that looser monetary policy cannot lead to more output. They ignore price and wage rigidities and the distributive effects of price changes. Yet, from other perspectives, it is precisely because of these rigidities that the economy is often not at full employment.

When conservatives are not arguing that monetary policy is ineffective, they contend that it's counterproductive because the government always gets the timing wrong, as discussed above. However, conservatives would say that the problems of monetary policy are not quite as bad as the problems of fiscal policy, because monetary authorities can change policies more quickly than governments can cut taxes or reduce spending.

We noted earlier that Keynesians acknowledge a trade-off between inflation and lower unemployment, but focus on unemployment because the costs of low to moderate inflation are small. The conservatives believe inflation has high costs (although they haven't provided any strong evidence of this).[16] In any case, the Phillips curve is vertical, at least in the long run.[17] Attempts to change the unemployment rate are futile. Today, while the concept, relevance, and nature of the long-run, vertical Phillips curve remains debated,[18] it seems clear that the government can affect the level of output and unemployment in the short run.

To most conservatives, markets typically work well—so long as government doesn't mess things up. There's little reason for the government to intervene to increase growth or to stabilize the economy both in the long run as well as in the short run. If the economy is growing slowly, it's simply a reflection of preferences—individuals choose to enjoy consumption today rather than in the future. To those conservatives who recognize that there is *some* role of government in stabilizing the economy (especially in ensuring price stability), price stabilization is seen as a necessary condition for growth, and (provided that the government doesn't create other regulatory or tax barriers) a virtually sufficient condition.

In this sense, both traditional Keynesians and conservatives share a view: long-term growth is enhanced by getting things right today. However, the major policy objective is different for these schools. In the case of Keynesians, this means ensuring that the economy is as close to full employment as possible. It also means shifting the composition of output towards investment and away from consumption, if possible. In the case of conservatives, it means ensuring that the economy is as close to price stability as possible.[19]

Because conservatives see the market as fully efficient on its own, they tend to be especially opposed to most microeconomic interventions. In their view, these interventions interfere with market efficiency. The labor market provides an example. For many conservatives, unemployment arises from structural problems in the economy caused, for the most part, by government. Governments would do better to correct these structural failings than try to intervene directly in the economy to correct some alleged market failure.

The structural problem they cite most often is the lack of labor market flexibility. They argue that, in some cases, labor unions undermine flexibility. In other cases, government regulations such as the minimum wage and job protections create inflexibility. In still other cases, taxing firms on their labor discourages employment.

Other economists point out that neither theory nor evidence provides much support for these allegations, especially in developing countries where unions are typically weak, and minimum wages and job protections are absent or unenforced. There is a large informal sector in most developing countries,[20] which means that, in theory, government regulations and minimum wage should have little effect on the unemployment rate[21] (though they will, of course, distort the economy by shifting more resources into the informal sector). For these economists, the rigidities that exist are largely of the market's own making.

While conservatives oppose microeconomic interventions to stabilize the economy, Keynesians largely ignore them. Keynesians rely on standard monetary and fiscal policies to achieve macroeconomic objectives of growth, employment, and price stability. It's not that they oppose microeconomic interventions, only that, like the conservatives, they think of them as unnecessary. Microeconomic interventions are required to address microeconomic failures, like pollution, but not macroeconomic problems, like unemployment.

The heterodox theories, to which we now come, argue that there are microeconomic problems underlying macroeconomic problems, and that accordingly, microeconomic interventions might be an important part of an economist's toolkit in addressing macroeconomic objectives.

The Heterodox Approach

There are a variety of alternative approaches to the standard Keynesian and conservative frameworks. We'll refer to these as the heterodox approach.[22] Heterodox economists generally agree with the Keynesians that there is an important role for government in economic stabilization. But they argue for a wider variety of instruments. In their view, there are a large range of mechanisms through which policy can help achieve macroeconomic objectives.

Heterodox economists emphasize supply-side effects, the structure of the economy, the role of expectations, constraints (including constraints on cash flow and credit), a broad range of balance sheet effects, and the impacts of policies on income distribution. The heterodox approach reflects advances in economic theory over the past three decades, and stresses the importance of market limitations resulting from imperfections and especially asymmetries of information, such as the absence of risk (or insurance) markets and limitations on equity markets.

While the standard Keynesian approach discussed above emphasizes aggregate demand, the heterodox approach also notes the importance of aggregate supply. A decrease in *either* aggregate demand or aggregate supply could result in a reduction in the level of employment, given wage and price rigidities. In addition, shocks to the economy that adversely affect aggregate demand often simultaneously reduce aggregate supply. The heterodox approach notes the positive supply-side effects of many policies, while the Keynesian approach stresses only the impacts on aggregate demand. For instance, a financial crash lowers the demand for investment. But since it adversely affects balance sheets, it also affects banks' willingness to lend and firms' willingness to produce, that is, it affects supply as well as demand. Even non-cash-strapped firms may decide to cut back on production as their balance sheets worsen. In a long-run growth context, a rapid growth in aggregate demand can also have a positive supply effect due to productivity gains generated by dynamic economies of scale and the increased use of underutilized resources, such as labor. These links generate a dual feedback between growth and productivity that can result in both 'virtuous' and 'vicious' growth cycles.[23]

Traditional heterodox analysis in developing countries emphasizes specific problems associated with the diversification of the production structure, particularly technological learning and other costs of entry for new firms. It also emphasizes entry into sectors subject to increasing returns to scale on an industry-wide basis. In these sectors, growth in the size of the industry as a whole would raise returns for all the firms in the industry. These 'external economies' are mainly in manufacturing industries, but are increasingly prevalent in service industries. In this context, specific incentives to promote investment in these sectors may turn out to be more important than the traditional Keynesian determinants of investment.[24]

Like many of the conservatives, heterodox economists emphasize the need for a more thorough analysis of the behavior of firms and households. But while conservatives criticize the Keynesians for failing to *derive* the asserted behavior of firms and households from a rigorous analysis of how competitive, rational, profit-maximizing firms and utility-maximizing households with perfect information and the ability to insure themselves against all risks *should* behave, heterodox economists criticize the conservatives for using models of behavior that are out of touch with reality. Markets are often not competitive. Households are often not perfectly rational. Households and firms cannot purchase insurance in private markets against many of the most important risks they face, and they certainly don't have perfect information. There are often important differences in the information that they have access to (information asymmetries). Households and firms know this, and this affects their behavior. Models based on more realistic assumptions give rise to firm and household behavior that is more in accord with actually observed behavior—and provide an additional rationale for government to intervene in the economy, and additional tools for government and central banks to stabilize the economy.

Like the conservatives, heterodox economists place greater emphasis on the intertemporal context in which consumption and investment decisions are made. Lifetime income (or permanent income) matters. In turn, lifetime income depends on *expectations* about future income because individuals don't get paid today for future labor services, and can't buy insurance against variations in their real wages in the future. Investment, too, depends on expectations concerning future prices and wages as well as on effective demand.

For heterodox economists formation of expectations on future inflation and the indexation that often accompanies moderate and high inflation can be particularly important. Some economists have even advocated wage-price controls or 'jaw boning' (trying to influence through persuasion) to influence expectations. Others emphasize consensual processes in which labor, management and government meet to understand better the resource constraints facing the country.[25] However, we'll discuss below, distributional conflicts underlie many inflationary processes, and the way policy addresses inflation can have major distributive implications.[26]

For example, prior to Argentina's collapse, conservative economists often emphasized the role of fixed exchange rates in 'anchoring' expectations. The idea was that markets would believe that prices simply could not continue to increase with a fixed exchange rate as we'll discuss in Chapter 6. Even if they did, unemployment would grow and eventually put downward pressure on wages. Argentina dispelled this, for it showed that the so-called anchor, the fixed exchange rate, could break well before prices were able to fall enough; and that the suffering and distortions in the meanwhile could be enormous.

An awareness of the importance of intertemporal effects leads economists to shift their focus from income to wealth, and from the impact of policy and shocks on income to their impact on balance sheets. Heterodox economists also recognize the constraints under which households and firms operate. For example, there might be credit rationing, which means that the expenditures of firms and households will be limited to current cash flows.

The limitations in equity and insurance markets have led to the development of the theory of the risk-averse, credit-constrained firm.[27] This theory has been used to explain variability in supply as well as to provide a richer set of explanations for variability in demand than provided either by conservatives or Keynesians. For instance, since firms have to spend money on inputs before they sell their output, most production involves risk taking. Because firms often cannot divest this risk,[28] variations in the firm's ability or willingness to bear risk will result in variations in its supply curve.

From this perspective, demand and supply are intertwined. A shock to aggregate demand in one period will affect profitability, the firm's balance sheet, and aggregate supply in subsequent periods. The heterodox approach argues that stabilization policy needs to take these effects into account; and once these effects are taken into account, some monetary, fiscal, and exchange rate policies are less effective than they might seem, and others are more effective.

While the heterodox approach tends to strengthen and refine traditional Keynesian analyses of fiscal policy, its analysis of monetary policy differs markedly from both Keynesians and conservatives.[29] To heterodox economists, it's not so much the supply of money that matters as the supply of credit. Financial institutions, especially banks, determine who is creditworthy, how much to lend to each borrower, and under what terms. Government must pay particular attention to how its actions affect the ability and willingness of financial institutions to lend. Government policy does not just have an impact on the supply of credit through standard mechanisms (such as open market operations), it also has an impact through regulatory policies (such as capital adequacy requirements) and through direct constraints on credit availability, especially in developing countries.

The heterodox models provide an additional set of circumstances in which monetary policy may be ineffective and government will have to rely on fiscal policy. It may be difficult for monetary authorities to induce banks to lend more. This is especially true when banks view loans as highly risky or when their balance sheets are impaired in ways that make them unwilling to undertake risk. This may have been the case in Japan for much of the 1990s, the United States in 1991, and in numerous developing countries.

Heterodox models, focusing on balance sheets, cash flow, and credit constraints have provided a framework for addressing some of the most important issues in policy-making, about which the earlier models had little to say. For example, an increasingly important body of work focuses on deflation, as we discussed in Chapter 2. When an economy goes into a downturn and there is deflation (or inflation is less than expected), the redistributive consequences between debtors and creditors can be very large, and can lead to significant effects on both demand and supply. While the experiences in Japan in the 1990s and early years of the current century have called attention to this possibility, there were important earlier episodes of deflation in most of the world during the 1930s and in all crises prior to that. Heterodox models have provided a theoretical framework within which the effects of deflation can be examined and alternative policy solutions developed.

The heterodox models also see closer and more complex links between stabilization policies and growth.[30] For instance, stabilization policies that entail large variations in interest rates may also adversely affect the willingness of firms to borrow, thereby impairing future growth. This is especially true in developing countries where equity markets are underdeveloped.

DISTRIBUTION

There is a curious correlation between beliefs about the structure of the economy and the objectives (values) that are stressed. Conservatives, for instance, tend to ignore distributional issues, either because they believe that distributional issues do not matter much for the performance of the economy, or because they are unconcerned about distributional consequences. Conservatives argue that the government has the power to redistribute income efficiently. In this view, any adverse distributional consequence of macroeconomic policy can be corrected by efficient lump-sum transfers. Whether this is done is a matter of politics, not economics. Economics should be concerned with efficiency.

In contrast, the distributive effects of economic policies are at the center of heterodox thinking.[31] Who gains and who loses from a particular policy (and the different propensities to spend) are crucial determinants of the effects of a macroeconomic policy. Also, as emphasized, balance sheet (wealth) effects are equally important. For example, if workers lose from the inflationary effects of an exchange rate depreciation, the depreciation may have contractionary effects, contrary to the traditional Keynesian analysis. If many domestic firms are indebted in foreign currency, the adverse effects of the exchange rate depreciation on balance sheets may also reduce the investment response. Long-term dynamics are also crucially affected by income distribution.

Furthermore, when it comes to addressing problems posed by poverty, unemployment, and inequality, conservatives stress the distortionary effects of redistributive taxation—in effect recognizing that, in practice, there is no way to costlessly redistribute income. This implies that issues of distribution *cannot* be separated from issues of efficiency. Yet, even in developing countries where it's difficult to implement an effective redistributive income tax, most conservatives support a value-added tax, a tax that is not progressive.

There remain, of course, large disagreements about the magnitude of the costs of redistribution.[32] Fortunately, for most of the short-run analysis on which this book focuses we do not have to resolve these debates. A major issue raised by the heterodox position is that one cannot and should not ignore the distributional consequences of policy.

Summary

Despite progress in economic science, important disagreements remain about the conduct of macroeconomic policy. These derive from different objectives and different assumptions about the structure of the economy. The problem is that, quite often, the assumptions remain unstated and are, on occasions, almost forgotten. We'll look at the formal models behind these policy perspectives in Chapter 9.

This and the previous chapters have also emphasized three themes central to the critique of the Washington consensus and its macroeconomic policies. First, macroeconomic policy needs to look at a broad set of objectives—not just price stabilization but also growth, development, and distribution that extend beyond the short term. Second, it's important not to confuse means with ends, or intermediate variables with ultimate policy objectives—the most important of which is sustainable, equitable increases in standards of living. Third, macroeconomic policy needs to use more instruments—not just traditional fiscal and monetary instruments, but also microeconomic interventions, including tax structures and regulatory policies.

The following chapters will further explore how government should respond to various economic shocks. Equally important, we look at how policies can prevent shocks or enable the economy to respond automatically to them, and dampen rather than amplify them. We start by looking at whether macroeconomics for developing countries differs from macroeconomics for developed countries.

4

Is Macroeconomics Different in Developing Countries?

Macroeconomics was developed in, and for, industrialized countries. Both theory and policy were concerned with how monetary and fiscal policy should be used in industrialized economies to attain full employment, control inflation, and stabilize economic activity. But, as discussed throughout this book, there are important disagreements about the appropriate conduct of macroeconomic policy. Even in developed countries, macroeconomic policies have often not worked as well as their proponents promised. Developing countries often use this corpus of knowledge, with its competing schools of thought, without any significant modification. But it's by no means clear that applying these theories to developing countries is either justified or appropriate.

The basic macroeconomic aggregates—output, employment, inflation—are, of course, the same for both developed and developing economies, and so too are the basic identities[1] and equilibrium conditions. Savings must still equal investment, output must equal income, and aggregate demand is the sum of consumption, investment, government expenditures, and net exports. But for an understanding of macroeconomic systems, these identities need to be combined with an economic analysis of determinants of the behavior of firms, households, and governments. Here is where the differences arise. The nature of relationships between variables and the direction of causation (what determines what) are both a function of the setting and the context.

Objectives, Trade-offs, and Policies

Chapter 2 focused on macroeconomic objectives. We noted there that policy objectives differ somewhat in developed and developing countries. In industrialized countries, macroeconomic policy traditionally focused on full employment combined with price stability.[2] More recently, since the high inflation of the 1970s, there's been an increased focus solely on price stability, especially by monetary authorities. In some countries, full employment is no longer an integral part of the overall macroeconomic objective at all. Supporters of this approach presumably believe that if the government achieves price stability,[3] the market will automatically achieve full employment. But, as we discussed earlier, there's little reason to believe this is the case in either developed or developing countries.

In developing economies, macroeconomic policy traditionally focused on economic growth. From the 1950s to the 1970s, policy-makers and economists assumed that unemployment and underemployment were caused for the most part by a lack of capital. Accordingly, the policy emphasis was on savings and investment. After the developing country crises of the 1980s and early 1990s many economists and policy-makers shifted their focus to short-term macro-management. IMF stabilization policies focused on price stability and balance of payments adjustment, seemingly in the belief that if the government succeeded in achieving these objectives in the short run, long-run economic growth would follow. As we've said, the validity of this hypothesis still generates considerable debate.

As we noted earlier, economics is the science of choice—all economic policies have trade-offs. Developing and developed countries differ not only in the weight associated with different objectives but also in the nature of the trade-offs. For example, the trade-off between short-term macro-management and long-term objectives is much more important in developing countries than in industrialized countries: 'short-termism' can have more lasting effects because of greater market imperfections and inadequate social safety nets.[4] In particular, short-term-oriented macroeconomic policies that continue to be in place for several years may have adverse consequences for the performance of the economy in the long term, through the phenomenon of *hysteresis* (i.e. irreversibility of short-term changes). However, economists disagree on the extent or impact of this trade-off between short-term macroeconomic policies and long-term objectives, particularly on the extent to which contractionary policies today lead to higher or lower levels of GDP in the future. One school of thought seems to assume that the necessary trade-off is painful macro-policies today leading to long-term growth. We argue instead that lower incomes today are more likely to lead to lower incomes in the future.

The inflation–growth trade-off is a second point of debate. As we discussed in the previous chapter, 'inflation hawks' claim that higher inflation leads to significantly lower long-term growth. We pointed out that there is more evidence that shows inflation has little effect on growth, so long as the inflation rate is not too high.

A third, related debate is on the inflation–unemployment trade-off. Economists disagree about whether or not this trade-off changes over time, whether economic policy can affect it, and, if so, how. The evidence of a stable relationship between inflation and unemployment is far weaker in developing than in developed countries.[5] It's even difficult to conceptualize a negative relationship between inflation and unemployment when disguised unemployment in the subsistence agricultural sector, underemployment in the urban informal sector, and wage employment in the formal (manufacturing and services) sector co-exist in a spectrum without clear lines of demarcation.

It's possible to cite other examples in which short-term policies have long-term consequences. If financial liberalization, for example, leads to a persistent, if not mounting, overvaluation of the exchange rate, it may force domestic firms to close down.[6] By the time the overvaluation is undone, hysteresis effects could be strong. This means that re-entry becomes difficult since domestic firms must create new capacities to capture the opportunities created by the changed set of relative prices. But that is not all. The workers who are unemployed as a consequence of closures may lose their skills with the passage of time and become less productive when employment opportunities appear after a lag.

Constraints of Growth

Some economists believe that the growth–stabilization trade-off is larger in developing countries than in industrialized countries because of additional constraints on growth. There are two main issues: a shortage of domestic savings and a shortage of foreign exchange. Without adequate savings and/or the ability to borrow abroad, countries cannot invest as much as they need to sustain growth.[7]

Everyone seems to agree that neither the foreign exchange constraint nor the savings constraint is important for developed countries: if a nation like the United States wishes to invest more, it can borrow on international markets (as it has been doing massively over the past quarter-century). With flexible exchange rates and open capital markets, any firm can always obtain the foreign currency it wants, though the domestic currency may become so devalued that purchasing goods abroad becomes expensive.

In developing countries, though, a lack of foreign exchange and a lack of savings can limit investment. Developing countries often cannot borrow (they face credit constraints), or can borrow only at exorbitant interest rates. The United States and Western European governments have little trouble financing their deficits, whereas few developing countries can sustain a 5 percent government deficit for long. During economic slowdowns, the ability of a country to repay its debt falls, and the cost of borrowing rises. The result is that most governments in developing countries are forced to tighten fiscal policy during a recession and to run pro-cyclical fiscal policies.[8] Similarly, developing countries sometimes lose access to foreign exchange inflows which can create a crisis, as it did in East Asia in the late 1990s. On the other hand, one interpretation of the East Asia success during the high growth period of the 1970s and 1980s is that they simultaneously addressed the savings and foreign exchange problems. They had very high savings rates, and export-led growth generated large amounts of foreign exchange.

The literature on 'gap models' considers the relative importance of a shortage of foreign exchange and a shortage of savings, debates which of these constraints dominates, and explores the macroeconomic implications and consequences of their interactions.[9] An understanding of such macroeconomic constraints on growth is especially important in the context of developing countries because it highlights macroeconomic interactions between the short and long run.

Structural Differences and Macroeconomic Behavior

There are important differences in the structural characteristics of developing and industrialized economies. Some of the differences are obvious: the agricultural sector is far larger in most developing countries, particularly the poorest. In many developing countries, family farms and sharecropping dominate agriculture; in industrial economies large (often corporate) farms predominate. The industrial sector in developing countries is generally less diversified and industrial concentration tends to be higher than in a typical industrial economy. The service sector in developing countries includes a much larger proportion of informal activities. Many developing countries are also more open (exports represent a larger fraction of their GDP) and many are still dependent on (volatile) commodity exports.

Developed and developing countries are also likely to differ in the relative importance of different sources of growth. For developed countries, growth generally stems from the development of new inventions and their introduction into the economy. For developing countries, growth is generally related to (i) investment in physical capital; (ii) closing the knowledge gap that separates developing from developed countries; (iii) attracting or copying economic activities and technical innovations previously developed in industrial countries; and (iv) shifting resources from less productive sectors (typically agriculture but also urban informal activities) to more productive sectors.

The importance of physical capital investment and growth for developing countries reveals another important difference. From a Keynesian perspective, the main short-run macroeconomic problem in advanced capitalist countries is the inadequacy of effective demand. The economy can fully employ everyone as long as there is sufficient aggregate demand. Although, as we'll see below, these problems are present in many developing countries, the crucial problem they face is generally different. Even if productive capacity or capital equipment is fully utilized, the economy cannot absorb the existing labor force. In this view, the problem for many developing countries is the deficiency of productive capacity and not the anomaly of its underutilization. And, as we saw in the previous section, the availability of foreign exchange may become, under many circumstances, the principal factor limiting economic activity. Demand constraints do exist, as we'll see, but supply constraints—generated either by the availability of capital or by the availability of foreign exchange—are more important.

Furthermore financial institutions tend to be far more developed in advanced industrial countries than in developing countries.[10] In developing countries, for instance, firms rely more on self-financing than they do in developed countries, and equity markets are especially underdeveloped as a source of finance for new investments. In developed countries, there has been a growing move away from bank lending towards securitization, with firms borrowing from the market by issuing commercial paper or bonds. But, to the extent that firms in developing economies rely on outside financing (as they do in East Asia), they rely largely on bank finance.[11] This has some obvious implications: when firms self-finance their investments, and when households cannot borrow to finance housing, changes in interest rates are likely to have less of an effect on investment, consumption, and aggregate demand than they do in standard macro-models for developed countries.[12] When firms rely on banks for finance, but banking institutions are weak, then sufficiently large shocks to the economy can precipitate a banking crisis and an economic recession. In these circumstances, authorities must pay particular attention to the impact of monetary policy on bankruptcy rates.[13]

Part III of this book highlights the consequences of open capital markets, but suffice it to say here that they have been both a major source of disturbance for developing countries and an obstacle to responding to disturbances. Developing countries differ markedly among themselves in the degree of openness of their capital markets, and this has important macroeconomic consequences. Latin American economies tend to have very open capital accounts, while many Asian countries, such as China and India, have maintained capital controls. In Africa, countries generally haven't been able to attract the interest of foreign investors to begin with.

Given these large differences, it's not surprising that there are correspondingly large differences in short-term macroeconomic behavior. An issue that is at the center of this book is the degree of macroeconomic volatility that developing countries face. Considerable evidence shows that economic volatility is much greater in developing than developed countries. This is partly because developing economies are smaller, less diversified, and exposed to greater trade and capital account shocks. Developing countries are also less able to absorb shocks, and the structures of their economies are more likely to amplify shocks than dampen them.

Developed and developing countries also differ in the institutional arrangements for handling risk. Poorer countries face greater risks, but the arrangements for handling risk are not as well developed. The primary differences in how shocks get absorbed or amplified in an economy arise from capital market imperfections. One important function of financial markets is to transfer and absorb risk. Underdevelopment of these markets is one reason why developing countries are less able to absorb shocks than are developed countries. Equity markets are better at risk sharing than debt markets, but developing countries rely more heavily on debt.[14] Countries with very high debt–equity ratios (including many East Asian countries before the 1997 crisis) are highly vulnerable to certain kinds of shocks, and the process of adjustment is much more difficult because it entails recapitalizing financial institutions. Social security and social protection systems are also weaker in developing countries.

Poorer risk markets and weaker social protection systems have several important implications. Firms and households act in a more risk-averse manner, and shocks to one part of the economy (e.g. shocks that benefit one group at the expense of another) are not 'smoothed out'. This means the contraction of consumption or investment in one part of the economy can exceed the expansion elsewhere. The economy is likely to have weaker built-in stabilizers, so that shocks are likely to have larger effects. Given that the economy is likely to respond more sensitively to shocks, and that households and firms are less protected, it's more important to design economic policies geared to insulate the economy against shocks.

Similarly, if firms rely on debt finance (as they typically do in developing countries, as we previously noted), a negative shock (such as a drop in prices or a drop in demand) may lead to a large contraction of production and investment as credit becomes more difficult to obtain. (This is called the financial accelerator, as we'll discuss in the next chapter.) The extent to which shocks are amplified may depend on the extent to which firms rely on debt finance and the magnitude of leverage.

Other structural characteristics of the economy may also affect the extent to which shocks are dampened or amplified. Some countries have greater price rigidities that put a larger burden on quantity (income or output) adjustments. Differences in the degree of rigidity across sectors imply that there can be large changes in relative prices in response to a shock to the economy, and these changes in relative prices can have marked consequences.[15] Traditional macroeconomics has focused on the price of goods and services relative to money, but relative prices, say, between primary and manufacturing goods (which may be affected by the international terms of trade in commodity-dependent countries), between domestic and foreign goods (in which the exchange rate plays a major role), or between investment goods and consumption goods determine the composition of output. Large changes in relative prices force large changes in composition. Resources do not flow easily or costlessly from sectors where the relative price has gone down to sectors in which it has gone up. Contractions often proceed far more quickly than expansions, so that the aggregate effect in the short run of large changes in relative prices is a lowering of employment and output.[16]

Sometimes, there are mechanisms in developing countries that facilitate adjustment. Because agricultural markets are more important, and agricultural prices more flexible, sometimes shocks are better diffused in developing economies. In some countries, flexible migration between urban and rural sectors helps spread a shock in one sector through the economy.

In the 1997 East Asian crisis, the 'shock' resulting from the outflow of capital and the collapse of the stock market and real estate market was transmitted to the agricultural sector, as workers re-migrated, increasing the supply of rural workers. Workers in the rural sector bore some of the consequences of the shock in the urban sector, as the increased labor supply drove down rural wages.

Since most developing countries are very open, the analysis of short-term performance must be viewed through the lens of open economy macroeconomics. However, the analysis of macroeconomic fluctuations in small open economies illustrates many of the deficiencies of standard analyses. If the standard assumptions were true, countries would face infinite demand for their products. It would be easy to deal with problems of insufficient *domestic* aggregate demand by simply increasing exports. Policy-makers would then have to focus attention on aggregate supply. But it's simply not appropriate to borrow the small country assumption from orthodox trade theory. In practice, small open economies have not been able to insulate themselves from the consequences of changes in domestic aggregate demand, as this analysis might suggest.

Some developing economies (especially Latin American countries since the 1980s) have had depressed demand and significant underutilization of both labor and physical capital. East Asian nations joined Latin America in this macroeconomic failure during the Asian crisis. Strengthening aggregate demand in these countries might not have achieved full employment, but it would have significantly lowered both open and disguised unemployment.

In developing countries, it may also be difficult to separate the impact of shocks and policies that affect aggregate demand from those that operate through aggregate supply. For example, a drop in the demand for a country's exports (a demand shock) can lead to defaults and a weakened banking system that produces a contraction in credit supply; this then forces other firms to cut back on their supply. In addition, the links between demand and supply mean that there may be greater linkages between stabilization policy and growth. An economic downturn that results in lower profits will lower investment growth in the medium term even if interest rates are reduced. Also, as we saw in the previous section, an adverse export shock or a reduction in the availability of external financing during a crisis generates another sort of supply problem: the availability of foreign exchange may become the binding constraint on domestic economic activity—constraining the capacity of domestic macroeconomic authorities to expand aggregate domestic demand.

Differences in Instruments

The effectiveness of macroeconomic tools available to policy-makers also differs between developed and developing countries. We can see this in fiscal policy, monetary policy, and other macroeconomic instruments.

In developing countries, tax revenues derive much less from direct taxes such as income or corporate taxes, and much more from indirect taxes than in developed countries. Moreover, the tax base is almost always significantly narrower in developing countries, and tax compliance is significantly lower (due in part to tax avoidance and tax evasion, but also to a lack of information that can be used to monitor tax compliance[17]). As a rule, tax–GDP ratios in developing countries are much lower than in developed countries. So governments find it very difficult to increase their income through tax revenues, and the scope for stimulating the economy through tax cuts is reduced.

In the sphere of expenditures, the proportion of investment in total public expenditure in developing countries is higher than in industrialized economies because private investment in infrastructure is often not forthcoming. But developing country governments often end up slashing investment in difficult times because they find it very difficult to cut current expenditure. These countries pay a high price in terms of lost growth when they engage in excessive fiscal stringency. In industrial economies, the proportion of public expenditure going to pensions and other social programs is significantly higher than in developing countries. But because so many more individuals in poor countries are near subsistence, even small cuts in social expenditures can have large, long-lasting consequences. In developed countries, a cut in educational expenditures will lead to slightly larger class sizes, smaller wage increases for educators and other workers, and, arguably, a decline in the quality of education. In developing countries, a cut in education expenditures will mean that more children will not go to school at all.

Developed and developing countries have much more pronounced differences in the sphere of monetary policy, particularly in terms of reach, because money markets in developing countries are often segmented, if not underdeveloped. When monetary policy affects a more narrow part of the populace, the policy effectiveness is lower. With fewer households borrowing for housing, and fewer firms borrowing for investment, the response to changes in interest rates or even credit availability may be more limited.[18]

In some circumstances, however, the thinness of financial markets in developing countries might actually give a government additional policy instruments. In developed countries, there is increasing reliance on market mechanisms and skepticism about the use of 'window guidance' (where the central bank suggests to banks within the country that they curtail lending) and direct controls. They argue that banks do not listen to simple admonitions, and that direct controls are ineffective because firms and financial institutions figure out how to circumvent them. But such instruments may be more effective in developing countries.[19] For example, some economists believe that the *volume* of credit in developing countries is a more effective instrument of monetary policy than the price of credit. In a small banking system with relatively few banks, the central bank can easily administer a system of credit controls, or even a more targeted policy of, say, limiting credit to the real estate sector. With a less developed financial sector, circumvention of direct controls is more difficult.

The situation in some developing countries has changed in the past 20 years as the deregulation of domestic financial sectors has led to the emergence of more vibrant markets for financial assets. This should have made interest rates a more potent instrument, but, ironically, it hasn't. Capital market liberalization, which allows capital to flow easily in and out of countries, has curbed the freedom to use interest rates as a tool, since lowering interest rates can lead to capital outflows.[20] (See Chapters 6 and 10.) Industrial economies are not immune to the fetters of international financial markets, but the reach of their monetary policy is much greater. Still, developing countries, especially the emerging market economies, can enhance the use of monetary and fiscal policies (without impairing the allocative role of the exchange rate) by regulating capital flows, as we'll discuss in Chapter 10. China, India, Chile, Colombia, Malaysia, and Taiwan have all been successful at this.

It's also important to recognize that the interaction of fiscal and monetary policy in developing countries has somewhat different macroeconomic implications. For example, the inflationary impact of fiscal policy might be greater in at least some developing countries because a larger proportion of their fiscal deficit is financed through borrowing from the central bank. Similarly, the fiscal impact of monetary policy might be greater. When public debt is a large proportion of GDP and interest payments on debts are a large proportion of government expenditure, even modest changes in interest rates have a profound influence on the government's fiscal position.

Concluding Remarks

A central theme of this book is that economic policy must be attentive to the different circumstances of countries. To be sure, the laws of economics operate in both developed and developing countries: scarcity is a fact of life everywhere; demand curves are downward sloping; the interaction of demand and supply will determine price equilibrium in competitive markets. In this chapter, we've tried to highlight the point that the laws of economics may be universal, but economies function in markedly different ways. Moreover, there are systematic differences between developed and developing countries, and large differences among developing countries.

Differences are myriad, but good economic theory and good policy analysis attempt to identify the most salient and show how each leads to differences in economic performance and the conduct of policy. Now that we've highlighted several major differences, we'll elaborate on their implications in upcoming chapters.

5

Policy Instruments from Three Perspectives: Fiscal and Monetary Policy

The two most important ways governments attempt to stabilize the economy are through monetary and fiscal policies. Even when economists agree over whether these policies are effective, they still disagree about when they work, when greater reliance should be placed on one than the other, and the ways in which they exert their effects.

As we noted in Chapter 3, in standard Keynesian analysis, policy-makers faced with an economic slowdown should increase government spending, reduce taxes, and loosen monetary policy. By contrast, conservatives are skeptical of government intervention. They criticize the efficacy of government policies for stimulating the economy on several grounds: the policies are unnecessary, are ineffective and even counterproductive, and can't be implemented in a timely manner.

Prolonged episodes of unemployment have, however, by and large weakened support for the view that the economy automatically maintains itself at or near full employment. There's evidence[1] that in developed countries (such as the United States) downturns have been shorter, and expansions longer, in the post-World War II period than prior to World War I, when government intervention was less significant. There's also evidence that economic downturns are no longer predictable.[2] Both of these observations indicate that modern macro-policy is having an effect, at least in developed countries.[3] If downturns were predictable, governments could and should intervene with well-designed policies to stimulate the economy. But if downturns can't be predicted, then it's impossible for there to be *ex-ante* interventions.

Economic volatility is greater in developing countries than in developed countries, which suggests that there may still be scope for improved macroeconomic policy in developing countries. As we discussed in the previous chapter, developing countries face greater disturbances and have economic structures that make them less able to absorb shocks, and more likely to amplify shocks. Typically, they have fewer government-provided automatic stabilizers, such as unemployment insurance. They also face greater constraints in the conduct of macro-policy. For example, they face important constraints in financing deficit spending, which means they have less scope for fiscal policy, and financial systems tend to be much less developed, so that monetary policy may be both less effective and more distortionary. In short, the challenges of stabilization are greater, and the instruments are more restrained. Not surprisingly, the outcomes have, by and large, not been as good—volatility of output growth in most regions exceeds that of the Organization for Economic Cooperation and Development (OECD).[4]

In the discussion below, we take a closer look at policy instruments from the alternative perspectives. Our discussions focus on the effectiveness of each instrument and its ancillary effects, particularly on growth. We should note that, as we've pointed out in previous chapters, underlying many of the different opinions on these policies are different levels of concern about inflation.

Discussions of different policy instruments are often confused because governments have limited ability to pursue one policy independently of the others. The government may not be able to set fiscal, monetary, and exchange rate policy independently. For example, under a fixed exchange rate system, the exchange rate chosen by the government might not be sustainable, given the chosen fiscal and monetary policies. This is especially true with open capital markets, since monetary or fiscal policy choices can cause capital to leave or enter the country, putting pressure on the fixed exchange rate. Under a flexible exchange rate system, a change in fiscal or monetary policy will directly affect the exchange rate. The government needs to take this interaction into account in setting policies.

Much of the policy discourse is centered on what the government should *determine* versus what should be set by the market. For instance, when monetarism was in fashion, central banks set the money supply (or its rate of expansion), letting the market determine the interest rate. Today, monetary authorities more often set interest rate targets, engaging in open market operations to allow the expansion of the money supply to whatever it needs to be to generate the desired interest rate. Some monetary authorities engaged in inflation targeting are establishing rules that, in effect, even let the interest rate target be 'endogenous', or set by the market: it's simply determined by the gap between inflation and the inflation target. The inflation target is the object of policy choice.

This chapter will focus on the use of fiscal and monetary policies (including an analysis of the macroeconomic dimensions of prudential regulations). However, we will concentrate more on fiscal issues and will leave a full analysis of monetary policy to the next three chapters on open economy macroeconomics, which examine the interaction between fiscal, monetary, and exchange rate policies.

Fiscal Policy Controversies

Conservative Perspective: Why Fiscal Policy May Be Ineffective—Offsetting Actions

As we noted earlier, critics of fiscal policy often refer to 'offsetting actions' as a main reason why fiscal policy is ineffective. In their view, the private sector responds to fiscal policy in ways that offset its impact. For example, suppose the government lowers taxes to stimulate consumption. Conservatives argue that if the tax cut leads to a fiscal deficit, households will note the deficit, recognize that someday they'll have to repay this debt, and increase savings instead of consumption. In this scenario, tax cuts will not stimulate the economy.

This reasoning, known as the Barro–Ricardo hypothesis,[5] implies (in its strong form) that deficits don't matter at all and have no effect on interest rates because increased government borrowing gives rise to an exactly equal and offsetting increase in private savings. There are, however, only a few instances in which a limited version of this scenario seems to have taken place. The most notable is Japan in the 1990s, but this isn't a compelling example, especially for developing countries. Due to the historically high level of household savings in Japan, it's likely that a smaller percentage of Japanese households were credit and cash flow constrained than are most households in developing countries. Had Japanese households been so constrained, the additional cash provided by the tax cut would have likely gone towards consumption rather than savings.

Moreover, the relevant question is not whether a poorly designed tax cut is ineffective but whether there is *some* form of tax cut that can stimulate the economy. For example, a temporary sales tax cut could be an effective measure for stimulating consumption in the short run. A temporary tax cut is similar to a sale: as long as the temporary nature of the tax is credible, consumers, who know that prices will be increased when the 'sale' ends, will increase consumption today. Even in Japan, a *temporary cut in the consumption* tax did appear to be effective.

One of the reasons why the Japanese *income* tax cut wasn't very effective was that most Japanese workers believed that taxes would have to be increased again in the future.[6] The US Treasury urged Japan to announce that the tax cut was permanent; believing that doing so would lead to a larger increase in consumption. But talk is cheap, and there was no reason to believe that households would believe such an announcement. Households could see the soaring deficits, and this meant that the promise to make the tax cut permanent wasn't credible. On the other hand, the very fact that deficits were soaring meant that the announcement that the reduction in *sales* taxes was *temporary* was credible.

The assumptions under which the Barro–Ricardo hypothesis is true are highly restrictive. For example, the Barro–Ricardo analysis assumes that households and firms are not credit or cash constrained. In addition, empirically, the weight of evidence is against the hypothesis.[7]

Keynesian Perspective: Why Fiscal Policy is Effective

Standard Keynesian economics emphasizes that government expenditures (or tax cuts) lead to an increase in GDP that's a *multiple*[8] of the original expenditure. Most of the money paid by the government is re-spent,[9] and the more that's re-spent, the greater the multiplier. If savings rates are low, as they often are in very poor countries, then the proportion of funds going into consumption will be high, and the multiplier will be very large. Public expenditures will be particularly effective. By contrast, in East Asia, where savings rates have been very high, multipliers have been somewhat smaller.

Note the contrast between the Barro–Ricardo hypothesis—which says that all of the additional income will be saved—and the traditional Keynesian model. Barro–Ricardo says that there is no stimulation (the multiplier is zero).

Heterodox Perspective: Why Fiscal Policy may be Particularly Effective, Especially in Developing Countries

There's evidence that tax cuts do, in fact, stimulate consumption, as long as they go to those who don't have access to credit. There's also evidence that many households and firms are credit and cash constrained, especially in developing countries. If those households and firms could spend more money they would; so if the government gives a tax cut to these individuals, all of the increased income should be spent. In other words, their marginal propensity to consume is one. For example, if the government provides better unemployment benefits, it's likely that the unemployed will spend all or almost all of the benefit. Of course, when they spend the money, some of it will go to individuals (landlords, storeowners, etc.) who will not spend all of it. But the important point is that in developing countries the multiplier can be quite high.

When firms are cash or credit constrained, there also may be a *financial accelerator*. Increased government spending increases the profits of firms. When firms are cash or credit constrained they're likely to spend all, or most, of any extra income on investment. More than that, the value of equity will increase in anticipation of a stronger economy, making it easier for firms to gain access to credit. The increase in investment stimulated can be a multiple of the original increase in the cash flow of the firm—and the increase in investment in turn can give rise to a multiple increase in GDP.

Firms in developing countries are more likely to be cash or credit constrained than firms in developed countries. A large fraction of production in developing countries occurs in small and medium-sized enterprises (SMEs), which are more likely to be credit constrained. (There is evidence that SMEs are even credit constrained in advanced, industrialized countries.) Equity markets in developing countries rarely function well, so it's difficult for firms to raise new equity. (During an economic downturn it's even difficult to raise new equity in advanced industrial countries.) In some countries, like those in East Asia, where there is a well-functioning debt market, debt is typically limited to a given ratio of equity due to prudential behavior on the part of both borrower and lender. This means that an increase in the value of equity (as a result of, say, increased sales and sales prospects) enables firms to increase borrowing. In Asian countries, the financial accelerator can be quite large.

There is still another accelerator that can be important in developing countries. If firms' profits grow due to increased demand, they will also be better able to repay their existing bank loans. The improved financial position of banks enables them to engage in more lending; and the increased availability of capital leads to an expansion of production.

More recently, another major benefit of fiscal policy has come into play: it can help overcome a large *negative* accelerator, triggered, ironically, by prudential bank policies. When firm profits fall enough during an economic slowdown, they default on their loans. Banks' capital adequacy can eventually fall below the level required by prudential regulations. In such situations, banks have to raise more capital or cut back on lending. But it's hard (or very costly) for banks to raise new capital in these circumstances, so banks are forced to cut back on their lending.

Banking authorities, however, can engage in forbearance, that is, allow banks to continue to operate undercapitalized. (We should note that if banks are allowed to continue to operate in such circumstances, regulators need to monitor the banks to prevent them from undertaking excessively risky loans or looting the bank, i.e. moral hazard problems.[10]) Without forbearance, the drop in lending will reduce both aggregate demand and aggregate supply, causing GDP to fall.

Conservative Perspective: Why Fiscal Policy May Be Counter productive—Crowding Out

While heterodox economists have identified a number of reasons that fiscal policy may be more stimulating than traditional Keynesians had thought, conservatives argue that expansionary fiscal policy is not just ineffective; it may actually be counterproductive. When expansionary fiscal policy leads to an increased deficit it 'crowds out' private investment: the higher deficit leads to higher interest rates, and the higher interest rates reduce private investment.[11]

It's important to differentiate between the effects of deficits when the economy is in recession and those when the economy is at full employment; the latter case is when deficits are more likely to have an adverse effect. Crowding-out arguments are then persuasive because the size of the 'pie' is fixed. When the economy is operating at capacity, increased government expenditures must come at the expense of reduced consumption or reduced investment somewhere else in the economy. But our concern here is when the economy is *below* full employment. Then, crowding out is *not* inevitable. The size of the pie can increase so that government expenditures can rise without private investment decreasing.

Or, in the case of a tax cut, consumption can increase, without investment decreasing.[12]

In addition, *the crowding-out argument implicitly assumes that central banks cannot take offsetting actions to lower interest rates*. Yet central banks can do so by increasing the money supply. One of the concerns about government borrowing is that the debt will be monetized (the borrowing will be financed by, in effect, printing money) and the banking system will be allowed to increase money (and credit) excessively, to the point that inflation will set in.[13] Even when interest rates are close to zero and there are limits on the ability of monetary authorities to lower interest rates further (a Keynesian-type liquidity trap[14]), central banks can at least undo the higher interest rates resulting from government deficits. Moreover, in a small open economy, there's another reason why interest rates might not rise and there won't be crowding out: an inflow of capital[15] can prevent a rise in interest rates.[16] (We'll discuss this in more detail in Chapter 6.)

Heterodox (and Keynesian) Perspective: Crowding In

While conservatives worry that private sector responses will diminish the impact of fiscal policy as a result of crowding out, Keynesians, and especially heterodox economists, emphasize that private sector responses may actually enhance the effects. There may be 'crowding in'. For instance, higher government expenditures might stimulate the economy and improve the economic situation so much that there's room for more investment. Similarly, an increase in government investments that complements private investment (for example, spending on infrastructure) can increase returns in the private sector and stimulate private investment and the economy as a whole.

The success of China's expenditures during the East Asian crisis provides a case in point. Part of the reason for China's success was that current expenditures drew upon a set of strategic investment plans that focused on improving infrastructure. The improved infrastructure increased the returns to private investments. This, in turn, encouraged productive investments that stimulated China's long-term growth. India's experience with stabilization and adjustment, following its external debt crisis during the early 1990s, was somewhat different. Yet, it also provides clear evidence of complementarities between public investment and private investment, which suggests crowding in rather than crowding out.[17]

69

Conservative Perspective: Counterproductiveness—Loss of Confidence

Perhaps because the standard arguments for crowding out seem increasingly unpersuasive, conservatives have turned to arguments based on the hard-to-verify notion of confidence. In this view, government spending leads to lower private investment because investors see the rising deficits, lose confidence in the economy, and decide not to invest. Only resolute government action to counter the deficit can restore confidence, increase investment, and quickly restore the economy to health.

Despite how frequently conservatives invoke the confidence argument, there's remarkably little empirical research on the matter (including little research by the IMF which seems to rely on the confidence argument heavily). The evidence does show overwhelmingly, however, that cutting government expenditures leads to lower GDP in both developed and developing[18] countries. The direct impact of a cut in government expenditure on GDP are much stronger than the confidence effect. Expenditure reductions forced on Argentina and East Asia in the 1990s did not have the positive effects promised by the IMF, but instead produced the negative effects predicted by the more standard Keynesian models.

Heterodox (and Keynesian) Perspective: A Strong Economy Builds Confidence

It might be true that *short-term* investors and creditors might be more interested in the size of the fiscal deficit than in other variables. The most important issue for these investors is government's ability to repay its debt in the very near term. To the extent that government saves money by cutting the fiscal deficit, it will have more funds to pay back creditors in the short run—even if this hampers long-term growth. But these are precisely the type of investors who heighten market volatility and whom governments shouldn't want to attract.

Long-term investors look beyond the deficit to a range of variables, the most important of which is long-term sustainable growth. These investors recognize that reducing government expenditures usually decreases output and increases unemployment. To Keynesian and heterodox economists, policies that lead to long-term sustainable growth will naturally lead to greater confidence in the economy and more investment.

If countries borrow to finance productive investments that will generate returns in excess of the interest rate charges, then growth will be enhanced. Investors will recognize the economy's increased strength and should have more confidence in it.

Controversies among Conservatives about the Effects of Deficit Spending

More recently, conservatives have become deeply divided over the issue of deficit spending. As we suggested earlier, conservatives are generally less optimistic about the use of tax cuts or expenditure increases to stimulate the economy than traditional Keynesians. However, since the Reagan years, some conservatives have been using Keynesian-like analysis combined with supply-side reasoning to argue that reducing taxes during an economic downturn is a good thing. They make two claims: that general tax cuts are more stimulative than government expenditures and that deficits have little adverse effect on the economy, in both the short and the long run. Underlying these claims are two fundamental confusions.

The argument that tax cuts are more stimulative than increased expenditures can be dismissed easily: neither theory nor evidence supports it. To begin with, recessions are marked by reductions in the demand for labor. But the conservatives' argument is with regard to the *supply* of labor. The argument is that lowering tax rates might induce people to work harder. Not only is there limited evidence of this, the problem at hand is inadequate demand for labor, not inadequate supply. A greater supply of labor at the going wage would simply lead to more unemployment.

In addition, the multipliers—the extra GDP generated by an extra dollar of government spending or tax cut—associated with government expenditure are larger than the multipliers associated with tax cuts as long as the government uses most of the funds for home-produced goods. This is because a part of any tax cut (especially tax cuts for upper income individuals) goes into savings. Also, when the wealthy, especially the wealthy in developing countries, increase their consumption, they spend much of their money on imported goods, again reducing the Keynesian multiplier. Therefore, the effects of a tax cut or expenditure increases depend on the design of the tax cut or the composition of the expenditure increase.

The second claim is that deficits don't affect long-term growth because the effect of deficits on interest rates is small, and the effect of interest rates on investment is small. Note that the second part of the argument contradicts the usual supply-side view that higher after-tax returns elicit a large increase in investment.[19] This is why this group of conservatives focuses attention only on the first part of the argument—that deficits don't affect interest rates.

71

However, this part of the statement contradicts another main argument made by conservatives: crowding out. If deficits don't affect interest rates, crowding out shouldn't exist. In this, the new conservatives are in agreement with traditional Keynesian economists: when the economy's in recession and there's excess capacity, there's no reason why there needs to be any crowding out, any increase in interest rates, or any reduction in investment.

But if the economy is at full employment (the economic models used by conservatives generally assume it is), the pie is fixed, so that tax cuts crowd out private investment and hurt growth (unless the deficit is, in effect, fully financed by foreigners). The New Conservatives seem to want to have it both ways, that tax cuts stimulate the economy through increased consumption, but do not crowd out investment. At full employment, this is a logical impossibility.

Fiscal Policy in the Presence of Borrowing Constraints

Limitations Imposed by Borrowing Constraints and the Costs of Pro-cyclical Fiscal Policies

The fiscal policy controversies reviewed above have one basic underlying assumption: governments can borrow as much as they want. The alternative schools, though, have different views on how much governments should borrow. But even those who believe in the efficacy of fiscal policy in developed countries recognize that developing countries face a significant impediment to relying on fiscal policy during economic downturns (which is when, according to Keynesian and heterodox thinking, they should engage in deficit spending): their governments might find it difficult or expensive to borrow the funds necessary to finance government spending. Tax revenues automatically fall as the economy slows, and funds available to repay debts fall as well. As the ability of a government to repay its liabilities drops, the interest rate on borrowing rises.

One of the main reasons that the IMF was founded in 1944 was to help countries in depressed conditions finance deficits for economic expansion. The founders recognized the interdependence of nations, which means that a downturn in one country can have an adverse effect on others. They also recognized that capital markets are imperfect and some countries, especially those that are heavily indebted and need funds the most, are sometimes unable to borrow at all. The modern theory of capital markets, with asymmetric information and costly enforcement, explains how such credit rationing can occur.[20] When it does, countries are forced to engage in pro-cyclical fiscal policy: they are forced to cut their deficits during economic slowdowns, exacerbating the recession.

Note that the opposite problem happens during the upswings of the business cycle. As revenues recover, so does government spending. Governments tend to have better access to credit during expansions: they often increase the use of deficit spending during booms, contrary to the recommendations of all schools of thought. This implies that spending might increase on the basis of temporary tax revenues and new borrowings, which will make the contraction during the following downswing even worse.

There is widespread evidence that fiscal accounts are highly pro-cyclical in the developing world.[21] In Latin America, for example, out of 45 episodes of cyclical swings in 1990–2001, 12 were neutral, 25 were pro-cyclical, and only 8 counter-cyclical.[22] So, the broader problem faced by developing countries are the strong incentives for fiscal policies to behave in a pro-cyclical way. This effect is compounded by the pro-cyclical performance of public-sector revenues in the context of high GDP volatility.

At the same time, other pro-cyclical patterns have become more important than in the past, particularly those associated with granting government guarantees to the private sector. An example is explicit and implicit guarantees issued to financial agents and depositors in the financial system. Another is public-sector guarantees for private-sector investments in infrastructure (such as minimum revenue or profit guarantees, or explicit coverage of interest or exchange rate risks). Both implicit and explicit guarantees have three elements in common: (a) they are not always transparent; (b) they encourage *private* spending during booms (the implicit public-sector spending in the form of an equivalent 'insurance premium' is actually incurred during periods of euphoria, indicating that accrued public-sector spending during these periods is underestimated); and (c) disbursements (cash spending) are incurred during crises, increasing borrowing requirements and crowding out other public-sector spending.

The costs of pro-cyclical fiscal policies are high. During upswings, abundant financing may lead authorities to start some projects that have low social returns. During downswings, cuts in spending may mean that investment projects are left unfinished or take much longer to execute than planned, thereby raising their effective cost. In turn, extended cuts in public-sector investment may have long-term effects on growth.[23] To the extent that current spending is reduced during downswings, some valuable social programs may be cut, the existing structure for the provision of public and social services may became disjointed, and reductions in real wages may lead to the loss of valuable staff. In general, 'stop-go' cycles significantly reduce the efficiency of public-sector spending.

This means that a major aim of economic policy in developing countries should be to avoid pro-cyclical biases in fiscal policy. This can be consistent with the establishment of rules that guarantee long-term sustainability of the fiscal account, such as targets for the public-sector deficit and/or maximum debt-to-GDP ratios. (The definition of such rules is not an easy task, however, as demonstrated by the recent debates within the European Stability and Growth Pact.)

In particular, a focus on the *current* fiscal deficit (measured during the recession) is clearly inappropriate. Rather, it's essential to estimate 'the *structural* deficit', which evaluates what the budget would be without cyclical fluctuations[24] in a 'normal' (full employment) situation. For example, when tax revenues fall during a recession, the current fiscal deficit will worsen, but the structural full employment deficit won't be affected, and the government won't be forced to tighten fiscal policy further to meet its deficit target. If necessary, the international financial institutions could play a role in helping to finance any *current* fiscal deficit that arises. We'll discuss these issues in detail in the section on accounting issues in Chapter 8.

Deficit targets should be complemented by adequate mechanisms to manage public-sector guarantees. As argued earlier, public-sector guarantees have pro-cyclical effects. Deficit targets create a strong incentive for governments to promote private (rather than public) sector investment in infrastructure to circumvent the targets, even when there's no economic reason to do so. As we'll see in Chapter 8, a major problem in relation to these guarantees is that they generate significant distortions in public-sector accounting. The nature of fiscal targets should be chosen to avoid these problems.

To the extent that cyclical swings may reduce the efficiency of public-sector spending, it may make sense to determine structural targets on the basis of an essentially long-term criterion: the balanced supply of public and private goods. At the same time, due to the inevitable time lags in the decision-making process, *automatic* stabilizers may be preferable to discretionary changes. Well-designed social safety nets to protect vulnerable groups during crises (preferably as part of permanent social protection systems) and fiscal stabilization funds are the best-available instruments in this regard.

Fiscal Stabilization Funds

A first major instrument of counter-cyclical policy is fiscal stabilization funds to sterilize temporary public-sector revenues. The experience gained from the management of stabilization funds for commodities that have a significant fiscal impact (the National Coffee Fund of Colombia, the copper and petroleum funds in Chile, and the oil funds in several countries)[25] can be extended to develop broader fiscal stabilization funds.[26] A similar example is foreign exchange reserves, which provide 'self-insurance' against sudden interruption in external financing (as well as reduced currency appreciation).

The point of a stabilization fund is to put funds aside when the economy is in a boom period, to be used when the economy is in recession. However, economists disagree on when a country should be building funds and when it should be spending them. For example, in 2005 the province of Mendoza in Argentina was growing at or above the national average and running a fiscal surplus. Many economists recommended that Mendoza save the surplus above current expenditures into an anti-cyclical stabilization fund. However, the governor of Mendoza pointed out that unemployment at the time, while lower than elsewhere in Argentina, was still high, at between 7 and 8 percent. In his view, it made more sense to invest the surplus in employment-generating activities, since the economy was still way below full employment.

Some economists argue that most developing countries are almost always below full employment, and would never find the opportunity to build the stabilization funds. Others point out that there are two criteria that can help determine when the surplus should be spent rather than saved. The first is based on expectations about the future. If the economy is growing today and a slowdown is expected it would make sense to save an important part of the surplus. Employment would be lower today but resources would be available to support more employment generation tomorrow when the economy slows down. The second criteria is based on the expected returns of each project. The question is whether the government spending goes into investment and job creation or consumption. To the extent that the funds go into consumption, they are unlikely to lead to future growth, and it would be wiser to put the surplus into a fund. But, to the extent that the funds go into investment, the returns could be high for both current employment and future growth, due to the multiplier and crowding-in effects discussed earlier.

The major policy implication of the previous analysis is, however, that international financial institutions should help countries build stabilization funds that can be used as anti-cyclical tools.

Counter-Cyclical Tax Policies

To the extent that stabilization funds sterilize the additional revenues generated by a commodity or capital boom, they make fiscal policy at most cycle-*neutral*, as the additional revenues due to increased demand go into reserves. A complementary instrument, of clear *counter*-cyclical character, would be to design flexible tax rates, particularly to manage sharp private-sector spending cycles. The best candidate is obviously a tax on the source of the spending boom. This is the traditional argument for taxing exports subject to temporary price surges, which has served as the basis for the design of commodity stabilization funds.

A similar argument can be used to justify an increase in the tax on capital inflows during booms, as this is the major source of private-sector spending upswings today.[27] It is interesting to note that this argument is in addition to the arguments associated with the greater monetary autonomy that a tax on capital flows provides, which we'll analyze in Part III of this book.

An argument can also be made for temporary hikes of VAT rates during private spending booms and reductions of VAT rates during downswings.[28] In addition, heterodox economists have put forth other tax policies that can be used to reduce pro-cyclicality and give additional fiscal options to countries, as are discussed below.

Low-Cost Stimuli and Other Fiscal Policy Alternatives

Some countries are unable to borrow to finance a tax reduction during a downturn. These countries still have some fiscal policy tools that can be used to stimulate the economy. Two such policy tools are 'expenditure and tax shifting' and 'low-cost stimuli'.

'Expenditure and tax shifting' increases taxes on those who are less likely to reduce expenditures, and cuts taxes on those more likely to increase expenditures, thereby stimulating the economy. Increasing the progressivity of taxation does precisely this. As we've noted, giving a tax cut to low-income individuals is likely to stimulate the economy more per dollar of tax cut simply because poorer people are more credit and cash constrained. Spending more money on goods produced at home and less on goods from abroad will similarly help stimulate the economy.

Countries facing limitations on borrowing need to focus on policies that have a big bang for the buck, called *low-cost stimuli*. For example, as we saw in the case of Japan, a temporary sales tax cut can have a far larger effect than a temporary income tax cut. The importance of cash flows and credit constraints suggests some other examples of low-cost stimuli. We've already discussed tax cuts targeted toward the poor. In addition, increasing unemployment benefits for low-income workers can be particularly effective because virtually all such workers are credit and cash constrained. (In many countries, an increase in aid to regional governments and localities during recessions is also more likely to have a big stimulus effect, since sub-national governments are often subject to balanced budget fiscal frameworks or have more limited access to financing and have to cut expenditures or increase taxes without such aid.)

Public investment expenditures may have a double effect. First, there's the immediate stimulation to the economy. Second, if the public investments are complementary to private investments, as discussed above, increasing government spending will increase the returns to private investment, fueling additional investment.

Other low-cost stimuli focus on firms. The prototypical low-cost stimulus is the '*incremental* investment tax credit'. An incremental investment tax credit provides a tax credit on increases in investments (e.g. the tax credit might apply to investments over 80 percent of the previous year's investment). The incremental investment tax credit lowers the *marginal cost of investment*; just as an ordinary investment tax credit would (the government in effect picks up a fraction of the cost of the machine or other investment). At least in standard models, it has the same stimulative effect as a full investment tax credit, but the cost to the government is markedly less because the credit doesn't apply to the bulk (or the 'base') of an investment. (This, incidentally, is why US businesses have been distinctly uninterested in this kind of tax credit.)[29]

A *temporary* incremental investment tax cut can be even more effective in providing short-run stimulus to the economy. A temporary investment tax credit lowers the price of investing today relative to investing in the future. As discussed earlier, this is like a temporary 'sale' on investment goods and will encourage current investment (although partly at the expense of future investment).[30] We should note, however, that if markets are imperfect and firms' available cash (or net worth) limits their investment, the incremental investment tax credit (whether permanent or temporary) will not be as effective. When fewer funds are available, investment is stimulated less.[31]

Another low-cost stimulus is carry-forward or carry-back tax treatment. The government can extend the period of loss carry-forward (when tax deductions are not taken in the current year, but are used to reduce tax liabilities in future years) or carry-back (when deductions are used to reduce tax liabilities in earlier years). This has the positive effect of increasing economic efficiency[32] and makes the losses fully creditable to the extent that firms engage in investment. These policies might boost investment for yet another reason: in effect, they increase the extent of government risk sharing. Since the ability and willingness of firms to bear risk limits their willingness to invest, better risk sharing between government and firms enhances investment. The government can also provide direct credit to firms for investment (though obviously, it's important that this be well designed, so that the government is able to recover principal and interest).

In short, developing countries often have difficulties borrowing, which can impair their ability to engage in fiscal policy. But heterodox economists have proposed alternative fiscal policy tools, including tax structures, stabilization fund (insurance) policies, and new instruments that can minimize the pro-cyclical nature of fiscal policy and give the government some means to engage in counter-cyclical policy.

An Introduction to Monetary Policy Controversies

Conservative Perspective: Monetary Policy is Ineffective

As we've noted, conservatives, for the most part, believe that monetary policy is relatively ineffective. They believe that the economy normally operates close to full employment, so that any increase in aggregate demand cannot increase output; it can only push up prices.

The conservative models in which monetary policy has no effect include other extremely restrictive assumptions. For example, they assume risk neutrality on the part of all actors and assume that economic agents are not cash constrained. More importantly, the conservatives' position that monetary policy is ineffective shows a fundamental intellectual inconsistency with their ostensible worry about inflation. If real variables such as output were unaffected by monetary policy, there would be little concern about inflation as it wouldn't have any adverse effect on the economy.

Keynesian Perspective: Monetary Policy is Effective, Except under Certain Conditions

We've already suggested that, for Keynesians, monetary policy is an important tool in macroeconomic management. Keynesians believe that monetary policy is, in general, effective in periods of unemployment. But even in some periods of high excess capacity, Keynesians agree that monetary policy might be ineffective, but for different reasons.

First, under certain circumstances, lowering *real* interest rates may be difficult. For example, households and firms simply may hold onto any additional money the central bank prints, so the central bank may be unable to lower nominal interest rates by increasing the money supply. Second, as we've noted, when the economy is characterized by deflation and prices are falling, even low nominal interest rates can be associated with moderate to high real interest rates. At the beginning of the Great Depression, for example, prices fell at more than 10 percent per year; even if the government had been able to lower nominal interest rates to zero, real interest rates would have been high. More recently, Japan pushed nominal interest rates close to zero, but with prices falling at 2 percent per annum, real interest rates couldn't fall below 2 percent.

Heterodox Perspective: Credit is What Matters

More recent heterodox approaches suggest additional reasons why monetary policy might be ineffective (and additional ways in which monetary authorities can expand the economy). In particular, Greenwald and Stiglitz emphasize that credit, and not the money supply, matters for the level of economic activity. The banking system is central in determining the supply of credit. Even if the interest rate on treasury bills falls, banks may be reluctant to lend more when they believe their balance sheets are weak, or when they perceive the risk of lending to be very high (and therefore can achieve high, safer returns by lending to the government).[33]

On the other hand the heterodox approach also emphasizes several additional channels through which lowering interest rates may stimulate consumption. First, changes in the interest rate represent a redistribution of income from creditors to debtors. In the heterodox approach, distribution matters: debtors may have a higher marginal propensity to consume than creditors. If firms and households are credit constrained, lowering interest rates may mean that firms will have more money to invest and households will have more money for consumption.

Second, there may be balance sheet effects, as the value of assets such as stocks and real estate increase with lower interest rates. The increased wealth may induce households to consume more; and if banks and other lenders have rules that limit borrowing to a certain fraction of collateral, the increased value of collateral allows more lending—and more consumption. Third, if lenders have rules limiting lending, e.g. to an amount which individuals can service with, say, a certain fraction of annual income, then lower interest rates lead to increased willingness to lend, and again, the relaxation of the credit constraint leads to more spending.

Raising rates will have the opposite effect. In particular, monetary authorities need to take into account wealth effects and the impact on bankruptcy. Credit constraints usually arise from imperfect information on creditors' ability to repay loans. Information is local, which means that bank failures lead to informational loss that sometimes can become permanent. Restructuring banking systems therefore need to take the flow of credit into account.

Conservatives versus Heterodox (and Keynesians): Discretion versus Rules—From Monetary Targets to Inflation Targets

Since conservatives are skeptical about government's ability to manage economic policy, they tend to advocate simple rules for monetary policy. In the heyday of monetarism in the 1980s, the most favored rule prescribed expanding the money supply at a constant rate. Then it became clear that the demand function for money (velocity) was unstable and hard to predict, especially in developing countries. The constant rate of increase in the money supply led to high interest rate and economic volatility. The money supply rule lost favor, and today inflation targeting is preferred. However, there are also problems with inflation targeting that are not often discussed. For example, inflation targetting doesn't provide a smooth convergence to an equilibrium with both external and internal balance.[34]

We'll discuss some of the difficulties with inflation targeting in more detail in Chapter 7 on open economy macroeconomics. More generally, Keynesian and heterodox economists are skeptical of simple rules and believe that well-designed discretionary government policies can enhance economic performance.

Debates on the Effectiveness of Monetary Policy

Recent experiences confirm both the strengths and limitations of monetary policy. In general, economists view monetary policy as more effective in restraining an overheated economy than in expanding an economy in a deep recession. Monetary policy, for example, has not been effective in stimulating growth in countries experiencing deflation (such as Japan). In the United States, lowering interest rates from 2001 to 2003 did little to stimulate investment, but did induce households to refinance their mortgages. The reduced mortgage payments and the improved financial position of households enabled consumers to sustain their spending even as their stock market wealth diminished enormously. The stimulative effect was related in part to the cash balance/credit constraint effects that the heterodox approach emphasizes.[35]

As we've seen, the impact of monetary policy in developing countries is likely to differ from the impact in the United States and other advanced industrial countries. In many developing countries there is greater reliance on bank lending, and firms have less access to non-bank sources of finance. For example, they can't turn to the commercial paper market. (This is partly because small and medium-sized firms—the kind of firms that cannot turn to commercial paper markets in *any* country—predominate in developing countries.) Since monetary policy has its most direct impact through the banking system, its effects in developing countries can be more significant than in developed countries.

However, in some developing countries, the banking sector is extremely undeveloped and lending is relatively unimportant. Most firms rely on self-finance. In these circumstances, the impact of monetary policy on the economy is limited. The narrower the impact of monetary policy, the greater the costs associated with using it, since a few sectors are forced to bear the brunt of adjustment. Those sectors may face greater volatility, as interest rates rise and fall in an attempt to stabilize the economy.

Modern economic theory (and recent experiences, such as those in South East Asia in 1997) has emphasized an important set of adverse effects of contractionary monetary policy during crises—especially of large increases in interest rates. The first is the effect of interest rate changes on asset values (such as land or stocks). Furthermore, because different firms own different assets, firms' net worth will be affected differently, often in ways that even informed investors may find difficult to ascertain. Interest rate increases give rise to significant increases in uncertainty, further dampening economic activity. Because higher interest rates reduce the net worth of firms, they adversely affect demand not only directly, as the demand for investment and consumption is decreased, but also indirectly, as foreign importers of the country's goods worry that firms will not be able to deliver on their contracts. As we noted above, large increases in interest rates also weaken government finances when the stock of outstanding public debt is significant as a proportion of GDP. The consequent increase in interest payments on public debt can sharply reduce government's fiscal flexibility. All of these effects reinforce the response of the economy to monetary tightening to dampen the economy and restrain inflation.

The focus of our attention here, however, is the use of monetary policy to stimulate the economy. Lowering interest rates has just the reverse effect of what we described above. In this case, the uncertainty associated with changes in asset values implies that the stimulative effect of lowering interest rates may be less than it would otherwise be. There are also complications associated with the relationship between monetary policy, capital flows, and exchange rates, which we'll analyze in the following chapters.

In recent years, many economists in advanced industrial economies have advocated greater reliance on monetary than fiscal policy for stabilization. They argue that the political processes required to change taxes or expenditure levels are too slow, and that monetary authorities can act in a timelier manner. The limitations of monetary policy noted in this section, as well as the limitations on the use of fiscal policy discussed earlier, suggest that we need to find innovative means to use both of them under the severe volatility that characterizes these countries. Heterodox analysis is critical in this regard.

Monetary Policy when Banks are Unwilling to Lend

When monetary policy is ineffective, heterodox economists have emphasized that central banks still have other tools at their disposal to influence lending and credit. When credit rationing exists, what's relevant is not loan demand but loan supply; authorities need to implement policies to induce banks to increase lending. For example, changing regulatory policies, such as capital adequacy requirements and other banking regulations, can impact credit availability. As we'll see below, banking regulations have more macroeconomic implications than is usually accepted (their effects tend to be ignored in most macroeconomic analysis). For example, the credit contraction in the United States following the savings and loan bail-out was due at least in part to the changed regulatory environment. Modifying those regulations probably played some role in restoration of the supply of credit. Two issues may be particularly important for developing countries: the first is credit constraints specific to certain sectors of the economy, and the second is ways to encourage bank lending when credit constraints are more general.

Monetary policy is a blunt tool. Raising interest rates affects all sectors of the economy, those sectors that are experiencing bubbles, as well as those sectors experiencing fragile recoveries or still in recession. When inflation is due to supply shortages in sectors of the economy experiencing credit constraints, authorities can look to innovative ways to ensure that credit reaches these sectors rather than raising interest rates and slowing the economy as a whole. In this regard, the authorities can use tax policies or reserve requirements to try to encourage lending to these sectors. Alternatively, development banks are another tool that can help direct credit to areas in need.

In many developing countries, banks often have excess liquidity. Instead of lending, they find it more attractive to buy government bonds—or even buy the bonds of foreign governments or corporations. This is particularly important during crises: banks view lending to private firms as too risky just when the economy needs additional private credit to avoid a credit crunch. There are a variety of ways that governments and monetary authorities can, in such circumstances, encourage banks to lend. They can, for instance, tax excess reserves, or impose taxes on capital gains from currency changes to discourage banks from, in effect, engaging in foreign exchange speculation. They can take more explicit regulatory actions, such as not allowing banks to hold net foreign exchange assets (either loans or bonds). They can go so far as to actively discourage banks from purchasing government bonds (e.g. by limiting the amount of excess reserves that can be held in the form of government bonds, or by increasing the risk rating of such bonds).

The Macroeconomic Dimensions of Prudential Regulations

Prudential regulations have traditionally been thought of as a measure to reduce microeconomic risks. In recent years, however, increasing attention has been placed on risks that have a clear *macroeconomic* origin. Heterodox economists have designed ways to use prudential regulations as a tool for macroeconomic policy.

Banks use microeconomic risk management to reduce the risks associated with the individual characteristics of borrowers. Prudential regulations have been designed to encourage banks to manage these risks. But it's more difficult to reduce risks associated with the common factors that all market agents face, such as the effects of macroeconomic policies and the business cycle.

Moreover, traditional regulatory tools, including both Basle I and Basle II standards, have a pro-cyclical bias.[36] In these systems, banks have to provision capital against loan delinquency or short-term expectations of future loan losses. Since expectations of losses are low during economic expansions, these systems are not effective in hampering excessive risk taking during booms. Sharp rises in loan delinquencies during economic slowdowns (or crises) increase bank losses, or force them to increase provisions for those losses, reducing their capital and their lending capacity. This may trigger a 'credit squeeze' and exacerbate the downswing in economic activity.[37]

Given the central role that all these processes play in developing countries' business cycles, the crucial policy issue is how to introduce a counter-cyclical element into prudential regulation and supervision.[38] In this regard, a major innovation is the Spanish system of forward-looking provisions, introduced in December 1999. According to this system, provisions are made when loans are *disbursed* based on *expected* (or 'latent') losses. Such 'latent' risks are estimated on the basis of a full business cycle, and are not based on the current economic environment.[39] This system implies that provisioning follows the criteria that are traditionally used by the insurance industry (where provisions are made when the insurance policy is issued) rather than by the banking industry (where they're made when loan payments come due).

In the Spanish system, provisions[40] are accumulated in a fund[41] that grows during economic expansions and is drawn upon during downturns. As long as the fund has adequate resources, banks shouldn't need to make additional provisions for new loan losses during a recession. Although the accumulation and drawing down of the fund has a counter-cyclical dynamics, it actually just counteracts the cyclical pattern of bank lending. The system is, strictly speaking, 'cycle-neutral' rather than counter-cyclical, but it's certainly superior to the traditional pro-cyclical provisioning for loan losses.

Strictly counter-cyclical prudential provisions should complement such a system. These criteria could include holding excess provisions against loan losses when authorities think that there is a disproportionate growth of credit (relative to some benchmark), or limits on lending to sectors characterized by systematic (economy-wide) risks, such as the construction sector. Alternatively, direct restrictions on credit growth, or restrictions on new lending to certain risky activities, could be used. The regulations also could be supplemented by more specific regulations aimed at controlling currency and maturity mismatches (including those associated with derivatives), such as limits on foreign-currency-denominated loans to the domestic non-tradable sectors.

We'll examine some of the risks involved in these types of balance sheet mismatches in the following chapters. Insofar as developing countries are likely to face more macroeconomic volatility, there may be an argument for requiring higher capital/asset ratios, but provisioning against loan losses is probably a better solution.[42]

In addition, prudential regulation needs to ensure adequate levels of liquidity for financial intermediaries so that they can handle the mismatch between the average maturities of assets and liabilities. Such mismatch is inherent in the financial system's essential function of transforming maturities, but it generates risks associated with volatility in deposits and/or interest rates. Reserve requirements, which are strictly an instrument of monetary policy, provide liquidity in many countries, but their declining importance makes it necessary to find new tools.

An alternative system could be one in which liquidity or reserve requirements are estimated on the basis of the residual maturity of financial institutions' liabilities. The valuation of assets used as collateral for loans also presents problems when those assets exhibit price volatility because, in many cases, prices used to value collaterals may be significantly higher than *ex-post* prices. Limits on loan-to-value ratios and/or rules to adjust the values of collateral for cyclical price variations could avoid some of these problems.

We should emphasize that any regulatory approach has clear limits and costs that cannot be overlooked. Prudential supervision is full of information problems and is a discretionary activity susceptible to abuse. As we'll discuss in Part III, experience also indicates that even well-regulated systems in industrial countries are subject to periodic episodes of euphoria, when risks are underestimated. The recent 2001 crisis in Argentina is a specific case in which a system of prudential regulations that was considered to be one of the best in the developing world, working within the framework of a financial sector characterized by the large-scale presence of multinational banks, clearly failed to avert the effects of major macroeconomic shocks on the domestic financial system. The Argentinian case, in particular, underscores the importance of fiscal, monetary, and exchange rate choices, as we'll discuss in the following chapter.

6

Open Economy Complications

The previous chapter contrasted Keynesian, heterodox, and conservative perspectives on policy-making during an economic downturn. Both the Keynesian and heterodox perspectives argue for an active role for government. Conservatives are far more pessimistic about the government's ability to resuscitate the economy. On the one hand, they're worried that government policy is ineffective; on the other hand, they're even more worried that it might be effective—but in the wrong way. In their view, for instance, government policy could provide a stimulus to the economy just when the economy is becoming overheated.

In the previous chapter, the main controversies centered on the size of the multiplier, the extent of crowding out, the management of fiscal cycles in developing countries, and the relative effectiveness of monetary and fiscal policies. Although some open economy considerations were introduced, the analysis tended to leave aside the major complexities of open economy macroeconomics, particularly the interaction between monetary and fiscal policies and exchange rate policies.

Most developing countries are open to trade—imports and exports represent a large fraction of their GDP. Increasingly, developing countries have also opened their capital accounts to foreign capital flows, including long-term direct investment and short-term capital flows. Inflows (outflows) represent a greater (lesser) demand for a country's currency, and all else being equal, put pressure on the currency to appreciate (depreciate). This openness exposes the countries to risks, and increases the need for stabilization policy. But it may also make some stabilization instruments less effective, and impose severe constraints on the use of other instruments.

Despite the greater complexities associated with open economy macroeconomics, the policy conclusions discussed in the previous chapter remain remarkably unaffected. While Keynesians and heterodox economists believe that government should actively intervene, conservatives remain skeptical about the desirability of such interventions. But the complexity itself inevitably brings greater controversy. During the East Asia crisis, for instance, the IMF argued for massive increases in interest rates and large cuts in expenditures, just the opposite of the Keynesian prescription. The objective of this chapter is to shed some light on how economists can come to such diverse views on economic policy.

This chapter is divided into two sections. The first introduces exchange rate policy. The second looks at the complex interactions between interest rates, capital mobility, and exchange rates. The following chapter then focuses more explicitly on policy options in open economies.

The Macroeconomic Effects of Exchange Rates

Exchange rates are relative prices among the currencies of different countries.[1] In a global economic system, not all countries can lower or raise their exchange rates at the same time. When one currency weakens, another must be strengthening and at least one currency has to be strengthening against all the others. But small developing countries are at an advantage at least in this respect: they can choose an exchange rate policy without worrying about the responses of the major economic players—although they might still worry about responses from neighbors or immediate economic rivals.

Keynesian economics, with its focus on employment, tends to look more favorably on policies that result in weaker exchange rates because they increase the attractiveness of exporting by making the country's products cheaper abroad, and help domestic industries that compete with imports (import substitution industries) by making foreign goods more expensive relative to domestic goods. In a *full employment* economy, a weaker exchange rate will lead to a reallocation of the country's resources away from goods and services produced exclusively for the domestic market ('non-tradables') towards goods produced for export or goods that compete with imports ('tradables'). But in an economy marked by unemployment and underutilization of resources, the higher demand for exports and the increasing production of import-competitive goods can spill over into demand for non-tradables due to the increased income in the sectors that produce tradables. Moreover, many economists believe that there are more growth-related 'externalities' in the tradable sector, so that countries that pursue a policy of maintaining an undervalued exchange rate will grow faster. There is some evidence that that has been the case.[2]

Conservatives are more skeptical about the positive effects of weaker exchange rates, fearing that devaluations will lead to inflation since, for example, imports will be more expensive. In fact, many conservatives go one step further and argue that attempts at currency devaluation will be self-defeating in the absence of monetary tightening: one dollar might buy more pesos following the devaluation, but the gains can be completely wiped out if each peso is worth less due to inflation. Despite the nominal currency devaluation, the higher prices mean there will be no depreciation of the *real* exchange rate.

However, even if prices *eventually* adjust so that there is no change in the real exchange rate, the adjustments do not occur instantaneously. And in the interim, the country may benefit from the weaker real exchange rate. The two issues are: (*a*) how long will it take for prices to adjust, that is, how long will the economy enjoy the benefits of a weaker real exchange rate; and (*b*) what are the adjustment costs (including the costs of inflation) in comparison with the benefits (including the benefits of a weaker real exchange rate, even if that benefit is only short-lived).

Heterodox economists, while generally in favor of maintaining competitive exchange rates to stimulate growth, have raised a second objection to devaluation. This objection focuses on balance sheet effects. When a country (or the firms within the country) have borrowed and lent in foreign currencies, devaluations will change the value of the country's and firms' overall balance sheets. For example, this effect was particularly important in Indonesia during the Asian crisis. Many companies were unable to repay their large foreign currency liabilities after the currency devaluation raised the value of their debt in local currency terms. This effect led to widespread bankruptcies throughout the economy.

Currency devaluation → more demand for exports → more production.

Impact on Inflation

In general, the magnitude and durability of the effects of a weakening currency depends on its impact on inflation and the net effect on the real exchange rate. We begin our analysis by looking at the direct impact of exchange rate changes on prices. If we assume the exchange rate weakens, the devaluation will lead to higher prices of imported and exported goods. Imports become more expensive in local currency terms as do exported goods since firms generally receive a higher price in foreign markets in local currency terms. The magnitude of the inflationary impact is likely to depend on the proportion of imported goods in the economy, especially intermediate and capital goods. When imported goods are large, the devaluation can lead to increased costs of production in many industries. This may be a 'once and for all' effect: the higher prices of tradable goods are reflected in the domestic price indices at once, with no further impact on prices. But it could also lead to an inflationary spiral.

Whether inflationary worries are justified depends in large part on expectations, the structure of the economy (i.e., the extent of indexation, such as cost-of-living clauses in nominal contracts), and secondary effects based on how the government and other economic actors respond to the exchange rate movements. For example, workers may react to the initial inflationary effect by demanding higher wages. If a devaluation gives rise to an adjustment of nominal wages, an inflationary spiral may be set off. Higher wages will lead to further price increases. Another devaluation may be called for, leading to round after round of price increases.

It appears that, when there is sufficient slack in the economy (when unemployment, for instance, is high enough), devaluations have generally not given rise to sustained inflation, at least in recent years. We saw marked exchange rate devaluations without inflationary spirals in East Asia, Argentina, and Brazil after the East Asian and Latin American crises in the 1990s. The same was true for India, following its external debt crisis, earlier in the 1990s.

Expectations depend, at least in part, on history. The fact that recent history has shown that there is no reason that even large devaluations will be followed by episodes of sustained inflation means that, going forward, it is less likely that devaluations will give rise to indexation and inflationary expectations.

The Impact on Aggregate Demand and Growth

As we've noted, currency devaluations should boost export and import-competing sectors and raise income and output. Yet often, these effects take time to materialize, while the short-term effects on aggregate demand are contractionary.[3] This may lead to what is usually referred to as the 'J-curve': an initial contractionary effect of a devaluation followed by a period in which the expansionary effects prevail.

There are several reasons why the growth in exports and import-competing sectors often occurs with a lag. It takes time for exporters to find new markets. In addition, some of the more permanent effects may require that producers retool their businesses. Furthermore, if firms believe that the real devaluation is only temporary because of inflation, the devaluation will produce only limited new investments in exports or import-competing industries. Before firms are willing to invest, they need to be convinced that the increase in profitability that results from the devaluation will be sustainable.

There are also several reasons why the initial effect of devaluation may be contractionary. The first arises from the adverse effect the devaluation may have on real wages. If increases in wages lag the increase in prices of imported and exported consumer goods, aggregate demand and output will fall as consumers' purchasing power falls. (A similar effect is produced if the money supply is slow to adjust to higher prices.)

Another reason devaluations may depress economic activity is that they may increase the trade deficit in the short run. The deficit may rise in domestic currency terms, even though it may be reduced in foreign currency terms. This is more likely when the short-term response of rising exports and falling imports takes time to materialize. *In practice*, however, even though the positive impact of currency devaluation on exports often occurs with a lag (it takes time for exporters to find new markets abroad), imports often drop almost immediately. For instance, in the Russian and Argentinian devaluations, there was large and rapid substitution of imports with domestic products, leading to improvements in the trade deficit and large rebounds in output.

When domestic firms face credit constraints and have trouble borrowing, the short-term contractionary effects of a devaluation can be especially large. Export-oriented and import-substitution firms may not have the capital to pay for imported intermediate or capital goods, and may find it difficult to invest and increase capacity to meet the new demand.[4] Some theories suggest that devaluations can actually worsen credit constraints due to higher inflation, increased uncertainty, and the loss of foreign credit. Similarly, when domestic firms have large borrowings in foreign currencies, devaluations can also generate wealth losses, as discussed above in the case of Indonesia. Even short of outright bankruptcies, those with foreign debts are poorer and less willing to undertake risky investments; and banks, seeing that the balance sheets of firms are in worse shape, are less willing to lend.[5] We'll discuss these balance sheet effects at greater length in the next section.

Devaluations also entail significant redistribution, especially in the short run. Exporters benefit, while importers lose. Debtors in foreign currencies lose while those who own net assets in foreign currencies benefit. Also, as we've seen, wages may lag. The losers often become vocal opponents of devaluation, while the long-run benefits to the economy derived from devaluation (increased exports and greater sales of import substitution goods) may be harder to see in the short run.

The impact of devaluation also depends on how monetary authorities respond to any resulting inflation. If the monetary authorities respond by raising interest rates (as they might following strict inflation targeting rules), the devaluation's positive impact—the economic expansion of export and import-competitive sectors and possible spillovers to the rest of the economy—will be reduced. The answer to whether it's appropriate for monetary authorities to respond to the threat of increased inflation posed by a currency devaluation by raising interest rates is problematic, even when combating inflation is a goal. The key question, as discussed above, is whether the devaluation leads to a one-time increase in prices or whether it will lead to further price rises and an increase in the *rate* of inflation.

Overall, the benefits to growth from the devaluation typically outweigh the costs associated with mild inflation. The consensus is that normally the positive effects on exports and import substitution industries outweigh the negative effects, so that devaluations are expansionary in the medium to long run. Furthermore, governments can act to reduce or offset some of these adverse effects by implementing heterodox policies, such as providing additional trade credit or temporary investment tax credits for domestically produced investment goods, as we discuss later in this chapter. When other instruments for stimulating the economy are limited (as they typically are in developing countries), a weak exchange rate can be an effective instrument for economic growth and job creation. Exchange rate policy, then, is not simply a tactical matter of getting-prices-right but may turn out to be a strategic matter of a deliberately undervalued exchange rate, maintained over a period of time, to provide an entry into the world market for differentiated manufactured goods.[6] Several Asian countries have used such a strategic exchange rate policy to promote manufactured exports. Similarly, the build-up of the Chilean boom of the 1990s was clearly preceded by a weak exchange rate policy in the late 1980s and early 1990s.

Indeed, a competitive exchange rate is seen today as an essential ingredient of dynamic growth and employment in developing countries.[7] It allows domestic firms to benefit from rapid growth in international trade and attracts multinational firms searching for the best location for their worldwide sourcing of their goods. This may also have positive spillovers on domestic technological development, and lead to a process of learning how to produce with the best technologies available, and with the best marketing tools for the global economy. Furthermore, a competitive exchange rate means that spillovers of export production on other domestic sectors is enhanced, as exporters find it more attractive to buy the inputs and services they need domestically rather than from abroad. In a world of reduced trade barriers, import-competing sectors see a competitive exchange rate as their major (and perhaps only) source of protection.

This is the reverse of what sometimes happens with currency appreciation. A couple of decades ago, this issue was dealt with in the literature on the 'Dutch disease', more recently referred to as the resource curse.[8] This literature analyzed the long-term losses that a boom in the availability of foreign exchange, due to a discovery of natural resources or a capital surge, could have. The essential insight was that the booming inflows of foreign exchange lead to a real exchange rate appreciation that could permanently hurt other tradable sectors—exports as well as import-competing sectors—and could entail the permanent loss of technological and other spillovers from those sectors. Such 'de-industrialization' (as this effect was sometimes called) implies that booming inflows of foreign exchange may be a mixed blessing.

Real Balance Sheet Effects

As we've noted, the value of foreign currency liabilities rise in relation to domestic assets following devaluations. Debtors might have more difficulty repaying loans to foreign creditors. The increased bankruptcy that results will have adverse effects on growth and output in developing countries.

If a country is a net foreign debtor, the impact of this will generally make the country worse off. The value of its liabilities will increase, and the weaker balance sheet of indebted firms will depress consumption and investment. (This is one of the reasons the Asian crisis was so severe.) If a country is a net creditor, it will be better off on average because foreign-denominated assets will be worth more. But even if the country is a net creditor overall, some firms will be net debtors, and the economic consequences of their losses might more than offset the benefits of the firms that are better off. So the impact of a currency devaluation will depend heavily on an assessment of the balance sheets of domestic firms, households, and the government. Moreover, because creditors generally do not know the exact balance sheet of each firm to whom they lend, and firms do not know the balance sheet of each firm with which they interact, large devaluations give rise to extreme uncertainty.

A good institutional framework, however, can help minimize the balance sheet effects of devaluations. Prudential regulations in place prior to the devaluation can limit the amount of bank (and indirectly firms') foreign currency exposure. If the country has a good bankruptcy law—say modeled after chapter 11 of the US bankruptcy code, which allows fairly rapid corporate reorganizations—the costs on the country can be limited.[9]

In order to design effective economic policies, we need to appraise the situation of each particular country. For example, Japan is a net creditor. At the time of the Asian crisis, Thailand, Korea, and Indonesia were net debtors. The Thai firms that were most heavily indebted in foreign currency were the real estate firms and the banks that lent to them. Most of these firms were already bankrupt at the time of the crisis, so further currency devaluation had little marginal effect. The other major group of heavily indebted firms in Thailand were exporters, and they often gained more from the increased baht value of their exports than they lost from the increased baht value of their dollar-denominated debt. In Malaysia, most of the firms and banks had limited exposure to foreign assets or liabilities. In Indonesia, as we noted earlier, the devaluation of the rupiah had a large negative impact on domestic firms.

In contrast to Asia, in Latin America many governments have large foreign liabilities. In these countries, a currency devaluation will raise the government's cost of borrowing and increase its risk of default—sometimes so much so that countries are afraid to let their currencies weaken. The increased cost means that governments may have to cut back real domestic expenditures, so the *net* effect of the devaluation may be negative: the cutbacks in government expenditures may exceed the increase in net exports.[10] These balance sheet effects point to the importance of governments managing their foreign liability exposure.

Policy Implications

Initial conditions matter, a weak exchange rate may promote growth, but depreciating the exchange rate further may hurt growth due to the balance sheet effects mentioned above. But, often, the argument for a devaluation is that the currency is overvalued. The question is not whether the currency should be devalued but when. It's preferable to devalue gradually than to have a crisis (in which there is often overshooting). Slow, or creeping, devaluations also avoid major price shocks.

In addition, as we discussed above there are often large costs to preventing a devaluation. Raising interest rates to maintain the currency may have even more adverse effects on the economy than the devaluation itself. In the example of Thailand, discussed above, while the currency devaluation might have had little marginal effect on firms, the dramatic increases in interest rates weakened their balance sheets and led to significant bankruptcies. Furthermore, as we discuss below, the impact of tighter monetary policy becomes even more complicated when interactions with the exchange rate and capital flows are introduced.

The Interaction between Fiscal, Monetary, and Exchange Rate Policies in Open Economies

We begin our discussion of the interaction among monetary, fiscal, and exchange rate policies in open economies with an analysis of the fixed exchange rate regime that prevailed prior to 1971. Under a fixed (or pegged) exchange rate regime, policy-makers target the exchange rate and monetary authorities intervene in the foreign exchange market by buying or selling international reserves to maintain the peg. As we'll see, in doing so they severely limit their ability to pursue monetary and fiscal policies. Our discussion of fixed exchange rates can be viewed as a prelude to the more relevant, and far more complicated, discussion on flexible exchange rates which follows.

Under a flexible, or pure floating, exchange rate regime, the government doesn't need to buy or sell reserves. The exchange rate is endogenous (or determined by the market), but authorities influence it through fiscal or monetary policies. And, as we'll see, the effectiveness of monetary and fiscal policies in open economies is still limited by the effects of capital flows, though less so than with a fixed rate.

Most countries don't maintain either a pure fixed or floating regime. Rather, they engage in some type of managed or 'dirty' float. In these intermediate regimes, authorities intervene periodically (sometimes according to specified rules) by buying and selling international reserves, as in the fixed rate system. But they have somewhat more flexibility than if they operated under a pure fixed rate, and the effectiveness of monetary and fiscal policies is somewhere in between the two extreme cases.

Monetary and Fiscal Policies in Open Economies with Fixed Exchange Rates

Fiscal and monetary policies are likely to be less effective in open economies with fixed exchange rates than in closed economies. Let's first consider fiscal policy. Government use of fiscal policy in open economies is weakened because of an additional source of 'leakage', meaning that some income is spent on imports. (The multiplier is smaller.) The fiscal deficit is then translated into a trade deficit (the twin deficit problem). In a fixed rate system, the exchange rate can't adjust, and the country will have to borrow from abroad, or spend its reserves, to finance the deficits.

There's a basic macroeconomic identity that states that net foreign borrowing (combined with changes in the government's foreign currency reserves) must equal the difference between imports and exports. In other words, a country must borrow from abroad (or spend its reserves) to obtain the foreign currency it needs to finance its trade deficit. If a country can't borrow from abroad monetary authorities will have to spend their international reserves to prevent a currency devaluation, but this cannot continue indefinitely—eventually reserves will run out.

As we discussed in Chapter 5, it can be very expensive for developing countries (especially heavily indebted countries) to borrow, and some countries cannot borrow at all. This is because the risk of default, even by governments, is markedly higher in developing countries than in developed countries. As we noted, the absence of external financing can mean that some developing countries may not be able to use fiscal policy as a policy tool.

If the country can borrow abroad, the trade deficit can be financed by borrowing, but this too cannot continue indefinitely. As debt increases relative to reserves, the risk of default increases, and the cost of borrowing rises, so that continued borrowing becomes extremely expensive. With open capital markets, there may even be an attack on the fixed rate. More generally, if 'confidence' erodes, then capital flight may weaken the banking system, leading to a decrease in lending (unless monetary authorities can contravene), and lower GDP.[11] This is why countries with access to borrowing still face limits on the use of fiscal policy, and why developing country governments may be able to use fiscal policy for only a short period of time.

Of course, our concern here is for a *temporary* economic downturn in which the country has no intention of sustaining the trade or fiscal deficit. The argument that's often made that the trade deficit accompanying a stimulation of the economy is not sustainable is beside the point—it was never intended that such spending be sustained.

In a fully open economy with fixed exchange rates, the country can also lose its ability to control monetary policy, since the domestic real interest rate may be largely determined by international rates. *All else being equal*, if domestic interest rates are higher than international rates, funds will flow into the country to earn the higher returns, pushing the interest rate back down. Similarly, if the domestic rate is lower than international rates, money will flow out, pushing the rate back up. (The analysis is, of course, too simplistic as it ignores the differences in risk, such as default risk referred to above. Capital is generally not perfectly mobile, particularly because the perception of risks differs across countries. We'll discuss this and the full interaction between interest rates, capital mobility, and exchange rates in greater detail later in this chapter.)

In this simple open economy, then, lower interest rates may not only have the standard positive initial effect of increasing aggregate demand; they may also lessen capital inflows or even lead to capital outflows, *all other things being equal*. This in turn exerts downward pressure on exchange rates to depreciate. If the government wishes to maintain a fixed exchange rate, it will have to take other actions, such as imposing restrictions on capital flows, as we'll discuss in Part III of this book. Alternatively, the government can intervene directly in the market for foreign exchange by selling dollars and buying local currency. If the government has sufficient reserves, this can be a temporary palliative. But if the government doesn't have sufficient reserves—often the case for developing countries—this will give rise to destabilizing speculation against the currency. Speculators, feeling confident that the exchange rate cannot be maintained, sell the currency, pushing it even lower. Typically, the exchange rate eventually becomes unsustainable, and a crisis emerges. In these circumstances, it would make more sense for the government to allow the exchange rate to depreciate.[12]

Monetary and Fiscal Policies in Open Economies with Flexible Exchange Rates

Today, most developing economies have at least some degree of flexibility in their exchange rates. With flexible exchange rates and open capital markets, expansionary fiscal and monetary policies typically (but not always) lead to a depreciation of the currency. The weaker exchange rate increases exports and reduces imports, avoiding some of the 'leakage' that was the source of the reduced impact of fiscal policy with fixed exchange rates. (This, of course, may not be as simple as it looks, due to some of the adverse effects of devaluation on aggregate demand discussed in the previous section.)

In a floating rate system, the central bank doesn't have to spend its reserves to defend the exchange rate. However, there may still be limits on the use of fiscal policy, especially when borrowing is limited, for reasons similar to the fixed rate case: developing countries often find it expensive to borrow, and the cost of borrowing rises as debt increases.

Conservatives worry that the additional borrowing required for standard Keynesian deficit expenditures will so lower 'confidence' in the country that there will be capital outflows. The capital outflows may result in an 'excessive' devaluation, with large balance sheet effects. This outflow, it's argued, would weaken the economy even more than tight fiscal policy.

In this view, the government must raise interest rates to stem the outflows, even though this will slow the economy. We'll discuss the issue of investor confidence later in this chapter. For now, we'll just point out that the evidence supporting the conservative argument is limited.

The major benefit, though, of a floating rate regime (in an economy with unrestricted capital flows) is the degree of monetary autonomy it provides. A floating rate gives the central bank more control over monetary policy, generating some room for counter-cyclical macroeconomic policies (that stimulate the economy during a slowdown and slow the economy during a boom). As we mentioned above, in an open economy, *other things being equal*, lowering interest rates to stimulate the economy leads to capital out-flows. With a floating exchange rate, the currency can now adjust (given outflows, it devalues). The monetary authorities don't need to increase rates to defend the exchange rate. This allows them to regain some of their 'independence' or 'autonomy' in macroeconomic policy. Some of the pressure on interest rates gets transferred to the exchange rate.

But, even though a floating exchange rate allows a greater degree of monetary autonomy than a fixed rate, there are still limits to its use, especially if the government worries about potential second and third round repercussions, as we discuss below. While monetary policy-makers may *seem* to have more discretion, the potential adverse effects from exchange rate adjustments may actually limit the benefits derived from exchange rate flexibility. The only way to guarantee adequate degrees of freedom for counter-cyclical monetary policies may be to give up free capital mobility.

Impact of Interest Rates and Exchange Rate on Capital Flows

The reason why it's difficult to disentangle the effects of monetary and fis-cal policy on an open economy, particularly one with flexible exchange rates, is that the impact on capital flows is hard to predict. The general view is, that *other things being equal*, an increase in a country's real income gen-erated by expansionary macroeconomic policies is likely to induce capital inflows. So too, *other things being equal*, an increase in the interest rate asso-ciated with say a contractionary monetary policy will induce capital inflows and lead to an exchange rate appreciation (and, alternatively, a lower interest rate will result in capital outflows, and lead to a weaker exchange rate). But other things are never equal, particularly due to the complex interaction between interest rates and capital flows.

Standard Keynesian analysis doesn't explicitly deal with capital inflows. To the extent that it does, it assumes that their effects can be fully sterilized through monetary policy. In Keynesian analysis, investment is determined by interest rates and consumption is determined by national income (and perhaps by interest rates)—but not by capital flows. So long as the government can determine the level of interest rate, it can determine the level of national income. Capital flows may affect what the government needs to do to maintain the chosen level of interest rate, that is, they are of relevance to the conduct of monetary policy, but little else.

Modern economic theory has stressed, however, that what matters is not just interest rates but credit availability; and capital flows affect the resources available to households and firms, and even affect the lending activity of banks. Under conventional closed economy analysis, lowering interest rates leads to increased investment and higher growth. But, in an open economy, lower interest rates can lead to capital outflows and a weaker exchange rate. This, combined with the weakened balance sheets that often result from exchange rate devaluations, may limit credit availability and could attenuate, or even reverse, the normal impact of lower interest rates on aggregate demand. Any attempt by policy-makers to counteract the drop in demand by lowering interest rates further will be partially self-defeating, as the lower interest rates will induce even more capital outflows.

Modern economic theory has also stressed the importance of expectations. Raising or lowering interest rates can sometimes do very little to strengthen or weaken an overvalued exchange rate because of market expectations. If market participants expect large capital inflows into a country to continue (because of, say, foreign direct investment or privatizations), there may be little the central bank can do to dampen enthusiasm for buying the local currency and strengthening the exchange rate. Low interest rates in the Czech Republic during the mid-1990s, a period of high foreign inflows, did little to stop the currency from strengthening further.

While this chapter focuses on short-run effects, one of the themes of this book is that these cannot, and should not, be separated from longer-run growth effects. Under conventional closed economy analysis, raising interest rates to slow an economic boom leads to less investment and lower growth. In an open economy, the higher interest rates may attract capital inflows, increasing the credit supply and leading to higher investment and growth. But in an open economy, there are also two additional medium-term effects. First, as we discuss in Part III of this book, when the central bank raises rates, it usually raises short-term rates, attracting short-term capital.[13] These flows often go into consumption or real estate, rather than into long-term productive investment. The implication is that there may be little long-term positive impact on growth. Worse, the capital inflows often lead to a short-term bubble, and when the bubble bursts there are potentially huge drops in output. This effect, for example, was one of the factors behind the Asian crisis.

Second, as mentioned above, the increased inflows also lead to currency appreciation. This can slow the economy in the medium to long term[14] as export and import-substitution industries became less competitive. The result is that, despite a short-term boom, medium to long-term growth is in fact stymied, as predicted by the standard model.

Effects of Interest and Exchange Rates during a Crisis

Up until now, we have been assuming that increasing interest rates leads to higher capital inflows (though, often, only of a short-term nature). However, as we mention above, this presumption does not always hold, especially during a crisis. The deepening economic recession often caused by higher interest rates means that risk-averse investors find it less attractive to put money into, or keep money in, a country.[15] In crisis conditions, accordingly, higher interest rates increase the riskiness of lending, and may *lower* the *expected return to investors*, having just the opposite of the intended effect.

Higher interest rates then slow the economy through several channels: the normal Keynesian effect of lowering investment, and hence aggregate demand, is augmented by large adverse supply-side effects, as firms cut back production; weakened balance sheets of firms also have an indirect adverse effect on investment even for firms that do not turn to the capital market for finance. Increased bankruptcy rates worsen the balance sheets of banks. And the weaker balance sheet of banks, combined with the increased risk, leads them to lend less. The higher interest rates also put the finances of highly indebted governments at risk. In the end, if the major objective is to avoid a devaluation, high interest rates may not even help at all. Capital may not be attracted; indeed, higher interest rates may contribute to capital flight.[16] The capital flight in turn may reinforce the other downward pressures on the economy.

Another instance when raising or lowering interest rates might not have much of an effect on either capital flows or the exchange rate is when market participants have strong views about an imminent change in the exchange rate. For example, if market participants expect the currency to devalue 10 percent in the next week, short-term interest rates would have to jump to an annual equivalent of over 500 percent in order to stem short-term outflows (since investors will receive only 1/52nd of the annual rate in the week prior to the devaluation). But annual interest rates of 500 percent are obviously unsustainable, and few investors are willing to invest at these rates. If high interest rates are able to attract capital under these circumstances, it will generally be very short-term funds, and the expected real benefits associated with long-term investment may still not materialize.

Just as the effect of interest rates on capital flows during a crisis is often unclear, so, too, is the effect of weaker exchange rates. A weaker exchange rate means that domestic assets are cheaper for foreigners, implying increased inflows. A weaker exchange rate can also indicate that expectations of additional exchange rate depreciation are reduced, again inducing net capital inflows. On the other hand, it's possible that a weaker exchange rate leads to the expectation of a still weaker exchange rate in the future. (For instance, a depreciated exchange rate could be expected to give rise to inflationary pressures.) Or a weak exchange rate could be interpreted by investors as a sign of weakness in the economy—of other investors pulling money out. In these cases, the exchange rate might lead to net capital outflows. It's particularly difficult to ascertain which of these effects will dominate a situation, because the impact is highly dependent on 'investor confidence'. ✗ *investor confidence.*

Investor Confidence and Animal Spirits

As we mentioned earlier, conservative economists claim that increased capital flows and the strengthening of the exchange rate are a reflection of increased confidence. Confidence begets confidence and increases the demand for investment and consumption. Therefore, governments should implement policies (such as tight fiscal and monetary policy) that increase confidence.

Keynes, on the other hand, believed that business confidence was virtually unpredictable. He argued that 'animal spirits' were an important factor in determining investor sentiments. In the decades since, investors attempting to make their fortunes out of an understanding of market psychology have not fared particularly well, and economic models based on investor psychology have proven remarkably unsuccessful.

Even the links between exchange rates and macroeconomic 'fundamentals', such as trade deficits or fiscal deficits, are tenuous. Asset prices (including exchange rates) are shaped by expectations about the future and are sometimes the outcome of a 'beauty-contest' of the sort so aptly described by Keynes.[17] The links that exist are based on the perceptions of market players and are subject to expectations that can change rapidly.[18] Those that based their political recommendations on conjectures of how the policies will affect confidence are, at least at this juncture, resting their case on a weak reed.

Analysts and newspaper interpretations of changes in exchange rates—reflecting the way many investors think—reflect the prevailing lack of coherence. Sometimes adverse economic data lead to expectations of an exchange rate depreciation, sometimes to expectations of an exchange rate appreciation. In the former case, analysts will say, 'signs of a weaker economy led investors to believe that the monetary authority will lower interest rates'. In the latter case, analysts will say, 'signs of a weaker economy led investors to believe that reduced imports will improve the country's balance of payments'. In the first case, they obviously focus on capital flows (the capital account); in the latter, on trade (the current account).

During the East Asian crisis, the IMF anticipated that higher interest rates and fiscal tightening would attract more capital and strengthen exchange rates. In fact, investors saw the higher interest rates as a sign that the economies would weaken, and that returns to investing would fall. They looked at the anticipated effects on the real variables, their confidence was undermined, and this reinforced the direct negative effects.

Particularly problematic are arguments about how temporary market interventions will lead to long-run changes because of changes in investor confidence. The simplest version of this argument is that if authorities take 'tough' measures, such as raising interest rates, confidence in the central bank's resolve to fight inflation will increase. There will be an upward shift in the demand curve for the currency, and the exchange rate in the long run will be stronger, so that the exchange rate in the short run will be stronger as well. There are some circumstances in which this may be true, but there are other plausible outcomes. If market participants believe that the monetary authorities have misdiagnosed the economy's problem—that higher interest rates will lead to a worsening of the economy's situation—there may be little confidence that the policy will be sustained, and little confidence in the judgment of the monetary authorities. In these circumstances, the high interest rate may lead to a weaker exchange rate and be counterproductive.

As another instance, consider a temporary direct intervention in the exchange rate market to avoid a currency depreciation. Most central banks recognize that, generally, this type of direct intervention in the market is costly (it drains the country's foreign exchange reserves) and often fails to work (if the demand curve doesn't shift, then the stronger exchange rate won't be sustained), and the money spent supporting it will be wasted. As we'll see in the next chapter, intervening to maintain a weak domestic currency is less problematic, but may still be costly.

Those who support such temporary interventions seem to believe that market participants will see the government's resolve to support the exchange rate and change their views. Their demand for the country's currency will increase, and the exchange rate will, on its own, be sustainable *without intervention*. Moreover, proponents of this view often argue that such intervention is important to prevent contagion. If investors see one country's exchange rate fall, they might believe that other countries' exchange rates will fall as well.

There may be some circumstances in which the putative beliefs make sense, but there are equally or more convincing alternative responses. Why would investors, knowing that the exchange rate was stronger *because of government intervention that was not sustainable (and that was announced to be temporary)* believe that in the long run the currency would be more valuable? Might they not, seeing the dwindling reserves of the country, conclude otherwise? Or would investors, seeing that massive support was required to sustain Mexico's exchange rate (in the Tequila crisis of 1995), recognize that such support was unlikely to be forthcoming for other Latin American countries, and come to exactly the opposite conclusion—that depreciation in those countries' exchange rates was inevitable?[19]

Concluding Remarks

Different schools of thought have markedly different policy analyses and prescriptions, particularly when analyzing economies with open markets. What makes open market macroeconomics so difficult is that capital flows and exchange rates are affected by expectations, and these expectations are difficult to predict. Different market participants may have different expectations, and it may not be obvious what the aggregate effect will be.

Neither historical experiences nor rational expectations models provide much guidance as to how market participants' expectations will respond in any particular situation. Each situation has its own distinctive characteristics, and there is ample evidence that many market participants' expectations do not conform to the strictures of the rational expectations hypothesis, whatever they might imply in these situations, each of which appear to be *sui generis*.

In this world, at least in the short run, beliefs can be self-fulfilling. If everyone believes that the dollar is going to weaken, it will weaken, because these beliefs will lead people to sell their dollar-denominated assets. It's virtually impossible for fiscal and monetary authorities to anticipate every vagary of market expectations.

In this world of great uncertainty, it makes sense for monetary and fiscal authorities to focus on what is real: lower interest rates and increased government expansion will normally lead to real increases in national income, and these real improvements in the state of the economy will increase investor confidence and attract more capital. There may be exceptions where these first-order effects are undermined by perverse expectations or adverse capital flows. But the burden of proof should be on those who argue for an increase in interest rates, a lowering of government expenditures, an increase in taxes, or a strengthening of the exchange rate in times of an economic downturn, to show that these indirect effects are so large as to swamp the direct and positive effects of expansionary fiscal and monetary policies.

7

Exchange Rate Management and Micro Tools for Macro-Management

In the previous chapter we looked at open economy macroeconomics and the interactions between interest rates, currencies, and capital flows. We saw that capital flows and their effects on exchange rates have a large impact on the standard closed economy analysis. In some cases, traditional Keynesian effects are enhanced. For example, lowering interest rates might weaken the exchange rate, leading to higher exports. In other cases, lowering interest rates will dampen capital inflows, reduce the availability of credit, and *slow* the economy, contrary to standard closed economy analysis. Though it remains a theoretical possibility, there is, however, a strong presumption against this scenario: it's unlikely that raising interest rates in a recession will strengthen the economy, or that lowering interest rates will weaken it, at least in a sustainable fashion. The record is clear: in the face of an economic downturn, conservative contractionary policies reinforce the slowdown.

In this chapter, we examine alternative policy options for open economies. As noted above, the impact of these policies vary depending on the situation. In order to determine the appropriate response, we must determine which economic variables are the causes and which are the effects. Is the fiscal deficit causing the trade deficit, resulting in high foreign borrowing? Or is the trade deficit the result of high capital inflows, strengthening the currency? Are high local interest rates attracting foreign capital inflows, or is it exuberance for investing in emerging markets? Different answers to these questions will lead to different policy responses.

We should note that in other areas economists have gone to great efforts to distinguish causal changes from effects, but that in open market economies, all of these are frequently confused. For example, many analysts focus on the exchange rate when examining the large US trade deficit, while others begin by noting the large fiscal deficit. The latter argue that, given the low level of private savings and the negative level of government savings, the United States *has* to run a large trade deficit. Fiscal policy is said to be causing the trade deficit.

In another example, discussions about Argentina's current account deficit (the trade deficit minus net private transfer payments to foreigners) often began by noting that the Argentinian peso had become overvalued under the country's fixed rate system. The overvalued currency (the exogenous variable) led to low levels of exports and high imports. The high trade deficit necessitated excessive foreign borrowing and high interest rates to attract foreign capital. The overvalued exchange rate is said to have 'caused' the trade deficit. We should note that there were economists who argued that Argentina's fiscal deficit caused its trade deficit, in a similar way to the US example above. But Argentina's fixed currency system meant that the exchange rate couldn't adjust to changes in demand. The only way it could have eliminated the trade deficit would have been to decrease national income to a low level (with high unemployment)—precisely the policy recommended by many conservative economists.[1] These debates reiterate the point that all the variables are linked, making it difficult to delineate the exogenous variable.

As the above examples show, the policy regime (fixed versus flexible exchange rate, whether monetary authorities follow a rule of a fixed money supply or a fixed interest rate) determines the outcome of any 'shock' to the system—how the economic system responds to various kinds of disturbances. (And indeed, one of the major criteria for evaluating alternative policy regimes is the analysis of how the system responds to the shocks.) Moreover, each of the above examples leads to different policy responses. In the US example, policy-makers worried about the trade deficit should concentrate on cutting the growing fiscal deficit. In the case of Argentina, policy-makers should have addressed the overvalued exchange rate and devalued the currency before it was forced into a crisis.

We start this chapter with an introductory discussion of overall macroeconomic management for open economies, including inflation targeting. We then look at how countries can attempt to manage the exchange rate. We end with an analysis of other policy options in open economies, including heterodox microeconomic interventions.

Macroeconomic Management in Open Economies

External Balance and Full Emloyment

When the economy's in a recession, the government generally wants to stimulate the economy to attain full employment (or 'internal balance'). But at full employment, the country may still have a problem of 'external balance'. A problem of external balance is not determined by whether a country's current account is in deficit, but whether the deficit—and the capital flows that finance it—are sustainable. There's a problem of external balance if a country must continually borrow, and the level of borrowing is unsustainable. Whether a particular level of borrowing is sustainable will also depend on how the money is spent, as we discuss below.

In a fixed exchange rate system, reserves are the control variable. If a country is running a deficit without sufficient financing, it will have to spend its reserves to maintain the fixed rate. The question here is whether the financing of the deficit is sustainable over a period of time. In a floating rate system, the currency adjusts and the central bank doesn't spend reserves intervening in the market, but there's still an issue of sustainability. So long as the country runs a trade deficit and foreign investors have limited interest in investing in the country, the currency will be subject to downward pressure.

Some countries, like the United States, have maintained large trade deficits for extended periods of time, without a serious problem. But the United States is a special case. Given that the US dollar serves as international money, it can borrow abroad in its own currency to finance its deficit. Other countries seem to have problems after only a short period of a relatively moderate trade deficit. While sufficient depreciation may eventually eliminate the trade deficit, this will take time, and the requisite depreciation may not be viewed as politically or economically acceptable.

Theoretically, a government can achieve internal balance or full employment and external balance, but to do so it must closely coordinate monetary, fiscal, and exchange rate policies. If,[2] for example, the government wishes simultaneously to achieve (a) full employment, (b) external balance, and (c) budget balance, then there is a determinant level of interest rate, exchange rate, and government expenditure (and taxes) that the government must set. The government has three objectives and three instruments.[3] This can be thought of in the following way: at full employment output, there is a unique exchange rate (given import and export functions)[4] at which the trade deficit is sustainable. And, there is a particular interest rate that can sustain that exchange rate, given full employment output and 'expectations'.[5] That interest rate determines the level of investment, and together with the level of net exports (determined by the exchange rate), there is a unique level of government expenditures (with taxes to finance those expenditures) that sustains the full employment level of output.

Although the government does have enough tools to achieve both full employment and external balance, achieving the appropriate mix may not be easy, particularly given the uncertainties associated with capital flows that we analyzed in the previous chapter. Given the complexity of these interactions, policy-makers often proceed by focusing first on certain intermediary variables, in hope that by getting those 'right' it will eventually (in a relatively short time) be possible to achieve the real goal of full employment with external balance.[6] Thus, in several recent crises, the IMF has focused on restoring the stability of the exchange rate and correcting the trade deficit. To critics who argue that the Fund is ignoring the far more important objectives of full employment and rapid growth, the Fund would presumably reply that those goals could only be achieved if the trade deficit and exchange rate instability have been dealt with. But if the country wishes to maintain the exchange rate, then the only way to do so *in the standard models* (without microeconomic interventions) is to lower national income: given the exchange rate, there is a determinate demand for the country's exports, and hence the only way to achieve external balance is to reduce imports to match those exports. But the only way to reduce imports—if exchange rate adjustments and tariffs and other trade restrictions are precluded—is to lower income.

Stiglitz[7] refers to these policies as beggar-thy-self policies, because you lower your own national income to reduce your trade deficit. In beggar thy neighbor policies, the country improves its situation—in this case, its external balance—at the expense of weakening its neighbors. But it makes no difference to its neighbors whether the country cuts its imports because of protectionist barriers or because its income has gone down. Here the country cuts its imports by weakening itself. The fact that so many countries have found themselves in recessions after implementing these policies is, in this view, not an accident. It's the inevitable consequence of a policy framework that sees stabilization of the exchange rate and the elimination of the trade deficit as the first order of the day.

But, just as the government can provide more stimulation to the economy with a given level of deficit by adjusting the structure of taxation as we discussed in Chapter 5, so too there is some scope for adjusting the structure of demand with microeconomic interventions—that is, for looking beyond traditional fiscal and monetary policies. As we'll see below, these additional policy tools reinforce the general heterodox position: achieving multiple macroeconomic objectives is far easier if the government uses the full panoply of instruments at its disposal, including microeconomic interventions. While there is a cost to such interventions, those costs pale in comparison to the costs from unemployment or from the crises that often follow large external imbalances.

Inflation Targeting

As mentioned above, to achieve full employment and external balance, it's crucial to coordinate monetary, fiscal, and exchange rate policies. Further, part of what's at issue is determining the best 'thermometer'. As noted in earlier chapters, the standard definition of full employment is the highest level of employment which, if sustained, will not give rise to increases in inflation. There's a great deal of uncertainty about how to determine the full employment level. Many economists argue that the best way to ascertain the level of full employment is to note whether inflation is increasing. If it is, then aggregate demand is excessive, and the economy needs to be dampened through monetary tightening.

This has led to the currently popular monetary regime called inflation targeting—the government or monetary authority announces a target for the inflation rate, and the monetary authorities commit to achieving this target. Inflation targeting divides responsibilities between government and a monetary authority, so that each policy-maker focuses on a single objective. In particular, the monetary authority focuses on inflation and the fiscal authority focuses on external balance. The problem, though, is that dividing responsibilities reduces coordination.

The issue of the efficiency or stability of the inflation-targeting rule is more complicated than can be addressed in this volume. It concerns, for instance, the extent to which (and the circumstances under which) conventionally measured changes in inflation provide a good indicator of whether employment is above or below the full employment level (as defined above). There is, in addition, a more fundamental question: whether a policy structure in which monetary authorities focus on inflation and fiscal authorities focus, for instance, on external balance is a good way of achieving the ultimate objective of full employment with external balance.

Think of the problem as a sequence of moves. First, the monetary authority, taking the actions of the fiscal authority as given, adjusts interest rates to achieve the inflation target. This may result in a large external imbalance—and an overvalued exchange rate. Now it's the turn of the fiscal authority. Seeing the overvalued exchange rate, it cuts back expenditures or raises taxes, leading to a high level of unemployment. As unemployment appears, the 'inflation' targeting monetary authority then reduces the interest rate. But recall that the fiscal authority had just set fiscal policy at the right level, given the interest rate, to achieve external balance. At the new lower interest rate, there is now a trade surplus. Now, the fiscal authority reverses its course, increasing expenditures. But, the monetary authority had just set monetary policy at the right level, given fiscal policy, to achieve full employment. With the expansionary fiscal policy, there is now an increase in inflation. The monetary authority increases interest rates again.

It's unclear whether or not the economy will eventually converge to the 'equilibrium' in which there is simultaneously internal and external balance. And it's also unclear whether the monetary authority's initial move of increasing interest rates was a move in the right or wrong direction. What is clear is that the policy of 'assignment' of objectives, with the monetary authorities using inflation targeting, results in repeated over- and undershooting. If there is convergence, it can be a slow process. *Closer coordination*, with monetary and fiscal authorities cooperating, sharing information, and acting jointly can achieve a faster convergence to the desired objective.[8]

In this book, where we seek to provide an overview of macroeconomic policy, we cannot provide a full analysis of the dynamics. We'll spend a moment, however, explaining how inflation targeting *when successful* can result in large external imbalances associated with overvalued exchange rates. Consider, for instance, the case where firms decide to raise the amount they invest at a given interest rate, increasing aggregate demand. If monetary authorities believe the economy is already operating at full employment, they'll respond by increasing interest rates to dampen inflationary pressures. If the government manages the increase in interest rates 'correctly', so that aggregate demand is dampened just to the full employment level, there is a potentially large trade imbalance. All else being equal, the higher interest rate will attract capital inflows, causing the exchange rate to strengthen, imports to rise, and exports to fall.[9]

There is an alternative: the government can leave the interest rate and exchange rate unchanged, and cut government expenditures and raise taxes enough to offset the increase in private investment. This strategy would maintain external balance and full employment. If the macroeconomic authorities, fiscal and monetary, coordinate, they can examine the source of the disturbance and identify the appropriate response in a way that can quickly achieve both internal and external balance. In this case, the response to the kind of shock that gives rise to excess aggregate demand is for the fiscal authority to cut expenditures and for the monetary authority to do nothing.

On the other hand, if the source of excess demand is a sudden upsurge in exports, an exchange rate appreciation is what's required. But now, the monetary authority should not target the inflation rate, but the external imbalance. The authority should let the interest rate rise to the point where there will be external balance *at full employment output*. The fiscal authority will then have to adjust government expenditures (and/or taxes). If the monetary authority does this, full equilibrium, with both internal and external balance, can be achieved in two simple steps.

The implication is that the nature of the response to excess aggregate demand *should* depend on an analysis of the source of the disturbance. A rule that simply looks at the magnitude of the inflation rate is not likely to provide for a quick adjustment of the economy to the new equilibrium. The basic implication is that monetary authorities can't detach themselves from the broader objectives of macroeconomic policy, such as full employment and external balance. They must coordinate the appropriate response to the specific source of disturbance with the fiscal authorities. Dividing responsibilities between the two authorities in a simple way, as assumed in the 'inflation-targeting' rule, is not an effective way to manage macroeconomic policy.

Macroeconomic Objectives and Day-to-Day Management

Given the time lag between a policy's approval and its effects, much day-to-day management of the economy involves forecasting the future and assessing risks. On a day-to-day basis, conservatives focus on the threat of inflation and are quicker to tighten monetary and fiscal policy at the slightest signs of potential overheating. As we've noted, they argue that inflation is costly and likely to get out of control. Keynesian and heterodox economists respond that the evidence shows that moderate inflation has negligible costs and that a little inflation in one period does not lead to more in the next.

Keynesians and heterodox economists concentrate on unemployment, pointing out that unemployment has real social and economic costs.

While inflation inertia may be less of a problem than conservatives suggest, unemployment inertia—when high unemployment in one period leads to loss of job skills, making it difficult to lower unemployment in subsequent period—is more of a problem. Given all the evidence, they take a more cautious approach to fighting inflation and a more active approach to fighting unemployment. Clearly the two schools of economic thought balance the risks quite differently.

Given the connection between employment generation and the exchange rate in open developing economies, Keynesian and heterodox economists want to guarantee that the real exchange rate allows exporters and import competing sectors to be competitive. This implies that they may be more willing to intervene in foreign exchange markets, or willing to impose capital controls to guarantee a competitive exchange rate. Keynesian and heterodox interventions may be viewed as a case for including an element of 'real exchange rate targeting' in the design of macroeconomic policy.

Interventions in the Foreign Exchange Market

As we've noted, most Keynesian and heterodox economists favor a weak exchange rate to stimulate the economy during recessions. They also favor maintaining competitive exchange rates to achieve sustained growth in developing countries. Conservatives often favor strong exchange rates to reduce inflation. In either case, policy-makers face the question of how to manage the exchange rate.

Maintaining Weak Exchange Rates

Governments have an easier time sustaining an undervalued exchange rate than an overvalued one. They can lower interest rates to discourage capital inflows. Or they can intervene in the exchange rate market directly by buying dollars and selling the local currency. Maintaining an undervalued exchange through direct intervention produces a build-up of international reserves. This has a long-term benefit: it strengthens the country against future capital account volatility (it acts as a 'war chest').

But buying up international reserves has costs. The central bank has to sell domestic currency to buy the reserves, and this increases the money supply. To keep the money supply within limits, authorities may choose to 'sterilize' the monetary effect of the foreign exchange intervention by selling domestic assets and buying the additional currency from the market.

The mechanisms generally used (e.g. open market operations) are costly as they involve issuing central bank bonds, which pay interest, to absorb the excess liquidity.[10] Furthermore, these interventions may lead to higher interest rates, raising the overall cost of government funding. The higher rates might attract more capital, overheating the economy, and forcing even larger reserve accumulations. Raising reserve requirements on banks is a less costly means to sterilize but may lead to higher credit costs and to financial disintermediation (in which banks use unregulated mechanisms to channel liquid funds). There can be an additional cost to purchasing foreign currency reserves at an undervalued exchange rate: if the currency does eventually revalue, then the value of the foreign reserves will drop relative to domestic GDP. The question is whether and when the costs of sterilization can become too great to maintain and outweigh the benefits of a weak exchange rate. In the late 1990s, the Hungarian central bank, for example, felt that sterilization had become too expensive and let its exchange rate strengthen.

On the other hand, China has maintained an exchange rate that some have argued has been undervalued for extended periods. It now holds several hundred billions of dollars in reserves that could, presumably, earn a higher return if invested elsewhere (though the reserves themselves would not have existed if China had not had a policy of maintaining a weak exchange rate). Unlike Hungary, China has maintained its capital account restrictions, giving it more leeway to manage its money supply. But is China making a mistake by accumulating a quantity of reserves in excess of what it would need to stave off a speculative attack, especially since it restricts short-term capital flows? Should it stop accumulating reserves and let its exchange rate strengthen?

Arguably, China's first concern is to maintain its economy as close to full employment as possible. Given the high domestic savings rate, it has all the domestic resources it needs for as high a level of investment as it can efficiently manage. Its need for foreign capital goods is limited to those that it doesn't produce at home or those which it can obtain more cheaply abroad. Maintaining an undervalued currency makes imports more expensive and helps strengthen export and domestic capital goods industries. A stronger exchange rate could lead to lower profitability in the tradable sector, hurting employment, investment, and growth.

Moreover, a stronger exchange rate would lower agricultural prices, increasing the already large disparity between rural and urban incomes.

Though one might argue that direct subsidies might be preferable, the government's limited resources preclude that as an option (and, in any case, the opportunity cost of such expenditures is high).

Raising Interest Rates to Maintain Strong Exchange Rates (or Limit Exchange Rate Depreciation)

While it's possible for a country to maintain an undervalued exchange rate for extended periods of time, it's far more difficult for it to maintain an overvalued exchange rate, even for short periods of time. Direct intervention in the currency market is unsustainable. Both speculators and ordinary citizens know that the central bank has a limited supply of dollars to spend defending its currency. They'll want to move money out of the currency before the central bank depletes its reserves, putting further downward pressure on the exchange rate and requiring the government to intervene even more. If the devaluation is expected to occur in the not too distant future, a speculative attack will be mounted now.

Of course, in a purely floating exchange rate regime such destabilizing speculation wouldn't be possible: if everyone expects the devaluation, no one would be willing to buy the currency at the current level, and the exchange rate would devalue immediately. But as long as there's some central bank or government intervention to defend the currency, there's scope for profitable speculation as public-sector losses are matched by private-sector gains. The incentive to mount a speculative attack is present even when this form of intervention takes place under a 'dirty' floating exchange rate regime (in which governments intervene in the market from time to time), but it's very strong in fixed exchange rate regimes.

The standard prescription to stem exchange rate depreciation is to raise interest rates to attract capital into the country. Two questions have been raised concerning this conventional policy prescription: does it work, and are the benefits worth the costs? We discussed the effects of raising interest rates on capital inflows and the exchange rate in the previous chapter. The evidence[11] suggests at best a mixed record. In the case of East Asia, the interest rate increases, even combined with huge bail-outs, did not stem the large exchange rate depreciations.

The cost of raising interest rates to defend the currency depends on the structure of the economy, but can be high, as we saw during the Asian crisis. There are real balance effects, similar to the effects of currency devaluation. For firms with outstanding short-term debts, high interest rates affect their balance sheets. The high rates reduce the value of long-term assets (including real estate). In many cases, firms are unable to meet their obligations to repay domestic debt in local currency. This has a ripple effect through the economy, as economic problems in one firm get pushed to the firms it trades with.

In East Asia, when many firms became insolvent, a new problem, known as *strategic defaults*, arose. Some firms that actually could have repaid their loans made a strategic decision not to as they realized that they could not all be forced into bankruptcy. In this environment, banks couldn't make new loans. The economic downturn contributed to a general sense of uncertainty and risk. The changes in asset prices had distinct effects on different firms, because of their different asset structures. This aggravated uncertainty about the value of balance sheets and resulted in an even deeper downturn.

The heterodox approach emphasizes other reasons why interest rate increases to limit the size of devaluations may have a less beneficial effect on inflation than the conservatives claim. In the short run, the increased interest rate is a cost of production that may be passed on to consumers.[12] Moreover, monetary tightening results not only in adverse effects on aggregate demand, but also on aggregate supply: with less access to working capital, higher costs, and worsening balance sheets, firms will be less able and willing to produce. The lack of working capital and the balance sheet effects, combined with risk aversion, result in a drop in supply (a leftward shift in supply curves).

Raising interest rates may have a greater adverse effect on the economy than traditional models that focus solely on demand-side effects would suggest because of the adverse supply-side effects noted above. In addition, the demand-side effects may be larger than the models suggest, since exports might get a much smaller boost from the currency devaluation than expected. Exporting firms might not be able to obtain the working capital they require. Importers in other countries might judge the exporting firms to be unreliable suppliers because of the increased likelihood of bankruptcies of the exporters and their suppliers, so their demand might also fall (the demand curve for exports shifts downward).

In short, raising interest rates has similar adverse effects to devaluing the exchange rate on balance sheets, bankruptcies, and economic activity. But there are differences. First, the effects of raising interest rates are more pervasive, since many firms—especially small and medium-sized enterprises, which are at the heart of developing countries—only borrow domestically. Relatively few large firms borrow internationally, and many of these are in export sectors so that in the event of a devaluation they gain from the improvement in their profitability what they lose on their balance sheet.

Second, those who borrow in foreign-denominated currency have the option to buy 'cover' (insurance against a depreciation of the currency) while those who borrow domestically typically do not have any means of insuring against the risk of an increase in interest rates.[13] Third, by the same token, a policy of attempting to stave off devaluations by raising interest rates contributes to a moral hazard problem—it lessens the incentives to buy insurance against exchange rate fluctuation, thereby reducing government room for maneuver.

Fourth, there are high long-run costs to raising interest rates, since higher rates make debt financing riskier and limit the ability and willingness of firms to engage in it. In developing countries with limited equity markets, this means that firms will become more reliant on self-finance. The long-run efficiency of the capital market will be impaired, and long-run growth will be slowed. Finally, appropriately designed monetary and regulatory policies can restrict firm exposure to foreign exchange rates; it's more difficult (and costly) to design monetary policies that restrict exposure to interest rate fluctuations. Firms would have to restrict their short-term borrowing (and there are even risks to long-term borrowing, since it has to be renewed).[14]

If the increase in the interest rate were able to stabilize the exchange rate, then one would have to weigh the costs of the high interest rate against the benefits and costs of limiting the extent of the devaluation. (There is an especial concern about 'overshooting' in a crisis, where the exchange rate falls more than it 'should', as a result of, say, excessive pessimism, and there is a manifestation of the excess volatility often observed in unfettered asset markets. As we explain below, there are high costs associated with this volatility, but there are also significant costs associated with avoiding an exchange rate depreciation.) It's *conceivable* that the economic consequences of preventing excessive devaluations—avoiding, for instance, the adverse balance sheet effects—might outweigh the direct negative effects of the higher exchange rate and high domestic interest rates. But, in most countries that have intervened to strengthen the currency, little or no evidence has been presented that these balance sheet effects outweigh the normal direct negative effects.

This discussion helps explain why raising interest rates to limit a currency's depreciation is often a lose-lose policy: few if any of the benefits of a strengthened exchange rate are achieved, but the country faces all the costs of higher interest rates, including a decline in GDP.

Interventions to Smooth Out Exchange Rate Fluctuations

The point of government intervention in the currency market is often not to maintain an overvalued or undervalued exchange rate, but to *smooth* exchange rate variations. Many developing countries are particularly concerned about the volatility of the *real* exchange rate, and try to avoid what they judge as either excessive real depreciations or appreciations. Most countries also intervene to smooth short-term volatility. This form of intervention is especially useful in countries with illiquid markets, where one large foreign currency payment can cause the currency to jump.

The reasons to avoid real exchange rate fluctuations are clear: they are not costless. As we've seen, appreciation pressures during periods of foreign exchange abundance (resulting from an increase in commodity prices or capital inflows) may have long-term de-industrialization effects, as the literature of the 'Dutch disease' indicates. Real exchange rate appreciation can also have large long-term costs if entry into tradable sectors has fixed costs (fixed capital investments or fixed costs of building a clientele in foreign markets), especially in the presence of capital market imperfections. A temporary currency appreciation may force a firm into bankruptcy; it cannot borrow against its future prospects, even if it would make economic sense for it to stay in business.

In economies that have net external liabilities denominated in foreign currencies, exchange rate fluctuations also have the real balance effects discussed above. These effects are pro-cyclical: real appreciation during the boom generates capital gains, whereas depreciation during crises generates capital losses. These balance sheet effects associated with currency fluctuations increase the amplitude of economic fluctuations.

The exchange rate fluctuations are themselves a result of some of the same forces that give rise to the economic fluctuations: capital inflows can fuel real exchange rate appreciation, at the same time that they lead to a private spending boom, while depreciation may have the opposite effects. In broader terms, in open developing economies the real exchange rate is an essential element in the dynamics of the business cycles, as well as a crucial determinant of investment, growth, and employment. Governments and central banks may decide that such a crucial macroeconomic variable should not just be left to the whims of the market, especially when there is evidence that these market whims lead to excessive volatility.

Counter-cyclical monetary and fiscal policies could, in principle, partially counteract the pro-cyclical effects of capital flows and the balance sheet effects of real exchange rate fluctuations. But a crucial factor is the degree of monetary autonomy that different exchange rate regimes allow. As we saw in the previous chapter, fixed exchange rate regimes limit or eliminate monetary autonomy. We also mentioned the traditional view that flexible exchange rates provide room for autonomous monetary policies, but emphasized that the government must be mindful of the consequences of interest rate changes, since they can give rise to large movements in capital flows and changes in exchange rates. Those who believe in free markets might argue that free and unfettered markets always result in the optimal degree of exchange rate variability. There are market forces for stabilization. For example, speculators can make money if there is excess volatility which means that their demand should help reduce the volatility. That is why many economists believe that governments and central banks should not intervene in exchange rate markets.

Today, few economists accept the efficiency of market outcomes, especially in relationship to exchange rate markets, though there is not unanimity about the reason—is it market irrationality, periods of irrational exuberance alternating with irrational pessimism; or is it rational herding behavior? What is clear is that markets exhibit 'excessive' volatility—more volatility than can be explained by theories that assume efficient markets.

In addition, if futures and risk markets are not complete, the market equilibrium won't be efficient, even if expectations are fully rational. But arguing that there is potential scope for government intervention does not answer fully the question of how the government should intervene in exchange rate markets, or even whether it should.

The Debate on the Choice of the Exchange Rate Regime

In choosing an exchange rate regime, developing countries are faced with a trade-off between their need for stability and their need for flexibility.[15] The demand for stability comes from trade, investment, domestic price stability, and the need to avoid pro-cyclical balance sheet effects of exchange rate fluctuations. The demand for flexibility comes from the need to have some degrees of freedom to manage trade and capital account shocks. The relative benefits of flexibility versus stability are determined by both the external environment and by objective factors. For example, increased international instability (e.g. the breakdown of the dollar standard, a period of turmoil in world finance for emerging markets, or a world recession) will increase the relative benefits of flexibility, whereas a period of tranquility (e.g. the heyday of the Bretton Woods system, or a period of stable world economic growth) will increase the relative advantages of stability.

The relevance of these conflicting demands is not captured by the call to choose polar exchange rate regimes that has filled the orthodox literature in recent years—that is, either 'hard pegs' (e.g. currency boards, or in the limit, open dollar or euroization) or totally flexible exchange rates. Rather, the defense of polar regimes is based on the argument that any attempt to manage the conflicting demands on exchange rate policy is futile and should be given up altogether.

Hard pegs introduce built-in institutional arrangements that provide for fiscal and monetary discipline, and avoid the balance sheet effects of exchange rate fluctuations,[16] but at the cost of eliminating monetary policy autonomy. Under this type of regime, adjustment to overvaluation (however that might occur) is painful, and may lead to low growth rates. When the currency becomes overvalued, domestic prices and wages need to fall for the country to regain competitiveness. More price flexibility, which in this case means deflation (and recession) during crises, generates severe adjustment problems that we analyzed in Chapter 2; of particular concern is the rapid increase in real debt burdens generated by deflation. It may also generate a short-term bias in bank lending, which is necessary to rapidly reduce nominal portfolios during periods of monetary contraction. One of the alleged advantages of the hard peg was that it was supposed to be speculation proof. But the experiences of currency boards in Argentina in 1994–5 and 1998–2001, Hong Kong in 1997 (and, for that matter, of the gold standard in developing countries during the late nineteenth and early twentieth centuries) indicate that that was not the case.

On the other hand, the volatility associated with freely floating exchange rate regimes increases the costs of trade, and reduces the benefits of international specialization. As developing countries are largely net importers of capital goods, exchange rate uncertainty also affects investment decisions.

The frequency of dirty floats, or floating rate regimes with limited flexibility,[17] shows how authorities in the developing world often opt for striking a balance between the conflicting demands they face. Intermediate exchange rate regimes can take several forms: (a) quasi-fixed exchange rate regimes with large central bank interventions in foreign exchange markets; (b) managed exchange rates, such as crawling pegs and bands; and (c) dirty floats, in which monetary authorities intervene in the market from time to time.[18] All these regimes can be understood as including an element of 'real exchange rate targeting' in the design of macroeconomic policy, and many or most of them are often combined with some form of capital account regulations. To the extent that smoothing out real exchange rate fluctuations has a counter-cyclical effect, 'real exchange rate targeting' turns out to be complementary with the objective of smoothing real (output) volatility.

One of the advantages of intermediate regimes is that flexibility *can be graduated*, depending on the relative benefits of stability versus flexibility that we have analyzed. This implies that any intermediate regime has an embedded 'exit option'. (Of course, even a peg has an exit option, but as the Argentine experience showed, the cost of that exit was high.) Also, if some degree of exchange rate flexibility is available before an external crisis hits, it would provide scope for avoiding the real interest rate over-shooting that seems to characterize the transition away from a fixed exchange rate regime in developing countries.[19]

There are still risks associated with intermediate regimes. The scope for monetary autonomy is still limited. First, as with fixed rate regimes, intermediate options are subject to speculative pressures if they do not generate credibility in markets. Defending the exchange rate may be costly, as we discussed earlier in this chapter. This is particularly true of any pre-announcement (of the rate of the crawl, of a band, or of a specific exchange rate target). Second, macroeconomic autonomy still depends on the effectiveness of capital account regulations as a macroeconomic policy tool, an issue we deal with in Part III of this book. Third, similar to fixed rate regimes, intermediate regimes will generally require sterilized intervention in foreign exchange markets in periods of high inflows. This can be costly, as we discussed above. Finally, interventions in the foreign exchange market always face the difficult choice of distinguishing between a real (permanent) shock and a temporary aberration in the exchange rate caused by random fluctuations in market sentiment.

Different regimes have different benefits and costs. They expose the country to different kinds of risk. No exchange rate system is risk free. Like all economic policies, the choice of currency regime involves trade-offs. In this case, there is a trade-off between policy flexibility and some measures of macroeconomic stability. The optimal choice will depend on the objectives of the authorities, and on the macroeconomic, institutional, and political characteristics of the country in question.

Other Policy Options for Open Economies

In addition to direct intervention in the exchange rate market, governments have additional policy tools available in an open economy.

There are a host of interventions that governments can use for macroeconomic management in an open economy. So far in this book, we've discussed several heterodox measures as alternatives or enhancements to fiscal and monetary policy. In this chapter, we'll consider a broader group of policies. Some of these are similar to the microeconomic tools presented in Chapter 5, and some, as we shall see, are considered quite controversial.

Public-Sector Liability Management in Developing Countries

If domestic debt markets are thin, governments might be tempted to finance expansionary fiscal policies through borrowing abroad. But this exposes them to greater future risk as a result of exchange rate changes, and undermines the role of exchange rate changes as part of the adjustment process. One of the reasons why the countries of East Asia did so well for so long—and avoided some of the volatility that marked countries elsewhere in the world—is that their high savings rate enabled them to invest at a high rate without borrowing from abroad, and this meant that they were relatively insulated from some of the volatility of global financial markets. Indeed, the extent of the East Asian crisis was largely a result of capital market liberalization, which was something, given their high savings rate, they need not have done. For countries with high external borrowings, one medium-term goal is to develop local capital markets and encourage domestic savings.

If foreign capital markets were well functioning, developing countries would be able to borrow abroad in their own currency (or in a market basket of currencies highly correlated with their own currency). Well-functioning markets would enable the transfer of exchange rate risks to developing country lenders who can bear the risk more easily.[20] There have been a few instances in which this happened, but by and large developing countries have to bear the brunt of the risk of exchange rate and interest rate fluctuations. What matters is not so much the source of the funds but the risk associated with the debt, and given that foreign borrowing entails the imposition of these high risks, countries should limit their exposure.

Severe currency and maturity mismatches in public-sector debt structures are an important problem in many developing countries. Most long-term debt is denominated in foreign currencies, while domestic debt is generally short term. Yet with the exception of a few public-sector firms, the public sector produces services for the domestic economy (non-tradables) and public-sector investments are long term.

The maturity structure of public-sector *domestic* liabilities is extremely important, as has been revealed in several financial crises. The basic reason for this is the highly liquid nature of public-sector securities, which facilitates asset substitution and capital flight. When most debt is short term the country will continually have to borrow to roll it over. When the gross borrowing requirements remain high, the interest rate will have to increase to make debt rollovers attractive. Higher interest rates will then feed into the budget deficit, contributing to the rapid increase of debt service and the accumulation of indebtedness. In addition, rollovers of domestic liabilities may be viable only if the government takes on the risks of devaluation or future interest rate hikes, generating additional sources of destabilization. This was the case prior to the Mexican crisis of 1994 and the Brazilian crisis of 1999, when fixed-interest bonds were swiftly replaced by variable-rate and dollar-denominated securities. Colombia, which has slightly longer-term debt (it has a tradition of issuing public-sector securities with a minimum one-year maturity), did not experience a substitution of similar magnitude during its 1998–9 crisis.[21]

Another benefit of a fully developed local yield curve is that it facilitates private borrowing. Many lenders like to price their lending off sovereign debt interest rates. The existence of a government bond enables the market to more easily separate out sovereign risk from firm risk, and some assert that this facilitates corporate borrowing.

Although the fact that government revenues are largely related to domestic prices suggests that governments should borrow exclusively in their domestic currency, there are two reasons why this rule should not be strictly followed. The first has to do with macroeconomic management. The government should manage its external public-sector debt to compensate for the highly pro-cyclical pattern of external private capital flows. For example, during phases of reduced private capital inflows, the public sector can generally still borrow, thanks to its preferential access to external credit, including credit from multilateral financial institutions.

The second reason relates to the depth of domestic bond markets, which determines the ability to issue longer-term domestic debt securities. Well-functioning markets require the existence of secondary markets and market makers that provide liquidity for these securities. In the absence of these pre-conditions, the government faces a trade-off between maturity and currency mismatches. It may make sense to have a debt mix that includes an important component of external liabilities, despite the associated currency mismatch. In the long run, the objective of the authorities should be to deepen the domestic capital markets. Due to the lower risk levels and the greater homogeneity of the securities it issues, the central government has a vital function to perform in the development of longer-term primary and secondary markets for domestic securities, including the creation of benchmarks for private-sector debt instruments.

To be sure, there is nothing that is risk free. The domestic currency debt market may affect short-term capital inflows. The domestic government debt market can give foreigners easy access to short-term investment instruments, increasing capital surges during booms and adding to capital outflows during crises. A liquid treasury bill market provides investors with the ability to sell the currency short, making it easier for speculators to bet against the exchange rate. But these concerns are probably not of sufficient import that they should induce governments not to borrow domestically (when they otherwise would have). More to the point, there are different types of capital account regulations that can be used to address these risks. For example, authorities can ban foreigners from being allowed to buy short-term instruments and can mandate that foreigners hold long-term securities for over a year, as we'll discuss in Part III of this book.

Another problem is posed by the decentralized nature of most governments: many (or even most) sub-national administrations and public-sector firms expect to be bailed out in case of a crisis. This gives rise to an important moral hazard problem.

Specific legal limits and regulations are required, including clear rules on public-sector indebtedness, direct mechanisms of control of foreign borrowing, and rules establishing minimum maturities and maximum spreads at which public-sector entities can borrow. The Ministry of Finance or the central bank can play a leading role in either of these two areas, establishing rules that should apply not only to the central administration but also to autonomous public-sector agencies and sub-national governments.[22]

Microeconomic Interventions and Other Heterodox Measures

There are many heterodox interventions that developing countries can use to stimulate their economy such as tax, banking, and other regulatory policies. In an open economy, many of these policies affect the exchange rate, and have additional indirect effects through this channel.

The most obvious of these measures are direct restrictions or taxes on capital inflows and outflows. Temporary outflow taxes, for instance, may be used to discourage a rush of capital out of the country, temporarily strengthening the exchange rate. This will be discussed in greater detail in Part III of this book, on capital market liberalization.

Other microeconomic interventions can also change the composition of demand towards non-tradables and away from imports. Tax policies that encourage more spending on domestically produced goods and less on goods produced abroad will help stimulate the economy, and at the same time, strengthen the currency. In many developing countries, most luxury consumption goods are imported. A high sales tax on such goods discourages these imports. Government expenditures can also be weighted towards domestically produced goods. For example, preferential treatment of housing may shift demand more towards that sector.[23]

In countries with good corporate and personal income tax systems, the tax system can be used to regulate the economy. As we saw in Chapter 5, changes in tax rules can provide a 'low cost stimulus'—sometimes also increasing the efficiency of the economy at the same time. Similarly, increases in taxes on capital gains can be used to dampen a speculative boom. This can be especially useful in developing countries that want to maintain economic growth, but worry that there is excessive investment in, say, the real estate sector.

Sometimes (e.g. during crises) the government can go a step further and use forced lending. For example, it can force high income recipients and large private firms to buy government bonds issued at relatively low interest rates or, more controversially, it can make some government payments in the form of bonds instead of cash, which forces the receiver of government funds (a contractor or pensioner) to become a creditor to the government. These bonds are typically resold at a discount, so this practice is quite controversial and is often considered a ruse. But in time of crisis or severe adjustment problems, forced lending can be effective.

One of the main ways of stimulating the economy is to enhance the flow of credit, and one of the main ways of dampening inflationary pressures is to restrict the flow of credit. Many developing countries are in a position where administrative controls still work well—far more effectively than traditional channels of monetary policy. This is especially the case when the government tries to control excessive investment in say, the real estate sector, where speculators may be relatively insensitive to the interest rate. The administrative measures China employed in 2004 and 2005, for example, seem to have been relatively effective in curtailing the real estate boom—had the government relied on interest rate increases, it would have squelched investments in factories and other job creation at the same time, or even before, it had tamed the speculative boom.

A common problem in many developing countries is that domestic banks (including those that are foreign owned) do not lend enough, or lend enough in sectors or areas where funds are particularly needed. There may be high spreads between lending and borrowing rates, dampening investment activity. This is sometimes true even when the banks seem flush with funds: they prefer to put their funds into government securities, or abroad. The latter is especially common when currency depreciation is expected. Government banking regulations and tax policy can sometimes be used to address these problems. For instance, a high tax on capital gains derived from currency depreciations will reduce the incentive to hold assets abroad. Obviously, direct (banking and non-banking) regulations limiting foreign asset holdings can be even more effective. Capital requirements, requiring higher levels of net worth for foreign asset holdings, act like a tax, but do not generate any income for the government.

Regulations can also be used to encourage lending in job-creating sectors, or even in areas of the country where funds are in short supply. In the United States, for example, the Community Reinvestment Act requires banks to lend a certain fraction of their portfolio to underserved communities. Governments can also establish financial intermediaries, such as development banks, that are more responsive to the need for expanded credit to some sectors, especially during downturns.[24] There are other measures that the government can use to facilitate the flow of credit, such as issuing partial government guarantees.

The high spreads between bank borrowing and lending rates, which dampen investment, can be attacked in several ways. Most importantly, governments can strive to increase competition in banking. In developing countries, the government is a major user of banking services, and government can use its market power, awarding contracts for banking services to banks with the lowest spreads.

We have noted the impact that exchange rates and exchange rate volatility have on economic activity. Bank regulations that restrict banks from lending to firms with foreign exchange exposure may limit foreign-denominated borrowing, and this too may help limit the adverse effects of exchange rate adjustments. When the government wants to reduce the supply of foreign exchange, it can loosen government regulations on investment abroad or allow pension funds to invest more of their portfolios abroad.[25] This will lead to a weaker exchange rate, which, as we have seen, can stimulate growth.

This list of micro-interventions is not meant to be exhaustive. Our point is a simple one: there is no reason to limit attempts to stabilize the economy to the standard macroeconomic interventions. The claim is sometimes made that such microeconomic interventions should be avoided because they lead to distortions; however, there are several responses to this objection. First, in developing countries especially, there are limits to the effectiveness of the standard instruments; the losses from 'Harberger triangles' (the losses in efficiency from, say, tax interventions), pale in comparison with those arising from the underutilization of a country's resources. Moreover, developing countries are rife with market inefficiencies; even in developed countries, capital markets are characterized by imperfections, many associated with inherent limitations caused by imperfect information. Those who argue against these microeconomic interventions assume the economy is well described by a perfectly competitive model with perfect information and no distortions—an assumption inappropriate even for developed countries, but particularly irrelevant for the developing world. Well-designed microeconomic interventions can increase the efficiency of the economy at the same time that they contribute to economic stability.

Debt Restructuring

Many crises are the result of excessive debt burdens, either public or private. Lenders, worried about borrowers' ability to repay, refuse to roll over loans. Countries in these situations face a critical question: should they restructure (or default on) their debt?

Not surprisingly, the creditors, and those who represent their interests, say no: the costs of default will be enormous; the country will not be able to regain access to international capital markets for years; and the country will be a pariah, shunned by all respectable investors. On the other hand, the advantages of debt restructuring (especially when the restructuring is accompanied by a significant write-down in the amount owed) can be enormous. When much of the country's scarce tax revenues are spent on servicing foreign debt, there is little room for the stimulative fiscal policies required to restore the economy to full employment. A successful debt restructuring can free up budgetary resources.

For countries facing this dilemma, the critical question is: how great are the costs of restructuring? In the corporate sector, the principle that companies often are better off declaring bankruptcy and getting a fresh start is well recognized. The economic benefits of a fresh start, not only to the firm, but also to other stakeholders like workers and the community, have led many countries to enact bankruptcy laws that facilitate rapid reorganization of firms, without liquidation (chapter 11 in the US bankruptcy code.) Arguably, modern capitalism would have never been possible without bankruptcy laws.[26] East Asia (where the debt problems were largely in the private sector) suffered from the absence of bankruptcy laws that would have facilitated quick restructuring. Stiglitz has argued that countries should have bankruptcy laws that provide for expedited debtor-friendly restructuring when there is a macroeconomic disturbance (like the collapse of the exchange rate) underlying massive defaults—a kind of super chapter 11.[27]

It appears that some of the alleged costs of government defaults have been exaggerated. For instance, worries about lack of access to credit are exaggerated on two counts. First, countries facing a debt crisis typically do not have access to credit anyway and are unlikely to gain access for perhaps years to come, particularly if their economies remain weak. The question for them is not how much money they will be getting from Washington, New York, and other financial centers, but how much money they will be sending back to them in the form of interest payments and debt repayment. The net flow for most countries facing bankruptcy is out, not in. A restructuring would at least eliminate the net drain.

Second, the record suggests that countries quickly regain access to capital markets. Russian municipalities did so within two years of Russia's default in 1998. And this should come as no surprise. Capital markets are forward looking, so they look at future prospects, not past behavior. A discharge of past debts means the country is less burdened, and in that sense it is a better credit. Moreover, capital markets are competitive. If there were a single lender, he or she might have an incentive to refuse to lend to a defaulter, to teach a lesson to others. But in competitive markets, it's not in the interests of any single lender to be the one to provide the 'discipline'.

This is not to say that managing a restructuring is easy, especially in countries where pension funds and domestic banks hold large amounts of government debt. But there are ways that the government (especially through implicit or explicit insurance) can compensate domestic financial institutions partially or entirely for losses associated with the default, and still leave the country better off. This is especially true since the 'compensation' often takes the form of long-term government bonds, so that the government retains its ability to using existing resources to stimulate the economy.

Concluding Remarks

This, as well as the previous chapter, shows how alternative perspectives have markedly different policy recommendations for open developing economies. The differences between the three perspectives show up most starkly in their responses to financial and currency crises. The conservative approach focuses on confidence and concludes that reducing fiscal deficits will be good for the economy. The Keynesian and heterodox approaches suggest that reducing deficits can be bad for both the economy and confidence. Conservatives consider defaulting on debt or imposing capital controls or large devaluations the worst possible policies. From the heterodox perspective, rescheduling debt can provide funds for a country to finance expansionary fiscal policy, and capital controls might allow a country to maintain lower interest rates. In this view, restoring strength to the economy is far better for building confidence than the conservative measures.

Argentina is a case in point: during the years when the government adopted conservative policies, the economy continued to sink and confidence steadily eroded. After the default and devaluation in 2001, growth finally resumed. Conventional Keynesian analysis would have predicted that if governments had not tightened monetary and fiscal policy during crises, the large devaluations would have led to an increase in exports, strengthening the economy. Unlike the Keynesian approach, heterodox analysis also looks at the adverse effects of interest rate increases and large devaluations on firm and household balance sheets. It considers the effect of high default rates on the strength of the financial system. The heterodox approach would have predicted deep downturns (recessions or depressions) even if governments didn't resort to contractionary monetary and fiscal policies. From the heterodox perspective, IMF policies of high interest rates and strict enforcement of capital adequacy standards deepened the crisis not only for the reasons cited by conventional Keynesians, but also because of the adverse consequences for the balance sheets and cash flow and credit availability of firms and banks, which affected not just aggregate demand but also aggregate supply.

Heterodox analysis is far more worried about the long-term growth consequences of measures used to respond to crises. The high interest rates maintained during the Asian crisis led to high rates of default, with large losses of informational and organizational capital. Many of these countries issued bonds to help finance firm and bank restructuring, the costs of which were increased by the high interest rate policy. Countries that followed the IMF prescription wound up with large debt, which could potentially be a drag on future economic growth. For many countries in East Asia, which have weak security markets, debt was also the major way firms financed their rapid expansion prior to the crisis. The high interest rates induced firms to rely more on self-financing—the allocative efficiency of capital markets was undermined.

We hope that these chapters have shed some light on how economists come to such different views. In the following chapter, we'll look at the broader policy framework, and discuss issues that are relevant to all three schools of thought. We'll then turn to the differences in the formal economic models, and discuss the recent advances in the underlying economic theory that have helped shape the alternative policy perspectives.

8

Policy Frameworks

The preceding chapter focused on different economic perspectives. In this chapter, we look at the broader policy framework, and discuss three issues—accounting frameworks, risk and uncertainty, and the political economy—that have been largely overlooked by the mainstream 'conservative' and 'Keynesian' perspectives. These issues have an important impact on policy-making and need to be included as part of the policy framework, regardless of whether one takes a 'conservative', 'Keynesian', or 'heterodox' stance.

We begin the chapter with an analysis of accounting frameworks. Accounting frameworks are supposed to provide policy-makers with the information necessary to determine the state of the economy. A good accounting framework should be able to answer questions such as: are budgets in balance, and is the capacity of the economy growing? But, unfortunately, many of the commonly used frameworks do not provide the right information, at least as they're generally interpreted.

We devote the second section of this chapter to risk and uncertainty. Risk, uncertainty, and information imperfections are at the center of macroeconomic analysis. If there were no uncertainty, managing an economy would be easy. Policy-makers would know the state of the economy and its response to alternative policy instruments. The government would simply take actions to ensure full employment, price stability, and high growth. But risks do exist and can never be fully eliminated which is why heterodox economists emphasize the importance of uncertainty and expectations. In the first part of this chapter we'll address questions such as: what can government do to reduce the risks facing the economy, and how should government respond to the risks that remain?

In the final section of this chapter, we'll turn briefly to the questions of political economy. The political economy is integrally linked with policy-making. In early discussions of macroeconomic policy, the policy analyst determined what the government should do and hoped that the government would implement what was recommended. Contemporary economists have begun to analyze and model the behavior of both governments and the international financial institutions as 'actors' in the economic drama, and, increasingly, to also model the design of institutions. They look at the incentives that motivate bureaucrats to 'do the right thing' in implementing government policy.

Accounting Frameworks

Macroeconomic policy is often guided by a focus on both intermediate variables and *measures* of ultimate objectives (such as GDP). These measures are typically far from perfect. For example, increases in GDP may not be a good indicator of a rising standard of living. The link between these economic 'signals' and the real variables of concern, such as long-term sustainable growth, is both tenuous and controversial. Making matters worse, the accounting frameworks we use to assess both the ultimate goals and the intermediate variables can be misleading. At best, our macro-indicators are like using a thermometer to measure someone's health: when the temperature is high, it signals that something is wrong. But what's wrong might not be reflected in body temperature. The thermometer never provides a 'full diagnosis'.

Furthermore, accounting frameworks not only provide a description of the economy, they also influence policy. This section will explore the accounting frameworks currently used throughout the developing world, and discuss alternative approaches that might be more effective tools of economic policy.

Deficiencies of Existing Accounting Frameworks

Bad accounting frameworks pose a danger: they can lead to excessive fiscal stringency and restrict a government's ability to carry out badly needed investment and social programs.

Most countries maintain accounts of their budget or fiscal positions (similar to cash-flow statements for firms), but do not generally keep balance sheet accounts. The budget numbers are therefore used to serve several purposes. They provide an indicator of inflationary pressure, a measure of government borrowing requirements, and a signal concerning the government's balance sheet position. Ideally, there should be separate accounting frameworks for each of these uses. In reality, most governments use accounting frameworks that are a mélange; they provide only incomplete indicators for any of the questions of interest.

For example, bad accounting frameworks can suggest there's excess aggregate demand (inflation) when there isn't. Borrowing for investment has a different impact on economic well-being than borrowing for consumption, and should be recognized as such in the accounts. A *balance sheet* would measure assets and liabilities and net worth (the value of assets minus liabilities), and make this distinction clear. In the first case, assets would increase in tandem with liabilities; in the second case, they wouldn't.

One of the problems with this approach is that differentiating between true investments and consumption expenditures isn't always clear cut. For example, we typically treat expenditures on education as current expenditures (consumption), but they are really investments in human capital. Health care expenditures on children should also be considered an investment, while health expenditures on the aged should probably not. But such issues could at least be addressed with an appropriate framework.

Some of the most striking examples of accounting failures include: excluding foreign aid from government budgets; consolidating borrowing by government-owned enterprise with the rest of the budget; accounting for privatization; and responding inappropriately to budget deficits that increase after the privatization of social security. Even the standard measure of economic success, current gross domestic product (GDP), often suggests that the economy is doing better (sometimes much better) than it really is.

GDP Measurement Problems

GDP is the value of all goods and services produced in a country (measured as government spending, consumption, investment, and exports minus imports). The problem is that GDP can rise even as citizens become poorer because the government might be selling national assets to foreigners, borrowing abroad, or using up its scarce natural resources.

A better measure of overall welfare is gross national product (GNP). GNP includes income earned by domestic residents on investments abroad and subtracts income earned by foreigners on investments made within the country. Even better is net national product (NNP), which subtracts depreciation of the country's capital goods. Measures of national output that take into account the depletion of natural resources, the degradation of the environment, and the assumption of risks are even better measures of well-being.

Accounting for Foreign Aid

The most egregious example of inappropriate accounting frameworks—the treatment of foreign aid in developing countries—has produced a long-standing debate between the World Bank and the IMF. Consider the dispute over Ethiopia in 1997. Ethiopia had exhibited robust growth without inflation for more than five years. According to the World Bank, Ethiopia's budget was in balance, but according to the IMF, it had a large budget deficit.[1] The dispute revolved around the treatment of foreign aid, which the Fund insisted should not be included in the budget because the revenues weren't guaranteed over time. World Bank analyses, though, showed that foreign aid was actually less volatile than tax revenues.[2] The Ethiopian government offered the appropriate response: if revenues are highly variable, expenditures have to be highly flexible. Their expenditure programs had a high degree of built-in flexibility, and, for example, they constructed village schools and health clinics only when they received the revenues.[3]

Accounting for Social Security Privatization

Some policy reforms have worsened the government's official budgetary position while maintaining, or even improving, its true budgetary position. Again the standard accounting frameworks provide very misleading information about the state of the economy and the government's fiscal position. Consider the privatization of social security in many Latin American countries. Privatization redirected the inflow of social security contributions from the government to private accounts. As a result, the governments' budgets look worse: revenues decline, but countries continue to pay for current retirees (although these benefits have sometimes been cut back as well). For example, if Argentina hadn't privatized its social security system, some economists estimate that the country would have had no budget deficit—even at the time of the crisis.[4]

In reality, the government's future liabilities have been reduced, and the value of the reduction (the expected present discounted value) may even exceed the reduced cash flow. But since these contingent liabilities do not appear on the books, the gain from reduced future liabilities shows up nowhere. The increased apparent deficit leads some to conclude mistakenly that the budget is registering inflationary pressure so that other spending needs to be reduced.

In real terms, nothing much has happened. Individuals' disposable income remains the same; they're simply sending payments to private social security accounts instead of to public ones. Government 'saving' is down, but private saving is up by exactly the same amount. Indeed, if the government borrows from the private social security accounts, it is doing what it was implicitly doing before, that is, borrowing from the public social security accounts.

Accounting for Privatizations

Economists generally treat the proceeds of the sale of national assets (privatizations) as income that improves the fiscal position of the country. Privatization increases the government's revenue and reduces its borrowing requirements (at least in the short term). This accounting of privatization gives incentives for governments to privatize companies, even when there might be little real economic reason to do so.

If the focus of concern is the government's financing requirement, the budget would be a useful indicator of the impact of privatization. But if the focus is whether the country is better off from the sale, the budget is inappropriate, as it ignores the fact that the government's assets have declined. There are, of course, links between the two. If the government's net worth deteriorates, it may be more difficult to obtain finance in the future as the government's borrowing cost may increase.[5] If the proceeds of the sale are spent on consumption, the country will be poorer after privatization because its assets have been reduced.

Accounting for Contingent Liabilities and Government Guarantees

Poor accounting frameworks influence incentives in other areas as well. Most accounting frameworks don't take into account contingent liabilities (liabilities that will materialize only if a specified event occurs, such as pension liabilities, liabilities associated with deposit insurance,[6] or loans made to agents in difficulties). But not including these in the accounting framework can create strong incentives for budget chicanery. For instance, to avoid accounting for government expenditures, the government might lend money knowing the funds will never be repaid. These loans wouldn't be treated as expenditures, so the 'true' budget deficit would be underreported. In the United States, the Federal Credit Reform Act, enacted in 1990, requires that a fair estimate of the losses from any loan be added to expenditures in the year the loan is made.

A similar problem is faced in the case of private infrastructure projects with government guarantees (generally known today as 'public–private partnerships') for cost overruns, minimum traffic or exchange rate variations, among others. These have become increasingly important in the developing world. The contingency costs of such projects for the state are not usually accounted for, and they do not show up in current expenditures. Such guarantees imply that the government acts as an insurer of risks that the private investor might incur. The 'insurance premium equivalent' of such guarantees should be regularly estimated and budgeted, with the corresponding resources transferred to special funds created to serve as a backup in the event that the corresponding contingencies become effective. The estimated contingent liabilities should also be added to the public-sector debt. A 1996 Colombian law forces the government agency incurring the risk to make provision in an 'insurance' fund whose resources can be used if guarantees become effective.

The absence of any regular accounting of government guarantees for private-sector infrastructure projects generates an incentive to prefer such infrastructure projects even if they are not less costly to the government in the long run. Such public-sector-guaranteed private infrastructure investments might become a useful way to circumvent stringent fiscal deficit targets.

The way public-sector guarantees are accounted (or, really, *not* accounted for in most countries) illustrates another point: as political discourse has come to focus on certain measures of economic success (such as low public-sector deficits, or smaller public sectors), politicians may have an incentive to use some accounting standards, or to manipulate these measures to serve their ends. It's very much the way Enron and their accountants manipulated measures of profits to pump up reported profits in the United States' 'roaring nineties'. Many countries have implemented important institutional reforms to restrict the scope for this kind of manipulation. For example, they've made their statistical agencies independent. In the United States, the bi-partisan Congressional Budget Office (CBO) is supposed to provide an independent check on budget projections provided by the executive branch,[7] and accounting regulations can be written to stipulate how future costs are to be accounted for. But even when the numbers aren't deliberately manipulated, the figures produced by conventional accounting frameworks must be used with caution.

Accounting for State-Owned Enterprises

Another example, which also shows inappropriate accounting practices but with the opposite effect, is the way developing countries are sometimes forced to account for expenditures of state-owned companies. As the IMF has now acknowledged, it has long treated borrowing by government-owned corporations in Latin America differently from the way this borrowing is accounted for in Europe. In Latin America, there is a consolidated public sector deficit which categorizes this borrowing as an increase in the government deficit. In Europe, borrowing by public-sector firms is not consolidated with that of the public-sector administration.[8] This means that the budget numbers for Europe and Latin America are not really comparable—a Latin American country in a similar situation to that of a European country will appear to have a larger deficit. Investment by public-sector firms also implies that the public sector is accumulating assets, but such assets are not included in the accounts, which, as we've noted, generally refer to flows rather than balance sheets.

These accounting practices distort the incentives authorities face. Accounting for state-owned companies as part of the consolidated budget constrains expenditures on investments and, again, gives developing countries the incentive to privatize these companies to reduce the fiscal deficit, even when there's no real economic reason to do so. Even if there were reason to do so, it would be preferable to use receipts from such asset sales to repay public debt. But conventional accounting frameworks do not provide any credit for such sensible macroeconomics.

Other Examples of Accounting Distortion: Stabilization Funds, Land Reform, and Bank Recapitalization

There are still other examples of accounting distortions. As we discussed in Chapter 5, some countries, such as Chile, have created rainy day, or stabilization, funds which are designed to save surplus funds so they can be spent during an economic downturn. But if the budget treats these expenditures like any other form of deficit spending, it could look as though a country has exceeded the fiscal spending targets negotiated with the IMF. Not wanting to appear profligate could discourage countries from using the self-financed deficit spending that they need for recovery.

Brazil is a country with enormous inequalities in income, wealth, and the distribution of land. Land reform holds the promise of increasing efficiency, growth, and equality. But inappropriate accounting frameworks are impeding land reform. In one of the better designed land reform programs, the government borrows money to buy land from rich landowners, using its powers of eminent domain (the government's ability to buy privately owned land to turn it into public land) to force sales at fair market value. It then lends money to small peasants so they can buy the land. If the government charges an appropriate interest rate on the loans, there is no real fiscal burden on the government. Of course, there's some probability the peasants will default on the loans, but in that case, the government repossesses the land and then resells it.[9] Traditional fiscal accounting, however, treats the government borrowing to buy land as a liability; it doesn't acknowledge the mortgage that the government receives as an asset, no matter what the interest paid. Because the liabilities but not the assets are recognized, land reform shows up as deficit spending. Given the IMF's strict deficit targets, land reform becomes essentially impossible. Land reform must compete with all other expenditures even though it would be entirely, or almost entirely, self-financing with an appropriate accounting framework.

Here's another example: government expenditures to recapitalize the banking system don't directly increase aggregate demand and shouldn't lead to inflationary pressures. The expenditures affect aggregate demand only to the extent that banks expand their credit supply, as with any other monetary expansion. Yet bank recapitalization is often treated like ordinary expenditure. The key issue, again, is what information the budget deficit is supposed to convey. If it's supposed to convey information about government borrowing requirements, then the critical question is how the government plans to raise the funds to finance the recapitalization. In some cases, governments can recapitalize the banking system by issuing long-term bonds that are held by the banks; in effect, the funds are borrowed from the banks themselves. Because these bonds are not usually traded and are held by the banks for, say, 10 to 30 years, the recapitalization has minimal impact on the debt market.[10]

Some economists argue that, while the principal repayment shouldn't be included in the deficit, the interest rate should be included because the interest is paid annually while the principle is not due until the maturity of the bond. Again, we need to ask what information the budget deficit is supposed to convey. If it's supposed to convey information about aggregate demand, then the marginal propensity to consume of the recipients of the interest payments is the key factor. If the interest is paid to domestic lenders other than banks, then it would presumably add to aggregate demand just as any other source of income would. But if the interest is paid to the banks, then the effect on aggregate demand may be minimal; only if the owners of the bank see an increased value of the bank and accordingly increase their consumption will there be an increase in aggregate demand. And if the interest is paid to foreigners, then the impact on domestic aggregate demand would be negligible.

In short, the government can structure the bank recapitalization so that it doesn't adversely affect the government's (or anyone else's) ability to get financing for other purposes. In this scenario, there's no justification for including recapitalization expenditures in the budget as an indicator of 'financing requirements'. The link between the recapitalization expenditures—or even the interest paid on recapitalization expenditures—and aggregate demand is, at best, weak.

Accounting frameworks affect government policy and have enormous political consequences. Avoiding the wrong incentives that accounting practices generate may require an entirely different set of rules than those used in current fiscal programs. In particular, it may be better to target the current fiscal balance of the public-sector administration (through a structural 'golden rule', by which investment should be financed by government savings, or a structural primary surplus), together with the consolidated debt of the public sector, including all contingent liabilities.

Structural Deficits

Fiscal deficits naturally widen during an economic slowdown as tax revenues fall and the need for government expenditures rises. We've argued that governments shouldn't be forced to counteract the deficit increase by tightening fiscal policy during a recession. From this perspective, as we mentioned in Chapter 5, a focus on the *current* deficit (the nominal deficit measured during the recession) is clearly inappropriate.

Many economists now emphasize alternative accounting measures, such as 'the structural deficit'.[11] The objective is to estimate what public expenditure and revenues would be in a 'normal' (full employment) situation. This is a normal practice in the analysis of industrial economies' fiscal position by the OECD.[12] Structural deficits allow the economy's automatic stabilizers to work. When the economy slows down, the deficit increases and when the economy accelerates, the public sector should reduce its deficit or generate a surplus.

Estimating structural fiscal positions in economies subject to external shocks is not an easy task, however, as it may involve long-term GDP trends as well as trends of other crucial economic variables, such as commodity prices. Chile, for example, has adopted such structural accounting in recent years, relying on the evaluation of a panel of economists with mixed persuasions to advise on the trend of the crucial variables involved in the estimation.

It also makes sense for developing countries to focus on the *primary* deficit, the fiscal deficit minus interest payments. Interest rates can be extremely volatile and are often outside the control of developing countries. What is more, public debt that has accumulated over a long period of time means that a large fiscal deficit will persist for quite some time after correctives have been introduced. In highly indebted countries, much of the variability of the overall fiscal position depends on events outside the country (on emerging market interest rates around the globe). Developing countries would have to bear enormous internal adjustment costs if they had to reduce expenditure or raise taxes every time the market changes interest rates. Furthermore, countries need to focus on what they can control. The primary deficit shows more clearly whether an observed change makes the situation better or worse.

The IMF agreed to focus on the primary deficit for the first time in its loan to Brazil in 2002. But even there, to get the full picture, the focus should have been on the *structural* or *full employment primary* surplus.

Summary

Although accounting frameworks provide valuable information necessary for decision-making, conventional accounting frameworks are often misleading. They're designed to provide information relevant to several objectives, but this kind of all-purpose framework serves none of the objectives very well. Rather accounting frameworks should be designed to provide information for specific purposes. Moreover, current accounting frameworks provide ample opportunities for budget chicanery. Policy-makers who want to present an overly positive image can manipulate accounting frameworks. Finally, the accounting frameworks and the misleading information they provide often distort decisions. They often, for instance, impose excessive fiscal stringency which impedes social programs. Supporters of the current framework often argue that although current accounting practices aren't perfect, they still provide adequate information. But, while no system is perfect, there are alternatives that are far preferable to those commonly used.

Risk

Stabilization policy, broadly defined, attempts to do four things: limit the number of shocks to the economy, minimize their effects and enhance the economy's capacity to cope with them, identify circumstances in which discretionary interventions might help stabilize the economy, and design 'optimal' interventions. Traditional macroeconomic analysis, such as that presented in the previous chapter, focuses on the third and fourth of this list; this chapter focuses on the first and second.

Modern risk analysis of a complex system (and the economy is a complex system) is based on an analysis of the volatility of economic variables, and the interrelations among these variables (and their interdependence). It recognizes that policy-makers can reduce risk by relying on a wide variety of interventions.[13]

Reforms often Increased Instability

As we mentioned at the start of this book, some of the central economic reforms of the 1990s (whatever their merits might have been) increased developing countries' exposure to shocks. The most notable of these reforms was capital market liberalization, which subjected developing countries to the whims of international capital markets and speculators in those markets, as we'll discuss in Part III. But other reforms had similar effects. For example, the move from import quotas to tariffs exposed countries more to external commodity price shocks, as the volume of imports tends to be much more volatile under a system of tariffs than quotas.[14]

These 'shocks' are often the result of asset market bubbles that inevitably burst,[15] and have been closely associated with liberalization—especially financial market liberalization.[16] Liberalizations have often resulted in a race to become the dominant player in a market, and have frequently led to excess capacity. An example is the telecom boom and bust in the late 1990s in the United States.[17] By the same token, deregulation of financial markets has meant that banks undertake greater risks and face a greater probability of financial collapse—evidenced in the savings and loan (S & L) debacle in the United States in the 1980s. This, of course, increases economic instability.

Some of the reforms instituted throughout the developing world during the 1990s also weakened the economies' automatic stabilizers (items that automatically adjust counter-cyclically to changes in the economy). For example, income taxes fall when an economy goes into a recession, stimulating the economy. But a greater reliance on value added tax (VAT) in many countries made income taxes less progressive and weakened this automatic tax stabilizer. At the same time, weaker social protection systems (such as reduced unemployment insurance) weakened automatic expenditure stabilizers. Still other reforms introduced built-in *destabilizers*. For example, strong capital adequacy requirements for banks[18] without forbearance, whatever their benefits, make a contraction of credit more likely when the economy goes into a downturn. The quality of the banks' loan portfolio erodes as the economy slows. Banks have to increase reserves, decreasing available credit, just when it's most necessary.

Other reforms sometimes had strong destabilizing effects, depending on the circumstances. For example, individual (defined contribution) pension accounts transfer risk from corporations to households, that is, from those more able to bear risk to those less able bear it. This reduces the insurance aspect of pensions and will almost surely be destabilizing. In the event of a downturn in stock market prices, households will respond more strongly, cutting back consumption more than corporations would have cut invest-ment.[19] Labor market reforms that make it easier to fire workers can also produce greater volatility. Workers, especially the poor who don't have access to borrowing, will face greater income volatility and will likely cut their consumption in a downturn.

Not surprisingly, economic stability would improve if we were able to transfer risk from those less able to bear it to those more able to bear it. For example, stability would improve if new developments in financial mar-kets allowed the wealthy to provide wage insurance for the poor (who are more likely to be credit constrained). Disappointingly, improvements in capital markets, including the creation of derivatives, do not seem to have resulted in substantial changes in the allocation of risk in ways that stabil-ize the economy. Instead, they've provided new opportunities for poten-tially destabilizing speculation. (The most dramatic instance of which was the threat to global capital markets posed by the bankruptcy of Long-Term Capital Management in 1998.)

Risk and Policy

As we mentioned above, there is always risk, and the effects of economic policies are not completely predictable. In addition, there are often long lags between initially implementing a policy and seeing its effects. It often takes six months to a year before the effects of monetary policy are fully felt. So policy-makers have to estimate what the state of the economy will look like in the future. If they think that there will be inflation then, they must act now. But the economist's crystal ball is always cloudy. There's always a risk that, while today it seems that the economy will face inflation in six months, when the time comes, the economy will actually be very weak with no inflationary pressures. Tightening monetary policy today will then only deepen the economy's problems six months from now.

Economists and policy-makers must subject stabilization policy to a risk assessment. They need to know the risks associated with alternative policies, and should also be responsive to new information as it comes in.[20] No policy decision is set in stone. Policy-makers need, accordingly, to know how a particular action affects the ability to take future actions as more information becomes available; and how costly it would be to reverse course. Below, we lay out several risks that are important to policy-making.

The Risks of Inflation versus the Risks of Unemployment

Critics of conservative economics argue that conservative economists have focused excessively on fears of inflation, and haven't balanced the risks appropriately. This is especially true for countries that have had recessions with large excess capacity and few inflationary pressures. Russia provides a striking example. By 1998, output had declined 30 to 40 percent from the end of communism. The changing structure of demand and the lack of investment in the intervening years had clearly contributed to a decrease in the country's productive capacities. The question was whether Russia's productive capacity had contracted as dramatically as its output. If it had, it would indicate a level of economic devastation beyond that associated with the worst wars.

The IMF worried that any stimulation of the economy would lead to inflation. Critics argued that productive capacity had not fallen as dramatically as output, and while an increase in aggregate demand might lead to some inflation, it would also elicit an increase in aggregate output. The increase in output could restart the economy and enhance future growth. When the ruble devalued in August 1998, the critics of this strategy were proved correct. Imports became more expensive, residents substituted imports with domestically produced goods, leading to higher output.

Risks in Debt Management

Another area where risk assessment is obviously desirable but often does not occur is in the procedure governments use to manage their debt. Governments often focus on interest cost and cash-flow management rather than on risk. For example, immediately before the Russian ruble crisis in August 1998, the government was paying a far higher interest rate on bonds denominated in rubles than on bonds denominated in dollars. The latter, too, paid a high interest rate which reflected default risk, but the interest rate on ruble-denominated bonds reflected the additional exchange rate risk. If one believed that markets were fully informed and risk neutral, the difference between the two interest rates would have represented the expectation of a devaluation.

A prudent Russian government borrowing in dollars would have set aside a reserve fund to cover the extra costs of the (expected) devaluation. But the IMF focused on the lower interest rates of borrowing in dollars and encouraged Russia to borrow in dollars. It ignored the currency risks. This might have lowered the probability of an immediate crisis slightly due to the appearance of the slight improvement in the budget, but the effect was short term. The likelihood of sustaining the exchange rate was, in any case, nil, as Russia's exchange rate was significantly overvalued.

This increase in Russia's dollar debt intensified the negative consequences of a potential currency devaluation. The gains made by the export and import substitution industries from the weaker exchange rate would be largely offset by the adverse effect on the country's balance sheet, as the value of its debts, in rubles, would increase substantially. Russia had sunk into a deep depression and would have even more trouble getting out of it. The increased dollar-denominated debt meant that there was an increased likelihood that Russia would default on its loans after devaluation. It should have been clear that encouraging Russia to move into hard currency bonds created significant risks, but the IMF paid scant attention to the risks and did not include them in any formal budgetary analysis.

Risk and Discretion

If the structure of the economy did not change,[21] then stabilization would amount to a standard control problem, albeit a complicated one. Economists could design rules that would specify what 'actions' (expenditures, taxes, and so on) to take in response to different observations of economic variables. All actions (such as increases in expenditures, cutting taxes, increasing the money supply, or lowering interest rates) could be automatic; the only stabilizers would be automatic stabilizers—although they would be more extensive and far more complicated than the stabilizers in standard models. For example, they might depend on levels of the economic variables, rates of change, and changes in the rate of change.

But the structure of the economy does change,[22] and economists have to assess the impact of these changes: has the NAIRU (the natural rate of unemployment) fallen, and if so, by how much? Is the 'new economy' real, and if so, how has the economy's potential growth rate changed?

143

Economists and policy-makers have to make judgments informed by past experience, but simple rules can't summarize all the appropriate responses. Discretionary policy (and not just automatic actions) has an important role to play.

The Design of Rules and Interventions

How the government designs its interventions is important. There are often long lags between government actions and their effects, and the impacts of government policies are often uncertain. Should the monetary authorities, for instance, 'target' an inflation rate, a growth rate, an unemployment rate, or a rate of increase in the money supply?

In a world without lags and uncertainty, the government would obviously target the variables of direct concern. If there's a trade-off between inflation and unemployment, it would simply pick a point on the trade-off curve. But if the relationship between inflation and unemployment is shifting, the level of unemployment may be higher or lower than expected for a given inflation target. In this simple setting, the choice of target depends on the costs associated with inflation variability versus unemployment variability: if the cost of inflation variability is low while the cost of unemployment variability is high, then there should be unemployment targeting, not inflation targeting.

As we argued in Chapter 2, it is the real variables that are of direct concern (unemployment, growth, incomes), and not the financial variables (such as interest rates, inflation rates, or exchange rates). These latter variables are of concern only to the extent that they affect the real variables. But the government may be able to observe, monitor, and control these intermediate variables more easily than the real variables. Still, if the relationship between the final and intermediate variables is volatile, it may not be desirable for authorities to target these variables.

Political Economy: Institutions and Institutional Constraints

If government has the capability to stabilize the level of economic activity, it must also have the capability to destabilize it. The government is an independent actor in the economy, with its own incentives. Whether it stabilizes or destabilizes the economy depends on the incentives it faces. In democracies, the voting choices of citizens determine the government's incentives.

Domestic Institutions

For those who see politics as the source of macroeconomic instability, the economy can achieve stability only if a body somewhat removed from the political process has responsibility for macroeconomic management, especially for monetary policy. The institutional arrangement of an independent central bank focused on inflation can keep in place commitments that might not otherwise be enforceable (the problem of 'dynamic consistency').[23] Economists with this view support the establishment of an independent central bank.

Critics of this institutional arrangement believe that it undermines democratic governance. Citizens consider few issues more important than the quality of macroeconomic management. Election econometric regression tests show this as the major determining factor in electoral success. Yet, by delegating authority over the economy to an independent central bank, the government is being held accountable for something over which it doesn't have authority. Moreover, we've seen that macroeconomic management entails trade-offs, with different decisions affecting the well-being of different groups. Such decisions are necessarily political, and should not be delegated to technocrats who are 'independent' from the government. Doing so undermines democratic accountability.

While economists and politicians have long discussed the desirability of independent central banks, they've spent much less time considering the importance of representativeness (or lack thereof) of these banks. The two concepts are distinct. The problem in many countries is that the governing body of the central bank is typically not representative of society and its broader interests. Financial markets, which are more concerned about inflation than about unemployment and growth, are disproportionately represented. It's not surprising that central banks put more emphasis on inflation than many economists do, and certainly more than many representatives of workers and small and medium-sized enterprises believe they should.

Governments that are more sensitive to the democratic process argue that they, and not the central bank, should set targets, such as an inflation target, because the decision involves trade-offs, such as the trade-off between unemployment and inflation. But even a government-specified inflation target does not depoliticize the conduct of monetary policy. The central bank is responsible for reaching the target, and missing it still can have costs that not everyone in society bears equally.

Some countries have narrowed the mandate of the central bank to fighting inflation. There is some evidence[24] that independent central banks with an inflation target do achieve lower levels of inflation—it would be striking if they didn't. But inflation is only an intermediate variable. The significant question is whether economies with this institutional structure achieve better performance in real terms, that is growth, unemployment, poverty, equality, or even the short-term trade-off between unemployment and the change in the rate of inflation—the 'sacrifice ratio'. This evidence does not show better performance.[25]

There is even the possibility that a central bank focusing on price stability might lead to greater instability in financial variables. Simple theoretical models suggest the following: with shifting demand and supply curves (common during crises like those in many developing countries in the 1990s), an attempt to stabilize prices can easily lead to destabilized output; price adjustments are meant to buffer quantity adjustments, and reducing the scope for price adjustments (in the process of fighting inflation[26]) places more of the burden on quantity adjustments.[27]

In the national context, an independent central bank is just one example of the intersection between economics and politics in the sphere of institutions and policies. There are other, equally significant, illustrations. The design and implementation of fiscal policy is often shaped by the constraints embedded in political economy. Many governments in developing countries find it difficult to increase their income through tax revenues, because important political constituencies with a voice have the capacity not only to evade or avoid taxes but also to resist taxes. In contrast, these governments may find it somewhat less difficult to decrease their expenditure, although there are asymmetries: it's often easier to cut investment expenditure than to cut consumption expenditure.

The Dual Constituency Syndrome

Increasing economic globalization and the integration of capital markets in the world economy affect governance and the constituencies to which national governments respond.

It's worrisome for democracy that governments in developing countries increasingly face dual constituencies when they make policy decisions. On the one hand, citizens vote for political authorities that promise to implement a platform that's designed before their election. On the other hand, once elected, the political authorities also seek the support of those with large financial interests. In effect, open capital markets give a greater say to foreigners and the wealthiest sectors of society, who can pull out their funds and destabilize the economy if they do not approve of government policies. Even governments who remain committed to serving the interests of workers may feel that they have no choice but to listen to the dictates of the financial market.

The Political Economy of International Financial Institutions

International financial institutions have played a large and controversial role in economic policy-making in developing countries. These institutions are, of course, public institutions, and issues of governance affect them, just as they affect any political institution. One can, and should, apply a political economy analysis to understand their behavior, just as one can, and should, for national governments. To do so, we need to look at the incentive structure that the institutions and those that work within them confront.

The G-7 (Group of Seven) nations have the largest voting block in these institutions, and the United States alone has what amounts to veto power on some crucial decisions within the IMF. Developing countries are underrepresented at some institutions (the Bank for International Settlements) and not represented at all at others (the Basle Committee on Banking Supervision). The United Nations Conference on Financing for Development, held in Monterrey, Mexico, in 2002, thus called for a greater voice and participation of developing countries in decision-making in the international financial institutions.

Countries are usually represented by their finance ministers, so that the interests of financial markets tend to be overrepresented in the decision-making process. Furthermore, bureaucrats' incentives are affected by open revolving door policies, with staff and officials coming from and, even more common, going to private financial institutions. Many democratic governments have put severe constraints on the revolving door in their own countries, to reduce the likelihood of conflicts of interest. Yet other governments, even if democratic, have not. And revolving doors continue to prosper.[28]

The international institutions have weak accountability to those most affected by their programs—those in the developing countries. Democratic accountability, transparency, and an openness to the views of civil society, as is usual in all democratic societies, are crucial for their ability to function in the interests of those that they serve.

Current representation imbalances might explain why so little has been done to improve the structure of the international financial system in ways that would promote stability and growth in developing countries. Standard economics argues that well-functioning efficient markets should transfer risk—including the risk of exchange rate and interest rate fluctuations—from poor developing countries to rich developed countries, which are more equipped to manage it. But, in fact, this hasn't happened. For example, Latin America was forced to bear the brunt of increasing interest rates in the United States in the early 1980s. This is a market failure, but, remarkably, one which has not been addressed within existing arrangements.

Similarly, the problems associated with the global reserve system are also increasingly being recognized. Developing countries hold a large share of their international reserves in US treasury bills, effectively lending hundreds of billions of dollars to the United States at low interest rates. Meanwhile, the international creditors lend money to developing countries at much higher interest rates. The result is an enormous transfer from poor and middle-income countries to the richest—a tragic irony, paralleled by the huge attendant trade and budget deficits in the United States. The growing indebtedness of the United States raises several questions. Will foreigners be willing to hold ever increasing amounts of US debt? What will happen, not just to the United States, but to the stability of the global financial system if foreigners lose confidence in the strength of the dollar, if they worry that it will depreciate in value in coming years?

Yet, while limited action has been adopted to correct these problems of global stability, capital market liberalization was encouraged or even forced on developing countries—a policy now widely recognized as contributing to global financial instability, as we'll discuss in Part III of this book. Similarly, developing countries have been encouraged into rapid trade liberalization, despite the fact that developed countries restrict imports of high interest to developing countries and massively subsidize agricultural production. Those responsible for macroeconomic policy in developing countries should be aware of the potential adverse effects that capital market and unfair trade liberalization can have on employment and macro-stability in their countries. They should make sure that countervailing measures for maximizing job creation—such as credit availability at affordable terms—are in place.

The object of this book is not to lay out an agenda for reforming international economic institutions.[29] Our focus here is macroeconomic policy. Yet we must recognize that the global economic system is biased against the interests of developing countries. Making international economic institutions more responsive to the concerns of these countries, especially the very poor within those countries, will require greater incentives for these institutions to respond to the concerns.

9

Formal Approaches

The preceding chapters took as their point of departure recent policy debates that have been informed by advances in economic theory. In this chapter, we'll examine the parallel discussion on the advances in the theory itself. Our discussion on theory will focus on the ways real world economies differ from the 'competitive equilibrium' model that has become the benchmark model.

Economists once based their thinking about stabilization on models of the business cycle[1] that depicted the economy as alternating predictably between periods of economic growth and recession. The evidence, however, doesn't support this behavior of the economy.[2] In fact, if growth and economic cycles were so predictable, governments could act to eliminate them. For example, if policy-makers knew that the economy went into recession every six years, the monetary authorities would engage in strong monetary expansion, say five years after the last trough. While there are not regular cycles,[3] the economy is subject to enormous fluctuations. There are a myriad of shocks; and although many of these are offsetting— the demand for products in one industry goes up, while the demand in another goes down—a few are of such a nature as to have macroeconomic consequences that affect the overall economy.

The current benchmark competitive equilibrium framework includes new classical, representative agent, and real business cycle models as discussed below. These models assume that all markets (including the labor market) clear. They also assume perfect information, complete markets (including perfect capital and insurance markets), perfect wage and price flexibility, perfect competition, perfect rationality, and no externalities. If these models accurately portrayed reality, the economy would be efficient and there would be no need for government intervention. There might be *fluctuations* in the economy. For example, the real business cycle literature[4] has attempted to show that simple 'calibrated' models can replicate observed patterns of movements in aggregate variables (including observed correlations), such as business cycles. There might be shocks to the economy, such as episodic increases or decreases in productivity, or shifts in preferences that lead to economic volatility. But perfect markets would then 'smooth' the economy (balancing costs and benefits).

Much of the macroeconomic modeling over the past few decades has centered on models that deviate very little from the perfectly competitive model. For example, wages and prices are still fully flexible. And while they may not assume that there's a complete set of markets, individuals behave as if there were. Individuals have rational expectations about wages and prices that extend infinitely far into the future. More broadly, even when information imperfections or asymmetries exist, they do not represent a fundamental problem. If markets are imperfect, so this thinking goes, intelligent market participants will find tools, such as complicated contracting provisions, to limit the consequences.

These models have serious inadequacies. The assumptions are unrealistic and it's difficult to reconcile the required macro-formulations with what is known about microeconomic behavior (without resorting to ad hoc assumptions about the nature of the stochastic shocks to preferences and technology). For example, in reality, shocks such as the productivity shocks referred to above have not been large enough to explain, on their own, the crises and prolonged recessions that many countries have experienced. Such models also typically leave key economic phenomena unexplained, such as why (involuntary) unemployment exists or why a reduction in the demand for labor takes the form of lay-offs rather than a reduction in hours worked.

As another example, real consumption wages (the purchasing power of wages, or nominal wages divided by the consumer price index) have exhibited relative stability over the business cycle even though unemployment has fluctuated. The models assume that markets are always in equilibrium and workers are always on their labor supply schedules. The fact that employment levels change while real wages remain stable[5] suggests *either* a close to horizontal labor supply schedule—a hypothesis rejected by microeconomic evidence—*or* implausibly large shifts in the labor supply schedule.[6] Similarly, changes in the level of employment combined with the relative stability of real *product* wages (compensation paid by firms divided by the prices received by firms) suggests implausible shifts in technology (or implausibly large variations in the stock of capital), as discussed above.[7]

The inadequacies of these models are, of course, even greater for developing countries—where information imperfections are more pervasive and more markets are missing or incomplete (e.g. insurance markets). One should, accordingly, be suspicious of policy prescriptions derived from such models. They provide few insights into the key stabilization problems faced by developing countries. Yet some of the policy stances we have identified as the 'conservative' approach are derived from such perfect market models, with only slight perturbations, or even worse, are based solely on incoherent modeling. For instance, during the East Asia crisis some conservatives argued that raising interest rates would attract more capital on the basis of models that assumed that debtor firms would not default, even though it was the fear of default that had motivated banks and other creditors to refuse to roll over their loans in the first place. More generally, it should be obvious that any economy that is going into a deep recession (e.g. because of excessively tight monetary and fiscal policy) is not going to attract capital from abroad. Instead, investors will be planning to take their money out of the country to find higher returns and less risky investments elsewhere.

The IMF itself calls attention to the excess leverage (or borrowing) of firms in developing countries and the weaknesses of the financial institutions, explicitly recognizing their vulnerability to financial distress. Nonetheless, the Fund still pushed for higher interest rates in East Asia. This put firms at greater risk, and saddled surviving firms with even higher debt equity ratios. Economic policy-makers emphasized the role of bad lending practices, but they relied on models that paid little or no attention to key details of the financial sector. In the simplified models, the entire financial sector was represented by an equation for money demand. The analyses ignored credit rationing, even though credit rationing frequently arises when there are information problems concerning borrowers. Information shortcomings accounted for at least part of the financial sector problems in the Asian crisis. This was reflected in the widely expressed concern over transparency.

We've noted that conservative models are often based on representative agent models, which are designed as if the economy had a single individual/household and a single firm.[8] Such approaches to modeling implicitly disregard many of the crucial aspects of macroeconomics. For example, these models have nothing to say about what form a reduction in the demand for labor will take (whether it will result in lay-offs or in a reduction in hours worked). In these models there's one individual, and that individual will work fewer hours. There can be no information asymmetries (different individuals having different information) and hence no credit rationing. With a single individual, the issue of risk sharing—and the problems in equity markets—do not arise.

In the real world, the social costs of economic fluctuations result largely from the fact that a few workers bear the brunt of the reduction in hours worked: they are laid off and cannot borrow to smooth consumption over time. Economists who use the representative agent model ignore credit rationing and vastly underestimate the welfare costs of economic volatility.[9] Similarly, representative agent models can't address the consequences of changes to the distribution of income—and so they can't represent the real consequences of price changes which bring about large redistributions. They can't address the impact of economic policy on inequality, or the impact of inequality on economic performance.

As we've noted, perfect markets models, including the variants that use representative agents, provide a poor description of advanced industrial countries, and are particularly irrelevant for developing countries. Accordingly, economic research since the 1990s has focused on identifying the most important limitations of the standard competitive model, particularly those that help to explain the nature of economic volatility.

Wage and Price Rigidities

Traditional Keynesian discussions focused on the role of wage and price rigidities (growing out of Hick's IS-LM framework). If wages don't fall when there is an excess supply of labor, there will be involuntary unemployment. Newer Keynesian models have sought to explain these wage rigidities.

Economists who believe in well-functioning markets argue that policymakers just need to restore full wage and price flexibility to return the economy to full efficiency and resolve the problem of unemployment. Economists in this tradition, accordingly, emphasize increased labor market flexibility.[10]

A focus on wage rigidities has been particularly convenient for the conservative policy agenda: it argues that government intervention and unions are the source of the problem. Limiting both would restore the economy to efficiency. These economists argue that the reason the economy might not be fully stable, even with labor market flexibility, is simply because it is buffeted by shocks, such as those associated with technological change.

While excessive labor market rigidities can lead to unemployment, two observations are in order. First, under the hypothesis that wage rigidities are the *only* problem in an otherwise perfectly functioning economy, restoring *full* wage flexibility would restore the economy to efficiency. It doesn't follow, however, that *more* flexibility will result in *more* stability in a real-world economy, where there are a host of other imperfections.[11] These are delicate matters of second-best economics. The 'theory of the second best' says that when there are multiple distortions in an economy, eliminating just one may not enhance overall welfare: when the first best solution is not attainable (due to market imperfections) a 'second best' solution is called for. As we noted earlier, greater wage flexibility in the absence of good insurance markets may be associated with greater economic volatility. Moreover, unemployment still exists even when there are no *artificial* sources of rigidities—no unions, or unions only in a few sectors, and no (enforced) minimum wage as in many developing countries.

Efficiency wage theories[12] provide an important set of explanations for why wages may not fall, even in the presence of high unemployment. In contrast to the more simplistic rigid wage models which simply *assume* rigidities, these theories emphasize how firms set wages, focusing on how employers might use high wages to attract a better workforce, motivate workers, and reduce labor turnover. They have important implications for stabilization policy. For example, in labor-turnover efficiency wage models, firms try to reduce the turnover rate by paying higher wages because it's costly to hire new workers; in some versions of this model, additional government employment might end up leaving the total unemployment rate unchanged as more workers are attracted into the urban sector.[13] In standard Keynesian models, increased unemployment benefits help stabilize the economy. In the Shapiro–Stiglitz incentive-based efficiency wage model[14] they lead to more unemployment because firms must raise wages to ensure that employees work hard and don't shirk. (We should note that while these effects may be present, in a downturn, they are likely overwhelmed by more standard Keynesian effects: as the economy goes into a recession, the costs to workers of being laid off increase significantly. They'll have more trouble finding work. Even with modestly increased unemployment benefits shirking is actually reduced.)

Traditional Keynesian analyses have focused on *nominal* rigidities (where money wages and prices are sticky),[15] while efficiency wage theories have focused mostly on *real* rigidities (where wages adjusted for inflation are sticky).[16] The problem, however, is that nominal wages and prices are *not* completely rigid. Today, most developing countries have fairly open markets with flexible exchange rates, so that the prices of their tradable goods have considerable flexibility. Even advanced industrial countries have exhibited considerable nominal wage and price flexibility: in the Great Depression, nominal wages and prices fell at a rate of 10 percent a year.[17] Again, in 2003, there were worries about deflation.

While older theories of fixed wages and prices are today seen as unpersuasive, it remains clear that wages and prices do not adjust instantaneously to market clearing levels. In particular, some prices and wages are set by firms, which typically adjust prices and wages slowly in response to changing circumstances. Other prices are set in 'auction' markets, where prices adjust relatively rapidly. This divergence means that large 'disequilibrium' fluctuations in relative prices can exist, and these can be a major source of disturbance to the economy.[18]

Incomplete Futures Markets and the Role of Expectations

In our discussion in Chapter 3, we stressed that different models of how expectations are formed (including the elusive 'confidence') help explain differences in policy prescriptions. In the competitive equilibrium economic model, individuals do not have to form expectations about future prices and wages: there is a complete set of futures markets (that specify wages and prices in the future for all possible states of the world). Most macroeconomic models have recognized that this is a fiction—futures markets are incomplete and simply do not exist for the medium and long term—and correctly emphasize the importance of expectations.[19]

Much recent research has focused on a special class of expectational models. In these 'rational expectation' models, expectations are rational: they are based on all available information, and are incorporated into beliefs about the future using the most sophisticated statistical models. Rational households' and firms' behavior, of course, is consistent (in these models) with those expectations. Many of the rational expectations models conclude that markets are efficient, that government intervention is ineffective, and that unemployment does not present a serious problem. It is important to recognize, however, that many of the conclusions of these models do not follow from the assumption of rational expectations. Instead, they are a consequence of *other* assumptions made in the model, such as complete wage and price flexibility, so that labor and product markets always clear. Neary and Stiglitz[20] have shown that even with rational expectations, if markets don't clear, increases in government spending can be effective at reducing unemployment—indeed, the multiplier (the extent to which output is increased as a result of an increase in government spending by a fixed amount) is actually greater with rational expectations.[21]

In addition, market behavior is often hard to reconcile with rational expectations. For example, there is irrational exuberance and irrational pessimism about stock prices.[22] Consider the 30 percent drop in stock prices in just a few days in October 1987: no event explains why the expected (present discounted) value of future earnings or dividends should have declined by that magnitude so quickly.

Moreover, bubbles can easily develop if futures markets project ahead only a limited number of periods—or if expectations have short-term rationality, but are not necessarily rational in the longer run.[23] When individuals see the price of an asset rise, they are willing to pay more for it because of the perceived capital gain. Expectations can be self-confirming— for a while. But all such bubbles eventually burst. Even if market participants know this, many cannot resist the temptation to participate in the market during the boom, (over)confident that they can leave before the bubble bursts. The higher prices induce more investment, and eventually the excess capacity that develops makes the prices unsustainable. As we've seen, many of the most serious fluctuations in the economy are associated with such boom and bust patterns, especially in the real estate sector.[24]

Incomplete Capital and Financial Markets

As we discussed earlier, many of the bubbles, and the crises that follow, have been systematically associated with liberalization, especially capital and financial market liberalization. We can see the links between instability and liberalization at both the micro- and macroeconomic levels. When a government eliminates or reduces restrictions in a market (as happened in telecommunications in the United States in the 1990s), a race begins. Market actors often believe in a first-mover advantage: they believe markets are not truly competitive, and the firm that establishes itself first will be able to earn monopoly profits. There is competition *for* the market, rather than competition *in* the market. And with competition for the market, the race to be the early dominant firm leads to excess investment and financial bubbles.[25]

Financial market liberalization often encourages bad lending practices: either banks engage in excessive risk taking, or the owners/managers loot the banks.[26] Although it can be difficult to differentiate between the two, the net effect is the same: a period of readily available funds is followed by a crash, as debtors don't repay their loans. Lending then contracts, the economy declines, there are more bad loans, and a vicious cycle is set in motion.

These microeconomic phenomena have large direct macroeconomic consequences, but there is perhaps an even more important macroeconomic reason that capital market liberalization in particular is often associated with instability. It leads to capital flowing into countries in good times and flowing out in bad times. Countries are forced to pursue procyclical fiscal policies. Chapter 10 describes in detail how short-term capital flows both induce fluctuations and impair the ability of governments to respond.

Incomplete Contracts

Closely related to incomplete futures markets is the fact that contracts, too, are incomplete. They generally have some missing provisions and don't account for all possible states of the world. Of particular concern is the imperfect indexing of credit contracts: most credit contracts have fixed interest rates and aren't indexed to inflation. A decrease in prices (or an increase in prices at a rate that's slower than expected) produces a redistribution of wealth from debtors to creditors because real interest rates increase as prices fall. Such redistributions can have large real effects and impose huge risk on both debtors and creditors. Just the recognition that it might occur affects behavior in important and costly ways. One reason why greater wage and price flexibility may lead to more economic instability is that, with falling prices and fixed interest rate debt contracts, more firms and households will be forced into financial distress.[27]

It's perhaps not surprising that when inflation has been highly volatile, markets have responded by indexing prices to the inflation rate to reduce the costs associated with the volatile inflation. In recent decades, some developing countries (such as Brazil and Chile) established indexation mechanisms for wages, real estate rents, loans and savings, and other contracts. However, as we pointed out in the analysis of the costs of inflation in Chapter 2, indexation mechanisms tend to generate inflation inertia.

157

This is the reason why efforts at disinflation in several developing countries have included the elimination of indexation clauses. Indexation of financial contracts may also help to lengthen the time horizon of financial contracts, but may not entirely eliminate the adverse effects that inflation has in shortening those horizons.

Constraints

The discussion in the previous sections has highlighted only a few of the more important examples of imperfections in capital and other markets. While imperfections of capital markets have long been discussed, the modern theory of asymmetric information has put such discussions on a firm footing.[28] It explains credit and equity rationing,[29] and accordingly, why firms act in a risk-averse manner; why balance sheet variables, cash flow, and the availability of credit matter; and why banks are important, for ascertaining creditworthiness, and monitoring and enforcing debt contracts. The theory of asymmetric information makes sense of observations and distinctions that have played a role in policy discussions for a long time. Firms, and policy-makers, often talk about the availability of credit, but in the standard competitive model, credit is always available; the only issue is 'price' (the interest rate which is charged) and it is always set to equate demand and supply.

Another example is the distinction that's often made between firms that are insolvent, and those that are liquidity constrained. With perfect information, a complete set of contracts, a well-functioning judicial system, and effective enforcement, there should be no distinction between the two: any firm with a positive net worth should be able to obtain funds at some price—the price appropriate to its risk. With asymmetric information and problems in contract enforcement, the owners of a firm may believe that the firm is solvent and that if the market *correctly* valued its prospects, its net worth would be positive; but of course, lenders may not share that view, and accordingly may not be willing to lend to the firm. Lenders may believe the firm is insolvent, even if the firms' owners do not. The reason the firm is illiquid is that critical market players believe the firm is insolvent. In these instances, policy-makers (central bankers) may come in with a bail-out. In effect, they believe that the firm is correct in its diagnosis, and are willing to override the markets' judgment.[30]

Behavioral Macroeconomics

Keynesian economists have long postulated that individuals exhibit 'money illusion' and are resistant to nominal wage cuts even if their real wages increase. In fact, there is some evidence of downward nominal price rigidities, even though rational actors should be willing to adjust prices downward when there is deflation. Imperfect and asymmetric information explains why product or goods, labor, and capital markets behave markedly different from the way envisaged in perfectly competitive models—even when all market participants act rationally.

Behavioral economics, which looks at actual behavior, at how decisions are made, argues that there are many instances—such as the example of money illusion just cited—where individuals systematically do not behave rationally. There can be significant consequences for the macroeconomic performance of the economy. This research has cast further doubt on the plausibility of the macroeconomic models underlying many of the conservative policy stances, for these models require both rationality and perfect information (or at least no asymmetries in information.)[31]

Dynamics

To a large extent, macroeconomics is about *adjustments*, including adjustments to shocks. The older literature on rigid wages and prices essentially assumed that wages and prices did not adjust, forcing the burden of adjustment on quantities. In fact, there are both quantity and price adjustments.[32] As we noted, wages and prices do adjust, but different wages and prices adjust at different rates. Asset prices adjust most rapidly; prices of 'commodities' (such as wheat) adjust more rapidly than do prices that are set in monopolistic and oligopolistic markets. The different speeds of adjustment mean that shocks to the economy can give rise to large changes in the short run to *relative* prices. At the same time, adjustments in product and labor markets typically occur in *nominal* prices, in the prices of the local currency.[33] This can give rise to excessively slow adjustments in *real wages* and other relative prices. For instance, in recessions, both wages and prices (in local currency) fall; but most firm decisions (e.g. hiring and production) as well as *real* aggregate demand depend on real wages, and so the falling wages and prices have little effect on the economy's output and employment.[34] (Increases in real money balances provide a little stimulation to the economy, either because individuals feel wealthier or because interest rates are reduced; but these effects are typically of second order.)

Many peculiarities in the short-run behavior of the economy relate to particular features of dynamic processes. For instance, as we noted in Chapter 6, exchange rate depreciations sometimes have a negative effect in the short run, contrary to the presumption that they should lead to an increase in effective demand. Much short-run policy-making focuses on the details of these dynamics. For example, we know that firms typically delay hiring new workers until late in the recovery from a recession when they become convinced that the recovery is real. In the earlier stages of recovery, firms rely more heavily on increasing workers' hours, even though this can be expensive, because of overtime pay. This is why many recoveries are, at one stage or another, described as 'jobless recoveries'. But the details of the dynamics can change from one cycle to another. In earlier downturns in the United States, firms tended not to lay off workers (a phenomenon called labor hoarding[35]) because of the high costs of hiring and firing workers. But in the US downturn in the early 2000s, firms seem to have responded to a fall in demand by laying off workers. There is a widespread view that this may be related to the more short-term focus of management: firing workers can increase current profits and stock prices, and hence management compensation.

Earlier, we discussed the importance of expectations in macroeconomics. How expectations actually adjust to changes in the economy is complex and controversial. One of the advantages of the rational expectations model is that it sometimes provides a clear answer; but unfortunately, that answer is often wrong, and in many of the most interesting situations, rational expectations provides little guidance. Those in East Asia during the crisis had no set of similar experiences to draw upon on the basis of which they could make a 'rational' inference. Different market participants and government policy-makers clearly had very different expectations about the unfolding situation and the effects of different government policies.

It is easy to see how expectations can sometimes give rise to instability, sometimes to slow adjustment out of a situation where the economy is underperforming. For instance, in a world with a complete set of markets, equilibrium might be restored by adjustments in wages and prices *in future markets*, but in the absence of those markets, behavior is determined by expectations of those wages and prices, and those expectations may not adjust, or may not adjust much. It is, in effect, rigidities in expectations as much as it is rigidities in current wages and prices that contribute to unemployment and lack of aggregate demand. If, for instance, pessimistic expectations about the future lead to a reduction in investment, and market participants simply do not change their expectations, it may take a very large adjustment in current wages and prices to restore the economy to full employment. If a weakening of the economy leads to less 'confidence', so that capital flows are decreased, and *if* a decrease in capital flows leads to a weakening of the economy (which, as we have argued, may well *not* be the case), then a negative shock can set off a downward spiral.

In short, market economies may not adjust either quickly or smoothly to disturbances. The dynamics of adjustment may be unstable. While there may be no consensus among economists about how best to model dynamics, including the dynamics of expectations, it is clear that empirical observations of high levels of economic volatility are consistent with simple and plausible models. We argued earlier that there is little basis for the confidence that many conservatives place in the efficiency of market equilibrium; by the same token, there is little basis for confidence in the efficiency of market adjustment processes.

Concluding Comments

Ideas matter. Economists' understanding of the structure of the economy is typically based on simple models that are intended to encapsulate the key features of the economy. These models are checked against reality, by comparing their predictions to what actually happens, and by testing directly the various hypotheses that go into them through econometric analyses. Models are constructed for particular purposes. One model might do a good job of forecasting average growth, but fail when it comes to predicting the turning points of cyclical fluctuations. Of course, the test of any model used for policies related to stabilization is its success in explaining and predicting the economy's fluctuations.

Today, there is no disagreement that good macro-models must be based on microeconomic principles. But there is disagreement over what this entails. Perfect competition models with perfect information are of dubious relevance for understanding developed economies; we should be even more skeptical about their policy prescriptions for developing countries. They fail to provide a good understanding of how labor, product, and capital markets operate, and not surprisingly, macroeconomic analyses based on flawed micro-foundations are themselves flawed.

Alternative models have been formulated that take into explicit account market imperfections—imperfect competition, incomplete markets and contracts, imperfect and asymmetric information. Although these models are still at an early stage of development, enough progress has been made to suggest that the new models provide far more insights than do perfect competition–perfect information–complete markets models into economic fluctuations and policies that reduce their frequency, duration, and magnitude. Alternative models indicate that government intervention is often desirable and effective. In these models, unemployment can occur as the result of market imperfections, and can have large social costs. In perfectly competitive–perfect information–perfect markets models, unemployment is always voluntary, and markets are always efficient.

The alternative models indicate that government policies should focus on *real variables*, such as unemployment and growth. The perfect competition–perfect information–perfect markets models focus almost exclusively on price stability. In the latter models, government is more often the cause of instability—government-sanctioned labor market rigidities, excessive profligacy, and loose monetary policy—while in the former models, the root causes are market failures and government intervention can improve the economy's performance.

A key difference in perspectives concerns the relationship between stabilization and growth. This is of crucial importance to developing countries. Conservatives often base their policies on the belief that stabilization—particularly price stabilization—is a prerequisite for growth. They argue that stabilization, accompanied by the associated policies of the Washington consensus (privatization and liberalization), almost automatically leads to growth. And the faster stabilization, privatization, and liberalization take place (the more 'pain' taken), the stronger long-term economic growth will be.

Critics of conservative stabilization policies contend that these policies (and the way they are implemented) rarely lead to growth. In fact, they often stifle long-term growth and development. There is considerable evidence in support of this position. At the very least, it is clear that the Washington consensus policies, including price stabilization, have not sufficed in many countries. Others have achieved growth without pursuing stabilization, or without pursuing it to the extent pushed by conservative economists. The tight monetary policies that are often associated with stabilization have often stifled investment and growth, even in countries that have liberalized and privatized. So too, responding to crises by raising interest rates to very high levels discourages debt financing; since equity markets are particularly weak in developing countries, this implies that firms rely more on self-financing, lowering growth and reducing economic efficiency.

In the next part of the book, we shall see how one part of the liberalization agenda, capital market liberalization, may not only have exposed countries to more shocks, but impaired the ability of the economy to respond. Liberalization has led to more instability, and this instability, and the way governments have had to respond to it under capital market liberalization, have actually led to slower growth.

Part III

Capital Market Liberalization (CML)

10

Capital Market Liberalization: The Arguments For and Against

For almost half a decade, capital market liberalization (CML) raged as a key battle in the debate on globalization—and for good reason. By the mid-1990s, the notion that free trade, or at least freer trade, brought benefits to both developed and less developed countries had gained acceptance in intellectual as well as policy circles.[1] When the Uruguay Round of trade negotiations (which created the World Trade Organization) ended in 1994, the Asia-Pacific Economic Cooperation (APEC)[2] and the Summit of the Americas agreed to create free trade areas. Meanwhile, the broader liberalization/free-market agenda was winning victory after victory on other fronts: the Uruguay Round had extended the scope of traditional trade liberalization to include services and the protection of intellectual property rights. Even social-democratic governments embraced privatization and deregulation.

During this wave of liberalization, capital market liberalization— eliminating restrictions on the free flow of volatile (particularly short-term) financial capital[3]—remained a major point of contention. The IMF sought to settle this issue too. At its annual meetings in Hong Kong in September 1997 it asked for a change in its charter to include a mandate to promote capital market liberalization, just as it had had a mandate (since its founding) to eliminate capital controls that interfered with trade.

The timing could not have been worse: the East Asia crisis[4] was heating up. Thailand had already succumbed. No sooner had the IMF delegates returned home than the crisis struck in Indonesia. Within little more than a year, it had grown into a global economic crisis requiring rescue packages of unprecedented amounts (more than $200 billion)[5] not only in Thailand and Indonesia, but also in Korea, Brazil, and Russia. And it was clear that hot speculative money—short-term capital flows—was at the heart of the crisis: even if these flows hadn't caused the crisis, they played a central role in its propagation.[6] Two of the large emerging markets—China and India—avoided the ravages of the global financial crisis and continued to grow at rapid rates. And both these countries maintained capital controls. As discussed earlier in this book, Malaysia imposed capital controls during the crisis, and as a result, its downturn was shorter and it emerged with less debt than other countries in the region.[7]

Today, the central intellectual battle over CML has for the most part ended. In March 2003, an IMF paper publicly acknowledged the risks inherent in CML.[8] There is now broad recognition that CML has not, in general, enhanced economic growth in developing countries, while it has exposed them to greater risk. But critical policy debates continue: under what circumstances is a country sufficiently developed to risk capital market liberalization? Should countries follow a straight and fast path to liberalization, or should they intervene in capital markets pragmatically throughout the process of development? Should countries that have partially liberalized reconsider intervening, at least under certain circumstances? Should liberalization necessarily be the long-term goal for all countries?

Although capital market liberalization might not produce the promised benefits, many economists and policy-makers still worry about the costs of intervention. Do these costs exceed the benefits? Under what circumstances? What are the best kinds of intervention? To answer these questions, we have to understand why capital market liberalization has failed to enhance growth, why it has resulted in greater instability, why the poor appear to have borne the greatest burden, and why the advocates of capital market liberalization were so wrong.

There is another reason for this chapter's detailed analysis of capital market liberalization: while a new understanding of the consequences of CML is reshaping many policy discussions among academics and international institutions, ideological and vested interests remain. The US Treasury has continued to push for capital market liberalization (e.g. it was included in the 2003 bilateral trade agreements with Chile and Singapore). Developing countries should be aware of all the consequences when they consider signing such agreements; at the very least, they will need to act to mitigate the worst effects. In 2004, there were even some renewed calls to give the IMF a mandate for capital account convertibility (or liberalization).

This chapter is divided into six sections. We start with the 'debate in brief', which presents the central arguments for and against capital market liberalization. In the next three sections, we look at the impact of capital market liberalization on stability, growth, and poverty. We then discuss the impact of the common international policy response to instability, known as 'bail-outs'. In the sixth section, we present a brief discussion on the interaction of capital market liberalization, political processes, and democracy.

The Debate in Brief

Arguments in Favor of Capital Market Liberalization

The most naïve—but at the same time most fundamental argument—put forward for CML was that free markets are inherently better than 'restricted' markets. Just as governments should eliminate barriers to trade, they should also eliminate barriers to the free flow of capital because doing so leads to better economic performance measured in growth, efficiency, and stability. That free markets are always better is almost an article of faith—although liberalization advocates occasionally appeal to economic doctrines such as Adam Smith's 'invisible hand', which asserts that free markets lead, as if by an invisible hand, to economic efficiency.

Other arguments for capital market liberalization were more specific: for example, developing countries are capital starved. Just as water naturally flows downhill, capital should flow from developed countries (where its relative abundance implies low marginal returns) to low-wage developing countries (where its relative scarcity implies high marginal returns).

A second argument was that capital market liberalization enhances stability as countries tap into a diversified source of funds. When a country faces an economic downturn and domestically funded investment drops, declining wages and asset prices will attract international funds, thereby helping to stimulate the economy.

A third argument put forth was that CML increases the welfare of domestic investors by allowing them to invest abroad and diversify risk. Still another argument was that open capital markets act as a disciplining force: countries that fail to pursue good policies will not attract funds, and so liberalization helps to keep countries on a solid reform path.

Arguments against Capital Market Liberalization: The Counter-Arguments

The case against capital market liberalization begins with the argument that advocates of CML are out of touch with both modern economic theory and the economic reality of developing countries.

169

Economic science places important caveats on free market doctrines.[9] Research over the past quarter-century has shown that markets often fail to produce efficient outcomes, and that capital markets, in particular, are plagued by market failures.[10] Countries are exposed to great risk when they liberalize. But the people of the countries—especially workers, small businesses, and the poor—have no way of protecting themselves against these risks. Even in developed countries, risk (or insurance) markets are imperfect, which is why governments play such a central role in providing a social safety net. But, insurance markets and publicly provided safety nets are weak or absent in most developing countries. Government interventions, not only in providing safety nets but also in reducing exposure to risks, can accordingly lead to welfare improvements. The advocates of free capital markets typically did not engage in the kind of detailed analysis necessary to assess whether government intervention (in particular, interventions in capital markets) could be welfare enhancing, given the market failures.

Consider their argument by analogy: since free trade in goods and services is beneficial, the free flow of capital must be good as well. But free trade in goods and free trade in financial assets are not equivalent.[11] In the discussion below, we shall highlight some of the ways that capital markets differ from ordinary markets. The trade analogy as a reason that CML should lead to growth or enhanced welfare is unpersuasive.

For opponents of CML, the notion that liberalization inevitably leads to faster growth because it leads to an inflow of capital is like assuming that an open birdcage will inevitably attract a bird. Instead, CML can make it possible for capital to flow out, as it did (massively) in Russia in the years after the fall of communism. The water analogy—capital will flow into 'capital starved' developing countries just as water inevitably flows downhill—was equally misleading. The market failures in many developing countries have meant that the marginal returns (adjusted for risk) to capital were often less in these countries than in developed countries.[12] Moreover, even if CML does encourage short-term capital inflows, the short-term capital inflows may not lead to sustained increases in economic growth, as we explain below.

The argument that capital market liberalization would be a stabilizing factor because capital flows would be counter-cyclical (and act as a counterweight to economic fluctuations by rising during economic slowdowns and falling during economic expansions) is also out of touch with reality. A wealth of evidence shows that capital flows are pro-cyclical: they exacerbate both economic booms and recessions. A standard banking dictum has it that bankers only lend to those not in need, money flows into countries in good times and out during crises. CML exposes a country to the irrationality of market sentiment based on the changing whims of short-term investors.[13] Worse still, CML exposes a country attempting to stabilize its currency to speculative attacks by hedge funds and other investors.

While short-term speculative flows are particularly unstable, the volatility of other capital flows also has severe consequences, as we'll see below. More broadly, capital flows to developing countries are subject not only to short-term volatility but also to *medium*-term fluctuations associated with successive waves of irrational exuberance and unwarranted pessimism that characterize financial markets. Not surprisingly, most of the recent macroeconomic crises in East Asia and Latin America have shown a close relationship with large swings in the flow of private financial capital.[14]

The third argument, that CML allows residents to diversify risk by investing abroad, focuses on the benefits for a small group of residents (generally the richer strata of the population) while it ignores the larger effects on society as a whole. There's no well-documented analysis of the relationships between portfolio risk diversification, domestic productivity, and economic growth. In fact, opening the capital account to residents can at times be very destabilizing. In the late 1990s, Chile (encouraged by a policy of liberalizing outflows during an earlier period of ample inflows) relaxed restrictions on domestic pension funds investing abroad. The pension funds then speculated against the national currency and deepened the balance-of-payments problems in the aftermath of the Asian crisis. Domestic pension funds and domestic investors were the main agents behind the massive capital outflows.

The fourth point put forward by the proponents of liberalization was that open capital markets act as a disciplinary force. However, this notion ignores the short-term focus of capital flows. Many financial market participants look to the near term because their returns are monitored continuously and bonuses are tied to short-term performance. But, a short-term focus is the very antithesis of what is needed for long-term successful growth. Capital market investors sometimes invest even when long-term fundamentals appear to be worsening, because the short term looks profitable. What matters from their point of view is that the crucial indicators (exchange rates and the prices of real estate, bonds, and stocks) continue to provide them with profits in the near term, and that liquid markets allow them to reverse decisions rapidly.

Market analysts often interpret economic policies from this short-term perspective. For example, they don't differentiate clearly between increases in indebtedness that result from expenditures on productive investments and those due to increased consumption. Similarly, market sentiment generally approves of reductions in indebtedness, even if the country becomes poorer as a result—as, for example, happens when public assets are sold, or privatized, cheaply (often to foreigners), as we discussed in Chapter 9. The markets focus on the reduced budget deficit and ignore the decline in government assets. Their short-term focus also leads them to overlook or underestimate the consequences of factors such as deterioration in a country's infrastructure, inadequate investment in education and technology, and growing inequality.

Finally, if you're going to have an outside disciplinarian, you want one who punishes you only when you've truly misbehaved. Under CML many countries learned with great pain that they could be punished even if they did precisely what the disciplinarians—capital markets, international financial institutions, and risk-rating agencies—considered correct. With open capital markets, even countries that have not yet fallen from favor can face crises due to contagion when international market sentiment changes.

CML does restrict what governments can do—but in ways that are often adverse to stability and growth. It limits, for instance, the ability of governments to use standard macroeconomic tools to reduce cyclical fluctuations, as we discuss below.

The Core Argument against CML: Instability

What is perhaps the most important argument against capital market liberalization can be stated in three words: *it increases instability*.

Capital market liberalization allows speculative capital to flood into a country. While the money flows in, the currency appreciates. The capital inflows may support short-term growth, but they can also lead to an unsustainable expansion of consumption, and to changes in the structure of production. The short-term capital tends to go into real estate and equity markets (not into long-term capital investment). This spurs price increases in these markets, and generates wealth effects that increase spending on consumption. The mix of a demand boom and strong currency induces growth in domestic non-tradable sectors (such as construction and services),[15] but weakens exports because domestic producers find it increasingly difficult to compete with foreign-produced goods.

Unfortunately, the capital inflows repeatedly turn into outflows. In the mid-1990s in Thailand, speculative inflows of capital led to a real estate bubble.[16] When the bubble burst in 1997, so did expectations of high and sure returns. The inflows stopped, and capital started rushing out of the country. In the late 1990s, Latin America was characterized by significant vulnerabilities due to high debt, high current account deficits, and currency overvaluation that had accumulated during the period of booming capital inflows. In 1998, a change in global sentiment towards emerging markets led to capital outflows.

Just as capital inflows may temporarily buoy an economy, capital outflows can depress it. They rob banks of their resources, forcing a credit contraction that monetary authorities often fail to offset. Sudden changes in capital flows can be particularly disruptive; exchange rates suddenly fall, resulting in huge dislocations that include large increases in the domestic value of dollar-denominated debt. Aggregate demand drops, forcing a contraction of output and employment. Central banks—which worry about the effects of currency depreciation on inflation—often raise interest rates to protect the currency. This leads to further declines in the economy. With tax revenue falling and foreign credits drying up, governments are then forced to cut back expenditures, aggravating the downturn even more.

This real-world scenario leads CML foes to their basic conclusion that capital market liberalization produces instability: capital flows, rather than being stabilizing, are destabilizing. During the crises of the 1980s and the 1990s capital generally flowed *from* developing countries *to* the developed world in search of better-known, low-risk assets, not the other way around.

Effects of CML on Monetary and Fiscal Policy

Standard recipes for dealing with a crisis call for central banks to reduce interest rates and for governments to stimulate the economy by increasing expenditures and/or cutting taxes. But countries that have opened their capital market often find it difficult to do either. Rather than lowering interest rates in a downturn—especially a downturn associated with a crisis—countries with open capital markets are typically forced to raise interest rates to stop capital outflows. The higher interest rates then have adverse effects on fiscal policy, particularly in countries where the government has high levels of short-term debt. Unless a government can increase its borrowing to fully offset the higher interest payments, other forms of expenditure have to be cut back. This reinforces the negative effects of monetary policy.

Even worse, foreign creditors may demand repayment of their loans: even at a higher interest rate, creditors may refuse to make credit available.[17] There is credit rationing. Then governments are often forced to *reduce* the level of the deficit and maintain primary *surpluses* to repay debt.[18] The actual level of spending on goods and services contracts even more, making the economic downturn even worse.

Restrictions on capital flows would, of course, give central banks some independence in monetary policy. During booms, they can raise interest rates without attracting a deluge of foreign capital. And, during downturns, they can lower rates without precipitating a massive outflow of capital.

Metaphors: Why Capital Market Liberalization is Dangerous and What Should be Done

In the early days of the liberalization debate, both sides often used metaphors to lay out their reasoning. While metaphors, of course, are hardly a substitute for economic analysis, they help make the concerns on both sides more accessible. Three transportation metaphors in particular capture the spirit of the debate.

One popular metaphor involved the automobile. Critics of CML maintained that if there is an isolated accident on a highway, you might infer that the problem is with the driver. But when there are repeated pile-ups at the same bend, the problem is more likely to be the design of the road. Supporters of CML countered that the appropriate response is to widen the highway, not to do away with cars and bring back the horse and buggy. They argued further that the problem is not so much with the design of the road as with the training of drivers, and this is where attention should be focused.

The critics responded that roads and cars have to be designed for ordinary drivers. If you need to be a racetrack driver with years of experience to survive the road, something is fundamentally wrong. Moreover, they continued, the only repair work on the road system proposed by international institutions was better road signs (improved information)—and even that initiative was half-hearted and incomplete since the United States refused to allow the posting of signs at the most dangerous turns (i.e. it refused to disclose information concerning the activities of hedge funds and offshore banking centers).

Another metaphor likened small developing countries to small boats on treacherous seas. According to opponents of CML, even well-designed and well-captained small boats are likely to be hit broadside by a big wave at some point and capsize. The IMF program of capital market liberalization made matters worse by sending leaky boats into the most tempestuous waters without a trained crew or life vests (safety nets).

A third metaphor had to do with aviation. The undersecretary of the US Treasury (who in the past had argued that failing to regulate capital markets was like failing to regulate nuclear power plants—you were inviting disaster) switched sides (and metaphors) and claimed that just because planes occasionally crash is no reason to give up flying. Critics of CML responded that governments take strong measures to ensure that pilots are well trained, that the planes are in good shape, and that the planes are suitable for the particular flight path—not every plane is allowed to cross the Atlantic.

The metaphors brought out many of the issues of the debate; they emphasized the instability associated with CML, the inadequacies of the existing policy responses, and the necessity of alternative solutions. These issues are discussed in more detail below.

Stability

As we've seen, advocates of capital market liberalization contend that it increases economic growth and efficiency and reduces risk. According to this thinking, CML stabilizes consumption and investment.[19] There may be some indirect evidence for this scenario in more developed countries,[20] but what made this argument remarkable is that CML proponents made it at the time when there was overwhelming empirical evidence against it for developing countries. As we've seen, short-term flows of funds are procyclical, exacerbating, not dampening, economic fluctuations.[21] There are several distinct but related reasons why capital market liberalization leads to increased instability.

Speculation, Bank Loans, Portfolio Flows, and Derivative Products

Liberalization exposes countries to the waves of irrational exuberance and unwarranted pessimism that characterize financial markets.[22] *In theory*, rational speculation, lending, and investment should be stabilizing: investors buy currency when the exchange rate is weak and sell when it's strong, thereby reducing the size of exchange rate fluctuations; otherwise they lose money. Markets, however, rarely exhibit such rationality.

Bubbles appear even in developed countries with well-functioning markets. In developing countries with thin or small markets, bubbles are easier to create, and their effects are more devastating.

One of the ironies of destabilizing capital flows is that they often afflict countries with seemingly good economic policies more than those with bad policies. Countries with good policies can obtain financing on favorable terms[23] and are encouraged to borrow. Then, of course, their higher level of debt makes them more vulnerable to excessive optimism and pessimism and changes in investor sentiment. Moreover, market sentiment about which countries have 'good' policies can change significantly over time. Argentina is a clear example. At its 1998 annual meeting, the IMF touted Argentina as a model developing nation under the guidance of its president, Carlos Saúl Menem. Shortly thereafter, when the problems in Argentina became impossible to ignore, the IMF berated Argentina for indulging corrupt politicians and choosing inept policies.

Furthermore, the most significant crises have been characterized by the shrinking availability of capital—foreign lenders refuse to roll over loans and cut new lending sharply. Banks' unwillingness to roll over trade and other short-term credit lines played a central role in the Asian crisis and has also figured in many other episodes.

Another source of instability is portfolio investments. Even though most bond issues themselves are medium to long term, bond financing is strongly pro-cyclical. This may reflect the short-term focus of many institutional investors who are active in the emerging bond market. The same is true of investments (also by institutional investors) in developing country stocks. When stock markets are doing well, additional funds flow in, reinforcing the boom, but when a stock market crashes, the opposite occurs.

The increasing use of derivative products is an additional source of instability associated with CML.[24] Although the accelerated growth of derivative markets has helped to reduce 'micro-instability' by creating new hedging techniques that allow individual agents to cover their microeconomic risks, it might have increased 'macro-instability'. Derivatives have reduced transparency, allowed large off-balance-sheet positions that are difficult to regulate, and have speeded up market responses to sudden changes in opinion and expectations.[25]

The role of speculation in recent crises has been widely debated. An IMF study in 1998[26] argued that speculative hedge funds did not play an important role in the 1997 Asian crisis, in part because they were simply too small to do so. Yet less than six months after the IMF published its study, the US government engineered a bail-out of the world's largest hedge fund, Long-Term Capital Management, on the grounds that this one firm was so large that its failure would greatly worsen the global financial crisis. This further undermined the credibility of those who claimed that capital market liberalization had little to do with instability.

Today, even the IMF recognizes that capital market liberalization has not enhanced stability as they had hoped—and predicted. Their 2003[27] study repeatedly emphasizes that theory predicts that CML *should* enhance stability, even though it hasn't, providing some insights into why the IMF was so misguided for so long. The basic problem with that 'theory' is that it is predicated on *perfect capital markets* (e.g. no credit rationing, no information imperfections) and *perfect intertemporal smoothing* (individuals living infinitely long or fully integrate their children's welfare with their own). The authors of the paper seem surprised to discover that CML does not stabilize consumption. Yet it has long been recognized that volatile capital flows are pro-cyclical, so that there would have been a real mystery if CML were associated with greater stability.

Market Manipulation

Some critics of capital market liberalization go further: they argue that the thinness of markets in developing countries exposes them to market manipulation. The Central Bank of Malaysia has contended that international hedge funds manipulated the Malaysian financial markets in the 1990s. And then there's the example of the infamous Hong Kong 'double play'. In August 1998, international banks and hedge funds attacked Hong Kong's exchange rate and stock market by selling both stocks and currency short.[28] They reasoned that they were almost sure to win: if the Hong Kong government responded as the IMF encourages governments to respond, by raising interest rates to defend the exchange rate, share prices in Hong Kong would fall.[29] The speculators would not make money off the currency, but they would make a killing on the stock market. If Hong Kong didn't respond according to script, the currency peg would break, the exchange rate would fall, and the speculators would make money in the currency market. At the same time, the stock market would likely fall in response to the currency crisis. Then they would win doubly.

The Hong Kong government foiled the plot by intervening in the market and buying up shares to keep share prices from falling. As a result, the speculators first lost money on their short positions in the stock market; then they lost more money as the currency market rebounded. At the time, the government's move was highly controversial, especially for those who lost money as a result; they used 'free market' arguments to bolster their position. For those who believe in the efficiency of free markets, prices should reflect the information of those in the *private* sector, and governments should never intervene in the stock market. Despite the fact that there were widespread reports of market manipulation and that it was clear that the markets weren't functioning the way they should, the Hong Kong government was accused of being dangerously interventionist. Standard & Poor's downgraded Hong Kong's credit rating from A+ to A.[30] Yet the Hong Kong government not only stabilized its economy, it made large amounts of money doing so. Hong Kong was in the position to intervene in the market because it had large reserves it could use for purchasing shares. Most developing countries though, are not so lucky.

Contagion

As we noted earlier, with open capital markets, countries are more exposed to the irrational exuberance, and pessimism, of foreign investments, even when manipulation is not a factor. Empirical studies[31] have shown that most of the shocks (both positive and negative) experienced by developing countries have been generated *externally* by factors such as sudden changes in investor 'appetite' for risk, or shifts in the prevailing mood (often affected by experiences outside the country affected). This exemplifies *contagion*: problems, or crises, in one country lead to problems elsewhere. Open capital markets expose countries to greater danger of a crisis from other countries.[32] During the boom of optimism in international capital markets in the 1990s, capital even flooded countries that had major macroeconomic problems; after the 1997 East Asian crisis, external financing dropped even in countries that seemed to have good 'macroeconomic fundamentals', such as Hong Kong.

Foreign Direct Investment (FDI)

Not all forms of capital flows contribute, or least contribute equally, to instability. It's important to distinguish between short-term capital flows and foreign direct investment (FDI). Foreign direct investors are usually interested in stability and the long-term performance of the domestic economy, while capital market liberalization refers to opening up markets to short-term and other volatile capital flows. As the policy of

China illustrates so well, a country can invite foreign direct investment and still restrict flows of short-term capital.[33] Foreign direct investment is often accompanied by access to foreign markets, new technology, and training. The new investments in plant and equipment associated with FDI generate jobs and real growth; by contrast, a country cannot build factories using short-term capital that can leave at a moment's notice.

However, it's worth noting that FDI also moves pro-cyclically (although not to the same extent as more volatile capital flows)[34] and can also increase instability. There are three primary reasons for this. First, much of what is classified as FDI is sometimes really 'finance'. For instance, privatizations and mergers and acquisitions are categorized as FDI, even though they often represent an ownership transfer rather than new investment. It's therefore important to distinguish between new 'greenfield' investments and mergers and acquisitions. Second, to the extent that FDI is geared toward the domestic market, it responds to an economic downturn in much the same way that domestic investment does. Finally, during a crisis, it's difficult for foreign direct investors to sell their assets. They therefore often use derivative products, such as currency forwards and options, to sell the local currency short as a hedge of their investment, adding to the run on the currency.

Capital account regulations, however, can be used to encourage the types of FDI that are most beneficial to the country while restricting riskier and more volatile flows, as we'll discuss in Chapter 12.

Balance Sheet Effects and Short-Term Booms

There are two additional sources of instability through which capital flow volatility translates into broad macroeconomic instability. First, capital inflows and outflows affect major macroeconomic prices—interest rates, exchange rates, and stock market values—and these have an impact on balance sheets and on investment, savings, and consumption decisions.[35] The balance sheet effects have received increasing attention in recent years. As we've seen, some of the most important involve the mismatch of the currencies in which liabilities and assets are denominated.[36] Balance sheet changes not only generate important wealth effects (impacting consumption and investment); they can even result in bankruptcy and financial disruption. For example, borrowing in foreign currencies, and using the funds to invest in domestic assets (like real estate), can lead to bankruptcies when the local currency devalues and the foreign liabilities increase relative to the value of domestic assets. When these adverse effects are large enough, the short-run dynamics are often brutal and not quickly self-correcting.

Second, capital inflows can have a positive effect in the short run, but a negative effect in the long run. On the positive side, when capital flows into an economy that has unutilized productive factors, the added capital can stimulate a recovery. It's important, however, not to confuse rising output and productivity based on the utilization of previously idle labor and capital with a structural increase in the speed of productivity improvements, or with enhancing the long-run strength of the economy. Much of the incoming capital may go to finance consumption rather than investment. (For instance, consumers might assume the improvement in the rate of income growth is permanent and increase consumption more than they otherwise would.) The country as a whole then becomes more indebted without a corresponding increase in its ability to service the debt. The end result is destabilization.

Productivity Shocks

Two other sources of instability are associated with medium-term fluctuations in the economy and arise even with rational expectations. They relate to how markets normally spread risks across generations, and how capital market liberalization amplifies the effects of shocks and undermines market risk-spreading mechanisms.[37] Consider an economy experiencing a period of unusually high productivity (a productivity shock) that increases the ability and desire to borrow (as in the United States in the 1990s). Capital flows into the country, and workers' incomes rise during the boom, both because of the productivity shock *and* because of the capital inflow. But when the bubble bursts and productivity returns to more normal levels, incomes will shrink as capital flows out of the country in search of higher returns and safer havens. The open capital market amplifies the effects of productivity fluctuations at home.

Capital market liberalization short-circuits some of the mechanisms that would naturally (and over time) smooth out the impact of disturbances.[38] With capital market regulations in place, higher incomes during a productivity shock lead to more savings as earnings are reinvested in the local economy. This drives down interest rates and boosts wages in subsequent periods. Some of the benefits of the productivity shock are passed on to the future. With full capital market liberalization, this does not occur because the (temporarily) higher earnings are often invested abroad.

Growth

The most compelling case against capital market liberalization, as we've noted, is that it leads to greater instability. Nonetheless, capital market liberalization still could be desirable if it led to faster economic growth.

Proponents of capital market liberalization maintain that open capital markets stimulate growth because of improvements in economic efficiency as well as increased investment, including investment in technology.[39] The expansion of aggregate income would then further increase domestic savings and investment, thereby creating a virtuous circle of sustained economic expansion. This 'virtuous debt cycle'[40] would contribute to converging levels of economic development among countries.

In order for CML to promote growth, though, capital inflows need to go into investment, and not be diverted into consumption.[41] In the 1970s and in the period 1990–7, capital did move to developing countries, but the basic conditions linking additional funds to growth were not met.[42] The capital inflows led mostly to increased consumption rather than investment. Moreover, much of the additional investment that did take place occurred in domestic non-tradable sectors that did not generate foreign exchange. With greater foreign debts unmatched by a greater ability to meet debt obligations, it's not surprising that balance of payment crises eventually developed.

An examination of the data, both over time and across countries, shows that CML is not associated with faster economic growth or higher levels of investment.[43] After World War II, global GDP growth per capita was high although, apart from the United States, capital markets were not generally liberalized.[44] More recently, as capital market liberalization has become more widespread, the pace of world growth has been falling: GDP per capita rose 1.8 percent in the 1970s, 1.4 percent in the 1980s, and only 1.1 percent between 1990 and 2003. These global trends are reflected in growth trends in Europe where liberalization occurred some three decades ago and in Latin America where it occurred more recently.

Additional direct evidence doesn't support the claim that CML increases investment. The fact that China has retained capital controls and has attracted more FDI than any other developing country undermines the claim that capital market liberalization is necessary for countries to attract foreign investment. Other countries that imposed capital controls, such as Malaysia and Chile, also continue to attract FDI.[45] Similarly, in the early to mid-1990s, Hungary attracted the greatest amount of FDI in Eastern Europe, even though it retained restrictions on short-term capital.

The case for why capital market liberalization may be bad for growth is even broader. As we've seen, CML increases instability, and instability is associated with a large average gap between potential GDP (full capacity) and actual GDP, reducing productivity, profits, and incentives for investors.

Furthermore, higher risk increases the return investors require, limiting long-term investment—such as investments in technology. Periodically, there is also enormous destruction of organizational and informational capital, as firms and financial institutions are forced into bankruptcy. That is why crises are often followed by an extended period of slow economic growth.

The instability and periodic crises associated with capital market liberalization have other costs: they force governments intermittently to cut back on investments in infrastructure and human capital. This stop-and-go investment pattern has high long-run costs. At the same time, countries are forced to maintain larger prudential international reserves in order to defend their currencies in case there's a crisis. Holding so much wealth in reserves has high opportunity costs.

An important theme of this book is that stabilization and economic growth cannot be separated: policies that lead to more instability or lower income today are likely to inhibit growth and output in the future. Economic volatility in general and crises in particular have huge costs. This is true even in the exceptional cases of fast recovery, the so-called V-shaped recoveries. A severe crisis can put a country onto a lower GDP growth path even after recovery. In brief: an economy that had a 7 percent growth trend and then suffers a 7 percent drop, experiences a net 14 percent gap from its trend. Figure 10.1 depicts the cases of Korea and Malaysia, two of the countries with the 'best-behaved' recoveries. Even these two economies have remained well below their earlier trends.

Poverty

The instability associated with CML often has significant distributional consequences. Even in developed countries such as the United States, the poor bear a disproportionate burden of increased unemployment.[46] This is even more the case in most developing countries where safety nets are inadequate or non-existent. The crises of the 1990s have amply demonstrated this burden: unemployment increased rapidly and real wages fell as economic activity declined. Not only low-wage earners but also small and

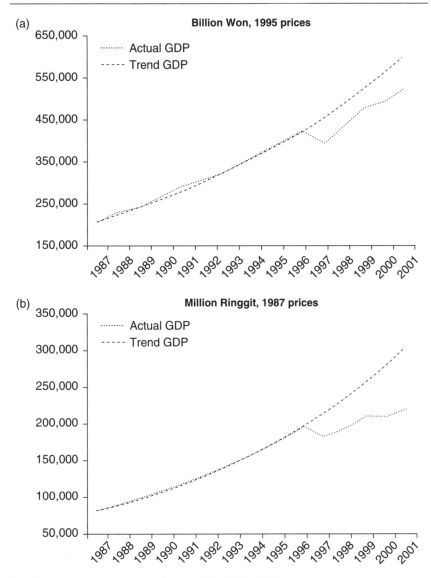

Fig. 10.1 (a) Korea and (b) Malaysia: GDP, 1987–2002.
Source: Ffrench-Davis (2004).

medium-sized enterprises (SMEs) suffer during downswings, as do middle-income wage earners and the self-employed.[47] The poor lose in other ways as well. There are losses from periodic cutbacks in public services and an enhanced sense of insecurity.[48]

Capital market liberalization hurts the poor in yet another way, especially in conjunction with restrictions on the flow of labor. With CML, the mobility of capital increases, but unskilled labor remains relatively immobile. This strengthens the bargaining position of capital relative to labor.[49] In doing so, it affects the ability of society to redistribute: any threat to increase taxes on capital can result in quick retaliation in the form of withdrawal of funds. This reflects a general principle of taxation: governments can impose only limited taxes on factors whose supply is highly elastic. Small changes in interest rates (the price of capital) can lead to large swings in the quantity of capital inflows, reducing the tax base.[50] Since governments are mindful of the sensitivity of capital to tax rates, they shift more of the tax burden to labor, especially unskilled labor, which is least able to migrate. We can see this bias in the reductions in taxes on capital gains and other returns on capital and their replacement with sales taxes (such as the value added tax, VAT).

International Rescue Packages Known as 'Bail-Outs'

In theory, lending by the IMF and other international institutions should be counter-cyclical, providing additional funds when private markets cut their lending. At least at times, this has not been the case; for instance, during the Argentinian crisis, the IMF asked Argentina to repay funds. But even when the loans themselves are counter-cyclical, they are tied to other policies ('conditionality') that have pro-cyclical effects. As these conditions impose severe restrictions on a country's spending, the loans have often done little more than increase the size of a country's international reserves. The funds are meant to give 'confidence' to international investors, but those benefits are often far outweighed by a loss of confidence as the country's economic performance declines.

Loans made by the IMF during a crisis are typically called 'bail-outs'. However, it's not so much the country that is bailed out of its difficulties (after all, the country is *lent* the money and will have to repay it), but the creditors (often of *private* debtors) who otherwise might not be repaid. The counterpart to the gains made by these creditors has been the losses encountered by the government, reflected in the additional debt that governments are left holding. The problems associated with this have been particularly severe when the loan money has been wasted on defending unsustainable currency regimes. The case of Argentina in the late 1990s is a prime example of wasting funds to defend an obviously overvalued currency.

Rescue packages raise 'moral hazard' problems. First, investors and creditors, expecting a bail-out, invest and lend without sufficient diligence in assessing a country's underlying risks. Second, domestic firms in many countries borrow in dollars even though their assets and revenues are in the local currency. By leading borrowers to believe the exchange rate will be defended, the bail-outs can undermine incentives for firms to buy insurance, hedge their currency exposure, or, even better, borrow in the domestic currency. The 'uncovered' exposure undermines the economy's natural adjustment mechanism (to e.g. trade imbalances) and impairs a government's ability to respond to a crisis. Normally (all else being equal), a decline in the exchange rate helps stimulate the economy, but when firms have large foreign exchange exposures, the stimulative effect on exports is offset, at least in part, by adverse balance sheet effects (which depress the economy), as we discussed in Chapter 6. Those with large foreign-denominated debts may even be forced into bankruptcy.

Even mega-bail-outs haven't worked as hoped. Some economists fault the accompanying conditionalities, which exacerbated the downturns. Others argue that the huge bail-outs weren't large enough. But it's doubtful that more money alone would have done the trick. Instead, it should have been clear that something had to be done about the underlying problem. Because speculative capital flows help to create crises, governments should have tried to contain these flows; they should have imposed some restrictions on capital markets.

The IMF used the existence of an externality—contagion—to justify bail-outs and other policies it pushed, like high interest rates. Relying on a health metaphor, the Fund argued that it had to worry about contagious economic crises just as public health authorities must worry about contagious diseases. But critics respond that the IMF was treating the symptoms rather than identifying the underlying source of the disease or the mechanisms through which the disease was transmitted. The international institutions' response to crises—ever-larger bail-outs—was like building bigger hospitals, but then not allowing doctors to use all the available treatments.[51] The irony is that the IMF, by advocating capital market liberalization, was actually bolstering short-term capital flows—one of the main mechanisms through which the 'disease' was transmitted.

Continuing the health metaphor, the IMF didn't adequately diagnose the mechanism by which the problem in one country spread to others. To the extent that trade relationships were a source of contagion, then policies that heightened fluctuations in incomes and volatility in trade (such as contractionary monetary and fiscal policies) increased the contagion. And while the IMF focused its attention on externalities among countries, it paid little attention to the more fundamental externality—between those engaged in short-term capital market transactions and the rest of society.

If the IMF had used rescue packages in conjunction with appropriate capital account regulations, some of the adverse effects might have been avoided. If lenders knew, for instance, that they might not be able to pull their money out quickly, they might have exercised greater due diligence and avoided some of the excesses that have marked investments in emerging markets.

Political Processes and Democracy

Another debate about capital market liberalization concerns its impact on democracy and democratic political processes. Some proponents of CML argue that open markets are more democratic because they give citizens the freedom to invest wherever they choose. Recent experiences in Brazil, however, show that matters are more complex. Opponents of CML argue that capital market liberalization undermined the democratic process by giving a large 'vote' (influence) to capital market participants abroad and to the wealthiest strata at home.

During the Brazilian presidential campaign of 2002, every time presidential candidate Luiz Inácio Lula da Silva made a remark that the markets 'didn't like', market participants sold off Brazil's currency, causing the exchange rate to fall, interest rates to rise, and voters to become increasingly nervous. One investment bank even created a 'Lulameter',[52] to measure the impact of a Lula presidency on the currency markets. Some observers claimed this was a concerted effort to influence the political process; others maintained that it was simply investors acting individually in their own self-interest.

Either way, capital market liberalization can put pressure on politicians so that they're afraid to propose policies that might be interpreted as not 'market friendly'. In politics, what matters is perception. Rationally, what could be more 'market unfriendly' than a long recession? And yet the policies short-term investors often 'demand' frequently involve contractionary monetary and fiscal policies that lead to extended downturns.

Consider the argument that we discussed earlier that capital market liberalization is desirable because it provides discipline. Who acts as economic 'disciplinarian' determines which policies get rewarded or punished, and this affects what a country does or does not do. In short, the choice of disciplinarian can shape the very evolution of society and politics. The underlying premise of 'market discipline' is that democratic processes can't provide an adequate check on economic policy-makers (or perhaps democracy even encourages bad policy) and thus countries should delegate economic policy-making to financial interests. Again and again, markets evaluate a country's performance against a benchmark reform agenda that, at the minimum, reflects the perspectives of particular interest groups and political players and is often even more myopic than politicians.

Open capital markets, at least sometimes, seem to exert veto power over economic choices. While it's true that governments need to take into account how their actions affect the attractiveness of investment, they should balance this with a concern about how the structure of their economic system affects the autonomy of a democratic political process and true national sovereignty.

These political objections to the *discipline* argument for CML augment the economic arguments presented earlier—that capital markets are myopic, and hence countries that are forced to listen to capital markets are forced to act more myopically. Capital markets are an erratic disciplinarian, and often punish countries when they shouldn't and don't punish countries when they should, thereby contributing to economic volatility and inhibiting long-term growth.

Conclusion

The advocates of capital market liberalization tried to force developing countries to liberalize without any analysis showing that it would enhance growth. They ignored both theory and evidence that CML imposed enormous risks; they had no guidelines indicating when countries might be able to bear those risks; and they had no prescriptions for how they might prepare to deal with the risks. The arguments for CML were based on a model that assumed an economy was perfectly competitive, fully efficient, and had a complete set of risk markets and the capacity for full intertemporal smoothing.[53] But in practice, capital markets are incomplete and imperfect, especially in developing countries. The next chapter will explore some of the central market failures associated with capital market liberalization.

11

A Formal Approach: Capital Market Failures

There is now a general recognition that capital market liberalization failed to help developing countries achieve economic growth and stability. The previous chapter looked at the arguments for and against liberalization. But, an important question remains: why did the supporters of liberalization get it so wrong?

The basic answer is simple: the advocates of capital market liberalization had an overly simple model of the economy in mind. Their model assumed efficient and complete markets. With perfect markets, capital market liberalization would be welfare enhancing. After all, allowing two parties to voluntarily engage in trade (in this case, a foreigner is lending money to a domestic investor) has to be welfare enhancing; either both sides must benefit from the trade or they wouldn't engage in it. And with complete insurance markets, the costs of any volatility associated with CML may not be that high, since the cost of the risk can always be transferred to those who are able to bear it most, and can be subdivided and shared throughout the global economy.

But markets are almost never perfectly efficient, and capital market liberalization may make matters worse.[1] There are problems with externalities: the trade may be beneficial for the two parties involved, but it can have consequences for the rest of society. In addition, insurance markets against the risks created by CML are weak or absent, especially in developing countries, and so there may be real costs associated with the increased instability.

This chapter will focus on major categories of 'market failures'. We'll examine the direct externalities associated with capital flows, and then look at how capital market liberalization can exacerbate the problems posed by coordination failures and broader macroeconomic failures. We'll also look at the effect of imperfect information on investor behavior, and examine the market failures associated with capital markets and the underlying reasons CML has failed to live up to the expectations of its supporters. We'll conclude with a discussion of the major objectives of government intervention, which serves as a background to our discussion of alternative modes of intervention in Chapter 12.

Externalities

A common thread runs through these types of market failures. In each case, there are discrepancies between the returns to market players and returns to society as a whole. Investors may gain even as society loses. These discrepancies make a case for government intervention. The case is especially strong in developing countries where banking and other financial institutions, governments ability to regulate them, and safety nets are all weak, and the ability of individuals and firms to obtain insurance against risks (and cope with their consequences) is limited. The volatility associated with capital market liberalization is likely to have an especially large cost in these countries.

Recognition of the large externalities associated with capital market liberalization is one of the primary reasons for the shift in thinking in the early 2000s. In the 1990s, for instance, workers saw their incomes plummet and small and medium-sized businesses went bankrupt as a result of abrupt capital outflows, soaring interest rates, and collapse of aggregate demand. Investors at home and abroad benefited (at least while the capital was flowing in), but over the longer run open capital markets imposed a huge negative externality on the rest of society in developing countries.[2]

Externalities take on a variety of forms. There are 'price' and 'quantity' externalities. Price externalities arise during periods of both capital inflows and outflows. During inflows the exchange rate often appreciates, harming exporters and those attempting to compete with imports. During outflows, governments often raise interest rates to limit the extent of currency depreciation. People holding foreign-denominated debt see the value of these debts, in terms of domestic currency, soar. Both the exchange rate depreciation and interest rate increases can force firms into bankruptcy, destroying jobs.

Quantity externalities are particularly acute when capital outflows lead to credit rationing: when capital leaves the country, banks may be forced to contract credit availability. Another quantity externality arises when a country's creditors look at the total short-term debt of the country and the ratio of outstanding short-term debt to reserves, and, believing that the higher ratio indicates a higher probability of a crisis, cut commercial credit lines.

Another externality arises because of the common prudential policy of holding reserves to match liquid liabilities. Evidence shows that the likelihood of a crisis increases significantly if foreign-denominated short-term liabilities exceed reserves. If market participants know or simply believe this, then a country that does not increase reserves as domestic firms increase their short-term foreign currency borrowing faces greater risk of a crisis.[3] This is one reason why several countries with a 'fully flexible exchange rate' keep significant reserves. The externality imposed on society is the cost of maintaining prudential reserves. A $100 million capital inflow that has to be offset by a $100 million increase in reserves imposes large financial costs on society. Those reserve funds are usually held in US treasury bills or other 'hard currencies', which have a much lower return than would be yielded by investing the funds elsewhere. When private domestic firms borrow short-term funds abroad, they don't take into account these costs borne by society.

There is an additional set of externalities associated with the impacts on *aggregate demand*. There are adverse shocks generated by, for instance, capital outflows, which we'll discuss in a later subsection.

In each of these instances, individual borrowers ignore how their additional borrowing affects others. Societies should insist that private firms pay the full social cost of their activity. Whenever there are discrepancies between public and private costs there is an argument for some form of government intervention. If appropriately designed, the intervention may not fully correct the problem, but it can at least improve overall well-being. The economist's natural 'intervention of choice' entails imposing a 'tax' to correct the externality and eliminate, or at least reduce, the discrepancy between social and private costs and benefits. In the mid-1990s, Chile and Colombia instituted taxes on capital inflows to moderate their volatility. These types of capital market restrictions reduce the level of activities that generate negative externalities. In the next chapter, however, we'll see that there are a variety of other interventions that also may be desirable.

Coordination Failures

A second market failure involves creditor or investor coordination problems. This is especially relevant during periods of capital flight. If you've invested in a country, it pays for you to stay invested as long as other investors are doing just that. But if you believe that everyone else is taking money out, and you believe that, as they do so, the country will face a crisis, it's in your interest to do the same. When all other investors pull funds out of a country, the currency will fall, the economy will weaken, the tax base will be smaller, the government will find it more difficult to repay its loans, and taxes will be raised. A Pareto-dominant equilibrium—an equilibrium that makes everyone better off—would probably be for all investors to leave their funds in the country, but given risk aversion, the equilibrium that naturally emerges entails capital flight.

The behavior of short-term capital during the Asian crisis provides an example. If all lenders had agreed to roll over their loans to Korea, Korea would have been able to meet its debt obligations relatively quickly (as the country clearly demonstrated over the next few years). But none of the lenders wanted to take the risk. When each refused to roll over outstanding loans, the country faced a crisis.[4] Another example was capital flight in Russia during the 1990s. Arguably, it was in everyone's interest to reinvest in the country and build a stronger legal and regulatory environment. Many investors, however, used open capital markets as an opportunity to get substantial amounts of their money out of the country. Open capital markets also increased the incentive of Russian entrepreneurs to 'asset strip', that is, to engage in transactions that allowed them to convert their assets into dollars that could be deposited in foreign banks.[5] As they did this, Russia's plight worsened. Because of the capital flight, those who stripped assets did in fact do better than those who attempted to create wealth inside the country by investing more. But the country as a whole was worse off.

Restrictions on capital outflows can eliminate the 'bad' equilibrium and ensure that an economy coordinates on the 'good equilibrium' where everyone reinvests. The interesting aspect of this intervention is that there are no additional costs of bringing about the 'good equilibrium'. When all players invest in the country, it pays each individual investor to do just that.[6]

General Macroeconomic Failures

We start with the premise that market economies are not self-regulating and do not necessarily quickly return to full employment after adverse shocks. Capital market liberalization exposes countries to additional shocks, increasing the likelihood of a recession. But, as we've seen, capital market liberalization also makes it more difficult for governments to respond to a recession in an effective way.

In the extreme case, a country can lose discretion over monetary policy completely: any deviation from international levels of interest rates results in a huge inflow or outflow of capital. In that situation, a government must rely exclusively on fiscal policy. But fiscal policy is often not as flexible as monetary policy, and as we've noted, in some cases, it has been ineffective. Moreover, fiscal policy often works best in tandem with monetary policy.[7] The double bind is that CML limits the use of fiscal policy as well as monetary policy. As we've seen, with the heavy level of short-term indebtedness which CML allows, just when a country needs additional funds to finance its deficit in a recession, foreign lenders refuse to lend, and indeed demand, the country repay outstanding loans.

The Effect of Imperfect Information on Investor Behavior

Since the late 1990s, economists have emphasized 'irrational exuberance'[8] and investor 'herding' as reasons for boom and bust periods of capital flows. If there were perfect information and market efficiency, these kinds of irrational market behavior wouldn't exist. While recent research shows that herd behavior *is* consistent with rational expectations when information is imperfect, the extent of herd behavior may well be greater than can be explained by these models.[9]

Since investors can't know future events, they make decisions based on expectations. These expectations are based on information about current conditions—information that's inherently incomplete and costly to process given the large amounts of data needed. Since some market participants have better access to relevant information and are better able to process it than others, it's rational for everyone to glean information about the desirability of investing from the actions and opinions of others.[10] The result is herd behavior. In addition, the major market players—investment banks, rating agencies, international financial institutions—use the same sources of information and tend to reinforce each other's interpretations.

This 'contagion' of opinions can lead to euphoria or panic, generating boom and bust cycles. When views converge, there is a risk of 'correlated mistakes': unexpected news that contradicts the general opinion is reported, and then all market players realize simultaneously that they were wrong and pull their funds out of a country. This type of correlated mistake has triggered numerous panics and crises. For example, the realization that

Thailand's reserves were close to zero was one of the culminating factors that triggered the Asian crisis in 1997.[11] A growing literature demonstrates how such investor behavior easily leads to bubbles.[12]

The Effect of Incomplete Domestic Financial Markets in Developing Countries

All countries—both developed and less developed—confront the problems of capital market instability. The United States maintained capital account regulations during the 1960's in order to limit capital outflows. It suffered an 'attack' on the dollar in 1971 and was forced to go off the fixed exchange rate system. In the mid-1990s, the United States worried about the fall of the dollar relative to the yen despite no apparent changes in the real economic positions of the two countries; and in 2003–4, Europe worried about the rise of the euro relative to the dollar. Capital movements were largely responsible for the exchange rate fluctuations that caused these concerns. All countries worry about capital market instability, but in developing countries the consequences are greater; it often leads to excessive lending, overheating, and high volatility. Moreover, as discussed earlier, there is greater potential for market manipulation.

One of the reasons that CML has such a large negative effect on developing countries is because the financial sector in developing countries often has currency mismatches between assets and liabilities. With only a few exceptions, the external debt of developing countries is issued in foreign currencies (and even domestic liabilities are sometimes denominated in such currencies). International creditors are often unwilling to take local market risks (or they demand such high compensation to bear that risk that local borrowers would prefer to bear it themselves), so they lend to developing countries in hard currencies, and the domestic borrowers assume the risk. The resulting 'currency mismatches' in the balance sheets of domestic economic agents (such as banks) can have enormous consequences.

Moreover, even creditors willing to lend in the domestic currency of the developing country are generally willing to lend short term, but not long term.[13] This leads to 'maturity mismatches'—the risk that creditors might not roll over short-term liabilities during a crisis, generating a liquidity crunch as borrowers are unable to repay their loans. But even if short-term debts are rolled over, domestic borrowers bear the cost of interest rate fluctuations (which they would have been able to avoid were they able to borrow long term). Finally, financial institutions in developing countries are often weak, and less able to withstand shocks. The induced volatility arising from capital market liberalization can easily lead to systemic problems in the banking sector.

Mismatches would cause less concern if the corporations or banks involved purchased insurance ('cover'). But in developing countries, currency risk often can't be insured, and if insurance is available the insurance terms aren't considered reasonable, or insurance is available only for short-term coverage.[14] The result is that developing countries bear the risk, although lenders in developed countries are better placed to take on currency risk since they can diversify their currency portfolios.[15]

This brings us to another fundamental market failure: in international capital markets, developing countries bear the brunt of exchange rate and interest rate risk even when the source of the fluctuations lies outside the country. This bears no resemblance to an optimal international arrangement, as the developed countries are better able to bear these risks.

The Effect of Institutional Weaknesses

The 1997 supporters of the effort to change the IMF charter to institute an agenda of capital account liberalization did, appropriately, add several caveats. They recognized that liberalization requires sufficiently strong and stable financial institutions, and this in turn means that a strong regulatory framework would have to be in place before liberalization. Still, it was clear that they thought most developing countries should liberalize their capital markets.

Today, recognition of the importance of those caveats has grown. Even economically advanced countries have found it difficult to establish sufficiently strong financial institutions and effective regulatory structures to avoid crises, as the financial crises in Scandinavia in the early 1990s and the savings and loan scandals in the United States in the 1970s demonstrate. These examples show that crises can easily occur in countries with a relatively high degree of transparency, and limited crony capitalism.

The growing use of derivatives has made the formulation of appropriate regulations more complex. The government-engineered, privately financed bail-out of Long-Term Capital Management (LTCM) in October 1998 demonstrates this. Many policy-makers believed that the bankruptcy of this one hedge fund, with an estimated exposure in excess of a trillion dollars, threatened global financial stability.[16] Much of the money put at risk by LTCM came from supposedly well-regulated banks. We'll discuss the sequencing of capital market liberalization in the context of institutional reforms in more detail in Chapter 13.

The Effects of Incomplete Equity Markets

When firms make decisions about how much to borrow, they need to take into account the size of fluctuations in both output and interest rates. The greater volatility of both these variables under CML means that firms make less use of debt financing. But the alternative—raising new capital by issuing equity—is difficult in developing countries. (This is also true in developed countries because information asymmetries make raising funds by issuing new equities very costly.[17]) In effect, CML has forced firms to rely more on self-financing, which then impedes the flow of capital from areas where it is less productive to areas where it is more productive. The result: capital is allocated less efficiently. This failure is particularly ironic because the major argument in favor of capital market liberalization has been that it increases efficiency in the allocation of capital.[18]

Capital market liberalization can lead to less efficient resource allocation in yet another way.[19] Governments usually raise interest rates in times of crisis if they have open capital markets—especially if they are following IMF strictures. (In the case of East Asia the increases were enormous.) Then even firms with moderate levels of debt equity ratios flounder and are sometimes forced into bankruptcy. There is an enormous economic cost to bankruptcy in these cases. It is not just inefficient firms that are forced out of business; even well-managed firms that made the one mistake of borrowing too much are forced into bankruptcy. The destruction of organizational and informational capital can set back growth for years.[20]

Conclusion

The previous discussion provides the rationale for intervening in capital markets. In simple terms, short-term and other volatile capital flows affect society beyond the market players engaged in the transactions (i.e. there are externalities associated with open capital markets). Thus, there is a role for government to reduce the instability and social costs; and governments need to address not only the consequences of short-term capital flows (the repeated crises), but also the underlying problem.

There are multiple purposes of capital market interventions, as we've noted throughout this chapter. First, capital account regulations can be used to stabilize short-term volatile capital flows. Interventions also give policy-makers more effective and less costly macroeconomic stabilization measures. As we've seen, the free flow of capital lessens, and can even eliminate, the scope for monetary policy. If, however, the government has set up effective restrictions on short-term capital movement, then the scope for monetary policy increases. Interest rates within the country can be lowered below the international level without precipitating an outflow of funds. Similarly, capital account restrictions provide greater scope for redistributive taxation of capital. In addition, effective capital account regulations can promote growth by discouraging long-term capital outflows. For example, when Russia's oligarchs shipped their money out of the country, it became more compelling for other investors (large or small) to do so as well, as we discussed under coordination failures. Of all the objectives of intervention listed, discouraging long-term capital outflows is perhaps the most difficult to achieve. Yet interventions can be effective even if controls are sometimes circumvented, as we'll discuss in the next chapter.

Given the past experiences of developing countries, the most critical issue today is not whether market interventions are desirable in theory, but whether, in practice, policy-makers can design interventions whose benefit to an economy outweighs any ancillary costs. The fact that some countries have intervened successfully does not tell us enough. We still need to know if there are interventions that can be designed and implemented by governments without highly sophisticated bureaucracies, and whether it will be possible to do so as capital markets become more complex. These issues will be taken up in the following chapter.

12

Interventions in Capital Markets

The previous chapter made a compelling case for the desirability of government intervention in capital markets, a case now accepted by most policy-makers and academics. There are still a number of unresolved controversies that the IPD Capital Market Liberalization task force debated vigorously at its meetings, including the fundamental issue of what kinds of capital market interventions governments should undertake, and more centrally, whether there exist *any* interventions for which the benefits exceed the costs. Given the importance that capital account interventions can play in macroeconomic policy-making, we devote this chapter to analyzing alternative modes of regulations.

Economists have a strong proclivity for price-based interventions (taxes and subsidies) as opposed to quantity-based interventions (administrative restrictions and controls). Price-based interventions are flexible, provide less opportunity for bureaucratic manipulation, and are in line with market incentives. The World Bank and, more recently, the IMF have accepted them as useful macroeconomic instruments. For example, after Malaysia implemented quantity-based capital controls in September 1998, the World Bank worked with Malaysia to convert those controls into an exit tax. Those who wanted to take their money out of the country could do so—at a cost. The government could (and did) reduce the exit tax over time, which meant that the intervention could be phased out gradually, with no major disturbances when it was completely eliminated.

But the case for price-based interventions is far from clear. Theoretical work in economics has shown that sometimes quantity-based restrictions can reduce risk more effectively than price interventions.[1] The reasoning is similar to the thinking of many environmentalists who support controls rather than fines on levels of pollution: they believe that there are large costs when pollution increases above a critical threshold and controls are the most effective way to ensure that this threshold is not exceeded. In the case of trade policy, the shift from (quantity-based) quotas to (price-based) tariffs exposed developing countries to an increased risk of balance of payments crises because import levels became more volatile. It also exposed producers to greater risk. Risk is, of course, key here: opposition to capital market liberalization derives from the risks to which it exposes developing countries. In the discussion below, we highlight that quantity interventions may be more effective in managing large capital account shocks. Ultimately, the choice of price controls or quantity controls depends on the particular situation faced by a specific country as well as its administrative capability. Under many circumstances, they can complement each other.

In addition to direct forms of interventions, such as taxes and restrictions on inflows and outflows, interventions in capital markets can also take on a variety of indirect forms. These indirect measures affect both the ability to borrow abroad and the associated returns. For instance, financial regulators can limit banks' short-term foreign borrowing or force them to match their foreign currency liabilities and assets. Regulators can go a step further and restrict bank loans in foreign currencies for firms that do not have equivalent revenues in those currencies, effectively imposing limits on total borrowing from abroad.[2] They can impose higher capital adequacy requirements to reflect the increase in risk. The government can also apply adverse tax or bankruptcy treatment to foreign-denominated borrowing.

There are arguments for and against each of the measures mentioned above. Some of the arguments put forward against restrictions, however, work equally well as arguments for restrictions. For example, anti-interventionists worry that certain measures might discourage borrowing by raising the costs. But that is, indeed, the purpose: to raise costs during an external financing boom in order to avoid the subsequent bust. This resembles the argument that taxing pollution will hurt businesses by forcing them to use more costly technologies to reduce pollution. Yes, it will, but reducing pollution is the reason the tax is imposed to begin with.

One of the arguments against capital market regulations is that they are ineffective because of circumvention. However, interventions don't have to be perfect to be effective. Opponents often argue that there are well-known ways of evading many types of capital market controls. But controls still work just the way an effective dam does. Some water makes its way around the dam; there's also some spillage, but the dam stops most floods and stabilizes the flow of water. Without the dam, the on-rush of water can cause death and destruction; with the dam, the regulated flow can be used to benefit the entire region.

Most of the well-known schemes used to avoid many forms of capital market controls do not undermine the ability of interventions to stabilize flows because most of the evasion tactics (e.g. under and over-invoicing) work slowly. They are like the flows of water going around the dam. In the long run, the aggregate amounts may be significant, but in the short run, the flows are still moderated. It's the huge flows (or surges) that cause the problem, and the dam still proves its worth.

Given that a measure doesn't have to be 100 percent successful in order to be effective, the question is whether the benefits of the intervention exceed the costs. And the crucial question is whether or not there are excessive ancillary costs. In the discussion below, we look at different types of interventions designed to stabilize capital flows and the relative benefits and costs associated with each.

Price-Based and Quantity-Based Regulations

As we've seen, despite the IMF's push for open capital markets, there were still countries that maintained capital market regulations during much of the 1990s. Malaysia placed restrictions on capital inflows in 1994 when short-term foreign borrowing surged; and on outflows in 1998 to protect its markets from contagion during the Asian crisis. India, China, Vietnam, and Taiwan all maintained more traditional restrictions on capital inflows that again helped insulate these countries from contagion during the crisis. In Eastern Europe, Hungary and Poland both instituted limitations on short-term capital inflows as part of the initial transition from communism.

The regulations varied across countries, but generally the controls served to segment (or separate) the domestic and foreign exchange markets, as we discuss below. Several different types of regulations have been used, including prohibiting domestic firms and/or residents from borrowing in foreign currency (except for some specific transactions such as trade financing and long-term investment); prohibiting foreign residents from holding domestic assets or, in some cases, debts denominated in the domestic currency (except for the domestic operations of foreign investors); and prohibiting domestic banks from holding deposits in foreign currencies or lending in foreign currency except when intermediating permissible external credit lines. Many of the interventions were traditional quantity-based restrictions that prohibited firms from borrowing abroad except under certain circumstances.[3] Chile and Colombia, however, implemented price-based interventions that discouraged inflows by raising associated costs.

In order to analyze the differences between price-based and quantity-based regulations, we'll begin by comparing the cases of Chile and Colombia to the case of Malaysia. In the process, we'll distinguish between restrictions on capital inflows and outflows, and examine how well (and under what circumstances) these techniques can be applied to other countries.

Price-Based Regulations in Chile and Colombia

The price-based intervention used by Chile and Colombia comprised an unremunerated reserve requirement (URR) on foreign inflows: for every dollar borrowed or invested from abroad, a certain percentage was placed in the central bank in non-interest bearing deposits.[4] Reserves could be converted into an explicit payment to the central bank, so that the URR was similar to a straight tax on foreign inflows.

The goal of this type of tax on inflows is to reduce the amount of short-term capital flowing into a country during an economic boom, not to stop funds from flowing out of a country during a crisis. Nonetheless, the expectation is that with less short-term capital in the country, bubbles are less likely to develop, and crises are less likely to occur. In the event of a downturn, there is less capital flight because less short-term money entered the country before the crisis.

The use of the URR in Chile and Colombia provide two experiments with price-based regulations. There's little agreement on whether or not the experiments were successful. However, there is some agreement on two points. First, it's generally agreed (even by the more critical authors) that the URR succeeded in changing the composition of external financing by reducing short-term flows and lengthening maturities. This improved the countries' overall liability profile while still maintaining longer-term direct investment. The URR changed the maturity structure of the flows, *even* if it did not affect the overall level.

There's also agreement that the URR allowed the authorities to maintain higher interest rates, and therefore made monetary policy more effective. With open markets, higher interest rates induce more short-term capital inflows, fueling the boom (at least for a while) and often leading to financial bubbles.[5] Because the URR acts as a tax, it reduces the returns to those who invest or lend. As long as capital flows are responsive to this cost, the URR should limit the amount of inflows at a given interest rate. Similarly, it allows the authorities to maintain higher interest rates at a given level of capital inflow.

There's less agreement about the impact of the URR on the total volume of flows and on other macroeconomic policy variables, particularly on the exchange rate. Some studies show that flows were reduced after the URR was implemented; others show that there was little impact on the total volume of capital inflows. Some studies show that, by reducing capital inflows, the URR reduced pressure on the exchange rate; others showed it had little effect.[6] However, much of the econometric evidence against URRs should be viewed with considerable skepticism. For example, much of the evidence that total capital flows were insensitive to the regulations comes from analysis that has an inadequate econometric specification.[7] In addition, part of the difficulty in evaluating the impact of interventions like the URR is that the impact must be evaluated against the 'counterfactual': what would have happened had the URR not been in place. Some casual observers have commented, for example, that the East Asia crisis and the global financial crisis seem to have affected Chile adversely in spite of the URR. This is true for several reasons, including the impact of the global shocks on the price of copper. But the key question is this: would the adverse impact on Chile have been much worse if there had been a simultaneous massive outflow of short-term capital? The answer is almost surely yes. The URR spared Chile from this disaster.

In Colombia, where the government actively modified regulations in response to changes in the economic environment throughout the 1990s, there's strong evidence that increases in the URR reduced overall inflows[8] and increased domestic interest rates.[9]

Chile and Colombia both structured the URR to penalize short-term inflows more than foreign direct investment (FDI) and other long-term investment. In the simple system adopted by Chile when it first instituted capital account regulations in 1991 (and by Colombia at a later stage), the same URR applied to any capital inflow, no matter the maturity of the loan or investment. The effective cost was higher for short-term flows than for long-term flows, since, for the latter, the fixed costs of the reserve requirement were spread out over a longer period. To strengthen the measures, Chile also required FDI and portfolio capital to stay in the country for a minimum of one year; Colombia directly regulated the amount of foreign funds that could be invested in the local debt and equity markets as well as the type of domestic securities that foreigners could buy.

In both countries, the URR was based on well-designed policies within a regulatory structure that local institutions were able to enforce. Policy-makers reacted promptly to changes in the economic environment and to new loopholes in existing regulations by modifying the details of the URR framework.

Overall, in terms of some (and probably most) of the principal objectives, the Chilean and Colombian experiments with price-based controls appear to have been successful. They were undoubtedly valuable in lengthening the maturities of flows and giving central banks more maneuverability to increase interest rates without risking additional capital inflows, thus effectively contributing to macroeconomic equilibria.

Malaysia's Quantity-Based Controls

In the early 1990s, Malaysia experienced a surge of capital inflows. In 1994, in response to these flows, it introduced outright restrictions on short-term inflows and prohibited non-residents from buying domestic short-term securities. The regulations proved highly effective in reversing the boom-ing capital flows of the previous years.[10] Similar to the URR, the Malaysian restrictions lengthened maturities and improved the country's debt pro-file.[11] Because the measures were so effective, the Malaysian authorities par-tially lifted the restrictions later that year, and dismantled them completely one year after they were first implemented.

In September 1998, in the midst of the Asian crisis, Malaysia again estab-lished quantity-based restrictions, this time on capital outflows rather than inflows.[12] A complementary set of restrictions was aimed at eliminating offshore trading of the local currency. The main objective of the intervention was to protect local capital markets from contagion during the crisis.

The 1998 Malaysian capital controls generated a significant amount of controversy when they were first introduced, as we'll discuss below. The Malaysian authorities, however, believed the measures were effective, so much so that, as in 1994, they began the process of loosening the restric-tions shortly after they were implemented. In February 1999, five months after the measures were introduced, the World Bank worked with Malaysia to replace the quantity-based restrictions with an exit levy (a tax on outflows). The regulations were structured to encourage longer-term investment, through a lower levy for liabilities with longer maturity.[13] In September 1999, the exit tax was changed to a flat rate, and by January 2001, Malaysia applied the tax only to portfolio flows held for less than a year. In May 2001, it was eliminated altogether.[14]

Kaplan and Rodrik (2002) provide the strongest argument for the effectiveness of the Malaysian regulations.[15] Drawing on previous studies, they showed that the regulations produced a speedier recovery, lower inflation, and better employment and real wage performance than most countries in the region that continued to follow IMF-styled programs. Malaysia's measures successfully closed the offshore ringgit market and reversed financial market pressure. By limiting capital flight, the restrictions gave the government space to enact expansionary monetary and fiscal policies, and these rapidly reversed the 1998 recession. In particular, lower interest rates (relative to what they would have been without the controls) had six main effects: (1) fewer highly leveraged firms were forced into bankruptcy (and more generally, the lower interest rates had a positive effect on both aggregate demand and supply); (2) because fewer firms faced bankruptcy, less stress was placed on the country's banks which were thus able to continue lending more than they would have otherwise; (3) fewer domestic firms had to be sold to international companies at bargain prices; (4) with fewer firms and banks in distress, the problem of corporate restructuring was reduced, enabling the economy to restart more quickly; (5) because more firms and banks had healthier balance sheets, Malaysia was in a better position to resume robust growth; (6) the government needed to spend less money on corporate and financial restructuring and could focus resources on increasing public investment. Again, this put the country in a better position to resume growth.

Opponents of the 1998 intervention argued that the main factor underlying Malaysia's recovery was a rebound in the external environment at the time Malaysia imposed restrictions.[16] In their view, Malaysia started from a stronger liability structure[17] than other countries in the region, which accounted for its better performance. Kaplan and Rodrik, however, showed that the Malaysian rebound was more robust than the rebound in other countries in the region, *even* controlling for the external environment—despite the fact that Malaysia didn't receive much multilateral support during the period. Interestingly, Malaysia's strong liability structure was most likely due to its 1994 capital controls and, more broadly, to central bank regulations restricting the foreign exchange exposure of banks and the corporations to which they lent.

Even critics who claim that Malaysia's quick rebound depended on the changed economic environment and not on capital controls admit that at the time when the controls were put in place, it was not clear that the external environment would improve relatively quickly. Given that uncertainty, the relevant questions at the time were whether the controls were a reasonable prudential action and whether they would have significant adverse side-effects. The critics predicted serious negative consequences—a slower recovery in the short run and less investment in the long run. But by the end of 1999, even harsh critics at the IMF[18] had to admit that the adverse effects they had predicted hadn't materialized.

Malaysia was in a strong position to implement capital controls in 1998 because of its previous experience, its strong administrative capacity and institutional infrastructure, and the government's political will to protect the local market. As with the URR, the ability to administer the regulations was crucial for their success.

A Comparison of Chilean, Colombian, and Malaysian Regulations

We noted earlier that although economists have a proclivity for price-based controls, economic theory has described circumstances under which quantity-based controls perform better. Within policy circles, however, a preference remains for price-based interventions, largely because price-based controls are believed to be less intrusive. The empirical evidence shows that both types of instruments can have positive effects, depending on the circumstances under which each mechanism is applied.

Figure 12.1 provides a simple way to view the effectiveness of the quantity-based controls in Malaysia and price-based capital-account regulations in Colombia and Chile.[19] A simple inspection of the graph indicates that the Malaysian quantity controls were extremely effective, both in reversing the strong expansionary effect of capital surges in 1994 and in halting the contractionary effects generated by capital outflows in 1998. The point that quantity-based controls can work more effectively is made equally clear by looking at countries that have long maintained more traditional types of capital controls. Some of the dynamic Asian economies—India, China, Vietnam, and Taiwan—have kept up traditional restrictions on capital inflows and outflows (with selective, flexible liberalization policies that vary from country to country). Most economists now agree that these controls were critical in insulating these economies from contagion during the Asian crisis.

The price-based controls in Chile and Colombia also show a marked effect. In Chile, the July 1995 regulations had a stronger effect than the smaller 1991–2 URR.[20] Colombia used price-based interventions more aggressively, and the effects were somewhat stronger than in Chile. (We should note, however, that overall the macroeconomic framework was

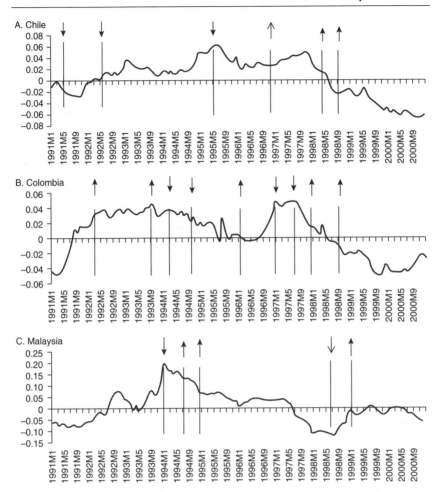

Fig. 12.1 Index of expansionary monetary pressures (IEMP)

Notes:

↓↑ Imposition or relaxation of restrictions on capital outflows, respectively (the direction of the arrows indicates expected effect on the index)

IEMP = $a^*(R) + b^*(e) - c^*(i)$

R = international reserves corrected by log trend

e = 12-month variation of the real exchange rate

i = real deposit interest rate

a, b, c = standard deviation of R, e, and i respectively

Ocampo (2003), 'Capital account and counter-cyclical prudential regulations in developing countries', in Ricardo Ffrench-Davis and Stephany Griffith-Jones (eds.), From Capital Surges to Drought: Seeking Stability for Emerging Markets, London, Palgrave/WIDER.

Source: Ocampo (2003*a*).

superior in Chile than in Colombia throughout the period of booming capital inflows of the 1990s.)

Both Chile and Colombia experienced capital outflows at the end of 1997, so that the tax on inflows was no longer necessary. Both countries reduced the URR until it was eventually phased out. As expected, this policy change didn't affect the outflows very much, since the main purpose of the URR is to reduce inflows during boom periods. (Even lowering the tax to zero can do little to stop outflows during periods of sustained financial panic.) An alternative solution would be to target outflows directly. But a tax on outflows might still be ineffective during a crisis, since the tax would need to be extremely large to outweigh the potential and quite significant financial losses that investors fear during a crisis. Regulating outflows directly might be a more efficient solution. Just as quantity-based restrictions work better than price-based regulations to lower pollution, quantity-based restrictions are more effective in preventing capital flight under these circumstances.

Regulating Inflows and Outflows

As we have noted, the regulation or taxation of inflows helps to limit outflow surges: if there is less short-term money in the country, there is less that can leave when expectations change and inflows turn into outflows. However, direct regulations or taxes on capital outflows are among the most controversial forms of capital market interventions, which explains in large part why there was so much criticism of the Malaysian restrictions when they were initiated.[21] One Singapore market participant complained that Malaysia had locked up his money, as if in a prison.

There are reasons why most economists prefer regulating inflows to outflows. First, regulating inflows helps prevent crises, and as argued extensively in Part II of this book, this should be the ultimate goal of policy-making. Second, regulating inflows involves less uncertainty and more transparency: creditors know the cost of their decisions before they invest.

Other arguments against controls on outflows are more debatable. In its May 2003 survey of capital controls, in an article that acknowledged the risks associated with capital market liberalization for the first time, *The Economist* magazine wrote: 'Experience suggests some rules. Refrain from blocking capital outflows (tempting as this might be at times of crisis). Such measures are usually oppressive, and deter future inflows of all kinds.'[22] Yet, despite *The Economist*'s assertion, evidence that controls on outflows deter future inflows is limited. This was most pronounced in the case of Malaysia. When the government initially instituted its restrictions, most analysts claimed it would reduce Malaysia's ability to attract capital in the future. They made dire predictions of a huge outflow of funds when the restrictions were finally removed and investors were free to take their money out of the country. But just the opposite occurred. When the government lifted the tax in 2001, the expected returns on investments increased. Investors are forward looking, and Malaysia's positive fundamentals (its current account surplus, high savings ratio, moderate external liabilities with a low share of short-term debts, and large international reserves—all of which the capital controls had helped create or sustain) and strengthening stock market drew *additional* funds into the country.[23]

The restrictions on outflows solved one of the market failures discussed in the previous chapter: the collective action, or coordination, problem. During crises, creditors and investors exhibit herd behavior and tend to pull their funds out of a country at the same time. The currency, interest rate, and stock market weaken and tend to overshoot substantially.[24] Investors and creditors get caught in the rush to pull out their funds, causing the markets to collapse. Since the markets usually rebound afterwards, investors would have been better off collectively if they had left their funds in the country. This is true even though it was in each individual investor's interest to exit at the time. By imposing controls on outflows, the Malaysian government solved the collective action problem. The overshooting stopped, and the markets rebounded.

The other criticism of regulations on outflows alluded to earlier is that it's unfair for governments to impose new regulations after an investment has been made, thereby changing the parameters of the original investment. The possibility that a government might impose exit controls increases investors' risks and thereby reduces overall investment. This is one of the arguments, however, that can be used in favor of the restrictions as well as against them. If the goal is to reduce short-term inflows during a boom, then the threat of potential controls on outflows in the future might have the desired effect. If this is the policy objective, though, regulations on inflows are a more appropriate policy tool, as we discussed above. But, as the Malaysian case shows, in the event of a crisis when other options are limited, targeting outflows might be an appropriate policy response.

Market Segmentation: Regulations as Second Best

The previous analysis (and the history of interventions) suggests that capital market regulations work mostly by segmenting the domestic capital market from international markets and capital flows. This is most evident with traditional quantity-based controls, but it played a role in Chile and Colombia's regulations (including the explicit objective of forbidding or discouraging the use of dollars for domestic transactions). Segmentation aims to protect the domestic economy from the volatility produced by capital market liberalization. In the best-case scenario this would be done without affecting current account or trade flows.

In the last chapter, we saw that a market failure prevalent in many developing countries is the lack of well-developed capital markets. A first best solution might include creating long-term foreign demand for assets denominated in the domestic currency, and developing good insurance markets as protection against exchange rate and interest-rate fluctuations. But these optimal solutions aren't likely in the near term. A second best response is to segment the domestic market from international flows. Since most developing countries don't have a stable source of foreign demand for local currency securities, their domestic capital markets are already somewhat segmented. But markets can be segmented even more through regulations (which are generally designed as if the segmentation doesn't exist). Segmentation can have positive macroeconomic effects for at least four reasons: it leads to stable demand for locally denominated assets; it reduces risks associated with foreign borrowing; it helps insulate the economy from pro-cyclical foreign borrowing; and it enhances the ability of government to control the macro-economy. All of these are related to the previous discussions of the effects of capital market liberalization.

Segmentation Results in More Stable Demand for Locally Denominated Assets, Contributing to Macroeconomic Stability

Domestic local currency securities are mainly, and sometimes only, used by domestic residents. It might make sense in the long run to develop an authentic long-term international demand for these securities (e.g. among institutional investors). But until the demand exists, most domestic holdings by foreigners will be short term and speculative. The primary risk for these holdings is the local currency, so foreign demand for domestic assets is largely determined by currency expectations. Any shift in international sentiment can end up destabilizing the foreign exchange market. It may make sense not to allow non-residents to hold domestic local-currency-denominated securities and to prevent the development of a premature offshore market for the domestic currency.

One might develop anyway, but additional regulations could reduce its attractiveness.[25]

We should note that domestic residents also shift their investments between domestic and foreign assets based on currency expectations (and interest rate differentials). But unlike foreigners, domestic agents have a clear long-term demand for the domestic currency and its associated assets. Capital market interventions can be used to segment the market and reduce the capacity of domestic residents to substitute foreign assets for domestic assets. This will stabilize domestic demand for assets denominated in the local currency. The growth or 'thickening' of the market itself will contribute to stability.

Segmentation Helps Insulate the Economy from Pro-cyclical Foreign Borrowing and its Destabilizing Dynamics

The second reason that market segmentation can have a positive macroeconomic effect is based on the pro-cyclical nature of the supply and demand for foreign currency loans. The transactions, revenues, and assets of many domestic residents are denominated entirely in the domestic currency. But there is a temptation for domestic entities to borrow in foreign currency when external loans are available because these loans often carry a lower interest rate. This currency mismatch between assets and liabilities creates considerable risk: any devaluation of the local currency will cause the value of foreign debt to rise. If the devaluation is large enough, local borrowers may be unable to repay their loans.[26]

External lending is most likely to be available during a boom, and lenders are likely to demand their money back in a downturn. Thus, the supply of funds intensifies economic fluctuations.

When borrowers expect the local currency to appreciate, they will have incentive to borrow in foreign currency because if the currency does appreciate as expected, their liabilities will fall in value. But when domestic agents borrow abroad, they often use those funds to buy local currency for their domestic transactions. This increases the demand for the domestic currency and fuels the currency appreciation.

Of course, there is an equally strong propensity for domestic residents to substitute foreign liabilities with debt in the local currency when a currency devaluation is expected. In this case, domestic agents need to buy foreign currency to pay back their foreign debts. This means they will sell the local currency, causing an even larger devaluation. So when domestic residents borrow in foreign currency, they increase currency fluctuations, multiplying the destabilizing effects of cycles in the availability of external financing.

Forbidding domestic agents who don't have foreign currency revenues to borrow in those currencies would also have a major positive macroeconomic effect: it would reduce fluctuations in the availability of external financing. Since foreign lenders often demand repayment when borrowers are least able to comply, restrictions would likely limit the overall adverse effects on individual borrowers over the course of an entire cycle.

Segmentation Enhances the Ability of Government to Control the Macro-economy

Segmentation gives a government greater influence over the exchange rate. The ability of policy-makers to use restrictive monetary policies during times of euphoria and to avoid excessively contractionary policies during crises (in other words, the level of a government's monetary autonomy) depends on limited capital mobility which, in turn, depends on the extent of market segmentation. Similar arguments apply to the exchange rate. The ability to manage the exchange rate provides a government with another essential tool for macroeconomic management. Moreover, segmentation also increases the effectiveness of exchange rate changes.

This is clearly the case when a country has large dollar-denominated debts. As discussed in Chapter 6, devaluation of the local currency has balance sheet effects that lead to a reduction in aggregate demand, and this offsets the devaluation's positive effect of increasing exports. So even when a government can affect the exchange rate, the effects on the macro-economy will be limited without segmentation.

The problems of exchange rate adjustment become even clearer in economies with widespread use of a foreign currency in the domestic financial market. Given the significant effect that devaluation has on the ability to repay dollar-denominated debts and on the stability of the domestic financial system, there's a strong incentive for governments to avoid currency fluctuations. The experience of Argentina in 2002 serves as an example: debtors with dollar-denominated debts were unable to repay their debts after devaluation; agents with net dollar assets were unwilling to give up their capital gains to subsidize the debtors; and the domestic financial system became temporarily paralyzed while legal and legislative controversies undermined the economy.

The Risks of Dollarization: A Digression

The problems we've discussed have led some analysts to argue for full dollarization, that is, replacing the local currency with the dollar. The major argument goes this way: replacing foreign-currency-denominated assets and liabilities with those denominated in domestic currency is pro-cyclical, so abandoning the domestic currency may be the best way to eliminate speculative movements altogether.[27] But this implies surrendering both monetary policy and the use of the exchange rate as policy instruments. We argue instead that it would be better to use improved macroeconomic policy and capital account regulations to stabilize demand for the domestic currency. Even if these instruments are imperfect and carry some costs, the costs are likely to be much lower than the costs associated with abandoning the domestic currency altogether.

We should note, however, that dollarization and, more commonly, domestic financial dollarization[28] are often the result of runaway inflation. Hyperinflation destroys the ability of the domestic currency to serve as a repository of value and generates a strong incentive for domestic residents to instead use a foreign currency for this purpose (although indexing domestic assets[29] and liabilities can restore the ability of domestic currency to act as such a respository). The magnitude of domestic financial dollarization after an episode of high inflation or hyperinflation depends in part on domestic policy. We know this because the various countries that experienced high inflation are not equally dollarized (in particular, compare neighbors Brazil and Argentina). Moreover, it's not true that dollarization can't be reversed. Chile, for example, is much less dollarized today than it was before the crisis of the early 1980s.

Soft Controls: Encouraging Market Segmentation

The direct interventions discussed above all serve the purpose of segmenting domestic markets from international markets. There is another category of direct restrictions called 'soft controls' that also aim to segment the market. Soft controls are restrictions on sectors of the economy that have effects on the foreign exchange market. For example, soft controls can require domestic funds, such as social security or pension funds, to invest their assets in domestic markets and can prohibit them from investing abroad. These restrictions limit the funds' potential to generate pro-cyclical disturbances.

This soft control has an additional positive effect on the economy. It creates a local demand for domestic securities, helps to develop the local capital markets, and builds a domestic capital base. In this way, soft controls can help remedy the market failure of underdeveloped and undeveloped capital markets discussed in the previous chapter.

This kind of control might become particularly relevant in the near future because of the growth of privately managed pension funds in many developing countries, especially in Latin America. In Chile (the pioneer in this area), such funds are equivalent to 70 percent of annual GDP. Most countries place limits on the extent to which domestic funds can invest abroad, and some have experienced new sustained growth in domestic markets in large part because of the resulting increase in demand for local securities. Once again, the Chilean experience demonstrates the stimulating role of pension funds on the development of domestic capital markets. But it also demonstrates how pension funds can generate macro-instability when the markets are not segmented and funds are allowed to invest abroad.[30]

Some economists oppose these soft controls because they limit the ability of domestic funds to diversify their assets. This is true, but all economic policies involve trade-offs. Building a local capital market and domestic capital base can, in the long run, increase the value of returns for all citizens. To the extent that domestic funds add to the pro-cyclical nature of open capital markets, they impose an externality on the entire population (as we saw in the previous chapter). Soft controls can help turn this negative process into a positive one for long-term growth.[31]

Costs Associated with Direct Capital Market Interventions

Although some economists have criticized the different forms of government intervention in capital accounts, empirical work on the costs of each type is limited. The most important question, however, is whether the costs of each instrument outweigh the benefits associated with managing the capital account.

Corruption

One of the main criticisms of the regulations, particularly quantity-based restrictions, is that they encourage corruption and cronyism.[32] The extent of corruption and the associated costs are difficult to quantify. But given the effectiveness of regulations in several of the countries that imposed capital controls, we can probably assume that the benefits to the economy outweighed the associated costs in those countries.[33]

As we noted earlier, administrative capacity is essential to making a capital account regime fully effective, and different kinds of restrictions may require different degrees of administrative know-how. The success of regulations in Chile, Colombia, and Malaysia depended on strong regulatory frameworks, efficiency and effectiveness in implementation, and the speed with which policy-makers adapted the regulatory framework to changing circumstances (e.g. as market players found new ways of circumventing regulations).

Administrative capacity is especially relevant during a crisis when policy-makers want to impose temporary controls. Without a regulatory framework, quantitative controls can generate serious credibility issues and may be ineffective. Given the cost of building administrative capability, a permanent regulatory regime, which governments can tighten or loosen through economic cycles, may work better than switching from one set of capital account regulations to another, or alternating controls with liberalization. The broader issue is that a government must maintain the autonomy required to impose capital account regulations or reimpose them when necessary.[34]

Impeding the Development of Domestic Capital Markets and the Restructuring of Domestic Financial Institutions

Critics of capital account restrictions worry that they can become obstacles to financial development.[35] A typical criticism of India's and China's quantity-based controls has been that they have inhibited the growth of the financial sector. Some critics have argued that open capital markets in these countries would have led to a faster restructuring of the local financial system. We could respond that this argument works equally well as an argument in favor of restrictions. China managed its transition with high growth whereas most of the countries that went through 'shock therapy' restructuring of the banking system (often accompanied by a collapse of the local financial system and forced restructuring) have had prolonged recessions. It has often taken them years to re-establish a strong financial system. China chose instead to restructure its banking system gradually, and capital restrictions helped make this possible.[36]

Higher Interest Rates from Capital Market Restrictions Hurt Small and
Medium-Sized Enterprises

Another set of criticisms, aimed particularly at price-based restrictions, has focused on the higher interest rates associated with interventions. In fact, one main goal of restrictions is to do just this: to give governments the room to raise interest rates during an economic expansion without attracting short-term capital inflows (and to lower interest rates during an economic slowdown). As we've seen, the immediate purpose of the restrictions is to prevent inflows from fueling consumption and creating financial bubbles (often in real estate). Yet, to the extent that the measures are associated with increases in interest rates, they can dampen lending throughout the economy. During a financial bubble, the government wants to raise rates to burst the bubble, but it also wants to encourage long-term investment, the development of small and medium-sized enterprises (SME), and productive foreign direct investment.

Two studies suggest that higher interest rates in Chile, associated with the URR, reduced lending to SMEs.[37] Of course, any increase in interest rates, or the use of monetary policy in general, during an economic expansion will undermine lending to SMEs.[38] But policy-makers must consider three important points when evaluating this criticism.

First, without capital account restrictions, what would the government have done about an overheating economy? If a government worries about inflationary pressures and believes that it cannot cut back much on government expenditures or raise taxes (as was the case in Thailand), it must raise interest rates. But under capital market liberalization, raising interest rates will probably have only a small effect since many borrowers (e.g. in the real estate sector) can attract funds from abroad. Then the government is forced to raise interest rates even higher, and anyone who lacks access to foreign capital (including small and medium-sized enterprises) bears the brunt of the adjustment.

Second, it's well documented that crises punish SMEs more than large local firms and multinational corporations.[39] From 1990 to 1997, the Chilean economy operated at full employment, together with an investment ratio 10 points above the average ratio recorded during the 16 years of the Pinochet dictatorship (1973–90).[40] In fact, Chile reached the highest investment ratio and growth rates in its history during the URR period, and SMEs enjoyed an exceptional environment in which to grow. It's hard to argue that SMEs are better off in a cyclical economy characterized by crises than in an economy that can avoid overheating and recession thanks to an active macro-policy.

Third, governments can turn to policies that mitigate the adverse effects of capital market restrictions. In addition to the URR, the Chilean government enacted measures to encourage long-term FDI. It could also have set up incentives to stimulate domestic lending to SMEs.[41] In conclusion, the evidence of reduced lending to SMEs in Chile is actually limited while the risks associated with open capital markets are significant.

Capital Account Restrictions are Not Fully Effective

We've already noted another set of arguments against capital account regulations: that the measures are not fully effective.[42] But, as discussed earlier, interventions with some leakage can still be valuable. Furthermore Chile, Colombia, and Malaysia showed how dynamic adjustments to capital account regulations can increase their effectiveness.

There is now increasing concern that financial market development, especially the expanded market for derivatives, has made it easier to circumvent restrictions. In fact, it might now be easiest to circumvent regulations in countries that have the most well-developed capital markets.

A simple example of this is the use of non-deliverable currency forwards (NDFs). Offshore NDFs are contracts that give investors the ability to sell or buy domestic currency at some time in the future and to invest in, or borrow at, short-term domestic interest rates. Like many derivative contracts, non-deliverable forwards can be difficult to regulate domestically because the contracts settle outside the country and often are not reported to authorities.[43]

The non-deliverable forward market is a particularly interesting example because Malaysia succeeded in restricting trading of NDFs through well-designed controls. When the government implemented its capital control program in 1998, there was a large offshore market for Malaysian ringgit in Singapore. To restrict these contracts, Malaysia prohibited borrowing between domestic and foreign firms. Foreign firms were unable to hedge their positions, the market became illiquid, and trading all but stopped. The restrictions shut down this market completely. The point is that restrictions can be used to limit the ability of investors to hedge their positions, which makes it difficult for a liquid derivatives market to develop. Despite this positive example, some economists still argue that in countries with well-developed domestic derivative markets (such as Brazil), only indirect forms of capital regulations are feasible or enforceable.

Indirect Forms of Interventions

In addition to direct quantity-based and priced-based regulations, governments can use a variety of indirect measures to control (or at least influence) capital account inflows and outflows. Prudential regulations on the banking system are one such tool. Numerous countries have limited the impact of exchange rate volatility on the financial sector by restricting banks' short-term borrowing from abroad. For example, bank regulators can prohibit domestic banks from lending in foreign currencies to firms that do not have matching revenues in those currencies (this was done in Malaysia). Additionally, regulators can require domestic financial institutions to maintain high liquidity (or reserve) requirements against their net foreign-currency liabilities. As with the URR, this reserve requirement acts as a tax on foreign-currency liabilities.[44] Regulators can set higher requirements for short-term borrowing to encourage longer-term liabilities. They can forbid currency mismatches in the portfolios of domestic financial institutions (regulators in several countries have already done this). To avoid domestic financial dollarization, they can also forbid financial institutions from holding deposits in foreign currencies.

For a more subtle approach, they can impose risk-adjusted capital adequacy requirements or additional prudential reserve requirements on foreign currency loans made to domestic agents who lack matching revenues. In countries with deposit insurance, the government can impose higher insurance premiums on banks that have riskier practices (they, or the firms they lend to, might have greater foreign exchange exposure). These regulations can discourage (although not eliminate) the indirect foreign exchange exposure of banks.

As with the URR, one of the costs frequently associated with stronger prudential regulations is a higher domestic interest rate due to the higher cost of financial intermediation. But the costs of prudential regulations, higher reserve requirements, and higher deposit insurance premiums simply reflect the higher risks of certain kinds of borrowing. Since society otherwise will bear most of the costs of this borrowing, the regulations reduce the disparity between social costs and private benefits. By discouraging excessively risky borrowing, overall economic efficiency is enhanced.

Some policy-makers worry that higher interest rates may result in less financing available for small and medium-sized enterprises. Again, all economic choices have trade-offs.[45] Moreover, it's actually large firms that are most likely to borrow abroad and have uncovered foreign exchange exposure. Competitive banks should pass the costs of prudential regulations relating to foreign exposure on to these large firms. This might discourage lending to these firms. By leaving additional room for expanding domestic credit, it might also increase the supply of funds available to small and medium-sized enterprises.

There's obviously good reason for prudential regulations to also take into account the foreign exchange exposure of firms that borrow from domestic banks. Otherwise, the risks assumed by corporations, particularly those operating in non-tradable sectors, can eventually translate into non-performing loans in domestic financial institutions. But a more systemic perspective also requires this same focus. Since banks traditionally mediate much of the capital flow in an economy, regulation of the financial sector has a significant economic impact. Unless the regulations focus adequate attention on the exposure of non-financial firms, the impact of the financial sector can be vitiated. For example, regulations that simply forbid banks from holding dollar-denominated liabilities might encourage firms to borrow directly from abroad. So banks must examine the entire asset and liability structure of the firms to which they lend (which they should do in any case). Since domestic firms borrow from domestic banks for the most part, if the banks put restrictions on the foreign exposure of the firms, this would act as an effective limit on foreign borrowing.

Regulation of non-financial firms might include rules on the types of firms that can borrow abroad (e.g. only firms with revenues in foreign currencies) and establishes prudential ratios for such firms.[46] Regulations might also include restrictions on the terms of corporate debt that can be contracted abroad (e.g. minimum maturities and maximum spreads) and public disclosure of the short-term external liabilities of firms.

In addition, the government can require full disclosure of all derivative positions.[47] Foreign-denominated debt can also be subordinated to domestic currency debt in bankruptcy proceedings. This would, of course, discourage foreign borrowing and raise its cost. But, as we've noted, there are strong reasons to discourage this borrowing: there are costs borne by society that go well beyond those engaging in the transactions.

An alternative (or complementary) approach is for governments to create adverse tax treatment for foreign-denominated borrowing, especially when it's short term. For example, countries that have a corporate income tax with tax-deductible interest payments might exclude foreign-denominated debt from the tax deduction or make interest payments only partially tax deductible.[48]

217

Limitations of Indirect Interventions

These alternative measures rely on a combination of banking regulations and complementary policies aimed at non-financial firms. The direct capital-account regulations we discussed earlier might be simpler to administer than such a system. Moreover, we should keep in mind that even well-regulated banking systems are subject to periodic episodes of euphoria (as the experience of many industrialized countries has shown). The 2001 crisis in Argentina is an example of a crisis in a country where multinational banks had a significant presence and where the system of prudential bank regulations was considered one of the best in the developing world.[49] This still failed to avert the effects of major macro-economic shocks to the domestic financial system.

Furthermore, risk assessment and traditional regulatory tools, including Basle standards[50] have a pro-cyclical bias in the way they operate. Because they require higher reserves to offset riskier positions, they tend to restrict lending during an economic slowdown (when the risk associated with all liabilities increases). The sharp increase in loan delinquencies during crises reduces the capital of financial institutions as well as their lending capacity. This, in conjunction with a greater perceived level of risk, triggers the 'credit squeeze' that characterizes such periods and reinforces the down-swing in economic activity and the diminished quality of the portfolios of financial intermediaries.[51] On the other hand, risk-adjusted capital requirements might be ineffective when there are fewer loan delinquencies during an economic expansion. Precautionary regulatory signals then become ineffective and do not impede credit growth.

Direct capital account regulations may work better because they are aimed at the actual source of the disturbance—pro-cyclical capital flows. For more developed countries with strong administrative capabilities, a combination of direct and indirect measures can succeed in restricting flows and helping to limit circumvention through derivative products.

Concluding Remarks

Overall, the experiences with capital account regulations in the 1990s were useful for improving debt profiles, giving governments more latitude in pursuing stabilizing macroeconomic policies, and insulating countries from some of the vagaries of capital markets. The previous chapter demonstrated that, given externalities and market failures, there is a strong case for capital market interventions if we can show that the proposed interventions don't have adverse side-effects that offset the potential gains. The cases we've considered in this chapter make evident that the benefits far outweigh the costs.

A key question for countries considering capital market interventions is what form the interventions should take. So far we've seen that many interventions are not mutually exclusive, and that governments can use a mix of instruments. The basic advantages of the price-based instruments used by Chile and Colombia were their simplicity, their non-discretionary character (i.e. their application didn't depend on the discretion of bureaucrats), and their focus on avoiding building up macroeconomic imbalances that eventually lead to crises. The more quantitative Malaysian regulations had a stronger short-term effect on reducing capital flows.

Traditional foreign exchange market interventions and quantity-based capital account regulations might be preferable when the policy objective is to significantly reduce domestic macroeconomic sensitivity to international capital flows. Quantity-based restrictions are also preferable in response to crises. In addition, based on the experience of the Asian countries in the 1990s, quantity-based restrictions might also be particularly effective in preventing crises. But as we've noted before, a regulatory framework and administrative capability must be in place in order for these regulations to work.

According to some recent thinking, all countries should liberalize their capital markets *at some point*. The open questions are when and what sequence of institutional reforms will work best. According to this view, the more developed countries should maintain open capital markets and use prudential regulations to control risk; meanwhile, the least developed countries should implement restrictions (even though they are least able to administer them). This chapter and the previous one have thrown into question the validity of this perspective. The following chapter will explore the relevance of 'sequencing' to address the risks inherent in international capital flows.

13

Capital Market Liberalization: Summary and Remaining Debates

Let's return to the spring of 2003, nearly six years after the Asian crisis began, when the IMF published a paper acknowledging the risks associated with capital market liberalization. At the same time, *The Economist* magazine, which had been a staunch supporter of liberalization, reversed its position and published an editorial and survey that came to the same conclusion as the IMF paper.[1] *The Economist* offered two reasons why liberalization had failed to live up to the expectations of its supporters: 'First, international markets in capital are prone to error . . . Second, the punishment for big financial mistakes can be draconian, and tends to hurt innocent bystanders as much as borrowers and lenders.'[2]

Many economists and practitioners had long argued that capital market liberalization should be approached with caution because of market failures and externalities, including those cited by *The Economist*. But it was only the force of circumstances—the international financial crises of the 1990s—combined with sustained critical analysis (much of it by members of the IPD network) that led to a rethinking of liberalization.

Although the 2003 IMF paper was a big step forward from the Fund's position in 1997, it still failed to address several key issues and outstanding controversies. Chapter 12 explored the debate about alternative forms of interventions.[3] In this final chapter of Part III, we'll draw on many of the discussions in earlier chapters to address several other unresolved disagreements. In particular, we'll focus on when a country is sufficiently developed to risk capital market liberalization, whether all countries should make liberalization their long-term goal, and whether capital market liberalization is reversible—even if it was a mistake in the first place, should countries that have already liberalized now stick with it.

We should note that these outstanding questions are not debates on whether, in the long run, countries should or should not integrate into the global economy. The relevant question here is *how* countries should integrate. As we've discussed, a country can regulate short-term capital flows while still remaining open to trade, foreign direct investment, and other long-term flows. (We'll discuss some of these other debates, such as trade openness, in other IPD volumes.) Capital account regulations are tools that can be used to manage one of the risks associated with globalization, the risk of globalized capital flows, without necessarily restricting its other facets.

Sequencing

There's a growing consensus that most developing countries do not have the prerequisites for successful capital market liberalization, and should first undertake other reforms. *But no consensus exists on a related issue: whether developing countries should see capital market liberalization as an eventual goal and as a mark of their developmental success.*

Proponents of liberalization often argue that it's not a question of whether countries should liberalize but when and how quickly they should do so.[4] The authors of the 2003 IMF paper argued elsewhere[5] that capital market liberalization should still produce the desired benefits if a government implements it within the 'proper' sequence of reforms. Much of this discussion[6] has argued that 'good governance' and appropriate institutions, especially strong financial institutions, are the critical factors for the success of liberalization.

Critics argue that CML should not necessarily be the long run goal of all countries and that there are better ways for developing countries to integrate into the global economy. Developing countries need a wide range of reforms before they can risk capital market liberalization. And small countries in particular may never be able to adequately protect themselves from the volatility associated with international capital flows—without using some form of capital account management. Even if most economists now agree that an adequate institutional framework must be in place before capital markets can be liberalized,[7] this doesn't mean that strong institutions and good governance alone suffice.[8] They may be necessary, but are they sufficient? Is there a wider set of reforms that are necessary before countries are ready to risk capital market liberalization? And how far can these reforms insulate small open economies from the volatility of international capital markets?

Given the economic structure of most developing countries, the caveat that they should have adequate institutions in place before liberalizing means that, at the very best, liberalization is a long way off. Furthermore, even advanced industrialized countries have found it difficult to establish fully effective regulatory structures and strong financial institutions. The Scandinavian countries are generally seen as having good governance, but that didn't prevent Norway, Sweden, and Finland from having a major crisis in the late 1980s. The United States is certainly viewed as having strong institutions, but it too experienced a financial bubble that burst in 2001.[9] The US economy is, of course, much stronger than most economies in the world, and the United States was better able to withstand the crisis. Still, subsequent reinterpretations of the data suggest that, despite the seemingly low unemployment rate, the post-bubble downturn in the United States had a huge cost.[10]

As we've discussed elsewhere in this book, developing countries have even less ability to withstand crises. (Their insurance markets are less developed and social safety nets are often non-existent. Their economies are less diversified and their capital markets are often underdeveloped.) Developing countries are also less able to respond to crises and have fewer macroeconomic tools to combat boom and bust cycles. For example, developed countries can use anti-cyclical deficit financing whereas most developing countries have only a limited ability to do so.

Even sound economic policies don't insulate countries from the surges of short-term capital flows. Reforms need to be able to increase a country's ability to withstand the shocks posed by capital flows and—since capital market liberalization will restrict the government's ability to use counter-cyclical monetary policy—give policy-makers the tools to respond. Sound financial systems, improved regulatory structures, and diversified economies[11] might help countries withstand some of the volatility associated with capital flows. But strong institutions alone cannot shield these countries from the pressure of speculative flows, even in the long run. Good governance will not reduce the volume of short-term capital inflows (it could even increase these inflows), eliminate the information imperfections inherent in capital markets, change the pro-cyclical nature of capital flows, or solve the other problems we've discussed in this book. Policy-makers need additional tools, which is what capital management provides.

This is especially the case for small countries that have tiny markets compared to the size of international capital flows. Large inflows can easily overwhelm macroeconomic policy in these countries. Paul Volcker, former governor of the US Federal Reserve Bank, compared small developing countries to boats on the tempestuous sea of global finance. A big ocean liner like the 'USS United States' can safely navigate through a storm, but even the sturdiest small vessel is likely to capsize. Volcker pointed out that 'the entire banking systems of Indonesia or Thailand or Malaysia are comparable to one good-sized regional bank in the United States. Their entire Gross National Products are smaller than the funds controlled by our largest financial institutions, including large mutual fund families and other investors.'[12]

We should note that the push for open capital markets is a relatively recent phenomenon. Most developed countries used some form of capital market account restrictions through the post-World War II period until the 1970s. Capital controls then became increasingly unpopular in the more general push towards freer markets (deregulation and liberalization), and many developed countries dismantled their controls.[13] The Netherlands, however, didn't remove all controls until 1986, and Belgium abolished its dual exchange market as late as 1990. Spain maintained some controls until 1991, and then, after a brief hiatus, reintroduced them temporarily in 1992 and 1993 when the peseta came under pressure during the European Monetary System crises.[14]

Is Liberalization Reversible?

While recognizing the validity of the arguments against capital market liberalization, many economists think that the issue is now largely moot. Most countries have liberalized, they say, and capital market liberalization is impossible to reverse. Even if it were possible, they continue, it makes little sense to do so because liberalized countries have already paid the large costs of adjustment. It might have been a mistake for them to liberalize in the first place, but—as the old economists' adage has it—bygones are bygone. In short, they believe, liberalization is a fact of life.

There is a grain of truth in this, but only a grain. Liberalization may induce firms and households to adapt, which would enhance their ability to withstand the problems associated with capital market liberalization. So once countries have made this 'fixed cost investment', liberalization becomes more desirable than it would be had they not made this investment. But after liberalization, most developing countries still have to withstand large shocks with high social and economic costs, while the government's ability to implement effective macro-stabilization policies has been impaired. For these countries, the benefits of many kinds of interventions in capital markets will still exceed the costs by a considerable margin. This includes indirect forms of regulation through the banking system or direct forms of regulation on pension funds. History matters, but liberalization is not irreversible, and it may even be desirable to reverse it.[15]

Capital Management at Different Stages of Development

As we mentioned earlier, a growing number of economists now believe that capital market restrictions might be appropriate for the least developed countries, but that more advanced countries have the institutional framework to withstand liberalization and would benefit from it. Others believe that the choice of when and how to manage the capital account depends on the specific circumstances in the country. In this section, we examine the appropriateness of different techniques for countries in different stages of development.

The Least Developed Countries

The question of capital market liberalization for the least developed countries is markedly different from that of middle-income countries. For example, the least developed countries rarely experience excessive capital inflows. Their markets tend to be small, often illiquid, and less of a haven for hot money. This illiquidity serves as a natural capital account restriction, somewhat insulating the countries from international volatility. The least developed countries in Sub-Saharan Africa were unaffected, or minimally affected, by currency volatility during both the Asian and Russian crises.[16]

That being said, in many of these countries, domestic capital flight has been extreme. Studies have estimated that capital flight from Sub-Saharan Africa has totaled more than 145 percent of the region's outstanding debt.[17] Although controls on inflows might not be necessary for these economies, well-designed restrictions on outflows could be important for development. While some policy-makers have argued that controls on outflows lose effectiveness over time as agents find ways to circumvent them, there is some evidence[18] that capital controls were effective in reducing capital flight in a number of developing countries in the 1980s.

In our discussion of 'market failures' in Chapter 11, we discussed capital flight as an example of a 'failure of coordination'.[19] Open capital markets give domestic agents the opportunity to take their funds out of the country instead of reinvesting to build the economy. As long as capital flight continues at the rates often seen in the past, it will be difficult for local economies to grow. Although everyone might be better off if all residents reinvested, no single investor has an incentive to do so. Effective regulations on outflows can encourage residents to reinvest.

The problem of capital flight in Russia in the mid-1990s serves to demonstrate the relevance of these assertions (even though Russia is a 'transition' and 'emerging' economy and not a least developed country). Those who obtained their wealth in privatizations that were widely viewed as illegitimate had an incentive to take their money out of the country as quickly as possible, 'stripping assets'. They worried that a successor government might try to reverse the privatization, or at least recapture some of the enormous gains. Open capital markets gave them the opportunity to take their money out. Meanwhile, some of the World Bank and IMF loans to Russia were reported as 'lost'. For example, immediately after the IMF lent Russia funds in 1998, an equivalent amount was tracked leaving the country through the open capital account.[20] Strong capital account restrictions would have made it more difficult for these funds to 'disappear'.

Although these policy tools might still be subject to some corruption and evasion, we should emphasize once again that regulations do not need to be 100 percent efficient to be effective. In fact, restrictions on capital outflows can help reduce certain kinds of corruption in other areas, especially the misuse of public funds and tax evasion.

International financial institutions could take on a new and useful role by helping countries devise and implement efficient regulations. (And international measures to restrict bank secrecy might also discourage capital flight associated with illegal activities.)

In more general terms, we can say that the least developed countries, which often do not have the institutions to withstand the volatility associated with open capital markets, also lack the administrative capacity for efficient interventions. These countries may find it easier to administer traditional quantitative restrictions that rule out specific forms of indebtedness (such as short-term borrowing abroad except for trade credit lines and borrowing in foreign currency by residents operating in non-tradable sectors) than price-based controls.[21] Restrictions generally work best when domestic financial development is limited (as is the case in these countries) because there is less room for circumvention through derivatives and other financial market transactions.

Emerging Market Countries

The currency crises in the 1990s hit emerging market countries particularly hard. Most of the debate on capital market liberalization has focused on the circumstances in these countries, which often have more developed capital markets and greater administrative capacity than the least developed countries. As we've seen, Chile, Colombia, Malaysia, Vietnam, China, Hungary, Poland, and India are among the countries that used various forms of capital account regulations with some success in the 1990s.

It's important for these countries to be able to adjust their interventions as economic conditions change or loopholes develop. For this reason, having a permanent but flexible regulatory regime in place (one that can be tightened or loosened through economic cycles) may well be the best choice for emerging market countries. The cost of building administrative capacity is not negligible, but as countries learn to adapt regulations and other interventions to changing circumstances, they also develop their administrative capabilities. This means that governments must maintain their autonomy to impose capital-account regulations and to reimpose them if necessary rather than dismantle them during periods of calm.[22]

Some economists argue that the real question is not whether more developed countries should or should not intervene in capital markets but whether interventions are still effective, given the growth of derivative markets and the globalization of financial markets. From this perspective, capital market liberalization is inevitable, as market players will find new ways to circumvent restrictions. As we discussed in the last chapter, other economists worry that derivatives and greater financial integration have increased the risks associated with liberalized capital markets so that the need for more capital management tools—tools not allowed under complete capital market liberalization—is greater than ever.

The growing use of derivative products has no doubt made the management of capital flows and the formulation of appropriate regulations more complex. The failure of Long-Term Capital Management (LTCM) exemplified the difficulty of monitoring these markets.[23] As we noted in Chapter 10, much of LTCM's funding for derivatives positions came from well-regulated commercial banks in one of the most highly regulated banking systems in the world.

Despite the increased complexities and the enhanced ability to circumvent capital market regulations, derivative products are unlikely to make regulations completely ineffective. The case of Malaysia has shown how an emerging market can use prudential regulations combined with direct controls to manage its capital account and even limit the growth of an offshore derivatives market. Countries with well-developed domestic financial markets can also manage the capital account indirectly, through banking regulations. A greater willingness to monitor hedge funds in the United States might have prevented the failure of LTCM from threatening to grow into an international financial crisis. And despite the difficulties in monitoring derivatives, few policy-makers or economists would argue that we should give up prudential regulation in the banking system.[24]

Some economists have long believed that traditional capital management techniques become less effective over time. They leveled this criticism at many of the controls used in the 1960s and 1970s in developed countries as well as some of the later regulations used in developing countries. But experiments in the 1990s showed how improved techniques could strengthen the effectiveness of regulations. And, as we've stressed, regulations don't have to be 100 percent effective to be successful, especially when one of the objectives is to prevent crises associated with massive *quick* movements of capital. Even if some policies lose potency over time, experience has shown that they can still help moderate capital flows, and their volatility.

Concluding Remarks

We conclude by reiterating that the conventional wisdom that the least developed countries should use capital account restrictions but then dismantle them as they build an institutional framework, is overly simplistic. Instead, each country needs to ask what is the best mix of interventions for its stage of development and administrative capacities. 'Monotonicity' in capital market regulations—a steady decrease in their magnitude—may not be desirable. The cycle of development might instead require initially increasing controls as a country builds its administrative capacity and develops its markets. Later, the forms of regulations might shift from traditional controls to measures that include indirect regulations. But whatever the progression, regulations need to be structured to fit the economic and institutional capacity of each country.

It is clear that there are externalities associated with capital flows for all countries, and these externalities make some form of intervention desirable, as long as it's possible to administer the intervention effectively, at reasonable costs, with limited adverse side-effects. As countries develop, not only do the costs and benefits of intervention change, but so too do the administrative capacities to implement effectively interventions. Even developed countries might choose to use some forms of capital account regulations.

Previous chapters have described an array of tools available to economic policy-makers for intervening in capital markets. Some affect the risk properties of the economy, for example, the extent to which it is exposed to changes in capital market sentiment or the extent to which such changes can be amplified or dampened. Others affect the scope of macroeconomic management by giving policy-makers greater latitude in sound macroeconomic management. And still others are the actual tools of prudent macroeconomic management themselves.

Economists now generally agree not only that capital market liberalization increases risk but also that there is little evidence that it brings the promised rewards. Yet, just as it seemed the IMF had acknowledged that liberalization should not be pushed on countries, the US government introduced open capital markets as a condition in its bilateral trade talks (e.g. the 2003 trade agreement with Chile and Singapore).

This reveals how international political processes often pay more attention to ideology and special interests than to economic science—to theory and evidence. Economists are partly to blame because they haven't done their part to present their analyses and results of their research to policy-makers and citizens in an accessible and persuasive manner. We intend this book (and the series of which it is a part) to be a first step in filling the gap.

The fact that international economic institutions pushed capital market liberalization so hard for so long also raises important questions about whose interests they are serving: are they serving the interests of their different member states in a balanced way? Are they excessively influenced by some schools of economic thought? It's often difficult to determine the appropriateness of a particular policy—just as it's difficult to second-guess a firm's management to ascertain whether it's pursuing policies that maximize shareholder value. We can put a firm's management to the test only under certain circumstances: for example, when we see clear conflicts of interest and abuse of management prerogatives (as was the case in the accounting, banking, and corporate scandals in the United States that became evident at the beginning of this century). Should we look at the advocacy of capital market liberalization in a similar light? If so, what inferences should we draw? What weight should be given to their assertions and recommendations in the future? What reforms does this suggest for the governance and operation of international economic institutions?

We can't pursue these questions in this volume, but they underscore the importance of the IPD project and this series of books: the public needs access to alternative perspectives on the key economic issues facing developing countries, perspectives that we hope will be less tainted by ideology and special interests. We firmly believe that few issues matter more to the lives, livelihoods, and future prosperity of hundreds of millions of people in the developing world.

Conclusion

14

Stabilization, Liberalization, and Growth

This book is about stabilization and liberalization policies in developing countries. In this final chapter, we bring together the various strands explored in the book, and highlight the links between stabilization, liberalization, and growth.

We emphasized early on that developed and developing countries have markedly different macroeconomic objectives and structures. We began from the premise that the ultimate objective of economic policy is to improve the long-run well-being of *all* of the people in the country, with particular emphasis on the poor. We argue here that real instability has high costs to the economy, and that real stability, rather than price stability, should be the focus of stabilization policies. We rejected the pursuit of price stability as an end in its own, since its relevance is based on the extent that it affects our ultimate objectives of growth, full employment, *real* stability or security, and the distribution of income.

We've also emphasized that markets, especially in developing countries, are imperfect. There's an important role for government, and we believe there needs to be a balance between government and markets. Macroeconomic policy has traditionally employed fiscal and monetary tools to achieve its goals. But, as we've emphasized in this book, there are additional microeconomic tools and structural policies, including capital account regulations, prudential regulations, tax policies, industrial policies, and improved accounting, that policy makers can also use to better manage the economy.

Economics is marked with divisions. As we've noted, there are divisions between macroeconomic policies and structural policies, and between stabilization policies and growth policies. Traditionally, stabilization policy focused on aggregate demand, and growth policy concentrated on aggregate supply. In particular, growth policies focused on increasing savings and investment, including investments in new technology. One strand of modern growth theory (associated with Solow in 1956) *assumes* a rate of technological change and population growth and argues that the long-term growth rate is entirely dependent on these assumed rates. This theory argues that (in a closed economy) the level of per capita income in the long run depends *only* on the savings rate.[1] Thus, issues of short-run stabilization don't affect long-term growth or (steady state) per capita income, and structural policies affect efficiency and may thus allow for one-time bursts in growth.[2]

There are reasons, however, why this analysis may be misleading. How the government pursues stabilization also matters. We've already suggested that there's evidence that lower income today is associated with lower income in the future,[3] so policy-makers should try to avoid policies that slow today's economy in the expectation of future growth. For example, in facing, say, a crisis, the government should *not* raise interest rates excessively because the high rates can impede current as well as future growth.

Similarly, structural reforms like capital market liberalization, may lead to increased risk, and given the imperfections of capital markets, they may lead to less efficient resource allocation. They increase exposure to shocks and may make the conduct of *real* stabilization policy more difficult. Overall volatility may increase, investment may be discouraged, and growth slowed. The social effects of the different phases of the business cycle may be asymmetric: employment and poverty may increase rapidly in recessions and recover more slowly and incompletely during upswings. As we have argued, there are also distributional consequences associated with alternative policy choices.

This chapter is divided into four major sections. In the first, we review why instability is bad for the growth of the economy. In the second, we review the argument that an excessive focus on price stability, as opposed to stability of output or employment, can be bad for growth. In the third, we argue that excess reliance on monetary policy as a tool for stabilization may be bad for long-run economic growth and examine the long-run consequences of failing to maintain the economy at as close to full employment as possible. In the fourth and final section, we bring together the various strands of argument put forward in this book: we first look at the issues of liberalization and macroeconomic policy through the lens of risk management, and then discuss the links between stabilization and liberalization, and between growth and poverty.

Links between Real Instability and Growth

Real instability exercises adverse effects on growth through several channels. Crises lead to the destruction of the net worth[4] of firms and banks, and reduce the willigness to undertake risks including banks' ability and willingness to lend, and firms' willingness and ability to invest. The important investments that would likely be foregone include risky investments that are also productivity enhancing, such as investment that develops and/or adapts new technologies. High levels of defaults and increased uncertainty about the economic environment also mean that banks and other financial institutions are less able and willing to extend loans. These effects can only be reversed, as balance sheets gradually get 'restored' to pre-crisis levels. When there's significant loss of organizational and informational capital, the effects may be even longer lasting. For example, in more extreme cases, as in East Asia, crises lead to corporate bankruptcies, which can undermine the financial sector, with a loss of organizational and informational capital that can't easily be reversed.

Throughout this book, we have also discussed several channels through which changes in financial sector variables (interest rates and exchange rates) affect real variables: (a) the reduction in demand for goods and services produced by domestic firms obviously hurts firm profitability; (b) large devaluations during currency crises hurt the balance sheet of firms with foreign-denominated debts; (c) increases in interest rates that often accompany crises reduce the values of domestic assets, hurting the balance sheets and profitability of virtually all domestic firms; and (d) uncertainties concerning the state of balance sheets and future profitability affect the ability and willingness of firms to borrow and invest and banks to lend.

Real instability also imposes large costs in labor markets. Just as uncertainty may discourage firms from investing in plants and equipment, volatility may discourage individuals from investing in human capital. Furthermore, as we noted earlier, when human capital deteriorates, workers remain unemployed or underemployed for more extended periods of time.

The effects of a crisis are often longer lasting. Capital constraints imply that, in developing countries, families may have to interrupt the education of their children in a crisis. Often, once interrupted, education doesn't resume, even when the economy emerges from the crisis. In some more extreme cases, the increased poverty of a crisis leads to increased childhood malnutrition.

There may also be important balance sheet effects on the government—again with long-run consequences. For instance, Malaysia, by imposing capital controls, was able to stabilize its economy and its exchange rate better, *without* raising interest rates. Because of the lower interest rates, there was less necessity for it to rely on fiscal policy than there was in other East Asian crisis countries. The lower interest rates meant that fewer firms went into bankruptcy, and banks' balance sheets were in better shape; there was less of a need for government bail-outs to the financial sector. As a result, Malaysia emerged from the crisis with less of a legacy of debt than did the other East Asian crisis countries.

Lastly, with increased volatility, governments are forced to set aside more funds in reserves (especially if they want to stabilize exchange rate movements). As we've discussed in earlier chapters, maintaining reserves has a high opportunity cost.

Some have argued that the cost of real instability is often exaggerated: during the boom, the economy grows faster than it would in a steady policy, largely offsetting the losses that occur because the economy moves more slowly in the subsequent downturn. But there are important asymmetries and hysteresis effects: the booms do not make up for the losses from recessions, nor do the gains by some make up for the losses of others.

The net effect has been weak or negative growth in economies that have experienced real and financial instability, through one or more of the channels described above.

Balancing Objectives: The Risks of an Excessive Focus on Price Stability

A central policy question is how governments should balance their multiple objectives. It would be nice if the same measures that improved stability necessarily improved growth as well. In the previous section, we argued that there are a variety of reasons why real stability is good for the economy. But, unfortunately, much of the debate about stabilization policy is not on how best to achieve *real* stability of the economy, but on how much weight to put on *price* or *exchange rate* stability. Some argue that price stability is *necessary* and *almost* sufficient for strong economic growth. Our analysis suggests that it's *real* stability that is linked with growth, and that price stability is not closely linked to *real* stability.

Inflation versus Output Stability

There is some evidence that countries that have focused on price stability[5] have *not* achieved greater output stability. During the period in which monetarism dominated central banking, it was clear that the focus on price stability often led to high volatility in (real and nominal) interest rates, with the adverse effects discussed more extensively below.

Assume, for instance, that a focus on price stability results in less volatility in inflation, but more volatility in output. Is investment more sensitive to volatility in inflation, or volatility in output? Most standard theories would suggest the latter (so long as inflation is kept within bounds). With floating or variable rate loans, the real interest rate (which standard theory says should be the focus of firms' concern) varies little.

Inflation, as has been repeatedly noted, is important mainly as it affects *real* variables of concern, like growth and inequality. Inflation is like a tax, and like any tax, there are inefficiencies associated with it. It remains an open question whether a moderate inflation tax may be, for some countries, a relatively efficient way of raising revenues to finance investment expenditures.[6] In general, the real costs associated with low to moderate inflation are limited.

But even if inflation has *real* costs, so do the measures governments take to reduce it. If stabilizing inflation leads to more unstable output or more volatile interest rates and substantially higher levels of unemployment, then the costs of stabilizing inflation may outweigh the costs.

Exchange Rate versus Output Stability

The East Asia crisis brought home the potential trade-off between exchange rate, price and output stability, and economic growth. One of the reasons for the concern about exchange rate stability is the fear that currency depreciation will lead to inflation. As we discussed earlier, recent episodes, for example in East Asia and Latin America, of large depreciations have not been followed by excessively high inflation, greatly allaying worries that depreciation will set in motion a process of persistent inflation. Evidently, market participants have been able to see these depreciations as one-off events.

In the case of a crisis, the concern is that the exchange rate should not fall *too* much. During the East Asian crisis, a further set of links between (short and medium-term) growth and exchange rates was identified. As we discussed earlier, the large currency depreciation adversely affected the balance sheets of firms with foreign-denominated debt, increased the risk of default, and led to the destruction of information and organizational capital. But the *means* by which this concern was addressed led to even worse adverse consequences. Interest rates were raised, with potentially more adverse effects on balance sheets and firm viability. On a priori grounds, it may not have been possible to ascertain which was worse: what was required was a close look at the structure of the economy. As it turned out, the posited trade-off really did not exist. The adverse effect on the economy of raising interest rates drove capital out of the country, weakening rather than strengthening the exchange rate.

The nature of the trade-offs depends critically on the circumstances of the country. When firms are highly leveraged with short-term debt, the adverse effects of raising interest rates are likely to be particularly marked. In Brazil, the firms were not highly leveraged, *but the government was*. Raising interest rates forced the government to increase its borrowings. The anxieties set off by the worsening fiscal straits of the government led to capital flight and a weaker exchange rate. In these circumstances, higher interest rates represents a lose-lose policy.[7]

Budget Balance versus Output Stability

Typically, when economies go into a downturn, tax revenues decline, and, if there are significant social protection programs, overall expenditures increase. As a result deficits may rise, even in countries that normally manage to balance their budgets, and may increase markedly in countries that generally run budget deficits. Standard macro-prescriptions hold that government should respond to a downturn by counter-cyclical fiscal policies—increasing expenditures or cutting taxes. This is precisely what China did in the East Asia crisis, as it saw a decline in its potential exports. China used counter-cyclical policy to strengthen the economy in the short run by making investments that enhanced long-term growth. This makes enormous economic sense: the social cost of investment at such times is very low. As we discussed in Part III of this book, capital account regulations gave China the scope to engage in countercyclical fiscal and monetary policy.

The Risks of Deficit Fetishism

The conservative 'deficit fetishism' assumes that policy-makers should respond to a crisis by cutting back on government expenditures to reduce the deficit. The argument is that reducing the deficit enhances confidence in the economy and the country's government and results in more invest-ment, quickly restoring strength in the economy, and leading to stronger long-term economic growth.

We know of no instance in which this confidence 'trick' has worked in a developing economy. On the contrary, as standard economics has pre-dicted, the contractionary fiscal and monetary policies typically worsen the downturn (evidenced by the experience not only in East Asia, but also in Argentina). Inevitably, in most developing countries, such cutbacks affect public investment in one form or another, and adversely affect long-term growth through this channel as well. But there are high costs not just to cutbacks in infrastructure. Cutbacks in food programs may lead to mal-nutrition, and a single episode of childhood malnutrition may have life-long consequences. Cutbacks in health may lead to increased prevalence of diseases, again with long-term consequences. Cutbacks in education may similarly hurt the prospects of an entire generation.

The Risks of Excessive Debt

Still, especially large debts can affect future economic growth, especially when the deficit is financed abroad. If the debt is short term, countries become hostage to the vagaries of the international financial market and lose the ability to engage in counter-cyclical monetary and fiscal policy, as we discussed earlier.

The Risks of Excessive Austerity

The United States' experience in the early years of the twenty-first century shows the risk of badly managed macro-policy. Badly designed fiscal poli-cies—huge tax cuts—provided little stimulation, but led to large debt. In many developing countries, policy debates have focused on the other side of the coin, the long-run costs of *excessive* austerity and how policy affects the mix of outputs. Obviously, countries have to live within their con-straints, but there are two criticisms previously noted that have some sub-stance: (*a*) accounting frameworks have sometimes imposed *unnecessary* stringency; and (*b*) the international economic institutions have been excessively preoccupied with fears of inflation, and have not appropriately balanced the risks. Excessive austerity has forced countries to cut back unnecessarily on high return public investments, led to higher levels of unemployment, and led to larger gaps between the economy's actual out-put and its potential output. All of this has harmed growth.

239

The Importance for Growth of Maintaining the Economy at Full Employment

As we have underscored in this book, there are high costs associated with *failing* to maintain the economy at full employment. There are high costs to governments responding to an economic downturn by undertaking macroeconomic policies that exacerbate rather than dampen *real* fluctuations. We have argued that the economy loses in both the short and the long run.

Maintaining the economy at as near full employment as possible leads to higher tax revenues, lower safety net expenditures, and a more positive fiscal position. It may lead to more capital inflows (less capital flight) and less depreciation of the exchange rate (and potentially even less inflation) than a policy that is *focused* on budget or trade balance, or on inflation or exchange rate stability.

The long-run benefits of maintaining the short-run strength of the economy are reflected not just in lower deficits and higher investment. In the labor market, 'learning by producing' may lead to increased productivity of firms and individuals. Growth begets growth.

Liberalization, Growth, and Short-Run Stabilization

There is another direction of causality that is often emphasized. Conservatives often argue that certain reforms in the economy, such as trade and financial market liberalization and labor market reforms, will result in a more flexible and dynamic economy. The economy will adjust better to shocks in the short run, simultaneously reducing inflationary pressures and lowering the 'natural' rate of unemployment, and growth will be enhanced in the medium and long run. To put it another way—supply-side reforms lead to better demand-side performance.

There is, in fact, little support for this view. On the contrary, financial market liberalization that leads to foreign ownership of banks with limited information about domestic producers may, at least in the short run, constrain the supply of funds going to such firms, impeding stabilization in the short run and growth in the long run. In this book, we've emphasized the opposite set of linkages: improved demand-side management has positive supply-side effects. Poor demand-side management can lead to more bankruptcies and less availability of capital (both through banks and other financial intermediaries), as it did during the East Asia crisis. The normal positive demand-side response through exports and the expansion of the import competing sector from the large devaluation was overwhelmed by the large negative supply shock.

How Stabilization is Pursued

There are important consequences of the way stabilization is pursued, to which we have already alluded. This is, of course, standard fare: reducing aggregate demand when the economy faces inflation by reducing government expenditures is often alleged to be better for growth than doing so by increasing interest rates, since the latter leads to reduced investment. But whether this is the case depends on which government expenditures are cut back: if it's high return investments in infrastructure, growth would have been enhanced by using monetary policy rather than a contraction in government investment. (Still better, of course, might have been increases in taxes.)

In this section, we summarize why excessive reliance on the use of monetary policy (high interest rates) may, in particular, have adverse effects on long-term economic growth. There are adverse effects on growth and output in both the short and long run. Using monetary policy or the exchange rate to stabilize the economy leads to large volatility in interest rates. Of particular concern are those situations where the consequences of a policy choice are long run, and not easily reversible. For example, the high interest rates imposed on East Asia led to massive bankruptcies (and predictably so, given the high level of indebtedness). Raising interest rates, as we noted, may force firms into bankruptcy; subsequently lowering them does not un-bankrupt them. There are long-term consequences for growth from these short-term policies.

Interest rate volatility[8] also limits the use of debt finance. The rapid growth in Korea and other East Asian countries depended on debt finance. In the absence of debt finance, firms would have had to rely on self-finance, and this would have limited their rate of growth. There is a further loss of overall economic efficiency, as the reliance on self-finance means that capital is less efficiently allocated.

Huge increases in interest rates such as those that occurred during the East Asian crisis will almost surely lead to less debt finance. There is more than a little irony that while conservative economists argue for the use of interest rate policies because they enhance the efficiency of the economy—the government does not interfere with the allocative decisions of the market in ways that it might were it, for instance, to use administrative

241

methods like limiting investment in speculative real estate or requiring higher collateral requirements[9]—in fact reliance on interest rates may lower the overall efficiency of the economy.

Today, there is widespread recognition that the conduct of monetary policy may have effects on output in both the short and long run. We noted earlier how the emphasis by central banks on monetarism had resulted in huge volatility in interest rates, with adverse effects not only on output in the short run, but on growth in the medium and long term.

Some have argued that switching to inflation targeting may improve growth and output performance. In particular, if markets believe that inflation is more likely to be within a narrow band, there can be much larger changes in unemployment before inflationary expectations (with resulting wage adjustments) are set off. Inflation targeting would then improve the trade-off facing policy-makers. The evidence on this, however, remains limited. Critics of inflation targeting, on the other hand, emphasize the risks: monetary authorities may be forced to increase interest rates when inflation increases, even though there is a widespread perception that the price increases are one-off, and not likely to give rise to an inflationary episode. More importantly, the appropriate adjustment to many kinds of disturbances to the macro-economy that would be associated with higher aggregate demand is *not* an increase in the interest rate. The full adjustment process associated with inflation targeting may be highly inefficient.

Stabilization, Liberalization, Growth, and Poverty

Risk

This book has looked at macroeconomic and structural policies through the lens of *risk analysis*. It should be clear by now why we have joined together the discussions of macroeconomic policy and capital market liberalization. Capital market liberalization has led to some of the most important macroeconomic shocks facing countries in the developing world. It is a *source* of instability. At the same time, even when the source of the shock to the economy was elsewhere, it resulted in the shocks being amplified—in marked contrast to what those who advocated capital market liberalization predicted, that it would lead to enhanced stability. And finally, it has circumscribed countries' ability to respond to shocks. The net result is increased real and financial volatility.

Of course, firms, households, and governments respond to increased volatility by taking defensive measures, such as building reserves or larger precautionary savings. These responses typically result in lower volatility, with a lower cost than otherwise would have been the case, but the volatility is still greater than it would have been without capital market liberalization.

Furthermore, these measures have their own costs, so that the adverse effects cannot be simply assessed by looking at the net increase in volatility. Real and financial volatility is bad for growth, but so too are the defensive measures taken—the high reserves and the limited resort to debt finance.

Stabilization, Distribution, and Poverty Reduction

We have repeatedly emphasized the distributional consequences of alternative policies. Different parties bear the risks associated with different policies. Policies that result in greater real instability (like capital market liberalization) have particularly adverse consequences on the poor. The deterioration of the labor market in a downturn is generally very rapid (through open unemployment, a worsening in the quality of jobs or in real wages, and a rise in informality), whereas the recovery is slow and incomplete. This is reflected in the long-lasting worsening of real wages in Mexico after the Tequila crisis. Still other effects work through long-lasting impacts on social conditions. Boom-bust cycles have ratchet effects on social variables. The fact that governments are often forced to cut back on social expenditures in an economic downturn (as part of their pro-cyclical pattern of expenditures) exacerbates, of course, the adverse effects on social conditions.

Interest rate policies have, of course, allocative effects; but they also have large distributional effects. Sometimes, the distributional effects are of an order of magnitude greater than the allocative effects. Raising interest rates, say from 5 to 15 percent, may not curtail speculative real estate investments, but it can have a devastating effect on manufacturing firms that rely on debt finance for working capital. In such cases, it is natural for governments to look for instruments that control the economy with smaller distributional impacts. Administrative interventions, for example, limiting real estate lending or capital controls, may on these grounds be preferable to reduce 'overheating' than simply raising interest rates. (For example, as we noted above, by resorting to capital controls, the Malaysian government was able to limit the extent to which it had to raise interest rates.)

243

There are also important distributional consequences for how government manages macroeconomic policy in the short run, and how it balances risks of inflation and unemployment. While it is often asserted that inflation is the cruelest tax on the poor, as we have noted, a more detailed look at the costs of inflation versus unemployment suggests that unemployment is much more costly for the poor, at least in many countries.[10]

A similar analysis applies to the consequences of an unanticipated currency depreciation, which in some instances results in an increase in the prices of imported basic necessities before the corresponding increases in wages, leading to increased poverty. On the other hand, a *weak* exchange rate, and perhaps even more so, an exchange rate that is *expected* to depreciate, stimulates investments in, and output of, exports and import substitutes. Accordingly, a weak exchange rate may be associated with employment creation and poverty reduction. This is especially the case for a country like China, in which there's an inadequately developed safety net. Job creation associated with exchange rate policy *is* the anti-poverty policy.

By contrast, the incidence of cyclical unemployment falls disproportionately on the unskilled and low-wage workers; typically (though not always) higher skilled workers can displace lower skilled workers, if the higher skilled worker is willing to accept a wage cut. By the same token, the incidence of budget cuts associated with excessive budgetary stringency may fall disproportionately on the poor if social spending falls within the area of budget cuts.

On average, of course, growth is associated with poverty reduction, and to the extent that stabilization policies promote or hurt growth, they may correspondingly reduce or increase poverty (relative to what it might otherwise have been). But some growth strategies are more pro-poor than others, and by the same token, some stabilization strategies are more pro-poor than others. Those that succeed most in stabilizing the real economy and reducing risk, are likely to be more pro-poor, precisely because the poor, who are least able to bear the risk, disproportionately bear the brunt of it.

Concluding Remarks

Market economies have always been subject to high levels of volatility. In spite of progress in economic science, we not only have failed to eliminate this volatility; there is some evidence that it may have become worse.

Some hundred countries within the developing world have experienced some form of crisis from the 1980s to the end of the century.[11] Nor has progress in economic science eliminated some of the central controversies concerning the appropriate conduct of stabilization policies—those policies designed to stabilize the economy, respond to downturns, and prevent inflation. In spite of the development of sophisticated econometric models to forecast the future of the economy, we remain uncertain not only about what will happen in each economy over the next few months, let alone the next few years; and we remain uncertain about the consequences of alternative policies.

In this book, we have emphasized that government policy should work to reduce the real and financial volatility of the economy, and maintain the economy at as close to full employment as possible. This reinforces the emphasis placed on the importance of real stabilization; but it also reinforces the emphasis placed on developing policies that reduce the exposure of the economy to risk and increase its ability to respond, especially automatically, to the risks it faces. That is why liberalization policy cannot be separated from macroeconomic policy.

But our analysis has also stressed that *how* the economy is stabilized makes a difference. And the effects are more profound and longer lasting than those identified in the usual discussions, which focus on how the mix of monetary and fiscal policies affects the division of the economic pie between consumption, investment, and government. Cutbacks in public-sector expenditures and large increases in interest rates—standard staple in the 'conservative' policy responses to the threat of increasing inflation—not only are often ineffective in the short run, but also have negative effects on long-term growth. Even though sold as increasing economic efficiency, they often do exactly the opposite, reducing the overall efficiency of capital markets.

From this perspective, it is easy to understand the strong criticisms leveled against capital market liberalization: it exposes countries to greater economic volatility and often forces them to respond in ways that further impede long-term economic growth and allocative efficiency of markets. It's also easy to understand the strong criticisms leveled against an excessive focus on price stability: not only does price stability not guarantee growth; an excessive focus on price stability may impede growth. *Stabilization* policy cannot be separated from growth policy. Failure to stabilize may hurt growth, but stabilization, in the traditional sense of the term (price stability and fiscal adjustment), does not necessarily lead to economic growth. Stabilization focusing on the wrong objectives and

245

using the wrong instruments can actually hurt growth and increase poverty. This is one of the reasons that a stabilization policy focused on growth and employment is of such importance.

Finally, the links between growth, stability, and poverty are complex, and are not adequately summarized in the mantra that stability and growth are good for poverty reduction, and the associated mantra that structural reforms are good for growth, which is in turn pro-poor. Some reforms, such as capital market liberalization, have not been good for growth; but even had CML been good for growth, it would not have been good for stability. Instability—*real instability*—leads to more poverty. While growth, in general, may be good, it matters how growth is achieved; if it is achieved through policies that lead to more instability, poverty may be increased.

While the issues raised in this book are likely to continue to be debated among economists and the public at large, what we do know is that the brunt of the risks is felt by different groups within society. There is not a single policy which Pareto-dominates all other policies. Accordingly, we cannot simply delegate to technocrats the task of finding that Pareto-dominant policy.

Economic policies inherently must be part of the political process. This book—and the work of the Initiative for Policy Dialogue macroeconomic and capital market liberalization task forces—are not intended to resolve these uncertainties, but to help lay out alternative views, to facilitate a democratic discussion of the alternatives, and more broadly, of the institutional frameworks within which the key macroeconomic decisions are made.

Notes

Chapter 1

1. Easterly *et al.*, 2001; Ocampo, 2002; Ocampo, 2005*b*.
2. By some accounts, the IMF was founded to ensure the stability of the exchange rate system. Interventions were directed at helping a country ward off an attack on its fixed exchange rate, by providing it with the dollars necessary to sustain its exchange rate. Instability of exchange rates opened up the threat of competitive devaluations, a form of 'beggar thy neighbor' policy in which each country would restore its economy through increased exports and reduced imports. We take the more expansive view that Keynes wanted to ensure global full employment. This meant that countries that ran surpluses (in some sense, produced more than they consumed) were the source of the problem of global insufficiency of aggregate demand. He proposed taxes and other sanctions be imposed on such countries (Galbraith, 2003). By the same token, a country that was facing a downturn and was unable to finance a deficit threatened others' welfare through a reduction in imports, regardless of the size of its current surplus or deficit. There was a global interest in ensuring that each country maintained the strength of its economy.
3. See Lane *et al.*, 1999 and *Wall Street Journal*, 20 Jan. 1999.
4. See IMF, 2003.
5. Capital Market Liberalization is discussed more extensively in Chapters 10–12 of this book.
6. See Chang, forthcoming 2006.
7. A Pareto-dominant policy makes everyone at least as well off, and some better off, than under *any* alternative policy.
8. One of the main charges leveled by critics of the IMF is that they do not have sufficiently nuanced policies; that even if charges of imposing one-size-fits-all prescriptions are exaggerated, the IMF has not been sufficiently attuned to the differences in economic circumstances. This was, for instance, one of the main concerns raised in the initial responses to the East Asia crisis, which, unlike the Latin American crises of the early 1980s, was not caused by large government budget deficits or loose monetary policy. The fact that corporations were highly leveraged meant that imposing high interest rate policies on East Asia would have drastically higher costs than such policies had had in Latin America. See e.g. Furman and Stiglitz, 1998. See also Taylor, 1988.

9. See Mayer, 2002 and 1990.
10. See e.g. Greenwald and Stiglitz, 2003.
11. See Kaplan and Rodrik, 2002; See also Jomo, 2001.
12. See Nayyar, 2002*b*.
13. Though there is a curious correlation: those who put less weight on the welfare of workers are more likely to argue that the likely adverse effects are smaller.

Chapter 2

1. See Stiglitz, 1999; Chang, 2001, ch. 1; Nordhaus and Tobin, 1973; Eisner, 1988; Sen, 1999; Nayyar, 2002*c*.
2. More accurately, if natural resources are being depleted, sustainable development requires that there be offsetting investments, so that the total capital stock of the country (natural, physical, and human) is not decreased. There are also a host of subtleties associated with weighing the well-being of different generations which we do not address here. Another important dimension of sustainable development about which we shall have little to say is *social sustainability*; economic policies may, for instance, contribute to the erosion of social capital. See e.g. Stiglitz, 2000*b*, and other papers in the volume.
3. See Stiglitz, 2000*a*; Chang, 2001, chs. 9 and 7; Stiglitz, 2001*b*; Bhaduri and Nayyar, 1996; Nayyar, 2003*a*; and Ch. 10 in this volume.
4. There is some controversy about what is meant by stability, which we will come to shortly. Needless to say, given our focus on *real macroeconomics*, our attention centers around volatility in the real variables—output, employment, and real wages; but much of the attention in policy circles focuses on stability in the level of prices or the rate of inflation.
5. There are other approaches that focus more on societal interactions. Even within an individualistic framework, individuals could face a loss of welfare as a result of envy. Their utility depends on the income of others, on their relative well-being, and their sense that society is being fair to them. More strongly, some may contend that societal well-being is not adequately captured by an individualistic social welfare function, even when it incorporates these envy effects.
6. It is easy to see why this matters for the social costs of unemployment: Assume an individual has two bouts of unemployment, each lasting a year. The two years' loss of income is still only 5% of the average individual's lifetime work, a loss equivalent to but two or three years' wage growth, and an amount that would be 'manageable' with limited stress. This understates the individual's loss of welfare from losing a job, since future wage prospects are also adversely affected (Farber, 1993 and 2003). In that sense, even countries with good unemployment insurance do not really provide adequate insurance against the risk of being unemployed; they only replace (and typically for a

limited time) income during the period of unemployment; they do not compensate individuals for their lower future expected wages.

7. Though there are marked differences among developed countries both in coverage and the replacement rate (the fraction of the individual's normal income that unemployment insurance replaces). For instance, in 2003, the unemployment insurance replacement rate as a percentage of average production worker (APW) was 41% for the United States; 78% for Sweden, 85% for Finland, and 71% for Japan. The duration of unemployment benefits also differs (maximum 6 months in the United States, at most 15 months in Sweden). Data are from OECD and the European Commission (2004). In 2003 about 40% of unemployed workers in the United States received unemployment insurance benefits. The average weekly benefit check was $262, which replaced, on average, 47% of a worker's previous salary. Workers received that benefit for an average of 16.4 weeks in 2003 (http://www.epinet.org/content.cfm/issueguides_unemployment_index). Among the OECD countries, the United States has the lowest replacement rate, barring Greece and Spain.

8. Because of the relatively short bouts of unemployment, if there were good insurance markets, or if individuals had large amounts of savings, or if they could borrow against future income, then they could smooth the loss of income over their lifetime, and accordingly the social costs of unemployment would be limited. But even in developed countries, none of these hypotheses is correct. (a) Although there is some *implicit* insurance provided by employers (they retain workers that they do not need on the job with pay for a least a short while), changes in mores, in which firms are encouraged to fire workers who are no longer needed, have lessened the extent of such insurance. Perverse incentives may play a role as well. When corporate executive pay depends on share value and share value reflects short-run profits, it pays managers to fire unneeded workers, even if in doing so long-term profits of the firm are reduced. (The shift in mores and incentive structures is likely to result in less labor hoarding, and to imply a smaller reduction in productivity in recessions—but larger impacts on unemployment.) (b) Even in developed countries, more than half of the population has no financial assets. Good public pension programs have reduced the need for savings for retirement, and thus made it even more difficult for individuals to buffer themselves against cyclical shocks. See Stiglitz and Yun (2002), who argue for the need for integration of the unemployment and pension programs. (c) There is now compelling evidence of the pervasiveness of credit rationing, especially for lower income individuals and small and medium-sized corporations. See Deaton, 1991; Ludvigson, 1999; Carneiro and Heckman, 2002; Mankiw and Zeldes, 1991; Zeldes, 1989; Cox and Jappelli, 1990; Holtz-Eakin et al., 1994; Bond and Meghir, 1994; Fazzari et al., 1988; Hubbard, 1998; Bacchetta and Gerlach, 1997; Attanasio et al., 2000.

9. Some economists (see e.g. Lucas, 2003) have argued that the costs of economic volatility are relatively low. But this is because they use highly simplified models

that ignore the central problems. In a representative agent model in which all individuals are identical, there is automatically full work sharing—so there is no unemployment; in a model with perfect information, there is no credit rationing, and individuals can smooth income over their lifetime. Such models can provide little guidance either on the costs of volatility, or on the policies that might reduce those costs. Other special models can be constructed (e.g. in which individuals are risk neutral) in which the costs of volatility are limited. The societal costs of reduced demand for labor are especially high because of the inequitable manner in which such reductions are typically borne: a few workers are laid off or fired, while most workers face a relatively modest reduction in hours worked. If there was complete work sharing, then the societal costs would be smaller; the costs of all individuals facing a 10% reduction in hours worked (with pay reduced commensurately) is far less than if 10% of the workers face a 100% reduction in hours worked, with the remaining 90% unaffected. There is a large literature explaining the lack of complete job sharing, which one might have thought would emerge naturally from an optimally designed contract. Most of these relate to some fixed costs, e.g. of keeping an individual on the payroll, or to efficiency wage concerns.

10. Though the literature on credit rationing in developing countries is somewhat less developed than that for developed countries. See Rosenzweig and Wolpin, 1993.

11. In Latin America, for instance, in the 1990s, the fraction of those in the informal sector increased significantly. From 1990 to 1997, employment in the urban informal sector grew by nearly 10% in Brazil and Mexico as a percentage of total employment. Informal employment grew from 35% to 45% of total employment in Venezuela and from 40% to over 45% in Argentina (ILO, 1999 and 2002).

12. See Nayyar, 2003*b*.

13. Even without return migration, surplus labor implicit in widespread underemployment subjects real wages in the rural sector to a downward pressure and does not allow them to rise; see Lewis, 1954.

14. For discussion on hysteresis in the European context, please see Blanchard and Summers, 1986.

15. The Clinton administration used this as one of its arguments for pursuing high employment policies. US Council of Economic Advisors, 1997, and Stiglitz, 1997.

16. See Aarts *et al.*, 1992.

17. Bureau of Labor Statistics, 2003.

18. Taking into account the uncertainty about how low unemployment can be pushed without inflation rising.

19. All of these terms are deliberately somewhat vague: we have not yet specified the trade-offs. Clearly, if there were no costs associated with maintaining the economy at full employment or in providing effective safety nets, all countries would do so. Much of the discussion in later chapters is directed at trying to

understand better the trade-offs. The purpose of this chapter is to help think through the various objectives.

20. Furman and Stiglitz, 1998.

21. Inflation thus acts as a tax on currency (non-interest bearing debt), which is distortive. But in assessing the costs of the 'inflation' tax, one must compare that distortion with the distortions associated with other ways of raising revenue. So long as inflation remains not too high and the additional costs arising from inducing individuals to put their money in interest bearing forms are not too high, this cost of inflation is not likely to be significant. (Data compiled from IMF, 2004.)

22. The concept of 'inertial' inflation owes a lot to the traditional Latin American structural school, which emphasizes the fact that inflation dynamics involve more than merely monetary mechanisms.

23. Kalecki's (1970, 1971) macroeconomic analysis of underdeveloped economies suggested the opposite: that moderate rates of inflation might enable an economy to attain a higher rate of growth than would otherwise be possible.

24. Country studies on inflation crises and stabilization programs can be found in Bruno *et al.* (1988 and 1991). For a more general discussion see Bruno (1995).

25. Levine and Renelt, 1992; Levine and Zervos, 1993; Bruno and Easterly, 1996 and 1998; Stanley Fischer, 1996.

26. The studies do not fully address many of the issues discussed in this section.

27. Many of the studies show no statistically significant relationship when inflation is below a certain threshold. This implies that one can't reject the hypothesis that there is no relationship below a certain level of inflation. Thus, Barro (1997) shows that there is no (or only a weak) statistically significant relation between economic growth and inflation when inflation is below 20%. Ocampo (2004*b*) finds that threshold to be 40% for Latin America since the mid-1970s. Others show a small but significant relationship, i.e. an increase of inflation from 3 to 5% might have a statistical relationship—statistically different form zero—but so small that so long as inflation does not change much, the impact on growth is barely perceptible.

28. There are many reasons that self-financing might develop. For example, difficulties in the enforcement of credit and equity contracts often lead to self-financing. Of course, if the inflation rate is not just high, but also variable, lending becomes riskier and the inflation variability itself can become a cause of self-financing.

29. The magnitude of the costs depends on institutional arrangements. For instance, some of the problems confronting borrowers in East Asia who suddenly saw nominal interest rates rise would have been far less if debt contracts had indexed interest rates (specifying a real interest rate), or if the maturity of the loan contract had been longer. In practice, few debt contracts are indexed. Even if they were, it would not fully resolve the problem since in crises there may be large movements in real interest rates. There are good reasons

having to do with moral hazard why many loan contracts are short term. Still, institutional arrangements—that differ markedly across countries—can have large effects, and it is not always obvious why one institutional arrangement has arisen in one country, but not in another. While there is little evidence that such institutional arrangements are optimal, it is clearly possible that the institutional arrangements may change with large changes in policy. (As an example we already noted briefly, the US conventional mortgage means that disinflation accompanied by correspondingly lower mortgage rates is associated with a large transfer from creditors to debtors.)

30. Further problems in interpretation are caused by the fact that many events often happen at the same time. There was a marked productivity slowdown in the United States beginning around 1973. While the timing suggested it might have had something to do with the price of oil, productivity did not increase when oil prices later fell, and it is hard to tell a story for why a shock in the price of a single commodity would have such pervasive effects on productivity. There were also demographic changes occurring at the time (more entrants into the labor force). The slowdown of growth most plausibly had to do with the decrease in productivity, which may have had something to do with the oil price shock, but less likely had anything to do with inflation.

31. In a sample of Argentina, Bolivia, Brazil, Chile, Colombia, Costa Rica, Dominican Republic, Ecuador, El Salvador, Guatemala, Honduras, Mexico, Nicaragua, Panama, Paraguay, Peru, Uruguay, and Venezuela for the years 1970–9, the (un-weighted) average of GDP growth rates is 5.2%, and of per capita GDP growth rates 2.6%.

32. There is an extensive debate about the cause of the lost decade. See Ocampo, forthcoming; Stiglitz (2003*b*) argues that it was not that the import-competing strategy eventually came to a dead end. Rather, the problem lay with the totally unexpected and unprecedented high levels of international interest rates that followed from the Fed's policies of the early 1980s.

33. See e.g. Greenwald and Stiglitz 1988, 1993*a* and 1993*b*.

34. Fisher, 1933.

35. Or more accurately, unexpected disinflation.

36. These results depend only on the actual level of inflation being significantly less than the anticipated level of inflation. But it is clear that 'deflationary psychology' is bad for the economy.

37. Akerlof *et al.*, 2000.

38. See e.g. Cecchetti, 1998.

39. The claim is that one cannot charge an interest rate on ordinary money. Proposals have been put forward, however, for doing so, e.g. by requiring legal tender to have a stamp affixed, once a year or so, which would cost say 2% of the value of the currency.

40. In the United States, they also benefit from unexpected deflation because of the particular design of US mortgage markets. The prevalent mortgage is a fixed

rate mortgage with an option to exchange that mortgage for a lower-rate fixed mortgage, should the long-term rates fall. It is a one-sided bet. The borrower wins the bet when the nominal interest rate falls. There is then a transfer of wealth from the lender to the borrower, and this may have real consequences. Mortgage refinancing reduces monthly payments, allowing individuals to spend more on other items. But the magnitude of the response is almost surely affected by the fact that it is a one-sided change—it would not have been as large if individuals had only variable rate mortgages. There is an implicit wealth transfer as a result of the exercise of the option. Any large balance sheet realignments, such as this, can have real effects not only in the short run, but also in the long.

41. In fact, because of problems in constructing the price index, there is a general consensus that retirees are *over-compensated* for inflation; i.e. when their true cost of living increases by 1%, their social security checks increase by as much as 2%. Changes in the way that the price index is calculated have reduced this over-indexing somewhat since the early 1990s, when the Boskin Commission report (1999) suggested it could be as much as 2%.

42. That is, if they do not, they will lose workers to firms who have adjusted wages in response to inflation. In addition, many firms pay higher wages than is absolutely necessary to attract and retain workers because they realize that workers who are paid better work harder, are less likely to quit, and are more efficient. In addition, wages have to be high to ensure that workers have enough nutrition to be productive. The efficiency wage is the wage that minimizes the overall costs of labor, taking into account the workers' responses to the higher wages. The wage firms pay—the efficiency wage—will also tend to rise with inflation. Shapiro and Stiglitz, 1984.

43. As noted earlier, a traditional focus (before money was largely interest bearing) has been on the costs to those who hold money. Poorer individuals are more likely to hold a larger fraction of their assets in non-interest bearing forms (currency), but the amounts are still, in general, small.

44. Some argue that in the long run, there is no trade-off. (The Phillips curve is asserted to be vertical.) While there is little convincing empirical support for this hypothesis, even if it were true, it does not preclude there being a trade-off in the short run.

45. Furthermore, if price stability is associated with greater output variability, it can undermine growth because of the increase in *real* uncertainty. The evidence on the link and the interpretation remain contentious. Most simple models suggest that if one stabilizes a price variable, the other variable will inevitably bear more of the brunt of the adjustment. Those who argue for inflation targeting seem to suggest that the commitment to stabilizing inflation has a salutary effect on the overall economic performance; if that is the case, mightn't a commitment to output stabilization—if effectively and consistently implemented—have an even more salutary effect? One needs to distinguish the benefit of *rules* from the question of, given that rules are to be

followed, what the optimal rules should be. Goldfeld (1982) examines compactly the point. The classic rational expectations models are Kydland and Prescott (1977) and Barro and Gordon (1983). See also Barro, 1985, and Clarida *et al.*, 1999.

It is clear that monetarism, a policy regime *intended* to lead to price stability, led to enormous volatility in real interest rates and output (partly because it failed even to take into account the consequences of shifts in the demand curve for money). A classic reference on the effects of targeting money supply aggregates on interest rates is Poole (1970). The empirical stability of money demand, established initially by Cagan (1956), was subsequently questioned by Goldfeld (1976). The debate is summarized in Judd and Scadding, 1982.

46. Or more accurately, raising interest rates significantly, to a level that was not anticipated: if firms anticipate the interest rates, they may be able to adjust their indebtedness accordingly (though, as we have noted, this too has its costs.) Note that there are often large costs to raising *nominal* interest rates, even when the increase in interest rates only offsets the increase in inflation, because of capital market imperfections and rigidities: there are cash-flow effects, which at least some firms cannot 'undo' by increased borrowing.

47. Of course, unemployment, like inflation, may be a symptom of deeper problems in the economy or in government macro-management. At the very least, the persistence of high levels of unemployment is indicative of a market failure; and modern analyses of unemployment try to relate this market failure to more fundamental market failures, like wage and price rigidities, and to link these with still more fundamental failures, like imperfections of information.

48. Speculators, recognizing this, often engineered a run against the currency.

49. Especially, as noted earlier, in the absence of insurance and other mechanisms to smooth consumption over time.

50. The statistical analyses model the economy as having a large random component. An economy is said to have 'mean reversion' if a higher than normal growth rate this year is followed by a lower than normal growth rate next year. An economy is said to have 'unit roots' if expected growth next year and in following years is unaffected by what happens this year. Hence, if this year is bad, the future simply builds on this weak basis. It never really recovers. The evidence seems to support a slight recovery. Such studies have mainly focused on advanced industrial countries. See e.g. Jorgenson and Yip, 2001; Romer, 1987; and Shigehara, 1992.

51. Formally, the question is: do the stochastic processes describing growth have (close to) a unit root? If they do, then lower income or growth today implies lower income in the future. This contrasts with the alternative hypothesis of trend stationarity (or mean reversion around a deterministic trend), in which a bad year today is 'made up for' by a good year in the future. An alternative hypothesis is that only shocks of sufficient magnitude have permanent effects but the economy is otherwise trend stationary. This hypothesis includes the

case in which a country exhibits a permanently lower output level after a negative shock that does not affect its trend. This hypothesis is consistent with our analysis. Empirical evidence is mainly available for developed countries. Two studies that include developing countries are: Ben-David and Papell, 1998 and Lutz, 1999. Both studies use samples from 1950 to 1990 and tend to reject the unit root hypothesis in favor of the existence of structural breaks with unchanged or lower trends after the shock.

52. That is, if there is close to a unit root to the stochastic processes describing the evolution of the economy.

53. Some of the growth issues referred to above also entail issues of efficiency. Without long-term contracts, there may be underinvestment in human capital, a problem that is exacerbated by extended periods of high unemployment.

54. This is consistent with the (near) unit root literature referred to earlier.

55. Surveys of the empirical literature on the relationship between crime and the unemployment rate in the United States are Freeman (1983 and 1994), Chiricos (1987). For more recent studies see Freeman, 1996, 1999 and Freeman and Rodgers, 1999; Raphael and Winter-Ebmer, 2001; Levitt, 1996. The link between crime and unemployment is not as thoroughly documented for developing countries. On the relationship between economic conditions and civil wars, see Collier and Hoeffler (1998).

56. The right to work is included in the International Covenant on Economic Social and Cultural Rights, the International Covenant on Civil and Political Rights, the International Labor Organization conventions, and in the Universal Declaration of Human Rights, whose article 23 is reported below:

> (1) Everyone has the right to work, to free choice of employment, to just and favorable conditions of work and to protection against unemployment. (2) Everyone, without any discrimination, has the right to equal pay for equal work. (3) Everyone who works has the right to just and favorable remuneration ensuring for himself and his family an existence worthy of human dignity, and supplemented, if necessary, by other means of social protection. (4) Everyone has the right to form and to join trade unions for the protection of his interests.

For links and references on the *rights* perspective on economic issues, see the UN Committee on Economic, Social and Cultural Rights (www.unhchr.ch), the UN Department of Economic and Social Affairs (www.un.org/esa/desa/htm), and the Center for Economic and Social Rights (www.cesr.org).

57. This is, of course, not the only deficiency with much of popular discourse. Often political discourse focuses on intermediate variables, like inflation or exchange rates; individuals often suffer from 'money illusion', see rising prices as eroding their purchasing power, without recognizing the effect of inflation on wages. Ordinary citizens are also unlikely to disentangle inflation as a *cause* and as a *consequence* (e.g. of the increase in oil prices). In that sense, the emphasis by outside advisers on inflation seems to validate the money illusion and the lack of attention to causality.

58. For instance, the Atkinson measure (building on the work of Rothschild and Stiglitz, 1970) analyzes how much societal income could be reduced to still generate the same level of societal welfare, if income were perfectly equally distributed.

59. The utilitarian or Benthamite social welfare function simply adds up the expected utility (a measure of their well-being) of different individuals.

60. For research quantifying the loss in welfare from insecurity, see Pratt (1964). He provides a money metric for assessing the risk premium associated with consumption variability; Rothschild and Stiglitz (1970) provides a more general framework for thinking about the losses of welfare associated with uncertainty. See also Atkinson, 1970; Atkinson and Stiglitz, 1980; and Rothschild and Stiglitz (1973) shows how those techniques could be applied to variability in income.

61. There is, for instance, evidence that deep and extended downturns are associated with higher suicide rates, higher divorce rates, and high rates of crime and violence. If individuals have utility functions that are not linear in leisure, presumably individuals should be averse to variability in hours worked, just as they are to variability in consumption; there is no consensus among economists on the significance of this.

Chapter 3

1. Disposable income is simply the income individuals have to spend, after paying taxes.

2. More recent work has shown that, even though individuals sometimes do not act in perfectly rational ways, their behavior is *predictable*. See e.g. Akerlof, 2002.

3. Stiglitz (1999*d*), explores alternative approaches to dealing with crises.

4. In some developing countries, there also may be some safety net expenditures that increase as the economy weakens.

5. Of course, if the government had been running a surplus, then the downturn would only have reduced the size of the surplus, or turned the surplus into a slight deficit. As we shall comment below, developing countries are increasingly recognizing the risks associated with depending heavily on borrowing, especially short-term foreign borrowing. As difficult and painful as it may be to run a surplus that can be used to create a rainy-day fund, such a policy increasingly looks more attractive than the alternative. See below.

6. In fact, the easing of monetary policy in the United States from 2001 on did help stimulate the economy, but not because investment was stimulated, but because households refinanced their mortgages. This effect would not be present in most developing countries, where mortgage markets are absent or underdeveloped. This is another instance of an important difference between macroeconomics for developed and less developed countries. Indeed, it would

presumably be weaker in countries where variable rate mortgages predominate, and/or in countries where there were significant pre-payment penalties. Thus, the effect of lowering interest rates in such a situation would also be weaker in many European countries.

7. That is, the increase in output is a multiple of the increase in expenditure. According to a recent review of the literature, expenditure multiplier estimates range from 0.4 to 1.6. The magnitude of the multiplier depends on savings rates and the openness of the economy. For small, open economies, the multiplier seems to be smaller than for large economies in which imports are a relatively small fraction of GDP, like the United States or Japan. See Hemming *et al.*, 2002.

8. US Council of Economic Advisers, 1995; Hall, 1996; Wallsten, 2000.

9. And even if policies are initially effective, they often have second-round consequences that undermine their long-term effectiveness.

10. In the United States, the obligation of the government to do so is reflected in the Full Employment Act of 1946.

11. There is one strand of thought that seems to suggest that correctly measured GDP increases if government cuts expenditures and taxes in tandem, as a result of the switch from unproductive government expenditures to private consumption. This contrasts with the standard Keynesian approach, which suggests that there is a 'balanced budget *multiplier*'.

12. This was the position of the Bush administration in pushing the tax cuts in the United States in 2001 and 2003.

13. Because higher after-tax wages mean that individuals are better off, they wish to take some of this increased 'well-being' in the form of leisure. (This is called the income effect.) See Goode, 1949. There is a more refined analysis that argues that lowering the tax rate reduces the *distortions* in the economy.

14. For a discussion of the classical dichotomy, see Teigen (1972). This notion was a mainstay of monetarism. See Friedman, 1956. For more recent discussions of this perspective, see e.g. Lucas and Sargent, 1978. See also Patinkin, 1952; Negishi, 1964; and Lloyd, 1970. In these views, the main real effect of an increase in money is negative—the adverse *real* effects of inflation. The Barro–Ricardo theorem can be extended, to show that *under highly restrictive conditions (analogous to those for which the original theorem is true)* all government financial policies are irrelevant. See Stiglitz, 1988 and 1983.

15. Some strains of *monetarism*—which holds that government should focus on the supply of money, for instance increasing it at a steady rate reflecting the increase in the productive capacity of the economy—reflect the same perspective. Monetarism was popular among the conservatives in the early 1980s. Like so many fads in economics, it has now gone out of fashion, with later generations wondering how policy-makers of an earlier generation could have been so attracted to such a simplistic policy framework.

16. See the discussion in Chapter 2.

17. See e.g. Friedman, 1968; Phelps, 1967.

18. For two opposing views, see Lucas, 1996 and Mankiw, 2000.

19. The language itself suggests 'hidden' trade-offs. When Keynesians say 'getting as close to full employment as possible', what they mean, of course, is *without setting off significant increases in inflation*; and when conservatives say getting as close to price stability as possible, what they mean is *without leading to significant increases in unemployment*. It might be possible to bring inflation down to zero, by pushing unemployment up to 20%, but in the minds of most, this is simply not acceptable.

20. See Card and Krueger, 1995. Though their results have been challenged, what is remarkable is how little evidence there is of the strong negative effects on employment predicted by the standard theory. Several explanations for this have been put forward: efficiency wage theory predicts that productivity will increase with wages, so that the net effect on labor costs may be markedly less than predicted by the standard theory. Alternative explanations focus on imperfections of competition in labor markets.

21. Similarly, social security taxes should not lead to unemployment, only to an adjustment in wages. See e.g. Stiglitz, 1999*e*.

22. There are a variety of heterodox approaches, with diverse interrelationships among them. Among them, we should emphasize the tradition that goes back to the work of Michal Kalecki; see, in particular, Kalecki, 1971. The most important implications of this tradition, combined with contributions from other schools of economic thought, have been developed by Lance Taylor; see, in particular, Taylor, 1991 and 2004. The Latin American structuralist tradition has also played an important role. See, in this regard, ECLAC, 1998; Sunkel, 1993; and Ffrench-Davis, 2000; Ffrench–Davis 2005.

23. The analysis of these links goes back to the work of Nicholas Kaldor; see, in particular, 1978. For a recent restatement of this link, see Ocampo and Taylor, 1998, and Ocampo, 2005*a*.

24. This is, of course, an essential insight of the Latin American structuralist school. The literature on balance vs. imbalanced growth in developing countries made an important contribution to this debate. The most lasting contribution is probably that of Albert O. Hirschman; see in particular Hirschman, 1958. See also Streeten, 1959.

25. See e.g. Bruno *et al.*, 1991.

26. This is an essential insight of the Latin American structuralist tradition in relation to inflation, and of the work of Lance Taylor. See previous references in both regards.

27. In standard economic theory with well-functioning capital markets, risk would be fully divested; the only risk that would matter would be correlation with the business cycle (a project would be evaluated only in terms of its expected return and its 'β'). In fact, firms do worry about 'own risk'—they act in a risk-averse manner. See Greenwald and Stiglitz, 1990*a*.

28. The imperfections can be explained through models of asymmetric information. See e.g. Stiglitz and Weiss, 1981; Greenwald *et al.*, 1984; or Myers and Majluf, 1984.
29. See, in particular, Greenwald and Stiglitz, 2003.
30. See Nayyar, 1995. See also Taylor, 1988 and Bhaduri, 1992.
31. See, in particular, the references to Michal Kalecki, Nicholas Kaldor, and Lance Taylor, and Amit Bhaduri above.
32. Conservatives emphasize statistical studies which show high savings and labor supply elasticities. Those who call for more redistribution cite studies that show low elasticities.

Chapter 4

1. Identities are equations that are always true, the result of basic definitions.
2. This is sometimes referred to as 'internal balance' as opposed to 'external balance', which is defined as equilibrium in the balance of payments, primarily with reference to the current account. The distinction between internal balance and external balance was first made by James Meade (1951). We discuss external balance as an intermediate objective in Chapter 7.
3. Some argue for the central bank focus on price stability on other grounds: it is more efficient to have each institution focus on a single target. Thus, fiscal authorities, in this view, should focus on unemployment. This approach reduces the difficulties of policy coordination.
4. For an analysis of this issue, see Nayyar, 1998.
5. See Jung, 1985; Katsimbris, 1990; Bagchi, 1994.
6. Such an overvaluation, with similar consequences, may be attributable to monetary contraction or fiscal expansion, as it was in the United States during the first half of the 1980s. And there was a literature that examined the *hysteresis* effects of the persistent overvaluation of the US dollar. The upshot of this literature was that overvaluation leads to an accumulation of adverse trade effects that ultimately need to be remedied through an over-depreciation. The reason is that, in the presence of *hysteresis*, a period of sustained undervaluation is needed to bring forth the required investment. For a discussion, see Dornbusch (1987).
7. There is an extensive literature on gap models. See e.g. McKinnon, 1964; Bacha, 1990; Taylor, 1994. In analyzing macroeconomic constraints on growth in underdeveloped countries, by contrast, Kalecki sought to focus on the wage goods constraint. See Kalecki, 1970.
8. In the United States, most states have balanced budget provisions in their constitutions, so they, too, have pro-cyclical fiscal policies.
9. Of course, in equilibrium, these constraints are always satisfied. Indeed, the constraints only exist *ex ante* but cannot be there *ex post* because there can be no gaps in accounting identities.

10. Correspondingly, the degree of 'monetization', the extent to which transactions are mediated by money, or the ratio of money to GDP, may differ.

11. Even the form of financial instruments can make a difference. In the United States, where most mortgages are fixed rate and do not have significant prepayment penalties, the lowering of long-term interest rates leads to refinancing; this played a large role in sustaining the US economy during the slowdown of 2000–03. But in the UK, a more common form of mortgage is the variable rate mortgage with fixed payments. Lowering interest rates would presumably have a much weaker effect.

12. Though, even here, there is some controversy about the extent to which and the mechanisms through which interest rates affect the economy. See Greenwald and Stiglitz, 2003.

13. The IMF's failure to do so in the East Asia crisis is one of the major criticisms of the IMF management of that crisis.

14. Modern theories based on the economics of information (information asymmetries) have provided an explanation both for the limitations in equity markets in general, and for why they play a much smaller role in developing countries than in developed countries.

15. See Stiglitz, 1999*f*.

16. For a discussion, see Nayyar, 1995.

17. For instance, in most developed countries, corporations rely on financial information to control their own operations; they are required by financial regulators to disclose information to shareholders; and a large fraction of transactions are mediated through financial institutions. This provides a rich information basis. See e.g. Stiglitz and Wolfson, 1988, paper presented for delivery to the American Accounting Association, Aug. 1987, and Sah and Stiglitz, 1992.

18. There may also be more distortions, especially when monetary policy is tightened, as the total reduction is concentrated on the small part of the economy that relies on bank lending.

19. Some who advocate reliance on market-based mechanisms have an overly simplistic view of the functioning of capital markets. They believe that capital should be allocated by auction, to those who are willing to pay the most for it, just like any other good. This ignores the fundamental distinctions between capital and other markets.

20. See Nayyar, 2002*c*.

Chapter 5

1. See Diebold and Rudebusch, 1992.

2. Diebold *et al.*, 1993.

3. For an argument suggesting that data selection bias accounts for the first observation, see Watson (1994).

4. Kose *et al.*, 2004.

5. Barro, 1974.

6. Some suggested that there was another reason that the tax cuts failed to stimulate much. Households may have interpreted the tax cut as a 'signal' that the economy was in worse shape than they had believed, and these changes in expectations led to a lowering of consumption (in effect, because of a lowering of expectations concerning future lifetime income).

7. For a compact presentation of both theoretical and empirical results, see Seater, 1993. Stiglitz (1988) shows that it holds only in the absence of information problems, credit or equity rationing. Most importantly, those who might end up repaying the debt must be the same as those who incur it; otherwise, there can be an important intergenerational redistribution, which can have real effects. Barro assumed dynastic utility functions; so that parents adjust the bequests they leave to their descendants to reflect the increased debt burden. This assumption is particularly questionable. At the very least, uncertainty about future repayments (e.g. whether the individual will have children or grandchildren) means that there will be real consequences to debt financing.

8. In the most simple macroeconomic model, where savings are the only 'leakage' of aggregate demand (i.e. the additional income of an individual or household that is not spent), the *multiplier* is $1/s$, where s is the savings rate. More generally, all leakages have to be included: not only private savings but also taxes and imports. We will return to this issue in Chapter 6.

9. If individuals have rational expectations, the effective leakage will be smaller; some of the savings will be spent, say, next period, and this will increase income in that period. Households today, recognizing this, will recognize the reduced need for precautionary savings, and so will consume more today. See Neary and Stiglitz, 1983. This simply emphasizes that the asserted results of the rational expectations school that policy is ineffective follow not from the assumption of rational expectations, but from assumptions about perfect markets/market clearing etc.

10. Akerlof and Romer, 1993.

11. Note that in the Barro–Ricardo world, there is no effect on interest rates, since the increased borrowing is matched by increasing savings by government. To the extent that there is some interest elasticity of savings, the increase in the interest rate resulting from an increased investment will be limited.

12. There is another reason that some crowding out might occur under certain conditions. The traditional reason given for crowding out is that the higher interest rate that results from government spending leads to lower investment. But in reality, there's limited evidence that investment is very sensitive to interest rates. See Chirinko, 1993; Hubbard, 1998. On the other hand, in some countries there may be some crowding out for 'institutional reasons', especially if there is credit rationing.

13. There are some models in which inflation can set in even when the economy has not reached full employment. Typically, this is because of structural rigidities; to the extent that these are important, full employment needs to be redefined

to include them, and government policy needs to be directed at removing the structural rigidities.

14. In a liquidity trap, the public holds onto money supplied to the economy rather than investing or spending. A liquidity trap could occur when the economy is in recession and interest rates are low, so that the expected return on investments are also low. If the recession is accompanied by deflation, there is an added incentive for consumers to hold spending on consumption.

15. An inflow of capital would raise the money supply—assuming the inflows are not sterilized (i.e. the central bank doesn't intervene in the market to keep the money supply from rising) as we discuss in the following chapter.

16. Similar results hold if we assume that it is the price of equity that drives investment rather than the interest rate. The portfolio approach (Tobin and William, 1977) suggests that an increase in the supply of bonds, with the resulting increase in the interest rate, normally leads to a fall in the price of equities, and it is the price of equities which drives down the level of investment. Evidence in favor of this approach is at best ambiguous (for a concise discussion of the measurement and identification problems, see Buiter, 2003). Again, if monetary authorities offset the interest rate increase, or if there is an inflow of capital from abroad, this effect will not materialize. Most investment is in fact not financed by the issuance of equity, and most firms pay some, but only limited, attention to its price. This is extremely relevant for policy design. The believers in the leading role of the stock price have been pressing for eliminating taxes on capital gains, reducing taxes on distributed profits and forcing higher shares of distribution versus reinvested profits. Opponents fear that these policies would lead to a poor outcome for financing of business investment, lower public income, and a worsening income distribution.

17. See Nayyar, 2000.

18. See Cooper, 1992 and Taylor, 1993. The effects in developing countries are complicated by limitations on the availability of finance, an issue which we turn to shortly.

19. Eaton and Gersovitz, 1981, proved that that is in fact the case. Easterly *et al.*, 2001; Gavin *et al.*, 1996; and Stein *et al.*, 1998, have shown that government fiscal policy seems consistent with such a hypothesis.

20. See Stiglitz and Weiss, 1981; and Eaton and Gersovitz, 1981.

21. Kaminsky *et al.*, 2004.

22. Martner and Tromben, 2003.

23. Easterly and Servén (eds.), 2003.

24. For countries that were neutral, the structural fiscal deficit remained unchanged through the improvement or deterioration of fiscal accounts. See ECLAC, 1998b; Ocampo, 2002, and 2005b, on which the analysis that follows relies.

25. See an evaluation of some of these experiences in Davis *et al.*, 2003.

26. ECLAC, 1998*b*.
27. Marfán, 2005. It should be emphasized that the tax collection could be done by the central bank (e.g. the equivalent tax for the unremunerated reserve requirements on capital inflows), and the revenues could be sterilized in the form of a quasi-fiscal surplus that is not transferred to the government.
28. Budnevich and Le Fort, 1997.
29. Except for those few firms which, even with the incremental investment tax credit, choose to invest less than, say, 80% of what they had invested in prior years. Obviously, by lowering the threshold, incentives are increased (fewer firms are excluded), but so too are the costs.
30. More generally, any tax change that affects relative prices (including intertemporal prices) can have real effects.
31. This suggests that an optimally designed tax system might have different provisions for large and small firms; large firms would be confronted with a net investment tax credit, small firms with a tax credit of the conventional form.
32. Auerbach, 1991; and Auerbach and Bradford, 2002, argue that limitations on loss carry-forward and carry-back are among the major distortions in the tax system.
33. There is a kind of liquidity trap, resulting not from the high elasticity of demand for money, but from a low elasticity of the supply of bank credit.
34. There are others: standard inflation targeting does not distinguish between increases in the inflation rate that are likely to lead to future inflation and those that are not.
35. This is another example of where the representative agent model provides inadequate guidance for macroeconomic behavior.
36. In relation to Basle II, see Griffith-Jones and Persaud (2005). Since credit ratings are also pro-cyclical, basing risk on such ratings, as proposed by Basle II, is also a pro-cyclical practice.
37. For this reason, the sudden introduction of strong regulatory standards during crises may worsen a credit squeeze. Although authorities must adopt clearly defined rules to restore confidence, the application of stronger standards should be gradual.
38. See Ocampo, 2003*a*, on which the analysis that follows relies.
39. Fernández de Lis *et al.*, 2001.
40. Under this system, provisions are estimated using either the internal risk management model of the financial institution or the standard model proposed by Banco de España. The latter establishes six categories, with annual provisioning ratios that range from 0% to 1.5%.
41. The fund is combined with traditional provisions for non-performing assets or for borrowers under stress, and with recoveries of non-performing assets.
42. See Liliana Rojas-Suarez in upcoming IPD Capital Market Liberalization Companion Volume.

Chapter 6

1. The relative price of the currencies of two countries is the *nominal* exchange rate.
2. Though there may be alternative explanations: maintaining an undervalued exchange rate leads to the accumulation of large reserves; countries with large reserves are less likely to have crises; and crises have very adverse effects on growth.
3. See Díaz-Alejandro and Velasco, 1988, ch. 1, and Krugman and Taylor, 1978, pp. 445–56.
4. As we note elsewhere in this chapter, large devaluations, especially when accompanied by large increases in interest rates, may have adverse effects even on exports, both because of adverse effects on supply and because importers, worried about supply reliability of firms near bankruptcy, reduce their demand.
5. Even if some firms in the economy are better off, their gains are more than offset by the losses of others.
6. For a discussion on such strategic forms of state intervention in countries that are latecomers to industrialization, see Nayyar, 1997.
7. See a recent defense of this view (with a particular emphasis on employment) in Frenkel (2004).
8. See, in particular, Krugman, 1990, ch. 7 and van Wijnbergen, 1984. See also a novel analysis of this issue that emphasizes how countries can avoid the Dutch disease through policies, in Palma (2005, ch. 3).
9. Elsewhere, Stiglitz has argued for a 'super chapter 11'—an even more expedited restructuring process which would come into play in the event of a macroeconomic disturbance. Miller and Stiglitz, 1999.
10. This is especially so, of course, if the country has an IMF program which focuses on the overall deficit, and not just the primary surplus.
11. We discuss the question of confidence at greater length below. Here, we simply note that it is difficult to predict the impact on confidence: normally, higher GDP strengthens confidence, and higher trade deficits lower confidence.
12. A weak (or depreciated) exchange rate means one rupee, baht, or peso can buy fewer dollars, euros, or yens. A strong (or appreciated) exchange rate means the opposite. We avoid using the terms 'low' or 'high' exchange rate, as they have opposite meanings in different parts of the world. In the United States and UK, a 'low' exchange rate usually means the same as what we just defined as a weak exchange rate, but in many developing countries this is called a 'high' exchange rate, as *more* bahts, rupees, or pesos are needed to buy a dollar, euro, or yen.
13. In developing countries capital markets are often underdeveloped, and longer-term instruments tend to be so illiquid that intervention in longer-term rates is extremely difficult. Of course, an increase in short rates affects longer-term rates, but the direction is ambiguous. To the extent that longer-term rates do rise, the higher rates often imply that the market perceives greater risk in the

long run, making it unlikely that the higher rates will attract new long-term funds.

14. This effect may take some time to materialize and may actually do so through destabilizing dynamics. The sequence has been well known in the developing world since the 1970s: higher inflows lead a temporary expansion accompanied by currency appreciation and rising current account deficit. Eventually, foreign investors stop financing the country due to rising risks, resulting in a crisis.

15. This is especially likely if domestic firms have high levels of short-term debt.

16. Again, the heterodox approach provides one of the few arguments for why higher interest rates may, even in these seemingly adverse circumstances, be effective: some businessmen (and speculators) with substantial funds outside the country are forced to bring in money to repay domestic loans (and currency shorts) that they can no longer afford at the high domestic interest rates.

17. See Keynes, 1936, ch. 12.

18. For a temporary action to lead to long-run shifts in the demand curves, the actions have to convey information that was not otherwise available, e.g. they have to provide a signal about the characteristics, say, of the decision-maker. For a more detailed discussion of these issues, see Stiglitz (1998: 9–58).

19. Alternatively, the central bank can sell existing domestic treasury bonds for the same purpose.

Chapter 7

1. In the *long run*, other variables adjust. For instance, some argued that, eventually, high unemployment would lead to lower domestic prices; the real exchange rate (which is what matters for exports and imports) would fall, bringing the economy back into external balance. But this required maintaining a high level of unemployment for a long period—longer than was politically sustainable.

2. This is the way the policy agenda of the government is often phrased, though as we emphasized in Chapter 2, the government should be focusing on *real* objectives, such as growth, employment, and distribution. The list of intermediary objectives often is expanded to a fourth variable, inflation; this is really subsumed in the first, which more accurately should be termed a level of aggregate demand at which there are no significant inflationary pressures. Budget balance and external balance are intermediary variables focusing on sustainability of policy; but, as we have repeatedly emphasized, deficits can be sustained if the funds are spent on investment. The analytic framework here can be used to analyze the determination of policy variables with alternative objectives and constraints.

3. Mathematically, one can think of there being three equilibrium conditions (three equations) in three unknowns. There are mathematical issues relating to the existence and uniqueness of the solution, which we pass over here.

4. The import function defines how much the country imports, as a function of national income (set here at the full employment level) and the exchange rate. (In principle, the interest rate too could matter.) The export function gives exports as a function of the exchange rate and other countries' incomes, which are viewed (from the perspective of a small developing country) as exogenous.

5. That is, the exchange rate is determined by the demand and supply for the country's currency. The demand for a country's currency has two components: that required to purchase goods from the country, related to the demand for that country's goods as exports; and that required for investment. A country's currency is an asset, the return to which depends on the interest rate and *expectations* of capital gains or losses. All other things being equal, an increase in the interest rate makes it more attractive to invest in the country.

6. Note the caveat: external balance is not really a policy goal but is taken here as a surrogate for 'sustainability'.

7. Stiglitz, 1999*a*: 1–38. See also Bhaduri and Nayyar, 1996.

8. The defense of the currently fashionable stance of independence and clean distinctions between the responsibilities, going so far as to preclude even commentary by the fiscal authorities about the stance of the monetary authority, is based on political economy.

9. There is an open question: can the monetary authority simultaneously intervene in the foreign exchange market to prevent the exchange rate from strengthening *without at the same time increasing the availability of credit*, thereby undoing its initial attempt to reduce aggregate demand. The central bank buys foreign exchange. If those selling the foreign exchange and buying domestic currency, for instance, deposit the funds into the banking system, there will be an increase in the monetary base which will lead to a further expansion of aggregate demand. This can be undone, by raising interest rates further, but that gives rise, in turn, to still more capital inflows. China seems to have managed to sustain an undervalued exchange rate without inflationary pressures, but it arguably has the ability to use direct controls, e.g. on credit expansion, far more effectively than can most market economies.

10. Alternatively, the central bank can sell existing domestic treasury bonds for the same purpose.

11. See Furman and Stiglitz, 1998, vol. 2: 1–114.

12. Even if, in the long run, the mark-up adjusts in response to market conditions, in the short run, many firms use mark-up pricing.

13. However, the exchange rate risk coverage available in the market may be limited, particularly in terms of maturities. Also, the preferred instrument to hedge that risk in developing countries is often central bank or government bonds denominated in foreign currency. If so, in the face of expectations of devaluation, the authorities may be forced to issue more of those bonds, effectively 'socializing' the exchange rate risks. (Indeed, this is equivalent to selling international reserves, but the effect may only come out with a lag.)

14. Moreover, long-term debt, while exposing firms to less interest rate volatility, also means that financial markets are less able to exercise discipline. See Rey and Stiglitz, 1993.
15. Ocampo, 2002.
16. See Calvo, 2001.
17. Reinhart and Rogoff, 2004.
18. For recent defenses of intermediate regimes, see ECLAC, 2000, ch. 8; Williamson, 2000; Ocampo, 2002; and Ffrench-Davis and Larraín, 2003. For interesting reviews of recent controversies on exchange rate regimes, see Frankel, 1999.
19. The phenomenon identified by Hausmann (2000), that the adoption of more flexible exchange is accompanied by rising interest rates, is only a feature of transition periods.
20. See United Nations Economic Commission for Latin America and the Caribbean (ECLAC), 1998, ch. VIII.
21. Ocampo, 2003.
22. One way foreign lenders can reduce the risk of lending in local currency is through diversification. Domestic creditors generally have a concentrated risk in their own currency, but foreign creditors can take advantage of the low correlations between emerging market local markets and reduce the risk of any one local currency investment. See Dodd and Spiegel, 2005.
23. The full equilibrium is more complicated. With a downward-sloping income-generation curve, while flows are decreased, aggregate demand is increased; to restore the economy to the full-employment level of aggregate demand, government expenditure can be cut, and while this may have some effect on capital flows (because of the improved budgetary position of the government), this effect is likely to be smaller than the effect on the income generation curve, so that the cut in government expenditure too will lead to lower capital inflows and an improved external balance.
24. The history of development banks is mixed. There are some successful development banks—CAFÉ, the Andean development bank, is often cited as one. There are others that have poor track records, sometimes with lending affected by politics or corruption rather than by commercial and development objectives.
25. Expectations of future exchange rates as well as future regulations can alter the effectiveness of some of these measures. For example, loosening regulations on investment abroad by residents may actually cause it to strengthen due to increased inflows, if residents expect the reform to strengthen the economy and therefore the exchange rate in the future. Domestic residents will have less of an incentive to take their funds out of the country today if they believe that the regulation is permanent. However, if the door is left open, when expectations change, there can be large and destabilizing outflows by residents. It is interesting that this happened in the otherwise well-behaved Chilean economy in 1998–9, during the contagion of the Asian crisis. (The main capital

outflows from Chile in that biennum were not foreign funds, but funds from the private social security firms.) See Ffrench-Davis and Heriberto Tapia, 2001; Williamson, 2003*b*, ch. 8; Zahler, 2003.

26. See Greenwald and Stiglitz, 1992.
27. 1992.

Chapter 8

1. For a discussion of this case, see Stiglitz, 2002*c*.
2. Collier, 1999.
3. Following this critique, the IMF exhibited a bit more flexibility on this issue for some time. However, later it published a study coming to opposite results than those of Collier, though using questionable statistical methods. See Bulír and Hamann, 2003.
4. See Baker and Weisbrot, 2002.
5. That is why some governments do not allow privatization revenues to be included in the government's *current* budget numbers; they are 'off budget' revenues.
6. Pension liabilities and liabilities associated with deposit insurance usually have revenues that cover the contingency. The problems that the government faces in these cases are when revenues are insufficient. An additional cost is the potential cost of financial crises on deposit insurance.
7. Though in recent years there have been some accusations of politicization of the CBO, when the Democrats controlled Congress, the CBO often provided a check even on a Democratic president.
8. Such differential treatment is sometimes defended on the basis that a government bail-out (assumption of the liability) is more likely in one case than in the other. We know of no statistical basis for such claims; if there were, presumably one should only include an actuarial estimate of the government's future liabilities, which in both Europe and Latin America would be substantially less than the amount borrowed. Moreover, recent government bail-outs of private enterprises in Germany, of the S & Ls in the United States, and the banking system in Japan show that even private indebtedness can represent a contingent liability of government. Again, presumably the appropriate treatment would be to provide some actuarial estimate.
9. The only loss is the actuarial value of the loss in rental payments during the interim—between the period when the loan goes into default and the time the land is resold—presumably a small fraction of the value of the underlying transaction itself.
10. There might be an impact on the government's overall credit rating, but since such bank recapitalization often entails little more than converting a contingent liability (e.g. associated with explicit or implicit deposit insurance) into a more explicit liability, even that is likely to be little affected.

11. See ECLAC, 1998; Ocampo, 2002.

12. Of course, the government still faces a problem of financing the *actual* deficit, not the deficit that would have occurred, had the economy been at full employment. So the government needs to monitor both budget measures.

13. See e.g. Greenwald and Stiglitz, 1989. In the area of financial market regulation, see Honahan and Stiglitz, 2001. See also Stiglitz, 2001*c*.

14. See e.g. Dasgupta and Stiglitz, 1977. See also Ffrench-Davis, 1968; Newbery and Stiglitz, 1984.

15. To some extent, asset market bubbles can be related to market failures such as the absence of futures markets. While, so long as future markets do not extend infinitely far into the future, asset market bubbles may occur, in fact, future markets are very limited, and asset market bubbles can and do frequently occur. In the absence of such futures markets, the differential equations describing short-run market equilibrium (the equality of returns, inclusive of capital gains) can be satisfied along a dynamic path in which such bubbles can appear. See e.g. Hahn, 1966. See also Shell and Stiglitz, 1967.

16. See Demirguc-Kunt and Detragiache, 1999; Kaminsky and Schmukler, 2001; Ocampo, 2002. Elgar and Rodrik, 1998.

17. Again, this problem can also be related to the market failure of the absence of long-term futures markets, which results in an investment coordination problem.

18. Capital adequacy regulations require banks to hold reserves against high risk.

19. In particular, households nearing retirement are likely to be induced to save much more in response to a marked decrease in their individual retirement account.

20. This is referred to as 'sequential decision-making'. Standard statistical theory suggests that it might, in some cases, even pay government to engage in some experiments to 'learn' more about the structure of the economy, or at least to consider explicitly the value of what might be learned from any policy.

21. So that the economy was well described by a stationary stochastic process. (A stationary stochastic process is a process in which the distributions of shocks to the economy stays constant over time.) The function would need to be well understood for stabilization to be reduced to a standard control problem.

22. So stationary stochastic processes don't describe the economy well.

23. More precisely, they affect transactions costs associated with certain changes in courses of actions, making those choices less likely.

24. Alesina and Summers, 1993.

25. See Fischer, 1996. See also Posen, 1998.

26. With inflation targeting, the central bank targets a publicly announced level of inflation. Central banks that do not use explicit inflation targeting might target the money supply or the exchange rate to fight against inflation.

27. There is a line of research which suggests that that is not the case, and has attempted to explain this seeming anomaly. Goodfriend and King (2001), for

example, argue that maintaining price stability guarantees that the economy always operates at its potential output. This result clearly arises from the simplistic assumption that they incorporate only one type of shock in their model. Gaspar and Smets (2002) argue that central banks should focus on price stability because of the time-inconsistency problem associated with ouput stabilization, because of the difficulty in assessing potential output, and because it facilitates agents' learning.

28. See Bhaduri and Nayyar, 1996.
29. For a discussion on the democratic deficit and the unfair rules in the world economy, see Nayyar, 2002*a*.

Chapter 9

1. These set of models are characterized by difference and differential equations that yield oscillations of regular periodicity.
2. See e.g. US Council of Economic Advisors, 1996.
3. See Furman and Stiglitz, 1999.
4. See Kydland and Prescott, 1982. Another example is provided by Hansen, 1985.
5. In the Great Depression, real consumption wages actually increased because of a fall in agricultural prices. In contrast, there is some evidence that real product wages (i.e. the costs of wages for producers) actually decreased during the Great Depression. See Greenwald and Stiglitz, 1988.
6. Alternatively, this could indicate implausible levels of dependence of today's labor supply on expectations concerning interest rates and future wages and prices and/or implausible expectations concerning such variables.
7. For a broader discussion of these issues, see Stiglitz, 1992.
8. In representative agent models, the agent, or consumer, is identical to everyone else in the economy. If the agent prefers good *a* to *b*, everyone in the economy would prefer good *a* to *b*.
9. See e.g. Lucas, 2003.
10. Both the conservative analytics and policy prescriptions were often confused about *transition* and *long-term* effects. For instance, provisions enhancing security of tenure (or better social security benefits) should not lead, in a competitive labor market, to more unemployment, so long as there was wage flexibility at the point of hiring. With such flexibility, the demand and supply of labor should always be equated—there should be no unemployment. Provisions affecting security of tenure might, of course, have costs, adversely affecting the efficiency with which labor is employed, that have to be set against the benefits, the reduced risk faced by workers. Government minimum wage legislation affects directly the hiring market only of very unskilled workers. There are, of course, *natural* sources of wage rigidity—such as the efficiency wage concerns discussed below—but no legislation can make these rigidities disappear. For a discussion in the context of the debate about the employment effects of social security, see Stiglitz, 1999*e*.

11. See Neary and Stiglitz, 1982. As we noted above, cross-country empirical studies suggest that greater wage flexibility may be associated with greater, not less, macro-instability. See Easterly *et al.*, 2000.
12. See e.g. Stiglitz, 1974 and 1982; Yellen, 1984; and Shapiro and Stiglitz, 1984.
13. Stiglitz, 1974.
14. Shapiro and Stiglitz, 1984.
15. The theory of nominal rigidities is in a most unsatisfactory state. Several authors have emphasized the presence of costs of adjustment to prices as an explanation for the failure of prices to adjust. But there are also costs of adjustments to quantities, and they are often far larger. (Indeed, the very terminology of this literature, referring to the price adjustment costs as menu costs, serves to deride their importance.) See Mankiw, 1985; and Akerlof and Yellen, 1985. Typically, the smaller the adjustment to prices, the larger the adjustment to quantities; because the costs of adjustment of quantities typically are of an order of magnitude greater than the costs of adjustment of prices, one should see more rigidities in quantities and less in prices. Hence, menu costs simply do not provide a plausible explanation of nominal wage and price rigidities. Greenwald and Stiglitz (1989) provide an explanation based on the relative magnitude of uncertainties that arise from the consequences of price changes (where rival responses are often unpredictable) being larger than those that arise from quantity responses (where the risk is mainly of larger or smaller than desired accumulations of inventory). More recent discussions of behavioral macroeconomics have abandoned the attempt to provide a rational explanation of price and wage rigidity, and returned to the older themes of 'money illusion', leading individuals to resist wage and price cuts in nominal terms. See e.g. Akerlof, 2002.
16. Though because of problems of coordination, there can also be nominal rigidities. See e.g. Stiglitz, 1985.
17. See Greenwald and Stiglitz, 1998.
18. See Stiglitz, 1999f. Moreover, with wages and prices both adjusting, real wages may adjust relatively slowly, so that flexibility in nominal wages and prices need not translate into flexibility in real wages. See Solow and Stiglitz, 1968.
19. This market failure can be related to the previous one: if expectations of future wages and prices depend on current wages and prices in an insufficiently flexible way, it means, in effect, that there is not full flexibility of wages and prices (as perceived today), and hence markets cannot fully adjust.
20. Neary and Stiglitz, 1983.
21. The reason is simple: what limits the size of the economic multiplier are 'leakages', e.g. increases in income that are saved and lead to increases in consumption in later periods. But if there is unemployment in the later period, the increased consumption in that period leads to increased incomes in that period, and individuals, rationally anticipating this, are accordingly more willing to consume more today.

22. See e.g. Shiller, 2000.

23. This was recognized long ago in the growth literature. See e.g. Hahn, 1966; Shell and Stiglitz, 1967. Moreover, when there are multiple equilibria, the economy may exhibit considerable volatility *even with rational expectations extending infinitely far into the future*. See e.g. Stiglitz, 1973. Also see the literature on sunspot equilibria: Shell and Cass, 1989; in short, even rational expectations ensure stability—smooth convergence to a well-defined long-run equilibrium state—only under highly restrictive conditions.

24. See e.g. Kindleberger, 1978.

25. The pattern of entry into such markets may also be affected by herding behavior, as each market participant, seeing others making the investment, infers that he or she has positive information about the prospects of the market. On the other hand, risk aversion in winner-take-all markets might be expected to lead to underinvestment in such markets. The repeated pattern of excessive investment is consistent with hypotheses concerning irrational exuberance, especially of entrepreneurs.

26. Alba *et al.*, 1998. On the theory of looting, see Akerlof and Romer, 1993. Even when liberalization does not provide greater scope for looting, liberalization reduces the franchise value of banks, and this leads to more risk taking. See Helmann *et al.*, 2001, 2002, and 1998.

27. Note that these redistributive effects simply cannot be analyzed within the context of a representative agent model.

28. Indeed, before the development of the modern theory of asymmetric information, some economists dismissed capital market imperfections as unimportant—they arose from the existence of transactions costs, which, in this view, were to be treated no differently from any other category of costs. See Stigler, 1967.

29. With equity rationing, firms can raise only limited amounts of new capital through the issue of new equity. As a result, risk is not as widely dispersed in the economy, which results in the effects of shocks to one part of the economy not being dissipated throughout the economy as much as would otherwise be the case. See also Greenwald and Stiglitz, 1990b.

30. There is one other reason that a firm can be liquidity constrained—even if it has positive net worth; lenders may believe that they cannot *enforce* a credit contract, so that even if the firm has the resources to repay (on average) the loan, the lender cannot extract the money.

31. See e.g. Akerlof, 2002.

32. It is important to recognize that quantities (capacity utilization) and prices (the real wage) may adjust simultaneously in a more general dynamic model. See Bhaduri and Marglin, 1990. The authors suggest that the Keynesian analytical framework for macroeconomics has a much wider theoretical as well as political range than is usually recognized. It can be extended beyond the conventional Keynesian model of 'cooperative capitalism' to the Marxian model of

'profit-squeeze', or even the conservative model of relying on 'supply-side' stimulus through high profitability and a low real wage.

33. Some developing countries have become highly dollarized, with prices in local currency adjusting quickly to inflation in the domestic currency.

34. See Solow and Stiglitz, 1968.

35. See Burnside *et al.*, 1993. Also, Solow, 1964.

Chapter 10

1. This was in spite of the fact that a close look at both theory and evidence provided a more skeptical view about the effects on growth, stability, distribution, and welfare more generally, as discussed below. Since the beginning of the new millennium, however, the broad consensus in support of these 'reforms' has frayed, especially as Latin America has faced another 'lost' half-decade. The region's GDP per capita in 2003 was 1.5% lower than its 1997 level. See Ocampo, 2004*a*; Stiglitz, 2003*b*. Even the case for trade liberalization has been questioned. See Rodríguez and Rodrik, 2001. Problems in deregulation and privatization in the United States and Europe, as well as in developing countries, have increased the skepticism towards these other items in the reform agenda. See Stiglitz, 2002*c* and 2003*a*.

2. The Asia-Pacific Economic Cooperation embraces 21 countries on both sides of the Pacific Ocean, including the United States.

3. It is important to recognize that the debate has focused primarily on restrictions affecting volatile short term capital flows—not foreign direct investment. While advocates of capital market liberalization sometimes argue that without capital market liberalization, countries will not be able to attract foreign direct investment, there is strong evidence rejecting this contention, as attested by India, China, and Chile, which all attracted greenfield FDI in parallel with capital controls. See the discussion below.

4. There have now been several accounts of the East Asia crisis. An account of the role of the IMF and the US Treasury is provided by Blustein (2001). See also ch. 4 of Stiglitz (2002*c*); Furman and Stiglitz, 1998; IMF, 1998; World Bank, 1999.

5. In the capital account crises of the 1990s, official financing totaled $8.7 billion in Argentina (Apr. 1995), $41.8 billion in Brazil (Dec. 1998), $36.1 billion in Indonesia (Nov. 1997), $58.3 billion in Korea (Dec. 1997), $51.8 billion in Mexico (Feb. 1995), $1.5 billion in the Philippines (July 1997), $17.1 billion in Thailand (Aug. 1997) and $4.5 billion in Turkey (July 1994) (see Ghosh *et al.*, 2002). On 20 July 1998 the IMF announced a total official financing of $22.6 billion for the Russian Federation (IMF Press release 98/31, 20 July 1998 and *Russia Reform Monitor*, No. 480, 21 July 1998). On 28 July 1999 an additional $4.5 billions of credit was announced after the failure of the 1998 agreement (IMF Press Release 99/35, 28 July 1999).

6. See Rodrik and Velasco, 2000.
7. See Kaplan and Rodrik, 2002; Wyplosz, 2002; Joshi, 2003.
8. Prasad *et al.*, 2003.
9. The case for capital market liberalization was often based on a conventional neoclassical model that ignores market failures and assumes markets allocate resources efficiently. Any restrictions would accordingly interfere with allocative efficiency.
10. Most of these market failures are related to problems of information asymmetries. See e.g. Stiglitz, 2002*d*.
11. See Diaz-Alejandro, 1985; Devlin, 1989.
12. For an elaboration of this point, see Stiglitz, 1989*a*, and Lucas, 1990.
13. Keynes had referred to investor sentiments as 'animal spirits', emphasizing their unpredictability. By contrast, many of the advocates of capital market liberalization emphasized the *rationality* of markets, using models *assuming* rational expectations. There is increasing research emphasizing the irrationality of markets. See e.g. Shiller, 2000. But even if markets are 'rational' in the short run, unless there is a full set of futures markets extending infinitely far into the future, there may be 'bubbles' in the short run. Even herd behavior may be consistent with rational expectations; see Chamley, 2004. Stiglitz (2004) shows that in an overlapping generations model with rational expectations, CML may lead to increased volality.
14. Such data depict, of course, only the actual patterns of capital flows. They show convincingly that capital flows have not been counter-cyclical. Other studies described below show that there have been large shifts in the willingness to lend or invest, caused largely by changes external to the developing country in question.
15. Non-tradables are goods and services for the domestic market and not for export, and which do not directly compete with imports.
16. The Thai example illustrates that some of the adverse effects of short-term speculative capital inflows might have been mitigated by more extensive government intervention *elsewhere* in the economy, e.g. through bank regulations on real estate collateral or capital gains taxation. This will be discussed later in this chapter.
17. The problem could, of course, occur even if governments borrow domestically, but governments typically have far more control over domestic financial markets.
18. The primary balance (which can be either in deficit or surplus) is defined as the fiscal balance (total income minus expenditures), other than interest payments.
19. CML would help balance transitory differences between output and expenditure, thereby attenuating the adjustment to permanent changes of relative prices. See Prasad *et al.*, 2003.
20. Kose *et al.*, 2003. It is important to recognize, however, that the evidence that they present is only very indirect. They ask: Is consumption volatility reduced

as capital market integration is increased? Any observed correlation may be spurious. They do not actually verify whether the capital flows themselves act in a counter-cyclical way.

21. Prasad *et al.* (2003) find that consumption volatility has increased with CML in 'financially integrated' developing countries.

22. The market failures behind irrational exuberance, unwarranted pessimism, and herding behavior will be discussed in the next chapter.

23. See also Ffrench-Davis and Ocampo, 2001; Reisen, 2003; Williamson, 2003*b*.

24. Some economists and practitioners argue that derivatives will decrease the effectiveness of capital controls. This will be discussed in Chapter 13.

25. Dodd, 2003.

26. IMF, 1998, ch. 1. For empirical evidence contrary to the IMF study, see Dungey *et al.*, 2002.

27. Prasad *et al.*, 2003.

28. Selling short means selling something you don't own (by, in effect, borrowing it from someone who owns it) with the hope of buying it back at a lower price.

29. High interest rates lower firm profitability. At the time of the Asian crisis, many firms in Hong Kong were highly leveraged, so that the impact of high rates could have had a devastating effect on stock prices.

30. Standard & Poor's downgraded Hong Kong's long- and short-term sovereign ratings to $A/A - 1$, from $A + /A - 1+$, on 31 August (Economist Intelligence Unit, 1998).

31. See Calvo *et al.*, 1993 and 1994.

32. There are other reasons for contagion. One is *trade*: an economic downturn in one country reduces the demand for imports, which hurts the country from which the goods come. This played an important role in the spread of the East Asia crisis from one East Asian country to another, given the high level of trade interdependency. The extent and consequences of the trade linkages seem to have been greatly underestimated by the IMF. It explains why the 'beggar-thy-self' policies that they pushed had such a devastating effect on the region. See Stiglitz, 1999*a*.

A second source of contagion arises from institutional imperfections—there are a limited number of institutions investing in developing countries. Risks are not fully diversified. And risks are often magnified through leverage. Thus the 1998 ruble crisis had repercussions for Brazil not because the existence of problems in Russia changed expectations concerning Brazil nor because of trade inter-linkages, but because a few institutions were heavily invested in both Brazil and Russia; the losses in Russia forced a portfolio rebalancing which resulted in sales of Brazilian assets. The various forms of contagion may be intermixed. Knowing that there are institutional imperfections, Brazilian investors may worry that a problem in Russia may lead to a problem in Brazil; they accordingly try to sell their Brazilian assets. Their beliefs are self-confirming.

33. Of course, one has to make sure that the regulations in place allow the eventual repatriation of profits and the original investment.
34. See World Bank, 1999.
35. Because these decisions involve trade-offs over time (e.g. individuals are deciding whether to consume more today or more in the future), these are referred to as *intertemporal decisions*. For a discussion of balance sheet effects, see Krugman, 2000; Aghion *et al.*, 2001. The general theory is set forth in Greenwald and Siglitz, 1990*a*, 1993*a*, 1993*b*, and 2003.
36. See IMF, 1998 and Rodrik and Velasco, 2000.
37. See Stiglitz, 2004.
38. One should contrast this analysis with that of the IMF study by Prasad *et al.*, 2003.
39. In the standard growth models, the long-term rate of growth in income per capita is determined solely by the rate of technological progress; growth in the short term is also affected by the rate of savings/investment.
40. Devlin *et al.*, 1995.
41. Large inflows during boom periods often lead to an overvalued currency, making imported goods cheaper, and encouraging consumption.
42. In this paragraph, we build on the research presented in Ffrench-Davis and Reisen, 1998, particularly in the 'Introduction' by the two editors and in the chapter by Andras Uthoff and Daniel Titelman, 'The Relation between Foreign and National Savings under Financial Liberalization'.
43. See e.g. Elgar and Rodrik, 1998. Two surveys of the contrasting results in the literature are Eichengreen, 2001; and Edison *et al.*, 2002. For a discussion on identification problems focused on Latin American countries, see Ffrench-Davis and Reisen (1998) and Frenkel (1998). Ocampo and Taylor (1998) give a theoretical perspective on the effects of liberalizing both trade and capital markets.
44. Maddison, 2001.
45. The issue of whether the imposition of capital controls *discourages* FDI remains mired in econometric and statistical difficulties. The literature is accordingly inconclusive. See e.g. Mody and Murshid, 2002; Montiel and Reinhart, 1999; Hernandez *et al.*, 2001; Carlson and Hernandez, 2002. The impact of capital account restrictions on interest rates will be discussed in Chapter 12.
46. Furman and Stiglitz, 1998.
47. There are still other mechanisms by which poverty may be increased. Higher volatility may increase unemployment, not only because of the slowness in adjustments, but also because, even with rapid adjustments, it may lead to an increase in the *equilibrium* unemployment rate. As we note below, in the Shapiro–Stiglitz efficiency wage model, an increase in volatility which shortens the expected lifetime of employer/employee relationships, unemployment must increase to induce workers not to shirk.
48. Insecurity is highlighted as one of the three central elements of poverty in developing countries in World Bank, 2001; see also Rodrik, 2001.

49. See e.g. Rodrik, 1997, and Stiglitz, 2002*a*.
50. We'll discuss the responsiveness of capital flows to interest rates in greater detail in Chapter 12.
51. Orszag and Stiglitz, 2002.
52. Goldman Sachs, 2002.
53. It is important to recognize that, in using the term market failure, we do not mean to suggest that there are some easy improvements in markets (eliminating these failures), after which capital market liberalization would be desirable. The market failures are endemic: they are limitations in the way that markets work *relative to some idealized world*, say with perfect information. Information will always be imperfect, so that market failures, in this sense, cannot be eliminated. Similarly, markets alone will never be able to undertake full intertemporal smoothing (unless there are individuals living infinitely long), since the generation alive at one date can never engage in a transaction with a generation alive at a much later date.

Chapter 11

1. To put it into the jargon of economics, they are not constrained Pareto efficient; there are government interventions that take into account the same limitations of information and the costs of acquiring further information, which, in principle at least, could make some people better off without making anyone worse off. See e.g. Stiglitz, 1989*b*. The general theory of the second best argues that whenever there are multiple distortions, eliminating one distortion may make matters worse. See Lancaster and Lipsey, 1957.
2. As already noted, it is likely that the design of the policy response increased the magnitude of the externality. For example, during the Asian crisis, the IMF explicitly argued for increasing interest rates to defend the local currency. This helped protect those with large foreign-denominated borrowings, but had huge adverse effects on firms that had prudently borrowed in local currency.
3. The IMF implicitly recognized the importance of this externality during the East Asia crisis, when it urged greater information about the total supply of outstanding short-term debt. In a standard competitive equilibrium model, such quantitative information would be of no relevance.
4. In the end, in 1998, some months after the massive bail-out that failed to stabilize the exchange rate, the US Treasury helped coordinate a rollover of Korean loans.
5. The problem was exacerbated by the political illegitimacy of the privatization, which meant that there might be long-run pressures to renationalize. Only by taking money out of the country could the oligarchs truly protect their ill-gotten wealth.
6. There are many examples of this kind of multiple equilibria, and such models have played an increasing role in explaining crisis. Among the early examples

was that of Diamond and Dybvig (1983), explaining bank runs. Of course, coordination failure is not the only source of instability or inefficiency, and with these sources of instability, it may pay investors to take their money out of the country or to engage in asset stripping, even in the absence of a coordination failure.

7. In addition, a switch to fiscal stimulation from monetary stimulation may affect growth, depending on whether public expenditures are efficiently spent on public investment.

8. See the classic Kindleberger, 2000 (first published 1978); and the more recent Shiller, 2000.

9. See Banerjee, 1992, and Bikhchandani *et al.*, 1992. For an application to portfolio allocations on international stock markets, see Calvo and Mendoza, 2000; Chamley, 2004; Caplin and Lehay, 1994.

10. See Ocampo, 2003*b*.

11. While the discovery of the foreign exchange position of the Thai central bank triggered the crisis, even if the Thai central bank had not been taking the positions it had, it is likely that there would eventually have been a crisis. The puzzle is why the market did not seem to recognize this. The stock and real estate markets had boomed in the mid-1990s, the exchange rate had appreciated, imports had surged, generating an increase in the external deficit, and financing—as recognized only *ex post* by the IMF and financial markets—was dangerously short term.

12. See e.g. Shiller, 2000. Much earlier, Hahn, 1966, and Shell and Stiglitz, 1967, showed that there could be multiple paths consistent with rational behavior *in the short run*; without capital markets extending *infinitely* far into the future, the economy could exhibit high levels of dynamic instability. While herding behavior is often attributed to investor myopia, these results suggest that bubbles may arise so long as investors do not look infinitely far into the future. However, even when investors look infinitely far into the future, it may not be possible for them to predict (on the basis of rational expectations alone) how the economy will evolve, if, for instance, there are multiple paths consistent with rational expectations. See Stiglitz, 1973.

13. Bank regulations in the advanced industrial countries encourage this. Long-term lending to developing countries is viewed as riskier than short-term lending, so banks have to hold more capital to satisfy capital adequacy requirements.

14. The problem is related perhaps to the 'irrationality' of market participants. They consider the implicit insurance premium excessive, given their view of the low probability of a devaluation of the currency. But why borrowers should believe that their estimate of the probability is more accurate than the markets' is not clear. There is a further difficulty: even when cover is obtained, there is a risk that the insurer will not be able to honor his commitment. The economics of information has provided explanations for the absence of

insurance markets, associated particularly with the existence of information asymmetries. The cost of ascertaining whether an insurance firm will honor its commitment to provide insurance is another explanation of the absence of insurance.

15. See Dodd and Spiegel (2005) for an analysis of risk diversification in developing country currency markets.

16. Those who defended the role of the government in the bail-out (and who resisted allegations that underlying the publicly orchestrated privately financed bail-out was crony capitalism and corporate mis-governance, American, rather than East Asian, style) did so because they believed LTCM posed a global threat. For a discussion of the LTCM bail-out, see Stiglitz, 2002c and 2003a.

17. See Greenwald and Stiglitz, 2003, and the references cited there; or Majluf and Myers, 1984. In developing countries, there are additional reasons for the lack of use of equity markets, such as the absence of a legal framework to ensure the rights of shareholders, including minority shareholders.

18. When information and contracting are incomplete, long-term relationships are at the heart of well-functioning markets. These long-term relationships (and the reputational capital which underlies them) motivate each party to do the 'right' thing: employees not to shirk on the job, employers to treat their workers decently. But the greater risk under open capital markets implies that the life expectancy of jobs and firms, and thus the labor relationship, will be far shorter than it otherwise would have been. Efficiency wage concerns force higher wages and higher *equilibrium* unemployment. See e.g. Shapiro and Stiglitz, 1984.

19. Still other channels are discussed at greater length below.

20. Typically, it is argued, bankruptcy does not result in the destruction of physical capital, but only its reorganization in more productive ways. But when there is systemic bankruptcy associated with high interest rates and/or a major economic slowdown, the prospects for efficient reorganization are diminished, and the chances of a delayed reorganization are enhanced. Without adequate oversight, there is a real risk of asset stripping during the extended period of reorganization.

Chapter 12

1. See Weitzman (1974), for a general discussion. In the context of trade interventions, see Dasgupta and Stiglitz (1977).

2. Only firms that relied on borrowing directly from foreign banks would be unaffected.

3. Exclusions included borrowing for approved purposes if certain conditions were met: e.g. a minimum maturity, and a maximum cost on the associated debt.

4. The URR averaged approximately 3% for one-year loans in Chile, and 13.6% for one-year loans and 6.4% for three-year loans in Colombia from 1994–8, significantly higher than the level often discussed for an international Tobin tax.

5. The phenomena was seen in many countries, including South Korea, Indonesia, and Thailand in 1997 prior to the Asian crisis; Mexico prior to the Mexican crisis; and the Czech Republic in the mid-1990s.

6. For papers which support the effectiveness of these regulations in Chile, see Agosin, 1998; Agosin and Ffrench-Davis, 2001; Larraín *et al.*, 2000; Le Fort and Lehmann, 2003; Palma, 2002; and Ffrench-Davis and Tapia, 2004. For a more mixed view, see Ariyoshi *et al.*, 2000; De Gregorio *et al.*, 2000; Laurens, 2000; Valdés-Prieto and Soto, 1998. Similarly, for strong views on their positive effects in Colombia, see Ocampo and Tovar, 1998; Ocampo and Tovar, 2003; and Villar and Rincón, 2003. For a more mixed view, see Cárdenas and Barrera, 1997; and Cárdenas and Steiner, 2000.

7. In some of these studies, the URR is not included as a determinant of interest rate spreads, but only as an additional factor affecting flows. There are two other common flaws. One relates to the treatment of changes in the external supply of funds; the other refers to the domestic macroeconomic absorption of different types of inflows. These two effects are controlled for in Ffrench-Davis and Tapia, 2004, where the URR is found to have had a significant effect on net inflows during capital surges. The indeterminacy of the effects of the URR on exchange rates may reflect the difficulties inherent in exchange rate modelling. See Williamson, 2000.

8. Ocampo and Tovar, 1998 and 2003.

9. Villar and Rincón, 2003.

10. Palma, 2002.

11. See Rodrik and Velasco, 2000.

12. Ringgit use was restricted to domestic transactions by residents. It became illegal to hold ringgit deposits abroad, and all such deposits held by nationals had to be repatriated. Trade transactions had to be settled in foreign currency. Ringgit deposits in the domestic financial system held by non-residents were not convertible into foreign currency for one year.

13. The levy had a decreasing rate for investments held for longer periods, and there was no tax on investments held for more than one year. For new capital inflows, an exit tax on capital gains was established (at 10%), with a higher rate (of 30%) for capital that stayed in the country for less than a year. The flat rate introduced in September 1999 was also set at 10%.

14. For a more detailed analysis of the Malaysian controls, see Khor (2004).

15. See Kaplan and Rodrik (2002) for the NBER. See Ariyoshi *et al.* (2000); Ötker-Robe (2000); Rajaraman (2003); and Joshi (2003) for additional evidence on the effectiveness of these regulations.

16. See Dornbusch, 2001.

17. The liability structure is defined as the make-up of outstanding debt—the amount of debt outstanding, the maturities of the debt, the interest coupons, etc.

18. IMF (2000).

19. Since a capital surge generates expansionary effects through three different channels—the accumulation of international reserves, an appreciation of the exchange rate, and a reduction in interest rates—the index weights the trends of these three indicators by their standard deviation during the period analyzed.

20. The level of the URR may account for this result. Valdés-Prieto and Soto (1998) find evidence of a 'threshold effect', which would explain why these regulations were only effective in reducing capital flows in 1995–6. (Of course, as we pointed out previously, one of the difficulties in this area is the counterfactual: what would the flows have been but for the URR? While the flows may have increased, they might have increased even more in the absence of the URR.)

21. See Edwards, 1999a; Dornbusch and Edwards, 1991; Dornbusch, 1998; Cuddington, 1986.

22. *The Economist*, 3 May 2003c.

23. After softening the controls in September 1999, Malaysia suffered immediate outflows of 5.2 billion ringgit, with an additional 3.1 billion flowing out of the country during the rest of the year. The net inflow of funds in the first quarter of 2000 was 8.5 billion ringgit, roughly equal to the total amount of funds lost after the lifting of the controls (Bank Negara Malaysia, 2001b). Throughout 2000, private long-term capital inflows increased and foreign direct investments remained stable (Bank Negara Malaysia, 2001a). Changes in levels of inflows may be more attributable to changes in the overall magnitude of capital flows from developed to less developed countries than to changes in the relative attractiveness of investments among developing countries.

24. When a currency weakens excessively, by say 30%, and then strengthens so that the total devaluation is only around 20%, the currency is said to overshoot. For example, according to a poll of the Citibank trading floor in 1989, traders believed that interest rate and currency markets react to bad news by overshooting by an average of 50%.

25. Malaysia, for example, was able to completely shut down the offshore market in ringgits.

26. The problem is exacerbated when there are prospects of, say, a government bail-out of a bank; the public bears some of the downside risk of the foreign exchange exposure.

27. Calvo, 2002; and Hausmann, 1999. See also Eichengreen and Hausmann, 1999.

28. We use the term 'domestic financial dollarization' to refer to the *use* of dollar-denominated assets and liabilities, not, as in Ecuador, the substitution of the local currency with the use of dollars (which we call dollarization, without further adjectives).

29. Indexing entails linking the price of the domestic asset to inflation: as inflation increases, the price of domestic assets increases proportionally.
30. Zahler, 2003.
31. Government regulations allowing for swaps—an exchange of assets, say, between the pension funds of one country and that of another—could help diversify risk, without putting any pressure on the exchange rate, and without subjecting countries to pro-cyclical capital flows.
32. See Rogoff, 2002; Johnson and Mitton, 2001; Rajan and Zingales, 2001; Forbes, 2004.
33. It is not only hard to ascertain the magnitude of the corruption, but also its costs. The allocative effects are associated with the distortions in production. But there are broader systemic consequences, for instance, associated with the legitimacy of government.
34. Ocampo, 2003b; Ocampo, 2002; Rajaraman, 2003; Reddy, 2001.
35. For cross-country evidence, see China and Ito, 2002.
36. The contrast with, say, Mexico, is marked. The government bail-outs were extremely costly to the government (13% of GDP), and even after the 'restructuring', there is an inadequate supply of credit, especially to small and medium-sized enterprises.
37. Forbes, 2003; Edwards, 1999.
38. Two methodological issues are also important: how SMEs are defined, and what is considered a financially constrained situation.
39. See e.g. Harvie and Lee (2002a).
40. Ffrench-Davis, 2002.
41. One such policy is the US Community Reinvestment Act which requires banks in poorer areas to lend a small proportion of their portfolio to local firms. Based on this idea, developing countries can require financial institutions to lend a small proportion of their portfolio to SMEs, either through tax incentives or direct regulations.
42. See Edwards, 1999a, 1999b; Dornbusch and Edwards, 1991; Dornbusch, 1998; De Gregorio et al., 2000. See also Harrison et al., 2002; and Dooley, 1996.
43. However, one can make them reportable to authorities, and one can make such reporting requirements enforceable by requiring reporting for these contracts to be enforceable in court, including having standing in bankruptcy court.
44. Note that the URR is applied to all foreign capital inflows, while this reserve requirement would be applied only to the liabilities held by domestic financial institutions.
45. We have argued, however, that there are social costs associated with these foreign exchange exposures. The tax or risk-adjusted capital adequacy requirement, if appropriately designed, would simply compensate for these external social costs. If the government wished to promote further lending to small or medium-sized enterprises, this should be done through explicit programs.
46. It is, of course, possible that some firms borrow exclusively from abroad. If only a few firms do so (with limited aggregate exposure), their default in the event,

say, of a large change in the exchange rate would have much less of an effect than if those firms borrowed domestically. There would be no collateral damage to domestic financial institutions except through the impact of the bankruptcy on the firms' suppliers. But in the unlikely event that large numbers of firms borrow extensively from abroad (and not from domestic financial institutions), there can still be systemic effects. Rajan and Zingales 2001; Forbes, 2004.

47. To do so, the government would need to add all the longs (investments) and shorts (borrowings) to get the net position and ascertain the actual extent of foreign-denominated borrowing.

48. For an analysis of these issues, see World Bank, 1999a; and Bhattacharya and Stiglitz, 2000.

49. Barth *et al.*, 2001.

50. Basle capital adequacy requirements recommend that reserve requirements be held against risky bank assets.

51. For recent analyses of these issues and policy options for managing them, see BIS, 2001; Borio *et al.*, 2001; Clerc *et al.*, 2001; and Turner, 2002.

Chapter 13

1. *The Economist*, 2003b.

2. *The Economist*, 2003a.

3. One of the conclusions from that chapter is that different interventions have different benefits and costs associated with them. The pertinent question is which tools are most appropriate for each country, given its economic structure, administrative capacity, and institutional framework.

4. Edwards, 1999a.

5. Rogoff and Prasad, 2003.

6. Johnston, 1998; Prasad *et al.*, 2003.

7. Some proponents of capital market liberalization suggest that open capital markets encourage the development of good institutions. In fact, this was a question posed in the recent article in the *Financial Times* by the authors of the IMF study, referred to below. The argument is similar to the one used in Russia in the early 1990s: that institutions would develop once other free market reforms were in place. And the example of Russia shows how miserably this argument can fail. There is very little evidence that deregulation and liberalization on their own encourage the growth of good institutions. In fact, Hoff and Stiglitz show that capital market liberalization may actually impede the development of the rule of law (see Hoff and Stiglitz, 2004).

8. More generally, good public and corporate governance and well-developed markets and institutions may contribute to economic efficiency; the issue at hand, however, is the extent to which they contribute to economic stability. For instance, the development of derivative markets may increase efficiency, but may also have actually contributed to instability. See Dodd, 2003.

9. Even before that, despite its strong financial and regulatory system, the United States had a mini-financial crisis; the S & L débâcle that came to a head in 1989, and cost American taxpayers between $100 and $200 billion.

10. There was not only massive misallocation of resources during the bubble, but the loss of output after the bubble broke in 2001—the disparity between the economy's potential and actual growth—was enormous. There was also massive 'disguised' unemployment—evidenced by data on discouraged workers, an increase in the number of individuals on disability, a decrease in labor force participation, and an increase in the number of individuals working part time because they could not get full-time jobs. See Stiglitz, 2003*a*.

11. Sometimes a *strong rule of law* is added to the trilogy of prerequisites for capital market liberalization. What is meant by a strong rule of law and the connections between that and the consequences of capital market liberalization are often not clearly delineated.

12. Volcker, 1998.

13. Growth in the post-liberalization period was lower than in the pre-liberalization period, though there are many factors that may account for this.

14. Bakker and Chapple, 2002.

15. Chile, for instance, might be well advised with the next surge of capital to reinstitute the URR tax described in Chapter 12. Faced with capital inflows and a large appreciation of the exchange rate, at the end of 2004 Colombia instituted a tax on capital that stays less than a year in the country.

16. See e.g. Harris, 1999.

17. Ndikumana and Boyce, 2003.

18. See Pastor, 1990; Boyce and Zarsky, 1988.

19. See section on Coordination Failures in Chapter 11.

20. *Wall Street Journal*, 1998.

21. Ariyoshi *et al.*, 2000.

22. See Ocampo, 2003*b*; and Reddy, 2001.

23. As stated earlier, those who supported the bail-out claimed that the failure of this one hedge fund could destabilize the entire international financial system.

24. One way in which reporting requirements can be enforced is not to allow court enforcement of unreported derivative contracts. There can be restrictions on lending by domestic financial institutions to firms and individuals with large (net) derivative positions.

Chapter 14

1. Of course, even in the short and medium term, growth will in general depend on the savings rate.

2. As economies move from within their production possibilities schedule towards the 'frontier'.

3. Recall the discussion of Chapter 2, where we discussed two alternative views: the economy as a *robust* spring, such that the further you push it down, the

stronger the recovery; and the economy as a *frail* spring, such that when the economy is pulled down too far, it becomes distorted and never returns to where it otherwise would have been. The evidence is that the economy is more like a frail than a robust spring. Econometrically, this means the economy exhibits *close to unit root:* lowering GDP by 5% today is likely to result in GDP 20 years from now being close to 5% lower.

4. There is some evidence that other factors of productions are, as well, affected negatively. For instance, the quality of labor may be lowered with unemployment. Moreover, public authorities are likely to reduce investments in technology and infrastructure if overall expenditures are cut as tax revenues fall and if more expenditures get directed towards buffering those affected by the crisis. Authorities' efforts to focus on long-term goals is undermined.

5. e.g. through establishing independent central banks focusing on inflation.

6. The fact, noted earlier, that the 'optimal' inflation rate may be greater than zero suggests that this may in fact be the case. Note that taxes like the VAT which induce relatively limited distortions in more advanced countries are likely to be far more distortionary in developing countries, simply because so much of GDP typically escapes taxation.

7. *Ex ante*, it may not always be possible to ascertain whether the economy is in a situation where higher interest rates will lead to a strengthened or weakened currency. The discussion of this section has emphasized, however, that there is at least a risk that monetary tightening will adversely affect exchange rates.

8. Especially when governments fail to pursue aggressively output stabilization policies.

9. Greenwald and Stiglitz (2003) explain why capital markets are *not* auction markets, with capital allocated to those willing to pay the most. Those willing to pay the highest interest rates may be those most likely not to repay the loan. If there were no problems with repayment and no imperfections or asymmetries of information, then the auction model might be appropriate.

10. Empirical studies have often been highly misleading. Periods of high inflation are often associated with real disturbances to the economy, such as the oil price shocks of the 1970s; these real shocks have real consequences, and in some cases, those consequences may be borne disproportionately by the poor. The question is not whether in inflationary episodes the poor have fared poorly, but whether, given whatever shocks, the poor fared better in those countries that maintained robust employment relative to those who fought inflation hardest.

11. There are at least four possible explanations for these seemingly perverse outcomes. The first is that policy-makers have not fully learned the lessons of how to stabilize the economy. The second focused on *political economy:* it is not a matter of knowledge, but of incentives. Conservative economists are more concerned with guaranteeing that creditors in the advanced industrial countries get repaid than in ensuring that the developing country remains at full employment. Third, capital and financial market liberalization has increased developing countries' exposure to risk. Note that even if economic management

had improved, the observed increase in stability would be limited. And finally, as the economy becomes more stable, firms are willing to undertake more risks—for instance, higher debt equity ratios—possibly largely undoing the original effects. But note that, in this case, there are still benefits from the improved 'ability' to manage the economy, not manifested in lower variability in output so much as in increased allocative efficiency and growth resulting from the higher debt equity ratios. In contrast to these experiences in developing countries, there is some evidence that economic volatility in the United States has been reduced: since World War II, expansions have been longer and downturns shorter.

References

Aarts, Leo, R. Burkhauser, and P. de Jong (1992), 'The Dutch Disease: Lessons for U.S. Disability Policy', *Regulation*, 15/2: 75–86.

Aghion, Philippe, P. Bacchetta, and A. Banerjee (2001), 'A Corporate Balance Sheet Approach to Currency Crises', CEPR Discussion Papers, 3092.

Agosin, Manuel (1998), 'Capital Inflow and Investment Performance: Chile in the 1990s', in Ffrench-Davis and Reisen (1998).

——and Ricardo Ffrench-Davis (2001), 'Managing Capital Inflows in Chile', in Stephany Griffith-Jones, Manuel F. Montes, and Anwar Nasution (eds.), *Short-Term Capital Flows and Economic Crises* (New York: Oxford University Press/UNU/WIDER).

Akerlof, George (2002), 'Behavioral Macroeconomics and Macroeconomic Behavior', *American Economic Review*, 92/3: 411–33.

——W. Dickens, and G. Perry (1996), 'The Macroeconomics of Low Inflation', *Brookings Papers on Economic Activity*, 1: 1–59.

————(2000), 'Near Rational Wage and Price Setting and the Long Run Phillips Curve', *Brookings Papers on Economic Activity*, 1: 1–60.

——and P. Romer (1993), 'Looting the Economic Underworld of Bankruptcy for Profit', *Brookings Papers on Economic Activity*, 2: 1–73.

——and J. Yellen (1985), 'A Near-Rational Model of the Business Cycle, with Wage and Price Inertia', *Quarterly Journal of Economics*, 100/5: 823–38.

Akyuz, Yilmaz, and A. Cornford (2002), 'Capital Flows to Developing Countries and Reform of the International Financial System', in Deepak Nayyar (ed.), *Governing Globalization: Issues and Institutions* (Oxford: Oxford University Press).

Alba, Pedro, and A. Bhattacharya, S. Claessens, S. Ghosh, and L. Hernandez (1998), 'Volatility and Contagion in a Financially Integrated World: Lessons from East Asia's Recent Experience', World Bank Policy Research Working Paper, 2008.

Alesina, Alberto, and L. Summers (1993), 'Central Bank Independence and Macroeconomic Performance: Some Comparative Evidence', *Journal of Money, Credit and Banking*, 25/2: 151–62.

Ariyoshi, Akira, J. Canales-Kriljenko, and K. Habermeier *et al.* (2000), 'Capital Controls: Country Experiences with their Use and Liberalization', IMF Occasional Paper, 190 (Washington: International Monetary Fund).

References

Arnott, R., B. Greenwald, and J. Stiglitz (1994), 'Information and Economic Efficiency', *Information Economics and Policy*, 6/1: 77–88.

Atkinson, Anthony B. (1970), 'On the Measurement of Inequality', *Journal of Economic Theory*, 2/3: 244–63.

——and J. Stiglitz (1980), *Lectures on Public Economics* (New York: McGraw-Hill).

Attanasio, Orazio, P. Goldberg, and E. Kyriazidou (2000), 'Credit Constraints in the Market for Consumer Durables: Evidence from Micro Data on Car Loans', NBER Working Paper, 7694.

Auerbach, Alan J. (1991), 'Retrospective Capital Gain Taxation', *The American Economic Review*, 81/1: 167–78.

——and D. Bradford (2002), 'Generalized Cash-Flow Taxation', NBER Working Paper, 8122.

Bacchetta, Philippe, and S. Gerlach (1997), 'Consumption and Credit Constraints: International Evidence', *Journal of Monetary Economics*, 40/2: 207–38.

Bacha, Edmar L. (1990), 'A Three-Gap Model of Foreign Transfers and GDP Growth Rates in Developing Countries', *Journal of Development Economics*, 32: 279–96.

Bagchi, Amiya K. (1994), 'Macroeconomics', *Journal of Development Planning*, 24: 19–88.

Baker, Dean, and M. Weisbrot (2002), 'The Role of Social Security Privatization in Argentina's Economic Crisis' (Washington, DC: Center for Economic and Policy Research).

Bakker, Age, and B. Chapple (2002), 'Advanced Country Experience with Capital Account Liberalization', International Monetary Fund Occasional Paper, 214.

————(eds.) (2003), *Capital Liberalization in Transition Countries: Lessons from the Past and for the Future* (Cheltenham: Edward Elgar).

Banerjee, Abhijit V. (1992), 'A Simple Model of Herd Behavior', *Quarterly Journal of Economics*, 107/3: 797–817.

Bank for International Settlements (2001), *71st Annual Report*.

Bank Negara Malaysia (2001*a*), *Annual Report 2000*, www.bnm.gov.my.

——(2001*b*), *Economic and Financial Developments in the Malaysian Economy in the First Quarter of 2000*, www.bnm.gov.my.

Barro, Robert J. (1974), 'Are Government Bonds Net Wealth?' *Journal of Political Economy*, 82/6: 1095–117.

——(1985), 'Recent Developments in the Theory of Rules versus Discretion', *Economic Journal*, suppl., 23–37.

——(1997), *Determinants of Economic Growth: A Cross-Country Empirical Study* (Cambridge, Mass.: MIT Press).

——and D. Gordon (1983), 'Rules, Discretion and Reputation in a Model of Monetary Policy', *Journal of Monetary Economics*, 12/1: 101–21.

Barth, James R., G. Caprio, Jr., and R. Levine (2001), 'The Regulation and Supervision of Banks around the World: A New Database', *Brookings-Wharton Papers on Financial Services*, World Bank Working Paper, 2588.

Ben-David, Dan, and D. Papell (1998), 'Slowdowns and Meltdowns: Postwar Growth Evidence from 74 Countries', *Review of Economics and Statistics*, 80: 561–71.

Bernanke, Ben, and F. Mishkin (1997), 'Inflation Targeting: A New Framework for Monetary Policy?' NBER Working Paper, 5893.

Bhaduri, Amit (1991), 'Keynesian and Classical Unemployment: A False Distinction', *Economic Appliquee*, 44: 43–9.

——(1992), 'Conventional Stabilization and the East European Transition', in S. Richter (ed.), *The Transition from Command to Market Economies in Eastern Europe* (San Francisco: Westview Press).

——and S. Marglin (1990), 'Unemployment and the Real Wage: The Economic Basis for Contesting Political Ideologies', *Cambridge Journal of Economics*, 14: 375–93.

——and D. Nayyar (1996), *The Intelligent Person's Guide to Liberalization* (New Delhi: Penguin Books).

Bhattacharya, Amar, and J. Stiglitz (2000), 'The Underpinnings of a Stable and Equitable Global Financial System: From Old Debates to a New Paradigm', Annual World Bank Conference on Development Economics 1999 (Washington, DC: The World Bank).

Bikhchandani, Sushil, D. Hirshleifer, and I. Welch (1992), 'A Theory of Fads, Fashion, Custom, and Cultural Change as Informational Cascades', *Journal of Political Economy*, 100/5: 992–1026.

Bisignano, Joseph R., W. Hunter, and G. Kaufman (2000), 'Lessons from the Global Financial Crisis', in J. Bisignano, W. Hunter, and G. Kaufman (eds.), *Global Financial Crisis: Lessons from Recent Events* (Boston: Kluwer Academic Publishers). 89–109.

Blanchard, Olivier J., and Lawrence H. Summers (1986), 'Hysteresis and the European Unemployment Problem', in Stanley Fischer (ed.), *NBER Macroeconomics Annual 1* (Cambridge, Mass.: MIT Press), 15–78.

Blustein, Paul (2001), *The Chastening: Inside the Crisis that Rocked the Global Financial System and Humbled the IMF* (New York: Public Affairs).

Bond, Stephen, and C. Meghir (1994), 'Dynamic Investment Models and the Firm's Financial Policy', *Review of Economic Studies*, 61/2: 197–222.

Borio, Claudio, C. Furfine and P. Lowe (2001), 'Procyclicality of the Financial System and Financial Stability: Issues and Policy Options', in *Marrying the Macro- and Micro-Prudential Dimensions of Financial Stability*, BIS Papers, 1.

Boskin Commission report (1999), 'Toward a More Accurate Measure of the Cost of Living', *Final Report to the Senate Finance Committee from the Advisory Commission to Study Consumer Price Index*, http://www.ssa.gov/history/reports/ boskinrpt.html.

Boyce, James, and L. Zarsky (1988), 'Capital Flight from the Philippines, 1962–1986', *The Journal of Philippine Development*, 15/2: 191–222.

Bruno, Michael (1995), *Inflation Growth and Monetary Control: Non-Linear Lessons from Crisis and Recovery*, Paolo Baffi Lectures on Money and Finance (Rome: Bank of Italy, Edizioni dell'elefante).

References

Bruno, Michael and W. Easterly (1996), 'Inflation and Growth: In Search of a Stable Relationship', *FRBSL*, 78/3: 139–46.

——— (1998), 'Inflation Crises and Long-Run Growth', *Journal of Monetary Economics*, 41/1: 3–26.

——G. Di Tella, R. Dornbush, and S. Fischer (eds.) (1988), *Inflation Stabilization* (Cambridge, Mass.: MIT University Press).

——S. Fischer, E. Helpman, N. Liviatan, and L. Meridor (eds.) (1991), *Lessons of Economic Stabilization and its Aftermath* (Cambridge, Mass.: MIT University Press).

Budnevich, Carlos and G. Le Fort (1997), 'Fiscal Policy and the Economic Cycle in Chile', *CEPAL Review*, 61.

Buiter, Willem H. (2003), 'James Tobin: An Appreciation of his Contribution to Economics', NBER Working Paper, 9753.

Bulír, Ales, and A. Javier Hamann (2003), 'Aid Volatility: An Empirical Assessment', IMF Staff Papers, 50/1.

Bureau of Labor Statistics (2003), Series title: Part-Time for Economic Reasons, http://www.bls.gov/opub/ted/2003/jan/wk4/art03.htm. Originally pub. 29 Jan.

Burnside, Craig, M. Eichenbaum, and S. Rebelo (1993), 'Labor Hoarding and the Business Cycle', *Journal of Political Economy*, 101/2: 245–73.

Cagan, Phillip (1956), 'Monetary Dynamics of Hyperinflations', in Milton Friedman (ed.), *Studies in the Quantity Theory of Money* (Chicago: University of Chicago Press).

Calvo, Guillermo (2001), 'The Case for Hard Pegs in the Brave New World of Global Finance', in Jorge Braga de Macedo, Daniel Cohen, and Helmut Reisen (eds.), *Don't Fix, Don't Float* (Paris: OECD Development Centre Studies).

——(2002), 'On Dollarization', *Economics of Transition Journal*, 10/2: 393–403.

——L. Leiderman, and C. Reinhart (1993), 'Capital Inflows and Real Exchange Rate Appreciation in Latin America: The Role of External Factors', IMF Staff Papers, 40/1: 108–51.

——————(1994), 'Capital Inflows to Latin America: The 1970s and 1990s', in E. Bacha (ed.), *Development Trade and the Environment, Volume 4. Economics in a Changing World* (London: Macmillan Press). 123–48.

——and Enrique Mendoza (2000), 'Rational Contagion and the Globalization of Securities Markets', *Journal of International Economics*, 51/1: 79–113.

Caplin, Andrew S., and J. Lehay (1994), 'Business as Usual, Market Crashes and Wisdom after the Fact', *American Economic Review*, 84/3: 548–65.

Caprio, G., Jr., and D. Klingebiel (1997), 'Bank Insolvency: Bad Luck, Bad Policy, or Bad Banking?' in Michael Bruno and Boris Pleskovic (eds.), *Proceedings of the Annual World Bank Conference on Development Economics 1996* (Washington, DC: World Bank).

——and D. Klingebiel (1999), 'Episodes of Systemic and Borderline Financial Crises', World Bank, mimeo.

——and D. Klingebiel (2003), 'Banking Crises Database', World Bank, mimeo.

Card, D., and A. Krueger (1995), *Myth and Measurement: The New Economics of the Minimum Wage* (Princeton: Princeton University Press).

Cárdenas, Mauricio, and F. Barrera (1997), 'On the Effectiveness of Capital Controls: The Experience of Colombia During the 1990s', *Journal of Development Economics*, 54/1: 27–57.

——and R. Steiner (2000), 'Private Capital Flows in Colombia', in Felipe Larraín (ed.), *Capital Flows, Capital Controls, and Currency Crises: Latin America in the 1990s* (Ann Arbor: The University of Michigan Press).

Carlson, Mark, and L. Hernandez (2002), 'Determinants and Repercussions of the Composition of Capital Inflows', Board of Governors of the Federal Reserve System, International Finance Discussion Paper, 717.

Carneiro, Pedro, and J. Heckman (2002), 'The Evidence on Credit Constraints in Post-Secondary Schooling', *Economic Journal*, 112: 705–34.

Cecchetti, Stephen G. (1998), 'Understanding the Great Depression: Lessons for Current Policy', in M. Wheeler (ed.), *The Economics of the Great Depression* (Michigan: W.E. Upjon Institute for Employment Research). 171–94.

CEPAL (1998), *Cincuenta años de pensamiento en la CEPAL: Textos seleccionados* (Santiago: Fondo de Cultura Económica y CEPAL).

Chamley, Christopher P. (2004), *Rational Herds* (Cambridge: Cambridge University Press).

Chang, Ha-Joon (ed.) (2001), *The Rebel Within* (London: Wimbledon Publishing Company).

——(2004), 'Institutions of Macroeconomic Management History, Theory, and Practice', IPD Working Paper.

China, Menzie D., and H. Ito (2002), 'Capital Account Liberalization, Institutional and Financial Development: Cross Country Evidence', NBER Working Paper, 8967.

Chiricos, Theodore G. (1987), 'Rates of Crime and Unemployment: An Analysis of Aggregate Research Evidence', *Social Problems*, 34/2: 187–211.

Chirinko, Bob (1993), 'Business Fixed Investment Spending: Modeling Strategies, Empirical Results, and Policy Implications', *Journal of Economic Literature*, 31/4: 1875–911.

Clarida, Richard, J. Gali, and M. Gertler (1999), 'The Science of Monetary Policy: A New Keynesian Perspective', *Journal of Economic Literature*, 37/4: 1661–707.

Clerc, Laurent, F. Drumetz, and O. Jaudoin (2001), 'To What Extent are Prudential and Accounting Arrangements Pro- or Countercyclical with Respect to Overall Financial Conditions?', in *Marrying the Macro- and Micro-Prudential Dimensions of Financial Stability*, BIS Papers, 1.

Collier, Paul (1999), 'Aid "Dependency": A Critique', *Journal of African Economics*, 8/4: 528–45.

——and A. Hoeffler (1998), 'On Economic Causes of Civil War', Oxford Economic Papers, 50/4: 563–73.

Cooper, Richard N. (1992), *Economic Stabilization and Debt in Developing Countries* (Cambridge, Mass.: The MIT Press).

References

Cox, Donald, and T. Jappelli (1990), 'Credit Rationing and Private Transfers: Evidence from Survey Data', *Review of Economics and Statistics*, 72/3: 445–54.

Cuddington, John (1986), *Capital Flight: Estimates, Issues, and Explanations* (Princeton: Princeton University Press).

Dasgupta, P., and J. Stiglitz (1977), 'Tariffs versus Quotas as Revenue Raising Devices under Uncertainty', *American Economic Review*, 67/5: 975–81.

Davis, Jeffrey, R. Ossowski, J. Daniel, and S. Barnett (2003), 'Stabilization and Savings Funds for Nonrenewable Resources: Experience and Fiscal Policy Implications', in Jeffrey Davis, Rolando Ossowski, and Annalisa Fedelino (eds.), *Fiscal Policy Formulation and Implementation in Oil-Producing Countries* (Washington, DC: International Monetary Fund).

De Gregorio, José (1998), 'Financial Integration, Financial Development and Economic Growth', mimeo (Department of Industrial Engineering, Universidad de Chile).

—— S. Edwards, and R. Valdés (2000), 'Controls on Capital Inflows: Do They Work?' *Journal of Development Economics*, 63/1: 59–83.

Deaton, Angus (1991), 'Saving and Liquidity Constraints', *Econometrica*, 59/5: 1221–48.

Demirguc-Kunt, A., and E. Detragiache (1999), 'Financial Liberalization and Financial Fragility', IMF Working Paper, 98/83.

Devlin, Robert (1989), *Debt and Crisis in Latin America: The Supply Side of the Story* (Princeton: Princeton University Press).

—— R. Ffrench-Davis, and S. Griffith-Jones (1995), 'Surges in Capital Flows and Development', in R. Ffrench-Davis and S. Griffith-Jones (eds.), *Coping with Capital Surges: The Return of Finance to Latin America* (Boulder, Colo.: Lynne Rienner Publishers).

Diamond, Douglas W., and P. Dybvig (1983), 'Bank Runs, Deposit Insurance and Liquidity', *Journal of Political Economy*, 91/3: 401–19.

Díaz-Alejandro, Carlos F. (1985), 'Goodbye Financial Repression, Hello Financial Crash', *Journal of Development Economics*, 19/1–2: 1–2.

—— and A. Velasco (1988), *Trade, Development and the World Economy. Selected Essays of Carlos F. Diaz-Alejandro* (Oxford: Basil Blackwell).

Diebold, Francis X., and G. Rudebusch (1992), 'Have Postwar Economic Fluctuations been Stabilized?' *American Economic Review*, 82/4: 993–1005.

—— R. Glenn, and D. Sichel (1993), 'Further Evidence on Business-Cycle Duration Dependence', in James H. Stock and Mark W. Watson (eds.), *NBER Studies in Business Cycles 28* (Chicago: University of Chicago Press and the NBER).

Dodd, Randall (2003), 'Derivatives, the Shape of International Capital Flows and the Virtues of Prudential Regulation', in R. Ffrench-Davis and S. Griffith-Jones (eds.), *From Capital Surges to Drought: Seeking Stability from Emerging Economies* (New York: Palgrave/Macmillan).

—— and Shari Spiegel (2005), 'Up From Sin: A Portfolio Approach to Salvation', in Ariel Buira (ed.), *The IMF and World Bank at 60* (London: Anthrem Publishers).

Dooley, Michael P. (1996), 'A Survey of Literature on Controls over International Capital Transactions', IMF Staff Papers, 43/4: 639–87.

Dornbusch, Rudiger (1987), 'Exchange Rate Economics', *Economic Journal*, 97: 1–18.

—— (1998), 'Capital Controls: An Idea Whose Time is Past', in S. Fischer and R. N. Cooper *et al.* (eds.), *Should the IMF Pursue Capital-Account Convertibility?* Princeton Essays in International Economics, 207.

—— (2001), 'Malaysia: Was it Different?' NBER Working Paper, W8325.

—— and S. Edwards (1991), *The Macroeconomics of Populism in Latin America* (Chicago: University of Chicago Press).

Dungey, Mardi, R. Fry, B. González-Hermosillo, and V. Martin (2002), 'International Contagion Effects from the Russian Crisis and the LTCM Near-Collapse', IMF Working Paper, 02/74.

Dyck, Alexander (2001), 'Privatization and Corporate Governance: Principles, Evidence, and Future Challenges', *The World Bank Research Observer*, 16: 59–84.

Easterly, William, and Luis Servén (eds.) (2003), *The Limits of Stabilization: Infrastructure, Public Deficits, and Growth in Latin America* (Palo Alto, Calif.: Stanford University Press and World Bank).

—— R. Islam, and J. Stiglitz (2000), 'Shaken and Stirred: Explaining Growth Volatility', in B. Pleskovic and N. Stern (eds.), *Annual Bank Conference on Development Economics* (Washington, DC: World Bank). 191–212.

—— M. Kremer, L. Pritchett, and L. H. Summers (1993), 'Good Policy or Good Luck? Country Growth Performance and Temporary Shocks', *Journal of Monetary Economics*, 32/3: 459–83.

Eaton, Jonathan, and M. Gersovitz (1981), 'Debt with Potential Repudiation: Theoretical and Empirical Analysis', *The Review of Economic Studies*, 48/2: 289–309.

ECLAC (Economic Commission for Latin America and the Caribbean) (1998*a*), *Cincuenta años de pensamiento en la CEPAL: Textos seleccionados* (Santiago: Fondo de Cultura Económica y CEPAL).

—— (1998*b*), *The Fiscal Covenant: Strengths, Weaknesses, Challenges* (Santiago: ECLAC).

—— (2000), *Equity, Development and Citizenship* (Santiago: ECLAC).

'EPI Issue Guide: Unemployment Insurance' (2004), *Economic Policy Institute*, rev. Available online:(http://www.epinet.org/content.cfm/issueguides_unemployment_ index)

The Economist (2003*a*), 'A Place for Capital Controls', 1 May.

The Economist (2003*b*), 'Survey: Global Finance', 1 May.

The Economist Magazine (2003*c*), 'A Place for Capital Controls', 3 May: 16.

Economist Intelligence Unit (1998), *Country Finance Hong Kong*.

Edison, Hali J., M. Klein, L. Ricci, and T. Sloek (2002), 'Capital Account Liberalization and Economic Performance: Survey and Synthesis', NBER Working Paper, 9100.

Edwards, Sebastian (1999*a*), 'How Effective are Capital Controls?' *Journal of Economic Perspectives*, 13/4: 65–84.

References

Edwards, Sebastian (1999*b*), 'How Effective are Controls on Capital Inflows?', An Evaluation of Chile's Experience', mimeo.

——(forthcoming) 'Financial Instability', prepared for the Copenhagen Consensus, May 2004, and forthcoming after revision in Bjorn Lomborg (ed.), *Global Crises, Global Solutions* (Cambridge: Cambridge University Press).

——and J. Frankel (eds.) (2002), *Preventing Currency Crises in Emerging Markets* (Chicago: The University of Chicago Press for the NBER).

Eichengreen, Barry J. (2001), 'Capital Account Liberalization: What Do Cross-Country Studies Tell Us?' *The World Bank Economic Review*, 15/3: 341–65.

——and R. Hausmann (1999), 'Exchange Rates and Financial Fragility', NBER Working Paper, 7418.

Eisner, Robert (1988), 'Extended Accounts for National Income and Product', *Journal of Economic Literature*, 26/4: 1611–84.

Elgar, Edward (2002), *Global Development Finance 2000* (Washington, DC: The World Bank).

——and D. Rodrik (1998), 'Who Needs Capital Account Convertibility?' in *Essays in International Finance no. 207* (Princeton: International Finance Section).

Emran, M. Shahe, and J. Stiglitz (2000), 'VAT versus Trade Taxes: The Inefficiency of Indirect Tax Reform in Developing Countries', IPD Working Paper.

Epstein, Gerald, I. Grabel, and K. S. Jomo (2003), 'Capital Management Techniques in Developing Countries', in Ariel Buira (ed.), *Challenges to the World Bank and the IMF: Developing Country Perspectives* (London: Anthem Press).

Farber, Henry (1993), 'The Incidence and Costs of Job Loss: 1982–91', *Brookings Papers on Economic Activity: Microeconomics*, 1: 73–132.

——(2003), 'Job Loss in the United States, 1981–2001', NBER Working Paper, 9707.

Fazzari, Steven (2003), 'Job Loss in the United States, 1981–2001', NBER Working Paper, 9707.

——G. Hubbard, and B. Petersen (1998), 'Financing Constraints and Corporate Investment', *Brookings Papers on Economic Activity*, 1: 141–206.

Fernández de Lis, Santiago, J. Martínez, and J. Saurina (2001), 'Credit Growth, Problem Loans and Credit Risk Provisioning in Spain', in *Marrying the Macro- and Micro-Prudential Dimensions of Financial Stability*, BIS Papers, 1 Mar.

Ffrench-Davis, Ricardo (1968), 'Export Quotas under Market Instability', *American Journal of Agricultural Economics*, 50/3: 643–59.

——(2000), *Reforming the Reforms in Latin America: Macroeconomics, Trade, Finance* (London: Macmillan/St Anthony's College).

——(2002), *Economic Reforms in Chile: From Dictatorship to Democracy* (Ann Arbor: University of Michigan Press).

——(2004), 'Macroeconomics-for-Growth under Financial Globalization: Four Strategic Issues', IPD Working Paper.

——(2005), *Reforming Latin America's Economics after Market Fundamentalism* (London: Palgrave Macmillan).

——and G. Larraín (2003), 'How Optimal are the Extremes? Latin American Exchange Rate Policies during the Asian Crisis', in R. Ffrench-Davis and

S. Griffith-Jones (eds.), *From Capital Surges to Drought: Seeking Stability for Emerging Markets* (London: Palgrave/Macmillan).

——and J. Ocampo (2001), 'The Globalization of Financial Volatility', in R. Ffrench-Davis (ed.), *Financial Crises in 'Successful' Emerging Economies*, (Washington, DC: ECLAC/Brookings Institution).

——and H. Reisen (eds.) (1998), *Capital Inflows and Investment Performance* (Paris: OECD Development Center/UN-ECLAC).

——and H. Tapia (2001), 'Three Varieties of Capital Surge Management in Chile', in R. Ffrench-Davis (ed.), *Financial Crises in 'Successful' Emerging Economies* (Washington, DC: ECLAC and Brookings Institution Press).

————(2004), 'The Chilean-Style of Capital Controls: An Empirical Assessment', Econometric Society 2004 Latin American Meetings 255, Econometric Society.

Fischer, A. (1996), 'Central Bank Independence and Sacrifice Ratios', *Open Economies Review*, 7: 5–18.

Fischer, Stanley (1996), 'Why are Central Banks Pursuing Long-Run Price Stability?' in *Achieving Price Stability* (Wyoming: Federal Reserve Bank of Kansas City), 7–34.

Fisher, Irving (1933), 'The Debt-Deflation Theory of Great Depressions', *Econometrica*, 1/4: 337–57.

Forbes, Kristin (2003), 'One Cost of the Chilean Capital Controls: Increased Financial Constraints for Smaller Traded Firms', NBER Working Paper, 9777.

——(2004), 'Capital Controls: Mud in the Wheels of Market Discipline', NBER Working Paper, 10284.

Frankel, Jeffrey (1999), 'No Single Currency Regime is Right for All Countries or at All Times', Essays in International Finance No. 215 (Princeton: Princeton University Press).

Freeman, Richard B. (1983), 'Crime and Unemployment', in J. Wilson (ed.), *Crime and Public Policy* (San Francisco: ICS Press).

——(1994), 'Crime and the Job Market', NBER Working Papers, 4910.

——(1996), 'Why Do So Many Young American Men Commit Crimes and What Might We Do about It?' *Journal of Economic Perspectives*, 10/1: 25–42.

——(1999), 'The Economics of Crime', in O. Ashenfelter and D. Card (eds.), *Handbook of Labor Economics—3C* (Amsterdam: North-Holland).

——and W. Rodgers III (1999), 'Area Economic Conditions and the Labor Market Outcomes of Young Men in the 1990s Expansion', NBER Working Paper, 7073.

Frenkel, Roberto (1998), 'Capital Market Liberalization and Economic Performance in Latin America', CEPA Working Paper, 6.

——(2004), 'Real Exchange Rate and Employment in Argentina, Brazil, Chile and Mexico', Paper prepared for the Group of 24, Washington, DC.

——and J. Ros (2003), 'Unemployment, Macroeconomic Policy and Labor Market Flexibility. Argentina and Mexico in the 1990s', presented at the ECLAC seminar on Management of Volatility, Financial Liberalization and Growth in Emerging Economies (Santiago, Chile, 24–5 Apr.).

Frey, Bruno S., and F. Schneider (1978), 'An Empirical Study of Politico-Economic Interaction in the United States', *Review of Economics & Statistics*, 6/2: 174–83.

References

Friedman, Milton (1956), 'The Quantity Theory of Money—A Restatement', *Studies in the Quantity Theory of Money* (Chicago: University of Chicago Press).

Friedman, Milton (1968), 'The Role of Monetary Policy', *American Economic Review*, 58/1: 1–17.

Furman, Jason, and J. Stiglitz (1998), 'Economic Crises: Evidence and Insights from East Asia', *Brookings Papers on Economic Activity*, 2: 1–114.

——— (1999), 'Economic Consequences of Rising Income Inequality', in J. Hole (ed.), *Symposium Proceedings—Income Inequality: Issues and Policy Options* (Wyoming: Federal Reserve Bank of Kansas City).

Galbraith, James K. (2003), 'Don't Turn the World over to the Bankers', *Le Monde Diplomatique*, May.

Gaspar, Vitor, and F. Smets (2002), 'Monetary Policy, Price Stability and Output Gap Stabilization', *International Finance*, 5/2: 193–211.

Gavin, Michael, R. Hausmann, R. Perotti, and E. Talvi (1996), 'Managing Fiscal Policy in Latin America and the Caribbean: Volatility, Procyclicality, and Limited Creditworthiness', Inter-American Development Bank Working Paper, 326.

Ghosh, Atish *et al.* (2002), 'IMF-Supported Programs in Capital Account Crises', IMF Occasional Paper, 210.

Goldfeld, Stephen M. (1976), 'The Case for Missing Money', *Brookings Papers on Economic Activity*, 3: 683–739.

—— (1982), 'Rules, Discretion, and Reality', *American Economic Review*, 72/2: 361–6.

Goldman Sachs (2002), 'The Lulameter', Emerging Markets Strategy, 6 June, New York.

Goode, Richard (1949), 'The Income Tax and the Supply of Labor', *The Journal of Political Economy*, 57/5: 28–437.

Goodfriend, Marvin, and Robert G. King (2001), 'The Case for Price Stability', NBER Working Paper, w8423.

Greenwald, Bruce (1998), 'International Adjustments in the Face of Imperfect Financial Markets', Paper prepared for the Annual World Bank Conference on Development Economics, Washington, DC, 20–1 April.

—— (1999), 'Aggregate Devaluation Impacts in Economies with Imperfect Financial Markets', in B. Pleskovic and J. Stiglitz (eds.), *Annual World Bank Conference on Development Economics 1998* (Washington, DC: World Bank).

—— and J. Stiglitz (1988), 'Money, Imperfect Information and Economic Fluctuations', in M. Kohn and S. C. Tsiand (eds.), *Expectations and Macroeconomics* (Oxford: Oxford University Press).

——— (1989), 'Toward a Theory of Rigidities', *American Economic Review*, 79/2: 364–9.

——— (1990*a*), 'Asymmetric Information and the New Theory of the Firm: Financial Constraints and Risk Behavior', *American Economic Review*, 80/2: 160–5.

——— (1990*b*), 'Macroeconomic Models with Credit and Equity Rationing', in R. Hubbard (ed.), *Asymmetric Information, Corporate Finance, and Investment* (Chicago: University of Chicago Press).

——— (1992), 'Information, Finance and Markets: The Architecture of Allocative Mechanisms', *Journal of Industrial and Corporate Change*, 1/1: 37–68.

—— —— (1993a), 'Financial Market Imperfections and Business Cycles', *Quarterly Journal of Economics*, 108/1: 77–114.

—— —— (1993b), 'New and Old Keynesians', *Journal of Economic Perspectives*, 7/1: 23–44.

—— —— (1998), 'Examining Alternative Macroeconomic Theories', *Brookings Papers on Economic Activity*, 1: 207–70.

—— —— (2000), 'Externalities in Economies with Imperfect Information and Incomplete Markets', in N. Barr (ed.), *Economic Theory and the Welfare State* (Cheltenham: Edward Elgar).

—— —— (2003), *Towards a New Paradigm in Monetary Economics* (Cambridge: Cambridge University Press).

—— —— and A. Weiss (1984), 'Informational Imperfections in the Capital Market and Macroeconomic Fluctuations', *American Economic Review*, 74: 194–9.

Griffith-Jones, Stephany, and A. Persaud (2005), 'The Pro-cyclical Impact of Basle II on Emerging Markets and its Political Economy', available at http://www.stephanygj.com/_documents/Pro-cyclicalimpactbasleII.pdf

Grossman, Gene M., and E. Helpman (2002), *Interest Groups and Trade Policy*, (Princeton: Princeton University Press).

Hahn, Frank (1966), 'Equilibrium Dynamics with Heterogeneous Capital Goods', *Quarterly Journal of Economics*, 80/4: 133–46.

Hall, Bronwyn H. (1996), 'The Private and Social Returns to Research and Development', in B. Smith and C. Barfield (eds.), *Technology, R&D, and the Economy* (Washington, DC: Brookings Institution and the American Enterprise Institute).

Hansen, G. D. (1985), 'Indivisible Labor and the Business Cycle', *Journal of Monetary Economics*, 16: 309–27.

Harris, Elliott (1999), 'Impact of the Asian Crisis on Sub-Saharan Africa', *Finance and Development*, 36/1.

Harrison, Ann E., I. Love and M. McMillan (2002), 'Global Capital Flows and Financing Constraints', NBER Working Paper, 8887.

Harvie, Charles, and Lee, Boon-Chye (eds.) (2002a), *Globalization and Small and Medium Enterprises in East Asia*, Studies of Small and Medium Enterprises in East Asia, Volume 1 (Cheltenham: Edward Elgar).

—— —— (eds.) (2002b), *Studies of Small and Medium Enterprises in East Asia, Volume III: Sustaining Growth and Performance in East Asia: The Role of Small and Medium Sized Enterprises* (Cheltenham: Edward Elgar).

Hausmann, Ricardo (1999), 'Should there be Five Currencies or One Hundred and Five?' *Foreign Policy*, 116: 65–79.

—— (2000), 'Exchange Rate Arrangements for the New Architecture', *Global Finance from a Latin American Viewpoint* (Paris: Inter-American Development Bank and Organization for Economic Co-operation and Development).

Helmann, Thomas, K. Murdock, and J. Stiglitz (1998), 'Financial Restraint and the Market Enhancing View', in Y. Hayami and M. Aoki (eds.), *The Institutional Foundations of East Asian Economic Development* (London: Macmillan), 255–84.

References

Helmann, Thomas, K. Murdock, and J. Stiglitz (2001), 'Liberalization, Moral Hazard in Banking and Prudential Regulation: Are Capital Requirements Enough?' *American Economic Review*, 90/1: 147–65.

————(2002), 'Franchise Value and the Dynamics of Financial Liberalization', in A. Meyendorff and A. Thakor (eds.), *Designing Financial Systems in Transition Economies* (Cambridge, Mass.: The MIT Press).

Hemming, Richard, M. Kell, and S. Mahfouz (2002), 'The Effectiveness of Fiscal Policy in Stimulating Economic Activity—A Review of the Literature', IMF Working Paper, 02/208.

Hernandez, Leonardo, P. Mellado, and R. Valdes (2001), 'Determinants of Private Capital Flows in the 1970s and 1990s: Is there Evidence of Contagion?' IMF Working Paper, 01/64.

Heyman, Daniel (2000), 'Major Macroeconomic Upsets, Expectations and Policy Responses', CEPAL Review, 70.

Hirschman, Albert O. (1958), *The Strategy of Economic Development* (New Haven: Yale University Press).

Hoff, Karla, and J. Stiglitz (2004), 'After the Big Bang? Obstacles to the Emergence of the Rule of Law in Post-Communist Societies', *American Economic Review*, 94/3.

Holtz-Eakin, Douglas, D. Joulfaian, and H. Rosen (1994), 'Entrepreneurial Decisions and Liquidity Constraints', *RAND Journal of Economics*, 25/2: 334–47.

Honahan, P., and J. Stiglitz (2001), 'Robust Financial Restraint', in G. Caprio, P. Honohan, and J. Stiglitz (eds.), *Financial Liberalization: How Far, How Fast?* (Cambridge: Cambridge University Press).

Hubbard, Glenn R. (1998), 'Capital-Market Imperfections and Investment', *Journal of Economic Literature*, 36/1: 193–225.

International Labor Organization (1999), *Key Indicators of the Labour Market–KILM7: Urban Informal Sector Unemployment* (Geneva: ILO).

——(2002), *Decent Work and the Informal Economy, Report VI*, presented to the Committee on the Informal Economy at the International Labour Conference (http://www.ilo.org/public/english/employment/index.htm).

International Monetary Fund (1998), *International Capital Markets—Developments, Prospects and Key Policy Issues* (Washington, DC: IMF).

——(2000), 'Recovery from the Asian Crisis and the Role of the IMF', IMF Issues Brief 00/05.

——(2003), 'Fiscal Adjustment in IMF-Supported Programs', *Independent Evaluation Office of the IMF* (Washington, DC: International Monetary Fund). Available online: (http://www.imf.org/External/NP/ieo/2003/fis/index.htm).

——(2004), International Financial Statistics (IFS) Database, International Monetary Fund.

Johnson, Simon, and T. Mitton (2001), 'Cronyism and Capital Controls: Evidence from Malaysia', NBER Working Paper, 8521.

Johnston, Barry R. (1998), 'Sequencing Capital Account Liberalization', *Finance and Development*, 35/4.

Jomo, K. S. (ed.), *Malaysian Eclipse: Economic Crisis and Recovery* (London: Zed Books, 2001).

Jorgenson, Dale, and E. Yip (2001), 'Whatever Happened to Productivity Growth?', *New Developments in Productivity Analysis, Studies in Income and Wealth*, 63: 509–40.

Joshi, Vijay (2003), 'India and the Impossible Trinity', *The World Economy*, 26/4: 555–83.

Judd, John P., and J. Scadding (1982), 'The Search for a Stable Money Demand Function: A Survey of the Post-1973 Literature', *Journal of Economic Literature*, 20/3: 993–1023.

Jung, W. S. (1985), 'Output-Inflation Tradeoffs in Industrial and Developing Countries', *Journal of Macroeconomics*, 7/1: 101–13.

Kaldor, Nicholas (1978), *Further Essays on Economic Theory* (London: Duckworth).

Kalecki, Michal (1970), 'Problems of Financing Economic Development in a Mixed Economy', in W. Eltis, M. Scott, and J. Wolfe (eds.), *Induction, Growth and Trade: Essays in Honour of Sir Roy Harrod* (Oxford: Oxford University Press).

——— (1971), *Selected Essays on the Dynamics of the Capitalist Economy* (Cambridge: Cambridge University Press).

Kaminsky, Graciela L., and S. Schmukler (2001), 'On Booms and Crashes: Financial Liberalization and Stock Market Cycles', World Bank Policy Working Paper, 2565.

——— C. Reinhart, and C. Végh (2004), 'When it Rains, it Tours: Procyclical Capital Flows and Macroeconomic Policies', NBER Working Paper, 10780.

Kaplan, Ethan, and D. Rodrik (2002), 'Did the Malaysian Capital Controls Work?' in Edwards and Frankel (2002).

Katsimbris, George M. (1990), ' "Output-Inflation Tradeoffs in Industrial and Developing Countries": A Comment and Additional Evidence', *Journal of Econometrics*, 12/3: 483–99.

Keynes, John Maynard (1936), *General Theory of Employment, Interest and Money* (London: Macmillan).

Khor, Martin (2004), 'The Malaysian Experience in Financial-Economic Crisis Management: An Alternative and Challenge to the IMF-Style Approach', IPD Working Paper.

Kindleberger, Charles P. (2000), *Maniacs, Panics and Crashes: A History of Financial Crises*, 4th edn. 1978 (New York: John Wiley and Sons, Inc.).

King, Robert G. (2001), 'The Case for Price Stability', NBER Working Paper, W8423.

Kochhar, Kalpana, L. Dicks-Mireaux, and B. Horvath (1996), 'Thailand: The Road to Sustained Growth', IMF Occasional Paper, 146.

Kose, Ayhan M., E. Prasad, and M. Terrones (2003), 'Financial Integration and Macroeconomic Volatility', IMF Staff Papers, 50: 119–42.

——— (2004), 'How do Trade and Financial Integration Affect the Relationship between Growth and Volatility?' Federal Reserve Bank of San Francisco Working Paper, 2004–29.

References

Krugman, Paul (1987), 'Is Free Trade Passé?' *Journal of Economic Perspectives*, 1/2: 131–44.

——(1990), *Rethinking International Trade* (Cambridge, Mass.: The MIT Press).

Krugman, Paul (2000), 'Balance Sheets, the Transfer Problem, and Financial Crises', in P. Isard, A. Razin, and A. Rosen (eds.), *International Finance and Financial Crises—Essays in Honor of Robert P. Flood Jr.* (Boston: Kluwer Academic Publishers).

——and L. Taylor (1978), 'Contractionary Effects of Devaluations', *Journal of International Economics*, 8: 445–56.

Kydland, Finn, and E. Prescott (1977), 'Rules rather than Discretion: The Inconsistency of Optimal Plans', *Journal of Political Economy*, 85/3: 473–91.

————(1982), 'Time to Build and Aggregate Fluctuations', *Econometrica*, 50/6: 1345–70.

Lancaster, K. J., and R. G. Lipsey (1957), 'The General Theory of Second Best', *Review of Economic Studies*, 24: 11–32.

Lane, Timothy (1999), 'IMF Admits Errors in Asian Crisis, but Defends Tight-Money Policy', *Wall Street Journal*, 20 Jan.

——*et al.* (1999), *IMF-Supported Programs in Indonesia, Korea, and Thailand: A Preliminary Assessment* (Washington, DC: International Monetary Fund).

Larraín, Felipe, R. Labán, and R. Chumacero (2000), 'What Determines Capital Inflows? An Empirical Analysis for Chile', in Felipe Larraín (ed.), *Capital Flows, Capital Controls, and Currency Crises: Latin America in the 1990s* (Ann Arbor: The University of Michigan Press).

Laurens, Bernard (2000), 'Chile's Experience with Controls on Capital Inflows in the 1990s', in Ariyoshi *et al.* (2000).

Le Fort, Guillermo, and S. Lehmann (2003), 'El Encaje, los Flujos de Capitales y el Gasto: Una Evaluación empírica', Central Bank of Chile Working Paper.

Levine, Ross, and D. Renelt (1992), 'A Sensitivity Analysis of Cross-Country Growth Regressions', *American Economic Review*, 942–63.

——and S. Zervos (1993), 'What Have we Learned about Policy and Growth from Cross-Country Regressions?' *American Economic Review*, 426–30.

Levitt, Steven D. (1996), 'The Effect of Prison Population Size on Crime Rates: Evidence from Prison Overcrowding Litigation', *Quarterly Journal of Economics*, 111/2: 319–51.

Lewis, Arthur (1954), 'Economic Development with Unlimited Surplus of Labour', *Manchester School of Economics and Social Studies*, 22: 139–91.

Lloyd, Collin (1970), 'Classical Monetary Theory and the Velocity of Circulation', *Canadian Journal of Economics*, 3/1: 87–94.

Lowry, Collin (1999), 'Epidemics Spread as Economies Crumble', *Executive Intelligence Review*, 26/16: 19–22.

Lucas, Robert E. (1990), 'Why Doesn't Capital Flow from Rich to Poor Countries?' *American Economic Review*, 80/2: 92–6.

—— (1996), 'Nobel Lecture: Monetary Neutrality', *Journal of Political Economy*, 104/4: 661–82.

—— (2003), 'Macroeconomic Priorities', *American Economic Review*, 93/1: 1–14.

—— and T. Sargent (1978), 'After Keynesian Econometrics', in *After the Phillips Curve: Persistence of High Inflation and High Unemployment*, Conference Series 19 (Boston: Federal Reserve Bank of Boston).

Ludvigson, Sydney (1999), 'Consumption and Credit: A Model of Time-Varying Liquidity Constraints', *The Review of Economics and Statistics*, 81/3: 434–47.

Lutz, Matthias G. (1999), 'Unit Roots versus Segmented Trends in Developing Countries Output Series', *Applied Economic Letters*, 6: 181–4.

McKinnon, R. (1964), 'Foreign Exchange Constraints and Economic Development', *Economic Journal*, 74: 388–409.

Maddison, Angus (2001), *The World Economy: A Millennial Perspective* (Paris: OECD).

Majluf, Nicholas S., and S. Myers (1984), 'Corporate Financing and Investment Decisions When Firms Have Information that Investors Do Not Have', *Journal of Financial Economics*, 13/2: 187–221.

Mankiw, Gregory N. (1985), 'Small Menu Costs and Large Business Cycles: A Macroeconomic Model of Monopoly', *Quarterly Journal of Economics*, 100/2: 529–38.

—— (2000), 'The Inexorable and Mysterious Tradeoff between Inflation and Unemployment', NBER Working Paper, W7884.

—— and D. Romer (eds.) (1991), *New Keynesian Economics, Vol. 2: Coordination Failures and Real Rigidities* (Cambridge, Mass.: The MIT Press).

—— and S. Zeldes (1991), 'The Consumption of Stockholders and Non-stockholders', *Journal of Financial Economics*, 29: 97–112.

Marfán, Manuel (2005), 'Fiscal Policy, Efficacy and Private Deficits: A Macroeconomic Approach', in José Antonio Ocampo (ed.), *Beyond Reforms: Structural Dynamics and Macroeconomic Vulnerability* (Palo Alto, Calif.: Stanford University Press and ECLAC).

Martner, Ricardo, and V. Tromben (2003), 'Tax Reforms and Fiscal Stabilization in Latin America', in Tax Policy, Banca d'Italia Research Department, Public Finance Workshop.

Mayer, Colin (1987), 'The Assessment: Financial Systems and Corporate Investment', *Oxford Review of Economic Policy*, 3/4: i–xvi.

—— (1990), 'Financial Systems, Corporate Finance, and Economic Development', in R. G. Hubbard (ed.), *Asymmetric Information, Corporate Finance and Investment* (Chicago: University of Chicago Press).

—— (2002), 'Financing the New Economy: Financial Institutions and Corporate Governance', *Information Economics and Policy*, 14: 311–26.

Meade, James (1951), *Theory of International Economic Policy: The Balance of Payments* (Oxford: Oxford University Press).

References

Miller, Marcus, and J. Stiglitz (1999), 'Bankruptcy Protection against Macroeconomics Shocks: The Case for a "Super Chapter 11" ', World Bank Conference on Capital Flows, Financial Crises and Policies.

Mishkin, Frederic (1999), 'International Experiences with Different Monetary Policy Regimes', NBER Working Paper Series, 6965.

Mody, Ashoka, and A. Murshid (2002), 'Growing Up with Capital Flow', IMF Working Paper, 02/75.

Montiel, Peter, and C. Reinhart (1999), 'Do Capital Controls and Macroeconomic Policies Influence the Volume and Composition of Capital Flows? Evidence from the 1990s', *Journal of International Money and Finance*, 18/4: 619–35.

Myers, Stewart C., and N. Majluf (1984), 'Corporate Financing and Investment Decisions When Firms Have Information that Investors Do Not Have', *Journal of Financial Economics*, 13/2: 187–221.

Nayyar, Deepak (1995), 'Macroeconomics of Stabilization and Adjustment', *Economic Appliquee*, 48/3: 5–38.

—— (1997), 'Themes in Trade and Industrialization', in Deepak Nayyar (ed.), *Trade and Industrialization* (Delhi: Oxford University Press).

—— (1998), 'Short-Termism, Public Policies and Economic Development', *Economies et Sociétés*, 32/1: 107–18.

—— (2000), 'Macroeconomic Reforms in India: Short-Term Effects and Long-Run Implications', in W. Mahmud (ed.), *Adjustment and Beyond: The Reform Experience in South Asia* (London: Palgrave).

—— (2002*a*), 'The Existing System and the Missing Institutions', in Deepak Nayyar (ed.), *Governing Globalization: Issues and Institutions* (Oxford: Oxford University Press).

—— (2002*b*), 'Capital Controls and the World Financial Authority: What Can We Learn from the Indian Experience?' in John Eatwell and Lance Taylor (eds.), *International Capital Markets: Systems in Transition* (New York: Oxford University Press).

—— (2002*c*), 'Globalization and Development Strategies', in John Toye (ed.), *Trade and Development: New Directions for the Twenty-First Century* (Cheltenham: Edward Elgar).

—— (2003*a*), 'The Political Economy of Exclusion and Inclusion: Democracy, Markets and People', in A. K. Dutt and J. Ros (eds.), *Development Economics and Structuralist Macroeconomics: Essays in Honour of Lance Taylor* (Cheltenham: Edward Elgar).

—— (2003*b*), 'Work, Livelihoods and Rights', *Indian Journal of Labour Economics*, 46/1: 3–13.

Ndikumana, Léonce, and James K. Boyce (2003), 'Public Debts and Private Assets: Explaining Capital Flight from Sub-Saharan African Countries', *World Development*, 31/1: 107–30.

Neary, Peter, and J. Stiglitz (1982), 'Expectations, Asset Accumulation and the Real-Balance Effect', presented at Dublin Meetings of the Econometric Society, Working Paper 1990, Sept.

——and J. Stiglitz (1983), 'Toward a Reconstruction of Keynesian Economics: Expectations and Constrained Equilibria', *Quarterly Journal of Economics*, 98: 199–228.

Negishi, T. (1964), 'Conditions for Neutral Money', *The Review of Economic Studies*, 31/21: 147–8.

Newbery, David M. G., and J. Stiglitz (1984), 'Pareto Inferior Trade', *The Review of Economic Studies*, 51/1: 1–12.

Nickell, Stephen, and B. Bell (1995), 'The Collapse in Demand for the Unskilled and Unemployment across the OECD', *Oxford Review of Economic Policy*, 11/1: 40–62.

Nordhaus, William (1975), 'The Political Business Cycle', *Review of Economic Studies*, 42.

——and E. Kokkelenberg (eds.) (1999), *Nature's Numbers: Expanding the National Economic Accounts to Include the Environment* (Washington, DC: National Academy Press).

——and J. Tobin (1973), 'Is Growth Obsolete?' in Milton Moss (ed.), *The Measurement of Economic and Social Performance*, NBER Studies in Income and Wealth, 38.

Ocampo, José Antonio (2002), 'Developing Countries' Anti-Cyclical Policies in a Globalized World', in Amitava Dutt and Jaime Ros (eds.), *Development Economics and Structuralist Macroeconomics: Essays in Honour of Lance Taylor* (Aldershot: Edward Elgar, 2002).

——(2003a), 'Capital Account and Counter-Cyclical Prudential Regulation in Developing Countries', in R. Ffrench-Davis and S. Griffith-Jones (eds.), *From Capital Surges to Drought: Seeking Stability for Emerging Markets* (London: Palgrave/Macmillan).

——(2003b), 'International Asymmetries and the Design of the International Financial System', in A. Berry (ed.), *Critical Issues in Financial Reform: A View from the South* (New Brunswick, NJ: Transaction Publishers).

——(2004a), 'Latin America's Growth and Equity Frustrations During Structural Reforms', *Journal of Economic Perspectives*, 18/2: 67–88.

——(2004b), 'Lights and Shadows in Latin American Structural Reforms', in Gustavo Indart (ed.), *Economic Reforms, Growth and Inequality in Latin America: Essays in Honor of Albert Berry* (Aldershot: Ashgate).

——(2005a), 'The Quest for Dynamic Efficiency: Structural Dynamics and Economic Growth in Developing Countries', in José Antonio Ocampo (ed.), *Beyond Reforms: Structural Dynamics and Macroeconomic Vulnerability* (Palo Alto, Calif.: Stanford University Press and Economic Commission for Latin America and the Caribbean).

——(2005b), 'A Broad View of Macroeconomic Stability', IPD Conference Background Papers.

——(forthcoming), 'Latin America and the World Economy in the Long Twentieth Century', in K S Jomo (ed.) *The Great Divergence: Hegemony, Uneven Development and Global Inequality during the Long Twentieth Century* (New Delhi: Oxford University Press).

Ocampo, and L. Taylor (1998), 'Trade Liberalisation in Developing Economies: Modest Benefits but Problems with Productivity Growth, Macro Prices, and Income Distribution', *Economic Journal*, 108/450: 1523–46.

——and C. Tovar (1998), 'Capital Flows, Savings and Investment in Colombia, 1990–96', in Ffrench-Davis and H. Reisen (1998).

Ocampo, José Antonio, and C. Tovar (2003), 'Managing the Capital Account: Colombia's Experience with Price-Based Controls on Capital Inflows', CEPAL/ECLAC Review, 81: 7–32.

Organization for Cooperation and Development and The European Commission (eds.) (2004), *Benefits and Wages: OECD Indicators—2004 Edition* (Paris: OECD).

Orszag, Peter, and J. Stiglitz (2002), 'Optimal Fire Departments: Evaluating Public Policy in the Face of Externalities', mimeo.

Ötker-Robe, Inci (2000), 'Malaysia's Experience with the Use of Capital Controls', in Ariyoshi *et al.* (2000).

Palma, Gabriel (2002), 'The Three Routes to Financial Crises: The Need for Capital Controls', in John Eatwell and Lance Taylor (eds.), *International Capital Markets—Systems in Transition* (New York: Oxford University Press).

——(2005), 'Four Sources of "De-Industrialization" and a New Concept of the "Dutch Disease" ', in José Antonio Ocampo (ed.), *Beyond Reforms: Structural Dynamics and Macroeconomic Vulnerability* (Palo Alto, Calif.: Stanford University Press and ECLAC).

Pastor, Manuel, Jr. (1990), 'Capital Flight from Latin America', *World Development*, 18/1: 1–12.

Patinkin, D. (1952), 'Further Considerations of the General Equilibrium Theory of Money', *The Review of Economic Studies*, 19/3: 186–95.

Phelps, Edmund S. (1967), 'Phillips Curves, Expectations of Inflation and Optimal Employment over Time', *Economica*, 34/135: 254–81.

——and G. Zoega (1995), 'The Incidence of Increased Unemployment in the Group of Seven, 1970–1994', in George Bitros and Yannis Katsoulacos (eds.), *Essays in Economic Theory, Growth and Labor Markets: A Festschrift in Honor of E. Drandakis* (Cheltenham: Edward Elgar).

Poole, William (1970), 'Optimal Choice of Monetary Policy Instruments in a Simple Stochastic Macro Model', *Quarterly Journal of Economics*, 84/2: 197–216.

Posen, A. (1998), 'Central Bank Independence and Disinflationary Credibility: A Missing Link?' *Oxford Economic Papers*, 50: 335–59.

Prasad, Eswar, Kenneth Rogoff, Shang-Jin Wei, and M.Ayhan Kose (2003), 'Effects of Financial Globalization on Developing Countries: Some Empirical Evidence', IMF Occasional Paper, 120.

Pratt, John W. (1964), 'Risk Aversion in the Small and in the Large', *Econometrica*, 32/1–2: 122–36.

Rajan, Raghuram G., and Luigi Zingales (2001), 'The Great Reversals: The Politics of Financial Development in the 20th Century', NBER Working Paper, 8178.

Rajaraman, Indira (2003), 'Management of the Capital Account: A Study of India and Malaysia', in UNCTAD (ed.), *Management of Capital Flows: Comparative Experiences and Implications for Africa* (Geneva: UNCTAD).

Raphael, Steven, and R. Winter-Ebmer (2001), 'Identifying the Effect of Unemployment on Crime', *Journal of Law and Economics*, 44/1: 259–83.

Reddy, Y. V. (2001), 'Operationalising Capital Account Liberalisation: The Indian Experience', *Development Policy Review*, 19/1: 83–99.

Reinhart, Carmen M., and K. Rogoff (2004), 'The Modern History of Exchange Rate Arrangements: A Reinterpretation', *Quarterly Journal of Economics*, 119/1: 1–48.

Reisen, Helmut (2003), 'Ratings since the Asian Crisis', in R. Ffrench-Davis and S. Griffith-Jones (eds.), *From Capital Surges to Drought: Seeking Stability from Emerging Economies* (New York: Palgrave/Macmillan).

Rey, P., and J. E. Stiglitz (1993), 'Short-Term Contracts as a Monitoring Device', NBER Working Paper 4514.

Rincón, Hernán, and L. Villar (2003), 'The Colombian Economy in the nineties: Capital Flows and Foreign Exchange Regimes', *Borradores de Economia*, 149.

Rodríguez, Francisco, and D. Rodrik (2001), 'Trade Policy and Economic Growth: A Skeptic's Guide to the Cross-National Evidence', in B. Bernanke and K. Rogoff (eds.), *NBER Macroeconomics Annual 2000* (Cambridge, Mass.: MIT Press).

Rodrik, Dani (1997), *Has Globalization Gone Too Far?* (Washington, DC: Institute for International Economics).

—— (1999), 'Where Did All the Growth Go? External Shocks, Social Conflict and Growth Collapses', *Journal of Economic Growth*, 4/4: 385–412.

—— (2000), 'Exchange Rate Regimes and Institutional Arrangements in the Shadow of Capital Flows', Sept.

—— (2001), 'Why is there so Much Economic Insecurity in Latin America', *CEPAL Review*, 73: 7–29.

—— and A. Velasco (2000), 'Short-Term Capital Flows', in Boris Pleskovic and Joseph Stiglitz (eds.), *Annual World Bank Conference on Development Economics, World Bank 1999* (Washington: World Bank).

Rogoff, Kenneth (1985), 'Optimal Degree of Commitment to an Intermediate Monetary Target', *Quarterly Journal of Economics*, 1/4: 1169–89.

—— (2002), 'Rethinking Capital Controls: When Should We Keep an Open Mind?' *Finance and Development*, 39/4.

—— and E. Prasad (2003), 'The Emerging Truth of Going Global' *Financial Times*, 2 Sept.: 21.

Romer, Paul (1987), 'Crazy Explanations for the Productivity Slowdown', in Stanley Fischer (ed.), *NBER Macroeconomics Annual* (Cambridge, Mass.: NBER).

Rosenzweig, Mark R., and K. Wolpin (1993), 'Credit Market Constraints, Consumption Smoothing, and the Accumulation of Durable Production Assets in Low-Income Countries: Investment in Bullocks in India', *Journal of Political Economy*, 101/2: 223–44.

References

Rothschild, Michael, and J. Stiglitz (1970), 'Increasing Risk: I. A Definition', *Journal of Economic Theory*, 2/3: 225–43.

——— (1973), 'Some Further Results on the Measurement of Inequality', *Journal of Economic Theory*, 6/2: 188–204.

Sah, R., and J. E. Stiglitz (1992), *Peasants versus City-Dwellers: Taxation and the Burden of Economic Development* (Oxford: Clarendon Press).

Seater, John J. (1993), 'Ricardian Equivalence', *Journal of Economic Literature*, 31/1: 142–90.

Sen, Amartya (1999), *Development as Freedom* (Oxford: Oxford University Press).

Shapiro, Carl, and J. Stiglitz (1984), 'Equilibrium Unemployment as a Worker Discipline Device', *American Economic Review*, 74/3: 433–44.

Shell, K., and D. Cass (1989), 'Sunspot Equilibrium in an Overlapping Generations Economy with an Idealized Contingent Commodities Market', in W. A. Barnett, C. Deissenberg, and G. Feichtinger (eds.), *Economic Complexity* (Cambridge: Cambridge University Press).

—— and J. Stiglitz (1967), 'Allocation of Investment in a Dynamic Economy', *Quarterly Journal of Economics*, 81: 592–609.

Shigehara, K. (1992), 'Causes of Declining Growth in Industrialized Countries', *Policies for Long-Term Economic Growth* (Wyoming: Federal Reserve Bank of Kansas City).

Shiller, Robert J. (2000), *Irrational Exuberance* (Princeton: Princeton University Press).

Solow, Robert M. (1956), 'A Contribution to the Theory of Economic Growth', *Quarterly Journal of Economics*, 70/1: 65–94.

—— (1964), 'Draft of the Presidential Address to the Econometric Society on the Short-Run Relationship between Employment and Output'.

—— and J. Stiglitz (1968), 'Output, Employment and Wages in the Short Run', *Quarterly Journal of Economics*, 82: 537–60.

Stein, Ernesto, E. Talvi, and A. Grisanti (1998), 'Institutional Arrangements and Fiscal Performance: The Latin American Experience', Inter-American Development Bank Working Paper, 367.

Stigler, George J. (1967), 'Imperfections in the Capital Market', *Journal of Political Economy*, 75/3: 287–92.

Stiglitz, Joseph E. (1973), 'The Badly Behaved Economy with the Well Behaved Production Function', in J. Mirrlees (ed.), *Models of Economic Growth* (London: Macmillan).

—— (1974), 'Alternative Theories of Wage Determination and Unemployment in L.D.C.'s: The Labor Turnover Model', *Quarterly Journal of Economics*, 88/2: 194–227.

—— (1976), 'The Efficiency Wage Hypothesis, Surplus Labor and the Distribution of Income in L.D.C.'s', *Oxford Economic Papers*, 28/2: 85–207.

—— and A. Weiss (1981), 'Credit Rationing in Markets with Imperfect Information', *American Economic Review*, 71/3: 393–410.

—— (1982), 'Alternative Theories of Wage Determination and Unemployment: The Efficiency Wage Model', in M. Gersovitz, Ranis G. Diaz-Alejandro, and

M. R. Rosenzweig (eds.), *The Theory and Experience of Economic Development: Essays in Honor of Sir Arthur W. Lewis* (London: George Allen & Unwin).

—— (1983), 'On the Relevance or Irrelevance of Public Financial Policy: Indexation, Price Rigidities and Optimal Monetary Policy', in R. Dornbusch and M. Simonsen (eds.), *Inflation, Debt and Indexation* (Cambridge, Mass.: MIT Press).

—— (1985), 'Equilibrium Wage Distribution', *Economic Journal*, 95: 595–618.

—— (1986), 'Theories of Wage Rigidities', in J. L. Butkiewicz, Kenneth J. Koford, and Jeffrey B. Miller (*eds.*), *Keynes' Economic Legacy: Contemporary Economic Theories* (New York: Praeger Publishers).

—— (1987), 'The Causes and Consequences of the Dependence of Quality on Prices', *Journal of Economic Literature*, 25: 1–48.

—— (1988), 'On the Relevance or Irrelevance of Public Financial Policy', in *The Economics of Public Debt*, Proceedings of the 1986 International Economics Association Meeting (London: Macmillan Press), 4–76.

—— and M. Wolfson (1988), 'Taxation, Information, and Economic Organization', *Journal of the American Taxation Association*, 9/2: 7–18.

—— (1989a), 'Economic Organization, Information, and Development', in H. Chenery and T. N. Srinivasan (eds.), *Handbook of Development Economics* (Amsterdam: North-Holland).

—— (1989b), 'On the Economic Role of the State', in A. Heertje (ed.), *The Economic Role of the State* (Oxford: B. Blackwell).

—— (1991), 'The Invisible Hand and Modern Welfare Economics', in D. Vines and A. Stevenson (eds.), *Information Strategy and Public Policy* (Oxford: Basil Blackwell).

—— (1992), 'Methodological Issues and the New Keynesian Economics', in N. Dmitri and A. Vercelli (eds.), *Alternative Approaches to Macroeconomics* (Oxford: Oxford University Press).

—— (1997), 'Reflections on the Natural Rate Hypothesis', *Journal of Economic Perspectives*, 11/1: 3–10.

—— (1998), 'Knowledge for Development: Economic Science, Economic Policy, and Economic Advice', in B. Pleskovic and J. Stiglitz (eds.), *Annual World Bank Conference on Development Economics* (Washington: World Bank), 9–58.

—— (1999c), 'More Instruments and Broader Goals: Moving Toward the Post-Washington Consensus', in G. Kochendorfer-Lucius and B. Pleskovic (eds.), *Development Issues in the 21st Century* (Berlin: German Foundation for International Development).

—— (1999a), 'Beggar-Thyself vs. Beggar-Thy-Neighbor Policies: The Dangers of Intellectual Incoherence in Addressing the Global Financial Crisis', *Southern Economics Journal*, 66/1: 1–38.

—— (1999b), 'Lessons from East Asia', *Journal of Policy Modeling*, 21/3: 311–30. (Paper presented at the American Economic Association Annual Meetings, New York, 4, Jan. 1999.)

—— (1999d), 'Responding to Economic Crises: Policy Alternatives for Equitable Recovery and Development', *The Manchester School*, 67/5: 409–27.

References

Stiglitz, Joseph E. (1999*e*), 'Taxation, Public Policy and The Dynamics of Unemployment', *International Tax and Public Finance*, 6: 239–62.

—— (1999*f*), 'Toward a General Theory of Wage and Price Rigidities and Economic Fluctuations', *American Economic Review*, 89/2: 75–80.

—— (2000*a*), 'Democratic Development as the Fruits of Labor', *Perspectives on Work*, 4/1: 31–8.

—— (2000*b*), 'Formal and Informal Institutions', in P. Dasgupta and I. Serageldin (eds.), *Social Capital: A Multifaceted Perspective* (Washington, DC: World Bank).

—— (2001*a*), 'Failure of the Fund: Rethinking the IMF Response', *Harvard International Review*, 23/2: 14–18.

—— (2001*b*), 'Participation and Development: Perspectives from the Comprehensive Development Paradigm', in Farrukh Iqbal and Jong-Il You (eds.), *Democracy, Market Economics & Development: An Asian Perspective* (Washington, DC: The World Bank).

—— (2001*c*), 'Principles of Financial Regulation: A Dynamic Approach', *The World Bank Observer*, 16/1: 1–18.

—— and J. Yun (2002), 'Integration of Unemployment Insurance with Retirement Insurance', NBER Working Paper, 9199.

—— (2002*a*), 'Employment, Social Justice and Societal Well-Being', *International Labor Review*, 141/1: 9–29.

—— (2002*b*), 'Financial Market Stability and Monetary Policy', *Pacific Economic Review*, 7/1 (Feb.): 13–30. (Speech given at the HKEA First Biennial Conference, Hong Kong, 15 Dec. 2000.)

—— (2002*c*), *Globalization and its Discontents* (New York: W.W. Norton & Company).

—— (2002*d*), 'Information and the Change in the Paradigm in Economics', *American Economic Review*, 92/3: 460–501.

—— (2003*a*), *The Roaring Nineties: A New History of the World's Most Prosperous Decade* (New York: W.W. Norton & Company).

—— (2003*b*), 'Whither Reform? Towards a New Agenda for Latin America', in *Revista de la CEPAL*, 80: 7–40.

—— (2004), 'Capital-Market Liberalization, Globalization and the IMF', *Oxford Review of Economic Policy*, 20/1: 57–71.

Stokey, Nancy (2003), ' "Rules versus Discretion" after Twenty-Five Years', *NBER Macroeconomic Annual 2002*, 9–45.

Streeten, Paul (1959), 'Unbalanced Growth', *Oxford Economic Papers*, 9 (June): 167–90.

Sunkel, O. (ed.) (1993), *Development from Within: Toward a Neo-structuralist Approach for Latin America* (Boulder Colo.: Lynne Rienner Publishers).

Svensson, Lars (1997), 'Optimal Inflation Targets, "Conservative" Central Banks, and Linear Inflation Contracts', *American Economic Review*, 87: 98–114.

Taylor, Lance (1988), *Varieties of Stabilization Experience: Towards Sensible Macroeconomics in the Third World* (Oxford: Clarendon Press).

308

——(1991), *Income Distribution, Inflation, and Growth: Lectures on Structuralist Macroeconomic Theory* (Cambridge, Mass.: MIT Press).

——(1993), *The Rocky Road to Reform: Adjustment, Income Distribution and Growth in the Developing World* (Cambridge, Mass.: The MIT Press).

——(1994), 'Gap Models', *Journal of Development Economics*, 45: 17–34.

——(2004), *Reconstructing Macroeconomics: Structuralist Proposals and Critiques of the Mainstream* (Cambridge, Mass.: Harvard University Press).

Teigen, Ronald L. (1972), 'A Critical Look at Monetarist Economics', *Federal Reserve Bank of St Louis Review*, 10–25.

Titelman, Daniel, and A. Uthoff (1998), 'The Relation between Foreign and National Savings under Financial Liberalization', in Ffrench-Davis and Reisen (1998).

Tobin, James, and B. William (1977), 'Asset Markets and the Cost of Capital', in Richard Nelson and Bela Balassa (eds.), *Economic Progress, Private Values and Public Policy: Essays in Honor of William Fellner* (Amsterdam: North-Holland). 235–62.

Turner, Philip (2002), 'Procyclicality of Regulatory Ratios', in John Eatwell and Lance Taylor (eds.), *International Capital Markets—Systems in Transition* (New York: Oxford University Press).

United Nations Economic Commission for Latin America and the Caribbean (ECLAC) (1998), *The Fiscal Covenant. Strengths, Weaknesses, Challenges* (Santiago: ECLAC).

US Council of Economic Advisors (1995), 'Economic Report of the President' (Washington, DC: United States Government).

——(1996), 'Economic Report of the President' (Washington, DC: US Government Printing Office).

——(1997), 'Economic Report of the President' (Washington, DC: US Government Printing Office).

Valdés-Prieto, Salvador, and M. Soto (1998), 'The Effectiveness of Capital Controls: Theory and Evidence from Chile', *Empirica*, 25/2.

van Wijnbergen, Sweder (1984), 'The Dutch disease: a disease after all?' *Economic Journal*, 94/373: 41–55.

Villar, Leonardo, and H. Rincón (2003), 'The Colombian Economy in the Nineties: Capital Flows and Foreign Exchange Regimes', in Albert R. Berry and Gustavo Indart (eds.), *Critical Issues in International Financial Reform* (New Brunswick, NJ: Transaction Publishers).

Volcker, Paul (1998), 'Emerging Economies in a Sea of Global Finance', Statement before the Joint Economic Committee, United States Congress, 5 May.

Wall Street Journal (1998), 'Financing Capital Flight', 14 July: 1.

——(1999), 'IMF Admits Errors in Asian Crisis, But Defends its Tight Monetary Policy', 20 Jan.

Wallsten, Scott J. (2000), 'The Effects of Government-Industry R&D Programs on Private R&D: The Case of the Small Business Innovation Research Program', *RAND Journal of Economics*, 31/1: 82–100.

References

Watson, Mark W. (1994), 'Business-Cycle Durations and Postwar Stabilization of the U.S. Economy', *American Economic Review*, 84/1: 24–46.

Weitzman, Martin L. (1974), 'Prices vs. Quantities', *Review of Economic Studies*, 41/4: 477–91.

Williamson, John (2000), *Exchange Rate Regimes for Emerging Markets: Reviving the Intermediate Option*, Policy Analyses in International Economics 60 (Washington, DC: Institute for International Economics).

—— (2003a), 'Exchange Rate Policy and Development', IPD Working Paper.

Williamson, John (2003b), 'Proposals for Curbing the Boom-Bust Cycle in the Supply of Capital to Emerging Markets', in R. Ffrench-Davis and S. Griffith-Jones (eds.), *From Capital Surges to Drought: Seeking Stability from Emerging Economies* (New York: Palgrave/Macmillan).

Woodford, Michael (2000), 'Pitfalls of Forward Looking Monetary Policy', *The American Economic Review*, 90/2: 100–4.

World Bank (1999), *Global Economic Prospects and the Developing Countries, 1998-99—Beyond Financial Crisis* (Washington, DC: World Bank).

—— *World Development Report, 2000/2001* (Washington, DC: World Bank, 2001).

Wyplosz, Charles (2002), 'How Risky is Financial Liberalization in the Developing Countries?' *Comparative Economic Studies*, 44/2–3, 1–26.

Yellen, Janet L. (1984), 'Efficiency Wage Models of Unemployment', *American Economic Review*, 74: 200–5.

Zahler, Roberto (2003), 'Macroeconomic Stability under Pension Reform in Emerging Economies: The Case of Chile', *Proceedings of the Seminar on Management of Volatility, Financial Globalization and Growth in Emerging Economies* (Santiago: ECLAC).

Zeldes, Stephen P. (1989), 'Consumption and Liquidity Constraints: An Empirical Investigation', *The Journal of Political Economy*, 97/2: 305–46.

Index